Montaigne among the Moderns: Receptions of the *Essais*

Montaigne among the Moderns: Receptions of the *Essais*

Dudley M. Marchi

Berghahn Books
Providence • Oxford

Published in 1994 by

Berghahn Books
Editorial offices:
165 Taber Avenue, Providence, RI 02906, U.S.A.
Bush House, Merewood Avenue, Oxford OX3 8EF, UK

Library of Congress Cataloging-in-Publication Data

Marchi, Dudley M.
Montaigne among the moderns : receptions of the Essais / Dudley M. Marchi.
p. cm.
Includes bibliographical references and index.
ISBN 1-57181-007-2 : ca. $49.95 (£35.00)
1. Montaigne, Michel de, 1533-1592—Influence. 2. Montaigne, Michel de, 1533-1592. Essais. 3. Literature, Modern—French influences. I. Title.
PQ1643.M33 1994
844'.3—dc20 94-29461
CIP

British Library Cataloguing in Publication Data
A CIP catalog record for this book is available from
the British Library.

ISBN: 1-57181-007-2

Printed in the United States.

Le vray miroir de nos discours
est le cours de nos vies.

— Michel de Montaigne

Contents

Preface vii

Introduction 1

Chapter One

Receptions of the *Essais*: Beginnings and Continuities 19

Chapter Two

Emerson and Nietzsche: Between Tradition and Innovation 103

Chapter Three

Pater and Woolf: A Modernist Renaissance? 185

Chapter Four

Conclusions: Montaigne among the Postmoderns 278

Bibliography 321

Index 335

Preface

Montaigne among the Moderns is a study that has generated several years of research and writing on a subject to which I have attempted to do justice, but by no means have exhausted. I owe a great debt to Antoine Compagnon for first introducing me to a serious reading of the *Essais* and the literary, philosophical, and historical issues which they embody. Both he and David Damrosch, who provided a myriad of brilliant insights into the comparative dimensions of the study, were exemplary teachers as they guided me through the early stages of the project as my dissertation directors at Columbia University. I likewise extend my appreciation to Gita May of Columbia University for her efforts at encouraging the study and for her scholarly expertise concerning Montaigne's reception in France. I would also like to thank Philip Watts of the University of Pittsburgh for discussing various aspects of the project and for offering valuable suggestions on the relationship of Montaigne to twentieth-century French writers. Colleagues Joan Hinde Stewart, Yvonne Rollins, Mary Ann Witt, Helga Braunbeck, and Michèle Magill of North Carolina State University deserve thanks for granting me precious hours to read and discuss sections of the manuscript at various stages of its progress. Special thanks to Philippe Desan of the University of Chicago, Marcel Tetel of Duke University, and John Burt Foster Jr. of George Mason University for their insightful editorial comments. My appreciation also extends to Philippe Sollers and Michel Chaillou, both of whom granted gracious and engaging interviews concerning Montaigne's importance to their own work as well as to French literary and intellectual history at the present time. My thanks extends also to Robert Riddell for having copyedited the manuscript with professionalism and insight. I am indebted to the

Research Committee of the College of Humanities and Social Sciences at North Carolina State University for having awarded me a Summer Stipend and a Research Travel Grant which permitted me to conduct the final stages of research at the *Bibliothèque Nationale* in Paris as well as at the *Archives Municipales de la Gironde* and *Bibliothèque Municipale* in Bordeaux. The committee's support also allowed me the opportunity to explore the town of Bordeaux, where Montaigne was a life-long citizen and mayor, as well as the country residence which was a sanctuary of his life and work — the *Château de Montaigne*. This on-site research into Montaigne's historical identity permitted a more direct understanding of the importance of his life and writing, not only to his time and place, but to our own. Finally, my gratitude to Beverly, Jonathan, and Robert, endless sources of inspiration and support without which this work would not have been possible.

August 1993
Raleigh, NC

Introduction

For he that hath not heard of Mountaine yet
Is but a novice in the schooles of wit.

— John Florio, Preface to the *Essays*, 1632.

> Il y a plus affaire à interpreter les interpretations qu'à interpreter les choses, et plus de livres sur les livres que sur autre subject: nous ne faisons que nous entregloser. Tout fourmille de commentaires; d'auteurs, il en est grand cherté. Le principal et plus fameux sçavoir de nos siècles, est-ce pas sçavoir entendre les sçavans? Est-ce pas la fin commune et derniere de touts estudes?[1]

To even begin to think about a study on writers writing on Montaigne, one must immediately consider his caveat (a state of affairs which seems to have reached crisis proportions in the academy): yet another book about one of the most widely interpreted authors in the French literary canon? Where will it end? On the other hand, to explore the richness of Montaigne's ubiquitous legacy is to bring us, not necessarily closer to the "sçavans" who have been explicating his work for over four hundred years (although it is my intention to achieve an enhanced understanding of Montaigne's interpreters), but particularly to the object of their efforts — the importance of the *Essais* to various times and places, our own included. Until now, there have been few systematic discussions of critical receptions of Montaigne's *Essais* and the relationship of his theories of reading, writing, and literature to writers and critics during the nineteenth and twentieth centuries in and outside of France.[2] In this study I will thus attempt to demonstrate that the *Essais* not only were an important source of material for certain modernist and postmodernist writers to comment upon or assimilate, but also play a significant role in their own work. In determining the extent to which similarities have developed through these writers' critical views and creative developments of Montaigne's work as they appropriated and extended certain of its aspects, it will help us to discuss the aesthetic and ideological relationships between the *Essais* and their own writings, both within and outside of the realm of direct imitative influence. Montaigne's work, as we will see, currently lives up to its now canonical reputation as an exemplary work of the European renaissance, yet also demonstrates a remarkable relevancy to current literary and intellectual activity.

There is an abundant scattering of commentary on Montaigne throughout more than four hundred years of literary history, including numerous studies on his presence in the work of a wide range of French writers and critics. There has been much less evaluation, however, of Montaigne's impact on writers of the nineteenth and twentieth centuries, particularly outside of France. One obvious reason for the scarcity of commentary on Montaigne's role in a modernist and postmodernist context is the frequent impossibility of empirical verification of such nebulous phenomena as influence, impact, and reception, and also the difficulty of working within and between different languages and cultural traditions. Yet the title *Montaigne among the Moderns* can be justified for at least three reasons. The first is that the subject is one that has been minimally considered in previous scholarship. In response to this gap in the history of the *Essais*' receptions, I am approaching the subject from a broad comparative perspective. I am not however disclaiming the useful specificity of historical circumstance, nor the great differences between the renaissance and modernist periods of literary history and a grouping of texts that span different centuries, countries, and languages. A diachronic study, yet one attempting to recognize the relationship of historical differences and similarities through intertextual evaluation, must do so, in order to be effective, by establishing strong points of contact between texts, writers, and ideas in order to demonstrate concretely the interrelationships. This leads to the second justification of the title: Montaigne's reception by modernist and postmodernist writers will help to establish a coherent field of inquiry which could serve as a future framework for the consideration of an expanded notion of "modernism" — less a term of literary periodization than a flexible paradigm of textual affinity and shared vision across historical, cultural, and linguistic boundaries. The third is that Montaigne is one of the most "international" writers ever — both in the assimilation of foreign writers and cultures into his own work and in the subsequent translations, critical receptions, and creative adaptations of the *Essais* by other writers throughout the world over the last four hundred years. This study thus strives to develop a revisionist perspective that also respects historical circumstance. Montaigne's "modernism" is thus at once an historical, philosophical, and aesthetic problematic. It necessitates a comparative approach to more fully evaluate its importance in literary studies. To avoid mere juxtaposition and accomplish clear comparisons and contrasts, I will demonstrate both affinities *and* differences between Montaigne and his modernist and postmodernist readers. Neither comparative relativism nor the privileging of an absolute historicist view of the *Essais* are autonomous goals. It is the conjunction of these approaches that may help to shine a clearer light on the *Essais* in a modernist context.

Montaigne is not only a canonical writer of the late European renaissance, but also an innovative modernist precursor in the company of Rousseau, Pater, Emerson, and Nietzsche. By first exploring the historical development of receptions of the *Essais*, it is possible to develop criteria with which to examine modernist and postmodernist receptions of Montaigne's work. The attempt then to establish parallels, shared concerns, stylistic and thematic affinities, as well as ideological convergences between various historically and linguistically dissimilar texts can be undertaken very much in the spirit of the "essai": a provisional attempt at a supple understanding of complex issues. The exploration of these shared concerns often touches upon fundamental problems of literature, philosophy, and history, problems in which there are many pitfalls, especially that of adopting a relativistic attitude toward numerous texts separated by historical and cultural circumstances. Yet comparison implies contrast and this second term is just as valuable in arriving at a more comprehensive evaluation of ideas and works that have had such widespread impact on so many readers. This study does not claim to have fully explored in an exhaustive manner all of the issues it raises — its intended contribution is rather to delineate previously ignored relationships between significant works and writers and thereby enhance our understanding of the nature of both the *Essais* and of various writers' appropriation of them. As we attempt to come to terms, from a cross-cultural perspective, with how the *Essais* have played significant roles in the works of these writers, we may see that Montaigne's influence in modernist and postmodernist writing is more pronounced than previously believed.

Although striving for a certain degree of scholarly objectivity, this study inevitably becomes prey to the very problematic that it sets out to examine. In adapting Hans Robert Jauss's concept of the "horizon-of-experience" to examine the reception and reactivation of texts, my own vantage point on the materials chosen partially determines their qualities. The circular hermeneutic of attempting to examine past texts from a present perspective, of the reciprocal nature of reading and interpretation, presents the danger of imposing an interpretive viewpoint on texts that say other things than what the critic wills them to say. A critical view of the past is often less an exercise in empirical historical understanding and more a perspective on oneself interpreting that understanding. In thus dealing with the multiply evolving receptions of the *Essais*, it has been helpful to keep in mind Margot Norris's warning to the critic who undertakes the study of modernist works: "The results of the critical efforts are not important ... but rather the compulsions and motives of the questors, their styles and methods, their quarrels, their self-justifications, and their own implication in the object of their study."[3] Her model text is *Finnegans Wake*, one of the indisputable monuments of high modernism. Written nearly four-hundred years earlier, the *Essais* are of the same radically innovative caliber in their invention of a major mode of writing and, as we will see, do much to prepare the ground and initiate problematics that later become central in the work of several key modernist and postmodernist writers. Many of these problematics are of such complexity that the approach to engaging receptions of the *Essais*, and the ensuing results, often become as important as the *Essais* themselves, ultimately helping us to better understand their widespread legacy.

Yet it is perhaps overly tempting to blindly pursue a deconstructive interpretation of the *Essais* — to categorize it as a work in perpetual motion and metamorphoses with no absolute, objective, or inherent meaning, one that easily lends itself to a process of creative interpretation refusing an absolute coherent image of its significance. Montaigne himself seems to invite such a critical approach to his writing by contradicting himself so often, and especially by impeding the systematization of the *Essais* into any consistent paradigm. The method of commentary developed here has thus been to first read writers in their connections to Montaigne's work on the level of critical contact. After considering this concrete textual evidence, it is possible to extrapolate from these writers' interpretive strategies in confronting the *Essais* and explore their interrelationships with Montaigne's work, and in some cases, even with each other's receptions.

There is also the constant danger in the interpretive quest of modeling one's own analytical approach on the text under consideration, of appropriating it to develop one's critical criteria. The pitfall of an overly developed faithfulness to the text is ever present, especially with a writer like Montaigne who demands the personal engagement of his readers. It must be countered with a constant awareness of the interactive process of interpretation, its problems, its precariousness, as well as its rewards. It is, thus, an intertextual approach to receptions of the *Essais* that can most effectively handle their pervasive impact. The genesis of the term intertextuality is generally attributed to Julia Kristeva: "tout texte se construit comme une mosaïque de citations et tout texte est absorption et transformation d'un autre text."[4] Structure is thus a network of interrelated components that take on meaning as they are gathered into a mobile whole.

The current widespread use of "intertextuality" as an analytical model is as varied as are its practitioners — I will thus develop a nuanced version of it, again that of Kristeva, one flexible enough to deal with the variegated materials of this study:

> Le terme d'intertextualité désigne cette transposition d'un (ou de plusieurs) système(s) de signes en un autre; mais puisque ce terme a été souvent entendu dans le sens banal de "critique des sources" d'un texte, nous lui préférerons celui de transposition, qui a l'avantage de préciser que le passage d'un système signifiant à un autre exige une nouvelle articulation thétique — de la positionnalité énonciative et dénotative.[5]

In this sense, I wish to go beyond the study of "influence" and examine the more dynamic area of the receptive transformations of the

Essais. The intertextual relationships will be conceived in this Kristevean sense: as transpositions and new articulations of textual systems contained in the *Essais*. In this conception, receptions of the *Essais*, like the *Essais* themselves, are not static essences, but rather webs of multidimensional cultural materials ("text" from the Latin *texere*, "to weave"), always demanding further development. Montaigne's *Essais* are sprinkled with references to his favorite literary, philosophical, and historical writers as well as many lesser-known writers — there are many explicit borrowings, but also many translucent ones, translations, vague references, allusions, summaries, and glosses. Moreover, Montaigne concerns himself not only with books, but also with people and events, contemporary incidents, and especially his own experience, thereby producing a leveling of authority in which all "texts" are of equal value. The intertextual approach helps to focus the issues and to discover that there are clear patterns that emerge in the numerous receptions of the *Essais*, the analysis of which helps to identify some coherent images of Montaigne's aesthetic and ideological positions; it is thus the essential means by which to accomplish a comparative reception study of the *Essais*. The *Essais* are in fact one of the most intertextual works ever, in the words of Terence Cave: "All literature, it can be argued, depends for its existence on the literary texts which preceded it, whether or not it draws directly on them as its sources, and the proposition is nowhere more palpably true than in the *Essais*."[6]

In what ways then are the *Essais* a multivocal text, one manifesting plural enunciation, always in search for its identity, always renewing dispersion and accenting fragmentation? And more importantly, how do the *Essais* produce these same qualities in numerous writers' attempts to interpret them? For the *Essais* are not only the unprecedented work of an exceptional author, but one without any true beginning or end, a quintessential "open" work written and rewritten for over twenty years by its author until his death, and one that invites its readers to continue redeveloping its exfoliating potential. Even as the *Essais* are the charming meanderings of a French provincial humanist, a canonical text of timeless wisdom, and one of the Western models for skeptical pragmatism, they also unsettle many of their own positions and subsequent attempts at critically articulating those positions. Montaigne abolishes spatio-temporal sequentiality, substituting for it the logic of movement and thematic association in a mode of unprecedented palimpsestic writing. His work manifests a problematic "intermingling of mood, tone, genre, and style ... simultaneous creation and recreation, imitation and invention, cutting across the regulations of conventional Platonic and Aristotelian critical theory."[7] Moreover, on nearly every page of the *Essais*, one encounters paradox: Montaigne tells us that he is not a writer yet spends most of his life writing; he speaks out against the vanity of all things, yet writes copiously about himself; in his essay on presumption he chooses a non-presumptuous person for analysis, himself; in his essay on repentance he tells us that he does not repent; he says time and again that he is horrified by innovation, yet in title, genre, tone, and subject matter he produced an absolutely new work; he tells us how he loves life, yet remains detached from it; he accepts the principle of becoming, yet searches for stability; he professes intellectual humility, yet takes great pride in his writing project — the enumeration could go on. Yet Montaigne's paradoxical investigations of a myriad of subjects, although hesitant, are not futile: "The presentation of antithetical patterns of thought does not necessarily reflect belief in a universe hopelessly fragmented and of irreconcilable views. In Montaigne's mind opposites coexist, reinforce each other, and actually harmonize into a composite flexible whole."[8] This is what I am provisionally proposing as the modernist identity of Montaigne: a paradoxical dynamism which has made him so appealing to some of the most original authors of the last several centuries.

The contribution of Montaigne to the modernist phenomenon is so broad that a definitive study of the relationship of the *Essais* to modernist and postmodernist writing is perhaps impossible. Yet Montaigne's work, while not an originary source, can be concretely associated with a number of modernist and postmodernist writers' attitudes and works. In this sense he is a "protomodernist," in the word of Gerald Monsman, the type of writer who should be considered "a modern whose greatest contributions often lie beyond the range or compass of sources either peripheral or direct."[9] I will therefore examine the indirect transformations of the *Essais* undertaken by modernist and postmodernist writers. This is a method of comparison that accomplishes the compilation of recorded opinions and factual documentation, yet goes beyond, by seeking to analyze the redevelopment of Montaigne's ideas and methods in the work of other writers. After reviewing important receptions of Montaigne's work in France, I will develop the issues raised in the context of a variety of modernist and postmodernist texts and examine to what extent Montaigne's presence actually *plays a role* in their development. I will give an overview of the network of problems, establish essential relationships, and then attempt to evaluate their significance. My goal is not comprehensiveness, but rather to focus on previously undiscussed points of contact by developing "case-studies" on the relationship of modernist and postmodernist writers and Montaigne in order to demonstrate the *Essais'* presence in twentieth-century literary and critical thought.

Writers ranging from Pascal to Emerson and Sainte-Beuve to Pater have shared a common response to the work of Montaigne: they all claim that he is speaking directly to them, that he is responding to their own concerns, serving as a guide and model in the unfolding of their own writing projects. What is it then about the *Essais* that makes them so adaptable and adoptable to various writers of different historical periods and of different countries? This is a recurring issue in this study, for which there will be numerous answers. There is of course the danger of reading Montaigne retroactively by imposing modernist or postmodernist conceptions upon the *Essais*, a text notorious for its ability to adapt itself to a wide range of literary and critical sensibilities, as will be discussed in Chapter One and pursued throughout the following chapters. The examination of the reception and influence of the *Essais* in modernist and postmodernist writing is thus a process operating in a reciprocal manner. It raises the question: do the *Essais* play an important role in modernist literature, or do readings of modernist and postmodernist writers, as well as recent poststructuralist evaluations of the *Essais* serve to constitute their putative modernity?

The choice of such a conceptual framework as "modernism," which has become somewhat of a cliché in literary studies, raises problems concerning a scheme of literary history that is by no means consistent. Yet I believe it is a useful one in which to examine modes of writing and thinking first suggested and carried out in the *Essais* as well as in some important works from the middle of the nineteenth century to the present. It permits us to consider the *Essais* in a context whose characteristics may be provisionally defined, thus providing a working organization of the topic. Few terms are as problematic as that of *modern*. Its Latin etymology *modo* ("just now") suggests its perennial recurrence as well as its resistance to historicist classification. The term *modern* has had various applications throughout Western history, from the ninth-century notion of the age of Charlemagne as a *seculum modernum*, to the *Querelle des Anciens et Modernes* of the seventeenth and eighteenth centuries, to the more emphatic modernisms of the nineteenth and twentieth centuries. Yet what distinguishes Montaigne's modernism and its interconnections to modernist and postmodernist writers are their shared notions of historical self-definition: a feeling of tradition disrupted and of authority in question, a sense of acute difference from one's predecessors and, especially, a conscious attempt to actively engage this state of affairs in writing.

The very concept of modernism is thus overwhelmingly complex. I will therefore neither propose an overly comprehensive definition, a hopeless task, nor develop a reductive characterization. Yet among the more obvious "modernist" elements of the *Essais*, which have also become the critical commonplaces of modernist studies, are the discontinuous nature of proposals, the undermining of narrative linearity, the relativity of truth, radical skepticism, the openness of discursive structure, the textuality of auto-reflexivity, the analysis of the self, and the crisis of representation. This is a profusion of issues requiring detailed attention in the context of specific intertextual relationships. Pursuing each one thoroughly would produce a diffuse evaluation of the *Essais*' importance to literary modernism. It is important to understand their general importance, yet focus on more specific and manageable criteria. Thus *M*odernism: a codified period of literary history, will often be supplanted by *m*odernism: a revised notion of a unique manner of textual production having several of its origins in the *Essais*, one subsequently redeveloped as a major genre in Western writing, the ubiquitous essay. The thorny question of the relationship of "modern" and "postmodern" in the context of the *Essais*' receptions will be addressed in Chapter Four as Montaigne's role in intellectual and literary activity today is considered.

The writers examined in this study raise questions about the nature of language and writing, and very often it is an obsession with the interaction of tradition and innovation that motivates these concerns. This dynamic is a significant impetus in a great deal of modernist and postmodernist writing and functions, as I intend to demonstrate, as a primary link that can be traced through works of writers whom I will designate as the "premodernists," Ralph Waldo Emerson ("Self-Reliance" and "Quotation and Originality") and Friedrich Nietzsche ("Vom Nutzen und Nachteil der Historie für das Leben" and *Ecce Homo*), the "high modernists" Walter Pater (*The Renaissance* and *Gaston de Latour*) and Virginia Woolf (*A Room of One's Own, The Common Reader,* and *Orlando*), and the "postmodernists" Michel Butor (*Essais sur les "Essais"*), Michel Chaillou (*Domestique chez Montaigne*), and Philippe Sollers (*Portrait du joueur*). In these and other works of the above writers, as in the *Essais,* there is a constant tension between a break with the past and its concomitant continuation. I see this as an essential relationship between many of their works and the *Essais.* The interplay between past and present is one of their central concerns and often motivates radical experimentation in thought and writing. The way these writers rearticulate the work of Montaigne in certain of their own works reveals fundamental points of contact with the *Essais.* These works display, on many occasions, the problematic of textual absorption and transformation while often producing radical stylistic innovation. Chapter One serves to establish the background of Montaigne's role among the moderns by tracing receptions of his work in France from the first publication of the *Essais* up to the middle of the twentieth century, detailing the more salient commentaries, discerning trends in attitudes toward Montaigne's life and work, and discussing several problematics that permeate these receptions. Chapter Two will examine how Emerson and Nietzsche establish literary and philosophical perspectives, in the context of which an analysis of Pater and Woolf (Chapter Three) and contemporary French and American writers and critics (Chapter Four) will help to clarify Montaigne's presence in twentieth-century thought and writing.

The methodology proposed here seeks to maintain the suppleness needed in order to confront a variety of texts and authors that diverge as often as they converge, yet aims to achieve a consistent evaluation while demonstrating the hitherto ignored pervasiveness of Montaigne's thought in Western literature and philosophy of the last one hundred and fifty years. An awareness of stylistic and ideological relationships between the work of the above writers and Montaigne's helps us to understand the *Essais*, an exemplary text of the European renaissance, in a wider cross-cultural spectrum, as well as the *Essais'* place in literary and intellectual history at the present time. The literary experience is constituted by Montaigne *as a problematic*: he challenges his readers to form their own judgments and forces them to make decisions which, like being human, may not be perfect. Thus, for example, Nietzsche's notion of *critical history* in "Vom Nutzen und Nachteil für das Leben," whereby writers are called on to produce a conflictual relationship to cultural precedent in order to create new works in the present, or Woolf's call for an idiosyncratic narration of history in the quest for self-knowledge, conceptualized in the essay "Montaigne" and executed in the novel *Orlando*, reproduce modes of thinking and writing as initiated in the *Essais*. Montaigne's depiction of his attempts to understand the world and himself is what has both fascinated and confounded his commentators over the last four hundred years. While Montaigne is not the primary source for the chosen works of the various writers discussed here, he is nevertheless a significant modernist precursor in the sense that he helped to inspire, through his *Essais*, a number of their attitudes.

The initial effect of the *Essais* on many of Montaigne's readers was, and still is, often one of shock or surprise: "It is the surprise, the new kind of seeing things, that strikes the recipient of modern literature first and foremost."[10] One indisputable quality of modernist and postmodernist writing is certainly that of unsettling expectations. This would be an overly comprehensive definition of modernism, yet it is one in which the *Essais* could be partially located. Another sweeping definition, whose validity I do not deny, also has direct relevance to the problems proposed in this study: "In their creation of forms modernists are radically experimental, in their thinking or values they are radically questioning of accepted orthodoxies."[11] These two broad characterizations, whatever their relative truth, consider only half of the modernist problematic, limiting its impulse to a rupture with past forms and to a dismantling of tradition. Yet in modernist and postmodernist writing is there not an equal (and even obsessive) appropriation of the past, its cultivation, and its dynamic transformation in individual works? I believe it is this opposition between the break with tradition and the idiosyncratic use of same that creates dynamic tensions and fruitful conflicts in the *Essais* and many modernist and postmodernist works that take their cues from Montaigne. The modernist impulse is of course perennial, and one could talk of the modernity of Heraclitus, Sappho, Longinus, Petronius, Villon, or of Montaigne, by virtue of their introduction of a new attitude into literature. Modernism is thus less of a period concept than a recurring phenomenon that begins to surface with greater frequency after the middle of the nineteenth century. I will demonstrate that Montaigne's work plays a role in this later occurrence of modernism in the work of the writers who appropriate Montaigne's discursive dynamics and thereby resituate the *Essais* in a new context.

Roland Barthes has framed the modernist problematic in a manner useful in a consideration of Montaigne's modernist identity:

> On verra, par exemple, que l'unité idéologique de la bourgeoisie a produit une écriture unique, et qu'aux temps bourgeois (c'est à dire classiques et romantiques), la forme ne pouvait être déchirée puisque la conscience ne l'était pas; et qu'au contraire, dès l'instant où l'écrivain a cessé d'être un témoin de l'universel pour devenir une conscience malheureuse (vers 1850), son premier geste a été de choisir l'engagement de sa forme, soit en assumant, soit en refusant l'écriture de son passé. L'écriture classique a donc éclaté et la Littérature entière, de Flaubert à nos jours, est devenue une problématique de langue.[12]

Not only the "problematics of language," but also those of interpretation and the concept of literature itself, are key issues in literary modernism and in the *Essais*. Barthes's historical delineation is one of the most widely accepted today when discussing literary modernism. But could these same qualities be present in the *Essais*, though in less programmatic form — qualities which, as will be shown, were often ignored, suppressed, or repressed for several centuries? The innovative elements of the *Essais* were only brought to life sporadically, yet often played an important role in the work of numerous writers. This study's examination of the relations between Montaigne and modernist and postmodernist writers' receptions of his work will enhance our understanding of this more problematized and historically comprehensive concept of modernity in literature. Montaigne relies on the past in an innovative manner in order to develop his own textual persona, writing over the past, and finally, even over his own work in order to create his all-encompassing self. It is in a similar way that the *Essais* are in turn read and appropriated as various writers reactivate intertextual fragments from them in order to develop their own works. It is in the context of this fragmentary appropriation of history and its innovative deployment that one can begin to piece together the elements of Montaigne's modernism.

Montaigne proposes that readers continue his writing: "par ces traits de ma confession, on en peut imaginer d'autres à mes despens" (II, xvii, 653). The writers to be examined here have continued Montaigne's writing, whether through critical interpretation or textual transformation. Thus, the issues of assimilation, influence, and interpretation will be common denominators in the determination of significant relationships between the *Essais* and modernist and postmodernist theory and practice in the context of works by writers who have accepted Montaigne's challenge to enter into dialog with the *Essais*. An understanding of these writers' relationships to the *Essais* will add an important dimension to the history of Montaigne commentary as accomplished by Alan Boase, Mathurin Dréano, and Donald Frame, yet will do so in a comparative manner. This study is certainly neither the definitive nor the only possible reception study of Montaigne's work in a modernist context. Neither is necessarily the "correct" one, since the critical undertaking can often follow its own course, straying from stratified models of academic discourse in the attempt to produce a new evaluation.

More formal definitions of the protean and elusive phenomenon "modernism" are unavoidably reductive; the term is best left flexible enough to admit that the very idea of modernism itself shifts perspective with each new critical articulation. New receptors create new readings, but as this study will attempt to demonstrate, they who "receive" are actually preparing their defensive position to parry and activate their own offensive strategy, to paraphrase Montaigne's tennis metaphor (III, xiii, 1088). Following Montaigne and his manner of actively engaging the work of past writers, the idea of "reception" should be endowed with this more active meaning. The critical enterprise is thus an interactive process of taking and giving in the same motion, thereby rendering the old questions of influence, precursors, originality, and imitation more complex and difficult to bring to unequivocal resolution. What has been called "the modernist reformation of the past" — the way an author can influence past literary works — can be seen often in modernist and postmodernist receptions of Montaigne's work.[13] Reading through the critical lenses of Emerson, Nietzsche, Pater, Woolf, Butor, Sollers, Chaillou, and others may help us to better understand features of the *Essais* not previously considered in such a comparative light, and perhaps not even fully understood by Montaigne himself. Thus, both the impact of the *Essais* on the work of these writers, and the way in which the *Essais* will be read after their receptions of them, is considerable. Reading writers through their contact with the *Essais* helps at times to clarify, and at others to complicate the critical focus; yet in both cases our awareness of the impact of Montaigne's work will be enhanced.

Written during a time of such daunting cultural spectres as "poststructuralism" and "postmodernism," and at a time when participatory reading has become so fashionable, *Montaigne among the Moderns* is all too susceptible to the danger of reproducing its author's own theoretical concerns in an idiosyncratic critical articulation of the *Essais.* This achievement, or failure, in this and other works, is a key to understanding the unfolding identity of the *Essais* and an important concern of reception studies as elaborated by Jauss, whose approach can help to justify an active understanding of the *Essais,* yet is also grounded in evolving historical circumstances. The *Essais* are in fact a text that shows itself again and again to embody the very dynamics of reception aesthetics. In "Literary History as a Challenge to Literary Theory," Jauss sees the critical enterprise as one of situating the literary work in its historical horizon, which he defines as the network of cultural meanings within which the work's interpretations are produced — meanings that, in fact, generate explanations of a work:

> In the triangle of author, work, and public, the last is no passive part, no chain of mere reactions, but rather itself an energy formative of history. The historical life of a literary work is unthinkable without the active participation of its addressees. For it is only through the process of its mediation that the work enters into the changing horizon-of-experience of a continuity in which the perpetual inversion occurs from simple reception to critical understanding, from passive to active reception, from recognized aesthetic norms to a new production that surpasses them. The historicity of literature as well as its communica-

> tive character presupposes a dialogical and at once processlike relationship between work, audience, and new work that can be conceived in the relations between message and receiver as well as between question and answer, problem and solution.[14]

The pursuit of a "processlike" relationship between the *Essais* and their various receptions allows the examination of the protean nature, not only of the *Essais*, but also of their interpretations — it also allows us to ask which qualities of the *Essais* motivated succeeding generations of commentators to discover something of themselves in them. Throughout this study, the term "reception," a problematic concept that is used differently among a variety of writers, will be nuanced in light of the meaning given to it by Jauss, namely as a term designating *a dynamic two-way exchange between readers and texts of different historical periods*. This aesthetics of transhistorical interaction is particularly characteristic of Montaigne's active relationship to his own precursors such as his father, his best friend Etienne de La Boétie, Plato, Plutarch, and Seneca, as well as the manner in which he encourages his readers to enter into dialog with the *Essais*. I follow Jauss in maintaining that literary texts and traditions are altered according to the various "horizons-of-experience" in which they are received. Thus the terms "influence" and "dialectical," although not abandoned in my analyses of the *Essais'* receptions, have been redeveloped in order to overcome the static one-way movement of thought implied in the former term, and the sense of final resolution in the latter, since, as will be discussed, the case of Montaigne's receptions is often more problematic than these concepts can adequately encompass; true, they are often of a "dialectical" nature, yet one without closure, leaving much to be resolved.

Montaigne and his heirs are concerned with the problems of tradition and originality and with assimilation and reproduction of cultural precursors, as are most writers, yet to an intensified degree. They are quintessential practitioners of a comparative approach to culture, engaging literature, philosophy, and history across national boundaries and between various disciplines, reactivating the existing monuments of their cultural traditions into new configurations that both regenerate and surpass them. The modernist and postmodernist readers of Montaigne develop certain modes of writing developed earlier, and to a less self-conscious degree, in the *Essais*.

Montaigne's work thus becomes an important link between their works as they attempt to reactivate cultural tradition, but with the goal of surmounting it, in order to produce their own innovative versions of tradition renewed. The cultural past is allowed to speak only through the intermediary of the writer's innovative positioning of the elements of tradition. Yet with each writer this relationship is unique, even while having affinities with other writers. These affinities are often related to their individual and correlative experiences with the *Essais*. Montaigne's modernism is embodied in his free interpretation of the parasitic relationship between explicit acknowledgment of cultural precursors and an implicit idiosyncratic deployment of their significance. That Montaigne alone engendered the issues raised here would be a ridiculously large claim. But a focused analysis of only several of the many possible Montaigne commentators, and their individual and collective relationship to the *Essais*, will help us to better understand Montaigne's presence in modernist and postmodernist writing and demarcate perspectives from which further evaluation may be accomplished.

Montaigne's writing, which he characterized as "crotesques, qui sont peintures fantasques, n'ayant grace qu'en la varieté et estrangeté" (I, xxviii, 183) have now become the centerpiece around which new textual arabesques, as embodied in four centuries of commentary and creative exfoliations, will be written, eventually covering over the centerpiece's original identity. Montaigne's presence in the work of the four writers under consideration in Chapters Two and Three is often not visible. He is absent yet remains an intertextual presence around which they develop their writing projects. Montaigne's explicit absence is thus a conspicuous presence, inspiring critical inquiry into his strange and variable role as a precursor to writers of major importance in modern Western culture. The goal of Chapter Four will thus be to establish a working conclusion concerning Montaigne's role as a significant precursor to literary and intellectual history today. Prepared in part by his modernist readers, and also developed anew by postmodernist representatives such as Butor, Sollers, and Chaillou, as well as by innovative academic critics such as Pouilloux and Starobinski, Montaigne offers suggestions for future comparative studies to be undertaken concerning his writing and its numerous receptions.

The consideration of modernism as less of an historical period than a recurring textual phenomenon generates the challenge of understanding how the *Essais* have played significant roles in works not previously assessed in a comparative framework. Montaigne's role in modernist and postmodernist writing may prove to be more pronounced than previously considered. In asking how the *Essais* may have affected them, we may also learn to better read problematic texts. A new critical reading of the conjunction of Montaigne and the moderns thus helps to achieve an evolved understanding of the work of the writers considered and their role in twentieth-century literature, theory, and criticism. This study hopes to add a dimension to both Montaigne studies and to modernist scholarship by accounting for a voice previously ignored in the study of modernism. Addressing the question of how the *Essais* are to be read today, as a reassuring text of canonical standing or as a threatening one of avant-garde dimensions, could help to particularize current debates on the politics of cuture as well as on the questions of modernist and postmodernist writing. Montaigne's relationship to literary, historical, and political traditions is interactive and constructive. His best readers have emulated these qualities in their receptions of his work. Perhaps it is more than ever useful to consider the *Essais* in this light — as a work that can help us to evaluate the monuments of tradition and the perennial philosophical debates which they embody in a constructional relationship to our own particular historical situations.

Notes to Introduction

1. Michel de Montaigne, *Essais,* eds. V.-L. Saulnier and P. Villey (Paris: Presses Universitaires de France, 1978), III, xiii, 1068. All further references to the *Essais* appear in the text with accompanying indications of book, chapter, and page.
2. Two notable exceptions are Jane Couchman, "Twentieth-Century Responses to Montaigne" (Ph.D. diss., University of Toronto, 1971) and Ruth Grace, "Montaigne's Twentieth-Century Critics" (Ph.D. diss., University of Michigan, 1964). Although these works are useful in this study as background material, they are positivist inquiries, documenting for the most part what, when, and where professional critics wrote about Montaigne and his work. In both studies, there is little attempt at critical evaluation or a comprehensive understanding of twentieth-century receptions of Montaigne, or of his influence, and the writers covered remain for the most part outside the scope of this work.
3. Margot Norris, *The Decentered Universe of "Finnegans Wake"* (Baltimore: The Johns Hopkins UP, 1976), 139.
4. Julia Kristeva, *Semiotikè: Recherches pour une sémanlayse* (Paris: Editions du Seuil, 1969), 146.
5. Kristeva, *La révolution du langage poétique* (Paris: Editions du Seuil, 1974), 61-2.
6. Terence Cave, "Problems of Reading in the *Essais," Montaigne, Essays in Memory of Richard Sayce,* eds. I.D. McFarlane and Ian MacLean (Oxford: The Clarendon Press, 1982). More recently, Diane Beckman has carried out a highly original intertextual analysis of Montaigne's work. See *"The Wild Man: Images of Liminality. Prolegomena to a Study of Gilgamesh and Montaigne's 'Des cannibales'"* (Ph.D. diss., University of North Carolina at Chapel Hill, 1993).
7. Rosalie Colie, *Paradoxica Epidemica* (Princeton: Princeton UP, 1966), xii.
8. See Marcel Tetel's introduction to the work of Montaigne: *Montaigne: Updated Edition* (Boston: Twayne Publishers, 1990), 12.
9. Gerald Monsmon, "Pater and His Younger Contemporaries," *Victorian Newsletter* 48 (1975): 1.
10. D. W. Fokkema, "The Code of Modernism," *Actes du Huitième Congrès de l'Association Internationale de la Littérature Comparée* (Stuttgart: E. Bieber, 1980), 680.
11. John Burt Foster, *Heirs to Dionysus: A Nietzschean Current in Literary Modernism* (Princeton: Princeton UP, 1981), 3.
12. Roland Barthes, *Le Degré zéro de l'écriture* (Paris: Editions du Seuil, 1953), 8.
13. Fritz Zenn, "Remodeling Homer," *Light Rays: James Joyce and Modernism,* ed. Heyward Ehrlich (New York: New Horizon Press, 1984), 71.
14. Hans Robert Jauss, *Toward an Aesthetic of Reception* (Minneapolis: University of Minnesota Press, 1982), 19.

Chapter One

Receptions of the Essais: Beginnings and Continuities

Vous le dirai-je? Ce que j'admire le plus en lui, c'est le don de se contredire dans tout ce qu'il dit. A ce signe on reconnaît un esprit heureux et bienfaisant. Les natures les plus riches, les plus fécondes, sont aussi les plus abondantes en contradictions. On ne peut être souvent d'accord avec soi-même, quand on est à soi seul un monde.

— Anatole France, Preface to *Montaigne,* 1923.

A comprehensive evaluation of the history of Montaigne's interpreters would be the material of a separate study. The goal of this chapter is to schematize the history of Montaigne's receptions from the first appearance of the *Essais* in 1580 to the middle of the twentieth century, detailing the more salient and influential commentaries. Important work has been done in this vein, to which this chapter is indebted.[1] The overall purpose here is to examine the contours of critical receptions of the *Essais* as they have evolved over four centuries of French literary and intellectual history. This is not an attempt to extract a homogeneous paradigm of reading from the abundance of Montaigne commentary — such a coherent framework does not exist. The history of the interpretation of the *Essais* is marked by heterogeneity, paradox, and complexity; yet within this elaborate network we will be able to discern dominant trends emerging from readings, misreadings, appropriations, suppressions, and intentional distortions of the *Essais.* In evaluating the history of Montaigne's interpreters in France from the late sixteenth century to the middle of the twentieth, I will attempt to reconstitute the critical background of the *Essais,* to which their various receptions outside of France will be compared and contrasted in subsequent chapters.

There are several recurring phenomena that affect the evolving identity of the *Essais'* receptions. The first is the impulse to perform radical editorial surgery on the *Essais* and reduce them to a collection of precise pronouncements on popular themes by removing personal anecdotes, self-portraiture, digressions, quotations, and other "imperfections" deemed unacceptable according to seventeenth and eighteenth-century rules of literary taste. The second moves closer to the problems involved in interpreting the *Essais.* The fact is that many of Montaigne's commentators produce paradoxical judgments, revealing ambiguity and ambivalence in the course of their arguments. The *Essais,* a text that often foils unequivocal hermeneutic resolution, produces similar judgments, which are likewise unable to finalize a position, and instead leave behind them a precarious balance of antithetical propositions. The third brings us closer to the possibility of evaluating how Montaigne has been interpreted so as to adapt to various readers' intellectual predilections and how these readers have used him to develop their own thoughts. The most striking characteristic of this latter tendency is that each successive historical period produces interpretations of Montaigne in its own image, modifying a text whose collage-like qualities seem easily adaptable to such variegated reconstitutions of their identity.

In the following chapters, as the focus shifts to more recent receptions of Montaigne's work, I will determine whether there are modernist characteristics of the *Essais* that play a role in the work of Emerson, Nietzsche, Pater, Woolf, Butor, Chaillou, and Sollers or whether these writers' horizons of formative norms serve to constitute the putative modernism of the *Essais.* Finally, I will discuss whether it is a shift or an evolution in concerns that occurs between these modernist Montaigne commentators and the writers to be discussed in this chapter.

One of the first commentators on the *Essais,* the relatively unknown Flemish jurisconsult Dominique Baudier (Dominicus Baudius), an ambivalent admirer of Montaigne, should perhaps be remembered for his characterization of the problematic situation that the very attempt to study the *Essais'* receptions presents. Even at the early date of 1601, he prophesied: "Il n'y a aucun écrivain sur lequel on porte des jugements aussi divers ou plutôt aussi contraires que Michel de Montaigne."[2] This diversity of opinion concerning the *Essais*, as seen in the voluminous interpretation of four centuries, is highlighted by shifting attitudes and contrary judgments as well as by a certain regularity in this inconsistency. As Jauss maintains, the literary work does not stand still, and offers its monumental essence to succeeding generations for reshaping: "It is more like an orchestration that strikes new resonances among its readers and that frees the text from the material of the words and brings it to contemporary existence."[3] One would thus expect, as with any literary work, interpretations of the *Essais* to be colored by many different "horizons-of-experience." Gustave Lanson develops this same idea in his reception of Montaigne: "Mais c'est précisément par là que se révèle la richesse d'une oeuvre. Les possibilités de suggestion et de signification en sont infinies. Chaque époque, chaque esprit, développe celles qui s'accordent avec sa nature et sa tendance."[4] Yet even judgments of the *Essais* from the same period often diverge widely, and even the same writer will contradict his or her own previous point of view, prompting one to explore just how the *Essais*, a text of shifting judgments and unstable conclusions, manages to generate critical interpretations that are, in their own turn, often caught up in Montaigne's often irreconcilable paradoxes.

Montaigne has always gained the attention of a wide range of writers. I will focus on, in the words of Mathurin Dréano, the "maîtres d'opinion,"[5] yet also seek to discern certain trends of thought developed by lesser-known writers and editors whose efforts expose other dimensions of the *Essais'* identity. Montaigne himself was pleased with the first reactions to the *Essais*: "La faveur publique m'a donné un peu plus de hardiesse que je n'esperois" (III, ix, 964). Henri III was his first important admirer and complimented Montaigne in person. During Montaigne's journey to Italy several months after the first publication of 1580, he was mildly chastised on a few minor points by the Roman Inquisition, praised for the quality of his work and, as a result, made an honorary citizen of Rome. These first readers of the *Essais* admired them as a manual for the teachings of Greek and Latin antiquity. The *Essais* were most often read with limited purposes in mind and, from the late sixteenth century onward, were generally regarded as a handbook of popular philosophy. One of the first written professional commentaries was by the bibliographer La Croix du Maine in 1584. It is surprisingly flattering considering that Montaigne was a new author, one who had chosen to pay for the publication of his first edition: "ce beau livre qu'il a intitulé *Essais*."[6] Among the other contemporaries who praised his work, Montaigne's most renowned admirer was Justus Lipsius. The Dutch professor brought Montaigne the approval of scholarly authority, calling him the "Thales Gallicanus" and holding his greatest merit to be the resuscitation and popularization of classical wisdom.[7]

Another contemporary, Etienne Pasquier, jurist and friend of Montaigne, singles out his stoicism for praise, yet loses patience with the many digressions of the later editions, and eventually accuses Montaigne of producing a poorly organized collection of provincial eccentricities, a "ramage Gascon."[8] Pasquier's letter to M. de Pelgé is the first example of a commentary on the *Essais* that is contradictory in its polite criticism and ambivalent praise.[9] Pasquier oscillates between the poles of adulation and reproach as he gives an account of his understanding of Montaigne's life and work: "Vous désirez savoir de moi quel jugement je fais des *Essais* ... je vous le dirai en un mot: rien ne me déplait en iceux, encore que tout ne m'y plaise" (389). After this equivocal opening, he discusses his main objections: there are the Gasconisms about which he admonished Montaigne during their meeting at Blois in 1588; he even expresses dissatisfaction that they were never corrected. Pasquier considers Montaigne's "peinture du moi" trivial, even egotistical ("je ne lus jamais auteur qui s'estimait tant que lui" — 393) and Book III inferior to Books I and II, countering Marie de Gournay's claim that it was the consummation and perfection of the first two. He goes on to criticize Montaigne's free and easy style as an exercise in "*Coq-à-l'âne,* pour s'être donné pleine liberté de sauter d'un propos à autre, ainsi que le vent de son esprit donnait le vol à sa plume" (390). Pasquier finally offers a limited endorsement of Montaigne as another Seneca ("un autre Sénèque en notre langue" — 394) and compiles a list of maxims selected from the *Essais* (mostly misquoted) over which he waxes ecstatic. He does not admire the digressive, self-revealing qualities of Montaigne's writing, nor his irregular yet captivating style, preferring to admire the *Essais* merely as a repertory of moral commonplaces. Pasquier's fluctuation between praise and blame, and especially his desire to extract from the *Essais* what he wishes and to discard the innovative aspects as frivolous, is a dominant characteristic of one of the very first receptions of Montaigne's work, the desire to suppress that which is most innovative in it: self-referentiality, stylistic freedom, and especially the idiosyncratic development of subject matter.

Villey maintains that in the first wave of the *Essais*' receptions, including the learned evaluations by Lipsius and Pasquier, the most admired quality was "la mise en oeuvre d'une morale toute laïque et païenne dégagée de l'autorité religieuse."[10] He is read as an author of the *exemplum,* as a compiler of the commonplaces of ancient wisdom. The first edition of the *Essais* does in fact give the sense of an accumulation of anecdotes from which the author draws moral lessons, without the independent affirmation of the self-portrait and lacking the complicated attempt to portray the human condition in all of its variety and contradictions, aspects that characterize the later editions.[11]

Thus, during the years from the first edition until Montaigne's death, there are generally appreciative receptions of the *Essais.* Opposition begins to appear after the publication of the third book in 1588, for the most part in the form of reservations about Montaigne's stylistic idiosyncrasies and what was perceived as his intellectual incoherence.[12] The most frequent praises of the *Essais* at this time fall in the realm of the history of ideas: secular morality founded on the classics, political and religious tolerance, and the revival of classical wisdom. The *Essais* became, in fact, a popular breviary: "un trésor de sagesse moderne, un fidèle miroir de la nature humaine."[13] Montaigne was thus cast in a humanist mold, an author whose work focused on human values and capabilities, with a hyperconscious return to classical ideals.

In the late sixteenth century there began to appear less favorable judgemnts of the *Essais.* There were two principal areas of contention that prompted the first oppositions. The first is religious: Montaigne's fideism, skepticism, and hedonistic self-portraiture conflicted with a move toward increased orthodoxy and dogma contemporary with the consolidation of power of the ultraconservative *Ligue* and the rise of the *Contre-Réforme.*[14] The second is stylistic: the lack of rigorous method (the critique of Malherbe), obscurity and obscenity (that of Scaliger), and his use of Latinisms, Gasconisms, and neologisms (that of Pasquier). These attacks prompted Marie le Jars de Gournay, Montaigne's most active literary executor, who published eight editions of the *Essais* after his death, to complain in the "Préfaces aux *Essais*" in the 1595 edition about what she considered to be their poor reception: "Je veux rechercher la cause du froid recueil que nos hommes ont fait aux *Essais.*"[15] Gournay spent the greater part of her life defending the *Essais,* yet at the same time prompted a great deal of derision to be directed toward herself as well as toward Montaigne. This was due to her often blind enthusiasm for the *Essais,* but especially to her tenacious efforts in defending and perpetuating that which was looked upon as most original in his work, and thereby most threatening to France's literary authorities. The many scathing attacks directed against Montaigne and the *Essais* by his critics justified such defense as Gournay's. Baudier was one of the first to berate Montaigne for his lack of coherent method: "Montaigne mérite tout au plus d'être regardé par les savants comme un de ces brouillons qui gâche l'étude et les lettres en s'y adonnant à tort et à travers."[16] This attack on Montaigne's compositional irregularity is a recurring motif in the commentaries of his detractors. It allowed many critics to avoid serious textual analysis, each being content to adopt the position that Montaigne's style was too unorthodox to merit attentive stylistic consideration.

Gournay was correct in maintaining that Montaigne was accused above all "de quelque usurpation du Latin, de la fabrique de nouveaux mots, et d'employer quelques phrases nonchalantes ou Gasconnes."[17] Montaigne's literary form was too open and personal for the *docte* interpreters to accept without reservations: "une botte contre les pédants et leur science matérielle."[18] The *Essais* were too idiosyncratically disorienting and deviated too often from accepted modes of literary discourse. This line of criticism began to manifest itself at the end of the sixteenth century and became an increasingly important issue in the seventeenth century, especially after the founding of the *Académie Française* in 1637. Villey sees this as the major problem for Montaigne's detractors: " … comment tolérer un esprit sans méthode, un auteur sans ordre, et qui encore se vante de son désordre?"[19] Gournay counterattacked Pasquier, Baudier, and Malherbe for being "impertinens juges," and particularly for their criticisms of Montaigne's language and style, which she believed to be misfounded and based on intentional misreadings of the text for ideological reasons. This antipathy toward the *Essais* was inspired, especially in the case of Malherbe, by his project of banishing from the French language what he considered to be the impurities that had arisen from the excessive attempts to enrich it during the sixteenth century. Malherbe reproached Montaigne in person for "l'usage de Gascogne, et non de nostre langue Françoise." Pasquier accuses him of using "de mots inaccoutumez," and Baudier declares that the *Essais* are "rempli de défauts."[20]

To summarize the position of Montaigne's detractors at this time: the *Essais* are lacking in methodical argument, scholastic rigor, and linear development. Montaigne is of course adamant in his critique of what he considered the ossified practice of systematic rhetorical argument. He develops his refutation of scholastic education in "De l'institution des enfans," calling for a more personally meaningful manner of expression, one depending less on arbitrary rules of procedure, and more on an individual's use of his own judgment:

> Qu'il ne luy demande pas seulement compte des mots de sa leçon, mais du sens et de la substance, et qu'il juge du profit qu'il aura fait, non par le tesmoinage de sa memoire, mais de sa vie. Que ce qu'il viendra d'apprendre, il le lui face mettre en cent visages et accommoder à autant de divers subjets, pour voir s'il l'a encore bien pris et bien faict sien. (I, xxvi, 151)

Montaigne's stylistic heterogeneity rattled his critics of the late sixteenth century, who were "scandalisés de ne trouver ici ni préambules, ni partitions, ni conclusions; point de ces divisions oratoires lourdement annoncées, méthodiquement suivies, qui donnent l'impression au lecteur — à tort ou à raison, d'ailleurs, — que le sujet a été examiné sous toutes les coutures, traité tout au long. C'est au mode de composition de Montaigne qu'ils s'en prennent."[21] Here is the greatest reservation about Montaigne's work, which resurfaces repeatedly as one of the key issues in the reception of the *Essais* for nearly four hundred years: the *Essais* transgress institutionalized modes of literary production by taking extravagant liberties with linguistic structures, and thereby threaten accepted modes of discourse. In the seventeenth century, it was considered an amusing yet disorienting work, and finally, a dangerous book in need of suppression. Montaigne's style was not regarded favorably, nor did it often play an explicit role in the work of other writers, outside of Pascal, Diderot, and Rousseau, until the nineteenth century.

The relationship of Gournay and Montaigne is complex and worth some attention. She was the first champion of the Montaignean cause, and a source from which the modern feminist spirit emanated in France. It is a curious fact that Montaigne, often accused of a misogynist dimension in his writing — by virtue of several general statements about women's role as being primarily reproductive and domestic — nevertheless addressed women readers and entrusted the posthumous fate of his work to a woman.[22] It is thus useful to consider this apparent contradiction and explore the question of Montaigne and feminism (to which we will return in Chapter Three in a discussion of Virginia Woolf's reception of the *Essais*). As Leschemelle demonstrates, for all of the advances of the humanistic revolution of sixteenth-century France, there was an accompanying intolerance, bigotry, and ignorance — all of which promoted religious fanaticism, witch burnings, along with the repressive notion of women's inferiority and the accompanying efforts to shackle them to domestic lives and childbearing while depriving them of an education. Montaigne was very much a "digne fils de son temps" and did not escape "tous les poncifs misogynes de son époque."[23] The *Essais* are in fact full of references to the inferiority of women and there is a near total absence of references to his mother, wife, and daughter, in contrast to the many eulogies for his father and La Boétie. No single passage can summarize Montaigne's attitude toward women, as a man of his time, better than the following: "La plus utile et honnorable science et occupation à une femme, c'est la science du mesnage" (III, ix, 975). He claims that women are inferior to men ("les natures plus faibles comme des femmes" — I, i, 8), possess dangerous sexual appetites ("un animal glouton et avide," — III, v, 859), and must be controlled in a marriage based on family propagation and marital duty ("on se marie plus pour sa posterité, pour sa famille" — III, v,

850). Montaigne, the sage, thus follows "les facons et les formes receus" (I, xxiii, 118) of his time; yet, on the other hand, Montaigne, the divided being, the paradoxical man, also demarcates a position that contradicts his explicit misogynistic pronouncements.

The first instance of his acceptance of women as intellectual equals can be seen in the fact that he dedicated five important chapters to learned women: "De l'institution des enfans" (Diane de Foix), "Vingt et neuf sonnets d'Estienne de la Boétie" (Madame de Grammont), "De l'affection des peres aux enfans" (Madame d'Estissac), "Apologie de Raimond Sebond" (Marguerite de Valois), and "De la ressemblance des enfans aux peres" (Madame de Duras). In these chapters, as Cathleen Bauschatz has demonstrated, Montaigne looks to women for concurrence and support as he attacks the haloed male-dominated institutions of his time: religion, education, medicine, and law.[24] In addressing these essays to women, Montaigne seems to be aware of their importance as readers who would more readily accept his radically divergent views on the sacred institutions of European civilization. Elsewhere, he claims that women should only be allowed to read poetry, history, and moral philosophy (III, iii, 823), thereby betraying his putative misogyny; for this is exactly what he preferred to read, as he tells us in "Des livres."[25] In terms of the Renaissance male hegemony, woman is defined in contrast to rationalism and the intellect, as frivolous, overly imaginative, and linked to bodily desires. Yet these are exactly the weaknesses Montaigne was accused of by his male detractors, in addition to being too indiscreet in his discussions of sex and general physiology, too ornamental, too free in his manner of expression, and especially too lacking in systematic method and the logic of reason. What is striking here is that if women are considered to be the antithesis of masculine reason, consistency, and other social tyrannies (what Montaigne outwardly adheres to in his various pronouncements of the shortcomings of women), these are the very strictures against which he furtively revolts. In many of his essays, he pokes fun at the incoherence of professors, outlandish medical practices, unjust attitudes toward New World inhabitants, and the incongruities of the French legal system. The paradoxical movement between misogynist *énoncés* and "feminized" *énonciations* (even Montaigne claims that the characteristics of his writing are "libres et desreglées" — II, xvii, 638) shows him to be pragmatic in paying lip service to the commonplaces of his time, yet simultaneously daring and subversive in granting women the role of intellectual authority by dedicating chapters to them, and especially by generating a personal and intimate discourse that counteracted the patriarchal norms of objectivity in style and virile subject matter. By turning to Montaigne's encounter and subsequent relationship with Gournay, we can consider the general outlines of Montaigne's "feminism" in a more particularized context.

Montaigne's friendship with Gournay may very well have helped to enhance, in his later work, his acceptance of women as intellectual beings. At the same time, Montaigne had a profound influence on the life and writing of this woman, who would become the most important feminist of her time.[26] Gournay met Montaigne in 1588. Their ensuing friendship and intellectual collaboration has several important aspects. The first is that it appears that Gournay actually wrote in some of the additions to the 1588 edition, as dictated by Montaigne during his several visits to her home in the fall of that year. It is, most notably, from this time (as Insdorf has documented) that some of Montaigne's more favorable comments on the female condition begin to appear (especially in the "feminizing" of certain passages of the "C-layer" of the *Essais* — which contain the final additions Montaigne made to the 1588 edition in the last four years of his life — as Cottrell has discussed). Whether or not a more progressive attitude toward women can be directly associated with his relationship to Gournay, and whether she helped to embed a feminist strain in the later stages of Montaigne's work, is of course beyond empirical proof. Yet around this time Montaigne did begin to make some egalitarian claims for women. It seems as if his newfound friend fulfilled the feminine side of spiritual friendship, the female counterpart to La Boétie, never experienced by Montaigne with his wife, and perhaps stimulated him to sincerely consider women in a less chauvinistic light. One can sense Gournay's effect on Montaigne's declarations at the end of "Sur des vers de Virgile," which surfaced later in her *Egalité des hommes et des femmes*. Montaigne first refers to Plato, who demanded the participation of both men and women in "tous études, exercices, charges, vacations guerrieres et paisibles, en sa republique," and then to Antisthenes, who "ostoit toute distinction entre leur vertu et la nostre" (III, v, 897). It is hard not to think of Gournay's life and writings, and also of the feminist mark left on the *Essais,* while reading "je dis que les masles et femelles sont jettez en mesme moule: sauf l'institution et l'usage, la difference n'y est pas grande" (III, v, 897). Whether or not she was directly responsible for such a progressive attitude, Gournay must, at the very least, have inspired Montaigne to reevaluate his previous attitudes toward women.

A second aspect of their relationship began after Montaigne's death as Gournay prepared what would become the definitive manuscript for subsequent editions of the *Essais* for the next two hundred years. The 1595 edition of the *Essais* also contained Gournay's preface, a long and extremely passionate defense of Montaigne's life and work. In it she champions Montaigne's intimate self-portrait, which did not appeal to a male literary establishment threatened by his private subjectivity, honesty, and personal intimacy. She eventually oversaw the publication of eight editions of the *Essais* and was a central figure in helping to establish the heritage of his work as well as a tireless defender against the narrow minds of such neoclassical literary critics as Scaliger, Malherbe, Racan, and others. Yet this is no mere father/daughter relationship, or patriarchal subservience on the part of Gournay. She actively engaged the *Essais* and the legacy of their author, even at times contradicting Montaigne, and ultimately using the experience to her own advantage. Her role as the definitive editor of the *Essais* for over forty years provided her with a steady income through most of her professional life. Her first work, a novella, *Le Proumenoir de Monsieur de Montaigne,* has nothing at all to do with Montaigne, nor with the *Essais;* she uses the fact that they took a walk one day and discussed love in Plutarch's *Lives* as well as in Claude de Taillemont's *Histoire des Champs Faëz* — works from which she takes her storyline. She also claims herself as the "fille d'alliance" of Montaigne on the title page — a useful device, along with the fact that she timed the publication of *Le Proumenoir* to coincide with her first edition of the *Essais* in 1595, to help herself, an young unknown woman writer, secure a reputation in a male literary world.

Montaigne inspires his readers "imaginer d'autres confessions à mes dépens" and Gournay accepts the challenge by appropriating the *Essais* for her own purposes. Along with this self-promotion in the wake of Montaigne's growing posthumous fame, there is the controversial passage in which Montaigne praises Gournay and publicizes his adoption of her as a "fille d'alliance." Part of the passage was a handwritten addition to a previous addition, and many now agree that it was most likely that Gournay embellished Montaigne's acknowledgment of her as she prepared the 1595 manuscript.[27] In thus supplementing Montaigne's praise for her, she inscribes her feminine self on the text of her "father" in order to immortalize her own name. Although full of praise for Montaigne, she must overcome him in order to establish her own identity. This is a move very much in the spirit of Montaigne's relationship to his own father, whom he praises highly in his work while abandoning at the same time the patronym Eyquem, renouncing the parliamentary position his father had acquired for him, and generally leading a life contrary to his father's own. Pierre Eyquem was a proud soldier, shrewd merchant, efficient manager of his estate, unquestioning admirer of humanism, and a loving husband and father; Montaigne was none of these. After his father's death, Michel was free to become Montaigne — the dynamic of overcoming the father in order to develop one's own unique identity has a metaphoric interrelation between Montaigne's and Gournay's lives and works. She would first promote the *Essais*, then surpass them by developing her own literary identity and ideological position that were far removed from Montaigne's own. Later, we will see a similar dynamic operating in Woolf's reception of Montaigne.

A third aspect of Gournay's relationship with Montaigne is her explicit respect and affection for Montaigne's mother, wife and daughter, Antoinette, Françoise and Léonor. She established a close relationship with them (something Montaigne himself was never to do) during her two-year stay at Montaigne's château where, along with Montaigne's Bordelais friend, Pierre de Brach, she prepared the *Essais* for publication. In her "Quatrains pour la maison de Montaigne," Gournay praises their admirable qualities and expresses gratitude for their friendship.[28] In this sense, Gournay gives life to the women whom Montaigne appears to have destined to oblivion (he rarely mentions them in the *Essais*, and never in any detail) by improving on Montaigne's shortcomings in the treatment of the females in his family. This, coupled with her adaptation of Montaigne's notion of the dynamic relationship of one's inherited materials (people and books) needed to produce one's own unique personality in writing, helped Gournay to produce her own discourse. Like Montaigne, she used that which helped to support her literary origins (in the case of Montaigne, his readings, in Gournay's, the *Essais*) and then continued to become increasingly independent in her self-expression, more or less leaving behind the foundations of her beginnings, although they remained embedded and nourished her own idiosyncratic extensions of them. Like the 1580 edition of the *Essais*, the "texte de base" which is very much a dialog with La Boétie and Montaigne's chosen authors of antiquity, Gournay's early career was a dialog with Montaigne and the *Essais*; the further she progressed in her work (much the same as Montaigne continued to revise and move beyond his early "exemplary" essays to develop the later ones characterized by self-portraiture), the more she developed her flourishing literary feminism, moving away from, even contradicting the *Essais*, and at times even ignoring some of the more blatant aspects of Montaigne's questionable attitude toward women, which contradicted her position as a feminist. We can see this dynamic operating in the evolution of her writings.

By 1597, Gournay had seen the successful publication of the *Essais* and of the *Proumenoir*, resolved several pressing family affairs, traveled to Belgium to promote the sale of both works, and was beginning a career as a professional writer, one who would eventually be considered the "Sirène de France," a thorn in the side of the male literary establishment.[29] She proved herself to be not only a writer of quality, but also a shrewd businesswoman, feminist polemicist, and literary authority who helped to found the *Académie Française*. She was able to survive financial hardships, public ridicule, and even the cruel practical jokes of her male adversaries. Her *Grief des dames* and *Egalité des hommes et des femmes* are important works that demarcate an important discursive space in the evolution of French feminism. Through all of this, she published important editions of the *Essais*, particularly the first posthumous edition of 1595, that of 1598 (containing Montaigne's handwritten additions to his own copy found in the château), that of 1617 (which was the first to include translations of the Latin quotations and cite their sources), and finally the 1635 edition, which was dedicated, perhaps ironically, to Cardinal Richelieu, no great admirer of the *Essais* or of Gournay. Gournay never ceased to defend Montaigne's stylistic "irregularities," which was one important reason why she was ostracized by the literary establishment. Independent and tenacious, she supported family dependents for many years and maintained as well a lifestyle commensurate with her status as a professional woman of letters, a rarity of her time. It was no small task to solicit monetary subventions for her writing in an environment hostile to women of free thought and independent means, and to do so until the age of seventy-nine. Her self-awakening to a literary career stems from her first reading of the *Essais* at the age of eighteen, at which time she became so captivated by their contents that she sought out Montaigne in Paris in 1588 to become his closest female collaborator — an extraordinary accomplishment for an impoverished, provincial, self-taught, aristocratic woman.

Gournay fought for Montaigne as she fought for women's rights and the *Essais* serve as a continual thread through her life and writing. The preface she wrote for the 1595 edition was immediately attacked as naive, self-serving, and overly enthusiastic. Gournay quickly retracted it from subsequent editions and even apologized for it in the 1598 edition, although she reinstated it in its entirety in the 1635 edition, attesting to the belief in what she had first written and now feeling more secure as an established writer who could do as she pleased. What she admired in the *Essais* and so passionately defended are their most original qualities, the very ones that made Montaigne's work distastefully presumptuous for the critics of the early seventeenth century, yet qualities that have endeared the *Essais* to so many readers and which are now more comprehensible than ever: his latinisms and regionalisms, which give the text a lexical richness, his frank discussions of sexual and physiological matters, his digressions, unique manner of composition, problematic ambiguity on religious and political questions, and especially his intimate self-analysis. Gournay promotes that which in the *Essais* would be officially suppressed during the seventeenth century and not really admired or understood until the nineteenth and twentieth centuries. Her own precarious position as an early feminist, and the increasing opinion that Montaigne was a *libertin*, did much to incur the wrath of the Malherbian circle of cultural authorities. In all of this, Gournay proved to be the most perspicacious and visionary of all Montaigne readers of her time, defending the *Essais* as a difficult modernist text *avant la lettre*.

Yet Gournay was no fawning disciple, and although she sought Montaigne's approval of the *Proumenoir* (which she never received), she came to extract from the *Essais* that which served her cause and contradicted other aspects when necessary — even using Montaigne's suggestions against him. Montaigne, although he saw women's role as primarily domestic and reproductive, also declared that they were "jettez en mesme moule" as men and even decried the pervasive injustice toward women: "les femmes n'ont pas tort du tout quand elles refusent les reigles de vie qui sont introduites au monde, d'autant que ce sont les hommes qui les ont faictes sans elles" (III, v, 854). Yet it is Gournay who puts into practice what Montaigne only hints at, motivating the heroine of the *Proumenoir,* Alinda, to refuse the patriarchal "reigles de vie" at the risk of her own well-being. Gournay picks up on Montaigne's suggestion and from it elaborates a new position, creating her own discursive space in the production of a feminist identity. Although the book was in many ways a *roman de chevalerie,* Montaigne's least favorite type of reading ("Quant aux Amadis et *telles sortes d'escrits,* ils n'ont pas eu le credit d'arrester seulement mon enfance" — II, x, 410 — emphasis added), Gournay always maintained a didactic purpose in the *Proumenoir* — pedagogy through example, so essential to Montaigne, also characterizes a good deal of this and other of her works.

Gournay's first important theoretical work is in fact on education. In *De L'Education des enfants de France* Gournay owes much to Montaigne's "De l'institution des enfans" and likewise claims that the key to social progress is in the intellectual formation of children through a humanistic education. Yet in what is perhaps her most important polemical work, *Egalité des hommes et des femmes,* Gournay far surpasses Montaigne's notions on education by declaring the intellectual equality of men and women and by demanding a formal education for the latter. *Egalité* is above all a work that explores the nature and identity of the feminine condition in a style that is much unlike Montaigne's. A rigorous and logical structure is maintained throughout the treatise — a good demonstration of how

Gournay grafts her own position onto points of reference found in the *Essais,* then goes beyond them, perhaps exceeding Montaigne's wildest expectations: "Le discours féminin de Marie de Gournay détourne le cours des divers hypotextes masculins dont elle se sert comme référence mais non comme modèle pour construire le texte de l'*Egalité*."[30] Gournay thus finds herself in a paradoxical situation and must forgive Montaigne by avoiding his pronounced reservations on giving women an education. Gournay seems to overcome the contradiction by ignoring it, transforming what is useful in the *Essais* to her own designs, and even accepting that, like Montaigne's declaration on the human condition, she too is "divers et ondoyant" (I, i, 9). In this sense, Gournay proves herself to be a very Montaignean author — the content of her writings is quite different from Montaigne's, yet the *Essais* are the work that most stimulated her liberated examination, individualism, analysis of passions, and debate of gender issues. Gournay's feminism, far beyond Montaigne's notion of the sexes, is nevertheless made possible by his demonstrating the possibility of free intellectual inquiry; her mode of literary production is founded upon his: the active reconstituting of one's precursors in a new and unique work.

It is perhaps in the 1626 collection of her works *L'Ombre de la Damoiselle de Gournay* that the "essayistic" dimensions of Gournay's literary project can be most clearly seen. This collection contained everything she had published since 1595, along with two autobiographical texts and a new feminist treatise, *Grief des dames.* This anthology of her works lent itself to many rewritings and expansions and was subsequently republished in 1634 and 1641. Its composition, described by Dezon-Jones in the following passage, was strikingly similar in quality to Montaigne's writing of the *Essais*:

> La constitution de ce recueil canalise les grands thèmes traités par Marie de Gournay autour d'une *grande souplesse de structure qui lui permet de multiples ré-écritures et expansions et des possibilités d'additions infinies,* sans que le lecteur perçoive les raccords de 1634 et de 1641. Dans son état de 1626, l'*Ombre* fait penser à un quilt composé de différents morceaux d'étoffe, aux couleurs variées mais complémentaires, patiemment assemblés au fil des années, et à partir de la juxtaposition desquels, s'organisent de grands motifs. (79 — emphasis added)

There is in fact more than a little Montaigneanism in Gournay's writing, especially in her treatment of moral, philosophical, or religious matters, in which she generally discusses a certain theme, around which she multiplies reflections based on personal experience, on her readings, and especially on the Latin and Greek quotations that call to mind different chapters of the *Essais*. Indeed, in almost every work she wrote she refers to Montaigne and the *Essais*. Yet Gournay will not let us forget, although she is greatly indebted to Montaigne, even referring overtly to the *Essais* several times in *Grief*, that she is "une femme qui parle."[31] Gournay's reception of Montaigne is thus at once faithful and devious, innovative in its use of Montaigne against himself — which, paradoxically, is what he calls on his readers to do ("à mes despens").

In *Les Advis ou les presens de la Demoiselle de Gournay*, written in 1624 (by which time she was a well-established writer), Gournay claims to have clearly rearticulated Montaigne's style and project: "estant fille adoptive d'un père qui s'est dépeind luy-mesme, je semble estre conviée par son example de dépeindre ou dire le prix de mon livre."[32] She finds in the *Essais* inspiration for producing her own ideas, which often run against their source. Like Montaigne, she is outwardly conservative (even more so in religious matters, as seen for example in her near reactionary *Défense des pères Jésuites*) but also an innovative "modern," as seen in her feminist project and in her efforts to counter the Malherbian strictures of purified lexicon, regularized syntax, and unequivocal meaning.[33] Gournay, especially in her *Traité sur la poésie*, demands a freedom of expression and a poetic license in order to portray a fuller and more natural expression of the complex human situation. Between the neoclassicists and the *précieux*, Gournay, like Montaigne, is a conservative radical, taking a middle path between the ancients and moderns, from which she produces a woman's version of Montaigne's unique discourse that could only scandalize the male hegemony of the time. Montaigne was subtle in his innovation, Gournay bold and daring in hers.

The modern spirit embodied in Gournay's promotion of women as writers and full human beings, though far beyond Montaigne's own notions in such matters, nevertheless arises in great part from her reading and rereading of the *Essais* over a period of sixty years, a text she knew more intimately than any other reader of the time. Her work, like Montaigne's was suppressed — the *Essais* officially,

Gournay's unofficially — because it did not fit in with what was deemed official culture. Gournay's importance in the history of Montaigne's reception cannot be overemphasized — it is a significant accomplishment for a woman of her time and place. Montaigne's role in the history of feminism is more complex and can perhaps never be formulated unequivocally due to the contradictory nature of his relationship to women in his life and writing. Yet we have seen that he prepares the way for Gournay and for the modern feminist spirit to flourish. More than any other person of her time, Gournay clearly announces Montaigne's modernity, particularly in the preface to the 1635 edition of the *Essais,* both in style and in subject matter: "Adjoustons, que cette égale et plaisante beauté de ce livre, *son nouvel air,* son intention et *sa forme incogneuës jusques à nos jours,* expriment assez, que quiconque l'ait escrit, l'a conçeu. *Nouvel air,* dis-je" (emphasis added).[34] Gournay's accomplishment in promoting the *Essais,* as well as her protofeminist project, was, however, largely ignored for several centuries.[35]

Montaigne had two other important disciples who were pivotal figures in the continued transmission of the *Essais* to a wider audience in the early seventeenth century. Their cases are much clearer and less problematic than that of Gournay. The theologian Pierre Charron's contribution was indirect. After Gournay, he was Montaigne's most devoted follower; in his most important work, *De la Sagesse* (1601), "he arranged and tabulated his master's living ideas like dead flowers in a herbarium."[36] The greatest effect of *De la Sagesse* "was to increase the dissemination and intensify the influence of the *Essays.*"[37] Charron sought to disseminate a popular wisdom founded on Montaigne's notion of self-analysis: "Bref, nous n'avons point de plus beau miroir et de meilleur livre que nous mesmes si nous n'y voulons bien estudier, comme nous devons, tenant toujours l'oeil ouvert sur nous, et nous espiant de près."[38] Yet Charron did not identify as closely with Montaigne as did Gournay and, although he was a friend of Montaigne's, wished to control what he considered to be the irregular dimensions of the *Essais.* To do so, Charron reduced them to a logical, scholastic text by producing a more linear reading of their contents and thus promoting the extraction of coherent doctrines, something Montaigne did not intend and that was subsequently used against him with negative consequences for the *Essais*' popularity. Villey shows us how Charron freely pillaged the *Essais* for material ("Charron a entrepris de les filtrer et de les refaire"), methodized their arguments, and faithfully adapted them to develop his own fideist notion of the separation of faith and reason, a position that came under vicious attack by the Jansenist movement.[39] He is thus another to adopt Montaigne's metaphor of the bees who transform thyme and marjoram into honey: "ainsi les pieces empruntées d'autruy, il les transformera et confondera, pour en faire un ouvrage tout sien" (I, xxvi, 152). He both renders a service to Montaigne by perpetuating his ideas and does him a disservice by distorting those ideas through a systematic recasting in a manner far from Montaigne's writings ("crotesques, qui sont peintures fantasques, n'ayant grace qu'en la variété et estrangeté" ... "libres et desreglées"). Charron's notion of the separation of faith and reason, along with his religious tolerance, was vigorously assaulted, and in turn, the same arguments used against him were used against the *Essais*, whose fideism was highlighted by Charron's appropriation, reduction, methodization, and popularization. Through this type of distortion, perhaps unaware of the potential negative consequences, Charron reduces Montaigne's complexity to dogmatic positions that the latter never really maintained, changing entire passages to alter their meaning; modifying, for example, Montaigne's dynamic "que sçay-je?" into a static "je ne sçay." Montaigne's paradoxes and conjectures thus become heavy-handed dogmas.

The *Essais*, read through the screen of Charron's reductive interpretation, became caricaturized and were consequently an easier target for attack. Charron's work enjoyed great success in the seventeenth and early eighteenth centuries and was as popular a source for the *Essais* as were the *Essais* themselves. They were thus read by the public at large, not in their original form, but in expurgated editions that provided slick neoclassicized versions, reducing the *Essais*' undulating textuality to rationalized, clarified, and homogenized dimensions. The *Essais* in this form disseminated a clichéd secular humanism among the public, which could only have had a positive pedagogical effect, yet were deprived of their impulse to show that dogmatic solutions to issues concerning the human experience in its cultural and institutional complexity are more problematic than a rigorous rationalism can ultimately resolve. The official version of the *Essais* in the first half of the seventeenth century presented a Montaigne who emulated its own standards of *le naturel, la raison, le bon sens,* and *la vraisemblance*. He was a model of how *to live* an authentic humanism: "Montaigne apparaissait comme l'éducateur de l'honnête homme."[40] The cultural authoritarianism emanating from Malherbe, Richelieu, and their disciples attempted to stylistically transform Montaigne into a writer of clarity and precision, banishing any untamed provincial individualism in the wake of *La Fronde*. The cultural canon was regularized while the monarchy centralized its political and religious control over France — Rabelais was all but banished, Ronsard and Du Bellay vigorously disposed of by Malherbe. Montaigne survived, but in expurgated form.

The other significant reception of Montaigne at the turn of the seventeenth century was by Jean-Pierre Camus. He calls himself the "natural" disciple of Montaigne and sprinkles the eleven volumes of his work *Diversitez* (1609) with quotations, eulogies, defenses, explications, and digressions on the *Essais*. *Diversitez* is in many ways a series of pastiches of the *Essais*. It was the work, along with Charron's, most responsible for the continued popularity of Montaigne during the seventeenth century. Camus correctly insists upon self-portraiture as Montaigne's central project and, along with Gournay, surpasses in perspicacity the critics who chastised the *Essais* on this point. Camus uses Montaigne's work to support his own fideism and skepticism, yet remains within the teachings of the Catholic Church. *Diversitez* is a series of dehydrated essays, abundant in quotations and authoritative references, yet with none of the playful movement between the "je" and the "nous" so prevalent in the *Essais*. It is moreover a very impersonal, abstract work, teeming with Montaignean commonplaces, yet with no explicit references to him. There is even an index that systematically orders the detailed contents of the work. The cases of Charron, a doctor of law, and Camus, a bishop, thus show two professional men attempting to produce more mainstream versions of the *Essais* (both became popular best-sellers) — using them for moral purposes, enriching themselves in the process, yet abandoning the *Essais'* more disconcerting aspects, central to the project of their author.

During the seventeenth century, Montaigne seems to have produced a myriad of competing interpretations. No important writer of the day could avoid passing judgment on his work. Receptions of the *Essais* thereby extended their life, but did so in a number of often conflicting ways. Boase's examination of Montaigne's commentators in the seventeenth century documents interpretations, assimilations, and possible influences concerning a wide range of writers. Most striking are the contrary opinions the *Essais* provoke, ranging from unlimited praise to virulent attacks. Even in the same writer, a love-hate relationship often surfaces when confronting Montaigne's work. As Boase puts its: "Hence the amusing spectacle of people who borrow from Montaigne with one hand and strike him with the other, while what they borrow and what they blame coexist in the *Essais*."[41] Marie de Sévigné, for example, singles out Montaigne for praise: "Ah! l'aimable homme! qu'il est de bonne compagnie, c'est mon ancien ami ... Mon Dieu, que ce livre est plein de bon sens."[42] Yet soon after, she disparages him as a dangerous writer because of his heterodoxy in religious matters as well his physiological frankness, and forbids her grand-daughter to read the *Essais*: "Je ne voudrais point du tout qu'elle mit son petit nez ni dans Montaigne ni dans Charron, ni dans *les autres de cette sorte* (emphasis added)."[43] Montaigne is thus characterized as one of those shocking, undesirable writers, even while his work, according to Sevigné, is full of good common sense.

The *Essais* were widely available in many forms during the seventeenth century before being placed on the Papal Index. According to Boase, approximately thirty-five printings appeared between 1600-1669. This is the time of their greatest accessibility and popularity; later they would be eclipsed for over a century. By virtue of their extensive self-analysis, the *Essais* were a primary model for the greatest preoccupation of the seventeenth century, the exploration of human motivation: "Toute notre littérature du grand siècle n'est qu'une perpétuelle analyse du coeur humain. Montaigne l'avait préparée."[44] The general reading public was seduced by Montaigne as an explorer of human nature: "C'est parce que les hommes du XVIIe siècle ont reconnu en Montaigne un maître du coeur, l'égal pour le moins des Sénèque et des Plutarque, qu'ils ont lu les *Essais*."[45] Ironically, Montaigne was most often attacked for his egotistical self-analysis. It is also his easy conversational style that provided this first great appeal to the general reading public. Several years before the proscription of the *Essais*, Huët, Bishop of Avranches, wrote: "Son esprit libre, son style varié et ses expressions métaphoriques lui ont principalement mérité cette grande vogue, dans laquelle il a été pendant plus d'un siècle."[46] The book was considered a bestseller and a classic, and found in most French household libraries. Yet despite their success, a countercurrent of antipathy to the *Essais* eventually eroded their popularity.

The most distorted critiques of the *Essais* in the seventeenth century, which would have have a profound effect on their reception, were those of Pascal, of the *Logique de Port-Royal* by Arnauld and Nicole, and of Malebranche. These writers' attacks ultimately smothered the popularity of the *Essais* under a blanket of harsh and often unjust criticism. In addition to these critiques, an increasing theological rationalism inspired by Descartes worked against the *Essais*. There was increased reaction to his fideism for; at this time, it was increasingly believed that the existence of God and the immortality of the soul could be proven by rational inquiry. The Cartesian influence on religion in seventeenth-century France, using the truth of reason to explain the truth of faith, did much to discredit Montaigne and his agnostic position that we can never know God yet must nevertheless accept his grace to overcome the infirmity of our condition — a position that rendered him incompatible with an increasingly dogmatic Christianity.[47] It was Montaigne's ambiguity on religious matters that often disturbed these readers. If one of his gestures is to inscribe a degree of undecideability in his text in order to engage active participation, then this move also produces the possibility that the *Essais* can be used in completely contrary ways, either for or against him. Montaigne's pyrrhonian skepticism, divided consciousness, and hermeneutic slipperiness often placed him in between oppositional forces — in this case either of Christianity (both the Jansenist and Jesuit modes) or secular *libertinage* — witness Cyrano de Bergerac and Théophile de Viau, both open enthusiasts of the *Essais* and both victims of a death inflicted by Richelieu's hegemony, which could not accept their ideological and stylistic opposition to its political practices and aesthetic doctrines.[48] It is at this time that the scales tipped toward the destruction of the *Essais*' reputation and their eventual abolishment in France.

A specific analysis of what Pascal's *Pensées* owes to the *Essais* would entail extensive attention, much of which has already been carried out.[49] What is difficult to come to terms with in Pascal's reception of the *Essais* is his ambivalence toward them and their author. They were a life-long obsession for him — he was alternately impressed and repulsed by Montaigne, and continued the latter's attempt to expose human vanity, weakness, and ignorance, yet without any of the essayist's self-referential indulgence. Overall, they had different purposes, and Pascal made numerous criticisms of Montaigne's accomplishment. He was tormented by the duality of the *Essais*, accentuating Montaigne's proposal that "nous sommes, je ne sçay comment, doubles en nous-mesmes, qui faict que ce que nous croyons, nous ne le croyons pas, et ne nous pouvons deffaire de ce que nous condamnons" (II, xvi, 619). Pascal could not rid himself of what he condemned, often using Montaigne's thought as a starting point for his own, while ultimately reproaching the latter's style, irreligion, and irrationality. The most important account of his relation to Montaigne is found in the conversation between him and Le Maître de Sacy.[50] Beyond that, as Brunschvicg has demonstrated, nearly all of the *Pensées* owe something to the *Essais*.[51] Pascal's debt to Montaigne is substantial, yet his attitude toward what he finds reprehensible in the *Essais* is severe. His most celebrated criticism can be found in *Pensée* 62:

> Parler de ceux qui ont traité de la connaissance de soi-même ... de la confusion de Montaigne; qu'il avait bien senti le défaut d'une droite méthode, qu'il l'évitait en sautant de sujet en sujet, qu'il cherchait le bon air. Le sot projet qu'il a de se peindre! et cela non pas en passant et contre ses maximes, comme il arrive à tout le monde de faillir; mais par ses propres maximes, et par un dessein premier et principal. Car de dire des sottises par hasard et par faiblesse, c'est un mal ordinaire; mais d'en dire par dessein, c'est ce qui n'est pas supportable, et d'en dire que celles ci ... .[52]

Pascal accuses Montaigne of writing unmethodically, and of doing so intentionally, by leaping from one subject to another: "il cherche le bon air." This criticism attacks Montaigne's method of composition, yet Pascal can forgive this defect more than he can his outspoken language (especially in "Sur des vers de Virgile") and, more importantly, his attitude toward death. These latter objections are put forth in *Pensée* 63:

> Les défauts de Montaigne sont grands. Mots lascifs ... Crédule, *gens sans yeux*. Ignorant, *quadrature du cercle, monde plus grand*. Ses sentiments sur l'homicide volontaire, sur la mort. Il inspire une nonchalance du salut, *sans crainte et sans repentir* ... On peut excuser ses sentiments un peu libres et voluptueux en quelques rencontres de la vie; mais on ne peut excuser ses sentiments tout païens sur la mort; car il faut renoncer à toute piété, si on ne veut au moins mourir chrétiennement; or, il ne pense qu'à mourir lâchement et mollement par tout son livre. (XII, 64-65, emphasis in original)

Pascal finds fault with Montaigne's credulity (perhaps overlooking Montaigne's subtle sense of humor when reporting fantastical accounts of antiquity, especially in "L'Apologie de Raymond Sebond," whose controversial leveling of humankind in the description of various animals' many superior qualities inspired acrimonious reactions to the *Essais*), and his lack of Christian piety in the face of death. In most of the specific references to Montaigne in the *Pensées*, Pascal's judgments are unfavorable. Yet in the *Pensées* there are more than one hundred and seventy allusions to Montaigne, the unorganized, credulous, and irreligious writer.[53] How can Pascal write so disparagingly of Montaigne, yet depend on him to such a great extent for his own work? How can he justify his censure of Montaigne, yet at the same time claim: "Ce n'est pas dans Montaigne mais dans moi que je trouve tout ce que j'y vois" (*Pensée* 64, XII, 66).

This inconsistent attitude demonstrates Pascal's foiled attempt to homogenize Montaigne's heterogeneous text: the failure of an effort to establish univocal discourse in a text charged with contrarieties. Pascal's efforts at interpreting Montaigne struggle against becoming as "divers et ondoyants" as the *Essais* themselves. For someone of Pascal's genius, a scientist, mathematician, philosopher and occasional mystic who had peered into the infinite expanse of cosmic being, it was a frightening thought to be totally responsible for oneself. He admires Montaigne's self-analysis, yet at the same time considers it a blasphemous act, since Montaigne places more importance on the relationship of his self to himself than on his self to God. They have the similar goal of self-understanding but achieve different results.[54] Pascal's ambivalent attitude justifies Montaigne's belief in the contradictory nature of the human condition, something the former, who sought mathematical certainty as his *modus operandi*, could not accept, nor escape. He wished to convert his readers against Montaigne, yet his contradictory reception, even as he strives for ultimate answers to the problems raised by Montaigne's preoccupation with human pride and presumption, is inevitably caught up in Montaigne's notion of the eternal instability of all things: "Le monde n'est qu'une branloire perenne" (III, ii, 804). Yet Pascal does reach a definitive solution to the problem of the misery of humankind without God, especially in the *Apologie de la religion chrétienne*, and shows that Montaigne, destitute of true Christian revelation, was a spiritually anguished *libertin*. Three hundred years later, Sainte-Beuve, Pater, Nietzsche, and even T.S. Eliot would regard the relationship of Montaigne and Pascal as an important context in which to consider the conflict between personal hedonism and religious devotion, between Pascal's more definitive, and perhaps more comforting conclusions on religious matters, and Montaigne's equivocal evaluations.

The Socratic precept as rearticulated by Montaigne in the *Essais* is a key to the *Pensées*: "Il faut connaître soi-même; quand cela ne servirait pas à trouver le vrai, cela au moins sert à régler sa vie, et il n'y a rien de plus juste" (*Pensée* 66, XII, 67-68). Yet Pascal for the most part speaks negatively of Montaigne in the *Pensées*, although his attitude in *L'Entretien de Pascal et Sacy* is considerably less scathing. Here, Pascal becomes a hesitant defender of Montaigne, notably on religious matters. He reveals that Montaigne is one of his most admired authors, yet willfully attempts to reduce the *Essais* to a singleness of purpose that better suits his need of establishing the universality of Montaigne's doubt. This is certainly the cornerstone to one of the most important *Essais* for Pascal, the "Apologie de Raymond Sebond," but such an overall coherent project distorts Montaigne's writing project. Pascal is seduced by Montaigne's suggestiveness and never finds his way out of the *Essais*, producing as a result of his reception of Montaigne his own equivocal text, *Les Pensées*. Pascal is however in accord with Montaigne's intellectual position concerning faith: "il a voulu chercher quelle morale la raison devroit dicter sans la lumière de la foi ... et en considérant l'homme destitu de toute révélation ... il met toutes choses dans un doute universel."[55] As a fideist himself, Pascal has no problem with Montaigne's similar position. He sees the skeptical attitude toward reason as compatible with Christian faith. In his argument of the wager, Pascal admits that human reason cannot solve the question of God's existence — thus one may as well believe in him. Nothing is lost if this proves to be wrong, yet if it proves to be correct, eternal salvation is at hand. Montaigne's separation of reason and faith thus conforms to Pascal's position except that Pascal's conclusion, and even his life, are tragic events in contrast to Montaigne's practice of serenely accepting paradoxical states of affairs. Yet neither one attempts to demonstrate divine being through reason. In Montaigne's terms "Il s'eslevera si Dieu lui preste extraordinairement la main; il s'eslevera, abandonnant et renoncant à ses propres moyens, et se laissant hausser et soubslever par les moyens purement célestes" (II, xii, 604), and in Pascal's "'Dieu est où il n'est pas.' La raison n'y peut rien déterminer: il y a un chaos infini qui nous sépare. Il se joue un jeu, à l'extremité de cette distance infinie, où il arrivera croix ou pile. Que gagerez-vous? Par raison vous ne pouvez faire ni l'un ni l'autre; par raison, vous ne pouvez défendre nul des deux" (*Pensée* 233, XIII, 146). Thus, Pascal, even as a man of science, critiques the rational method; divine principles are intuitive and unprovable and human reason is unable to rationally comprehend them: "... cette impuissance ne conclut autre chose que la faiblesse de notre raison, mais non pas l'incertitude de toutes nos connaissances comme ils [les pyrrhoniens] le prétendent" (*Pensée* 282, XIII, 204).

There is nothing remarkable in Pascal's acceptance of fideism; it had a pervasive influence in the first half of the seventeenth century. He does not completely abandon humanity after humiliating it, and even gives it some dignity by showing its spiritual superiority over nature by virtue of the power of consciousness in the famous "roseau pensant" *Pensées* (347 and 348, XIII, 261-262). Pascal argues, like Montaigne, that reason falls short in religious matters and that an understanding of God must be based on faith. Where Pascal diverges widely from Montaigne concerns the latter's self-indulgent humanism and pagan attitude toward death. Pascal appropriated what he needed from Montaigne, namely the latter's portrayal of human weakness, which he found useful for his obsession with the human fall from divine grace. Yet in Pascal's weighing of the possibilities, there is less acceptance of human inconsistency than is to be found in Montaigne's playful skepticism. As Pascal appropriated elements of the *Essais* in order to develop his own writing, he could only accept Montaigne's humanism to a point, after which he followed a theological path to work out ultimate relations with divinity. The *Essais* were an aid to Pascal's intellectual growth, yet his positions on the issues of reason opposed to faith, acceptance of death, and human weakness are much more severe than Montaigne's. He cannot justify self-portraiture as a goal in and of itself — self-knowledge for Pascal must lead to divine revelation. What Pascal needed from Montaigne is, thus, an awkward counterpart to what he refused to accept. He both extends and destroys the *Essais*, generating their presence into a new horizon, yet also setting up obstacles for their continued popularity. He ultimately considered Montaigne a heretic. Later, in the same vein, Sainte-Beuve accused Montaigne of hypocrisy. Montaigne's heterodox positioning of such issues as personal indulgence vs. public commitment and natural understanding vs. divine wisdom produced attacks on his work that go as far as to accuse him of blasphemy.

Pascal is thus the major writer of the seventeenth century to most fully appropriate Montaigne's thought, yet also the one to demonstrate how the *Essais* were a radical text, one difficult to come to ultimate terms with. After Pascal's death, many of his negative pronouncements on Montaigne were recast, distorted, and used as ammunition to attack the *Essais* in *La Logique de Port Royal,* which finally led to their proscription in 1676. Pascal's appreciation of Montaigne was be disregarded, and although he, along with Gournay, was the closest reader of Montaigne at this time, sharing with him a concern for self-knowledge, the conformity to custom, and the folly of human vanity, he succeeded in undermining the *Essais*' continued acceptance: "Pascal combat Montaigne rudement et superbement, il veut détruire l'effet du livre *Essais* sur les intelligences et les coeurs. Mais l'emploi qu'il en fait montre bien qu'il a reconnu dans Montaigne un esprit du même ordre que le sien."[56] Pascal thus failed to tame Montaigne's modernist impetus.

The beginning of the end of Montaigne as an officially recognized author in the seventeenth century occurred with the publication of the *Logique de Port-Royal* in 1662 by the Jansenists Antoine Arnauld and Pierre Nicole. In this work, the authors vituperate against Montaigne for his false sincerity, vanity, and lack of repentance. In the first edition, there are no specific attacks on Montaigne, but there are indirect indications concerning the faultiness of the Pyrrhonist position as delineated by Sextus Empiricus in *Hypotyposis*:

> Il est des choses obscures et cachées et l'on se trompe quelquefois grossièrement. Toutes choses sont obscures et incertaines, disent les anciens et les nouveaux Pyrrhoniens. Il y a de l'inégalité dans quelques actions des hommes. Il n'est qu'inconstance, disent-ils, que légèreté, qu'instabilité, que la conduite des hommes, mêmes les plus sages. Nous ne pouvons ce que nous voulons qu'à l'instant que nous le voulons: nous ne voulons rien librement, rien absolument, rien constamment.[57]

In the second edition of the same work four years later, after the authors were in possession of Pascal's manuscripts, the criticisms became vehement. Arnauld and Nicole not only adopt what is useful to them from Pascal, namely his strictures on Montaigne, but exaggerate them. Now, Montaigne's work is considered much more volatile than a "sot projet de se peindre." They consider the *Essais* the product of a hedonistic and irreligious libertine, his writings full of "paroles horribles et qui marquent une extinction entière de tout sentiment de religion" (330). In their Jansenist commitment to austere moral and theological conceptions of Christianity, and as arbiters of neoclassical discourse, Arnauld and Nicole condemn Montaigne outright, and then suggest that his work be proscribed:

> Il est plein d'un si grand nombre d'infamies honteuses, et de maximes Epicuriennes et impies qu'il est étrange qu'on l'ait souffert si longtemps dans les mains de tout le monde, et qu'il y ait même des personnes d'esprit qui n'en reconnaissent le venin. (331)

They thus attack him on moral and theological grounds by presenting his innovative ideas as irrational and blasphemous. Arnauld and Nicole also take to task Montaigne's personality and style and reprimand his obsession with self-portraiture ("un défaut de jugement aussi bien que d'un violent amour de soi-même" — 330), a problem as serious as his compositional irregularities ("cette confusion dans le langage" — 334). Their denunciation of Montaigne culminates in the following reproach:

> Pour les personnes du commun, c'est une vanité ridicule, de vouloir informer les autres de leurs petits avantages, et c'est une effronterie punissable, que de découvrir leurs désordres au monde, sans témoigner d'en estre touchés, puisque le dernier excès de l'abandon-

> nement dans le vice, est d'en rougir point, et de n'en avoir ni confusion, ni repentir, mais d'en parler indifféremment comme de toute autre chose; en quoi consiste proprement l'esprit de Montaigne. (332)

In addition to Arnauld and Nicole's call for censorship, Bossuet delivered an unequivocal diatribe against Montaigne in 1668:

> Je le vois bien, votre esprit est si infatué de tant de belles sentences, écrites si éloquemment en prose et en vers, qu'un Montaigne, je le nomme, vous a débités, qui préfère les animaux à l'homme, leur instinct à notre raison ... Mais, dites-moi, subtil philosophe, qui vous riez si finement de l'homme qui s'imagine être quelque chose, compterez-vous encore pour rien connaître en Dieu?[58]

Montaigne's ploy to undermine human vanity by demonstrating the many superior qualities of animals, as put forth in the "Apologie," was one of the greatest points of contention for Bossuet and other theologians of the seventeenth century, from whom there issued a continuous succession of attacks.[59] Yet the strongest and perhaps most unjust invective against Montaigne came from the metaphysician Malebranche.

In *La Recherche de la vérité*, published in 1674, Malebranche was not unaware of Montaigne's merits as a literary writer. In Chapter V, "Du livre de Montaigne" of Book II, *De l'Imagination*, Malebranche praises Montaigne's power of imagination, a quality that the former believes makes the book so original. Yet this very quality renders the *Essais* dangerous. Malebranche was a staunch adherent to Cartesian rationalism, and held that Montaigne does not persuade by reasoning, but entertains readers by appealing to their sentiments, thereby inciting their passions:

> Il n'est pas seulement dangereux de lire Montagne pour se divertir, à cause que le plaisir qu'on y prend engage insensiblement dans ses sentimens: mais encore parce que ce plaisir est plus criminel qu'on ne pense. Car il est certain que ce plaisir naît principalement de la concupiscence, et qu'il ne fait qu'entretenir, et que fortifier les passions; la manière d'écrire de cet Auteur n'étant agréable, que parce qu'elle nous touche, et qu'elle réveille nos passions d'une manière imperceptible.[60]

As an ascetic Christian and rationalist philosopher, Malebranche cannot forgive Montaigne for having written a book containing so much of his own self:

> Si c'est un défaut de parler de soi, c'est une effronterie, ou plutôt une espèce de folie que de se louer à tous momens, comme fait Montagne: car ce n'est pas seulement pécher contre l'humilité Chrétienne, mais c'est encore choquer la raison. (369)

He holds that it is an unforgivable vanity to have written at length on a subject other than God: "l'esprit et le coeur de l'homme n'est fait que pour Dieu" (368). Malebranche further accuses Montaigne of endangering the civilized social fabric of France by focusing on his personal and unique self, proudly exposing his faults, and thereby inciting his readers to impious actions and to abnegate social commitment in favor of self-indulgence.

Malebranche proceeds to expose several contradictions in the *Essais* in an attempt to discredit Montaigne; he asks, for example, how someone who complains of a faulty memory can memorize official speeches or refer to such a great quantity of ancient literature and philosophy. Yet Malebranche quotes Montaigne out of context and twists the latter's pronouncements to discredit him, not acknowledging that the development of paradox was at the heart of Montaigne's project of demonstrating the vanity and very impossibility of dogmatic systems of thought: "L'affirmation et l'opiniastreté sont signes exprez de bestise" (III, xiii, 1075). Malebranche's character is thus at great odds with Montaigne's. The former's most significant achievement was an attempt to construct a rational system of Christian philosophy, a blend of faith and Cartesian rationalism: as a result he could accept neither Montaigne's unmethodical procedure, his fideism, nor his Pyrrhonism. He does offer some backhanded praise at the close of the chapter: "ses idées sont fausses, mais belles. Ses expressions irrégulières ou hardies, mais agréables" (375). Yet Malebranche's attacks added fuel to the growing fire of dissension against the beautiful lies ("idées fausses mais belles") of the *Essais*.

There are thus two conflicting currents in Montaigne's reception in the seventeenth century. One rejects Montaigne, the other accepts him. Acceptance comes in the form of Montaigne as the essential precursor to the notion of the *honnête homme* as well as for his "connaissance de l'âme humaine."[61] At the same time, among intellectuals and religious censors, he was increasingly disparaged until it was forbidden to print the *Essais* in France.

For almost three quarters of a century, the *Essais* were the dominant work of French literature. Pascal, Bossuet, Nicole, Arnauld, and Malebranche succeeded in destroying Montaigne's official reputation, but his prestige among the reading public remained strong. The innovative dimensions of the *Essais* were considered subversive to moral purity and to the social structure. Their transgressive textuality exceeded the boundaries of acceptable literary and philosophical discourse and was suppressed accordingly. The *Essais'* placement on the Papal Index in 1676 was the result of various assaults on Montaigne by Malebranche, Bossuet, Pascal, and *La Logique de Port-Royal* as well as the burgeoning neoclassical insistence on discursive regularity. The proscription occured also because Christian skepticism was no longer accepted as valid by Gallican Catholicism. Montaigne was perceived at this time as a precursor to libertine rationality or even atheism — a thinker dangerous to the strata of political order and religious conformity. Montaigne's work continued to be available, but in expurgated form.

The two most popular editions of the *Essais* in France from 1676 to 1724 were the *Esprit des "Essais" de Michel Seigneur de Montaigne* (1677) of Charles de Sercy, and the *Pensées de Montaigne propres à former l'esprit des moeurs* (1700) of Artaud. The former packaged the *Essais* with a preconceived plan of stylistic simplification and of suppressing Montaigne's quotations and digressions. The latter accomplished a similar task. Both works disfigure the *Essais* to extreme degrees, reducing them to coherent treatises. In the words of Sercy:

> C'est pourquoi j'ai pris la liberté de travailler après lui, non pour le réformer, mais pour en faire une *agréable réduction,* dans laquelle il paroit dans toute la force et la vivacité de son esprit. Aussi n'y ai-je employé que ce qui m'a semblé plus digne d'être retenu, c'est à dire toutes les choses historiques et divertissantes, que j'ai déchargé autant que j'ai pu *de leurs ornements superflus.*[62] (emphasis added)

The "agréable reduction" and expurgation of all "ornements superflus" was the trend Montaigne's editors would follow for nearly a century and a half. It was the same impulse that would also affect much of Montaigne's academic commentary and editions of his work in the twentieth century, as critics and editors such as Lanson, Strowski, Gide, and more recently, Eva Marcu attempted to make an "agréable reduction" of Montaigne's textual heterogeneity by reducing it to a more readily accessible coherence. Sercy and Artaud even went as far as to modify several titles in order to encompass digressions they decided not to cut. "Des coches," for example, became "Des coches ou plutost des dépenses des princes et de l'industrie du nouveau monde," "Sur des vers de Virgile" became "Sur des vers de Virgile ou plutost de l'amour et du mariage." Twenty-five years later, the text of Artaud was even more regularized: archaisms were removed, chapters rearranged, and titles rewritten to an even greater degree. The *Pensées de Montaigne* is a handbook of concise thoughts, a work that transforms the *Essais* into a collection of maxims. The longest are only several lines and easily lend themselves to quotation out of context. Artaud's text enjoyed widespread popularity, and went through at least three editions in as many years. It was a primary source for readers of Montaigne at the turn of the eighteenth century. The most original qualities of the *Essais* were thus removed or modified to conform to contemporary tastes. Receptions of the *Essais* at this time went beyond the modifications that "horizons-of-experience" always impose on a received work and accomplished textual distortions in order to suppress the most innovative dimensions of Montaigne's writing. Consequently, the *Essais* went underground and traveled to England, where they were published in their next unexpurgated edition.

After over a century of controversy, the *Essais* were, by 1700, legitimized, stripped of their volatility, and made "presentable" to the reading public. The leisured aristocracy would continue to read Montaigne as an *honnête homme plein de bon sens* as the formalistic innovations and polyvalent paradoxes of the *Essais* were removed; the *Essais* would be used henceforth as raw material from which streamlined products were created. The most striking fact during the first century of Montaigne's reception is how often his merits as a literary writer were neglected in favor of the discussion that surrounds religious and philosophical questions and the propriety of self-portraiture. It should be said in favor of Montaigne's literary influence that there were important assimilations of his work, especially by Pascal and Gournay. There are also varying degrees of Montaigne's presence in the work of Gassendi, Racan, Molière, La Fontaine, La Rochefoucauld, La Bruyère, Saint-Evremond, and others.[63] As a result of the proscription of the *Essais*, it would take more than another century for Montaigne to regain his status as an important literary writer, although Montesquieu, Voltaire, Diderot, and Rousseau regarded his work as worthy of their attention. The principal reasons for this temporary eclipse of Montaigne were first, a widespread theological rationalism as inspired by Descartes, which produced a reaction against the fideist position and, second, Pascal's equivocal attack, subsequently distorted, then adopted in order to produce the narrow-minded assaults of the Port-Royal critics. Thus, the seventeenth century successfully assimilated, codified, and finally banished one of the most internationally influential French writers ever.

During the eighteenth century, Montaigne's work found itself involved with most of the important debates of the time, yet many of the *philosophes* had little use for what was regarded as his idiosyncratic individualism. Yet Montaigne's importance to eighteenth-century French literary history is nevertheless evident in the work of Montesquieu, Diderot, and especially Rousseau. However, these writers were most often less interested in reformulating his thought than in using carefully chosen aspects of it to promote their own; they were, as Dréano puts it: "moins intéressés de le connaître que de l'exploiter."[64] The *Essais* were considered to be so irregularly composed that only expurgated editions that suppressed the Latin quotations and smoothed out the stylistic irregularities were read. There were very few attempts at judicious evaluation of the *Essais* and they were generally misquoted and used out of context to serve the matter at hand. Montaigne's discursive method was considered to be irrational, although he was admired for having an "esprit très libre de philosophe" — meaning that his Pyrrhonism was useful for the anticlerical arguments of the day.[65] Comments by Vauvenargues and Voltaire, though full of admiration, were superficial and self-serving and did not go very far in evaluating *Essais*. It is Rousseau who owes the greatest debt to Montaigne in the eighteenth century, and he often appropriated the *Essais* more than he revealed. His case, as we will see, is far more complex than that of either Montesquieu or Diderot.

In the early eighteenth century, there are numerous instances of Montaigne's scattered presence in literature and criticism.[66] In 1724, for the first time in fifty years, an unexpurgated French edition of the *Essais* appeared, published in London by the Huguenot refugee Pierre Coste; it was republished often and served as the principal edition of the *Essais* in the eighteenth century. In 1733, a modernized version ("une espèce de traduction") by the Abbé Trublet appeared along with an article in which he justifies the necessity of correcting Montaigne's style and modernizing a vocabulary by then out of date.[67] In 1753, another neatly packaged version of the *Essais* appeared: *L'esprit de Montaigne ou les maximes, pensées, jugements, réflexions de cet auteur rédigés par ordre de matières*, by Pessalier. In his preface, he lists four major difficulties that discourage potential readers of the *Essais*: "Les digressions les égarent, les citations les ennuient, les répétitions les rebutent, le style les dégoûtent."[68] The *Essais* were once again chastised for the qualities that are now generally considered to constitute their greatest originality: self-portraiture, paradoxical formulations, digressive freedom, openness of discursive structure, and creative use of quotation. It is interesting to note that a genre that Montaigne began with, but radically transformed, namely that of the *leçon* — a writer's collection of quotable sayings based on his readings — was now the genre of choice to which the *Essais* were most often reduced.[69] There were altogether fourteen editions of the *Essais* in the eighteenth century, each with varying degrees of modification of the text's "irregularities" according to the temperament of the editor.[70] It was not until the edition of 1776 that the original text with all of the Latin and Greek quotations was once again published — the last time had been Gournay's edition of 1635.

Reduced versions of the *Essais* thus continued to appear throughout most of the eighteenth century. The publication of such editions indicates the overall incompatibility of Montaigne with the current of enlightenment rationalism coloring French intellectual life of the time:

> Evidemment, pour les philosophes qui ont foi en la dignité de l'homme, en l'excellence de sa nature, en la sûreté de sa raison, le pyrrhonisme de Montaigne ne peut être, comme l'écrit Guer, qu'un "système impertinent, un ruisseau bourbeux qui roule quelques paillettes d'or."[71]

Montaigne's work nevertheless remained an ubiquitous presence (as provided for by the Coste publications of 1724, '25, '27, '39, and

'45) and merited increasing attention from literary professionals and the *philosophes* who often used him as a weapon against Cartesianism (associated with Church doctrine) and the strictures of a lingering neoclassical aesthetic.

The most well-known French readers of Montaigne in the eighteenth century were Vauvenargues, Voltaire, Montesquieu, Diderot, and Rousseau.[72] Vauvenargues, in his essay "Sur Montaigne et Pascal," praises Montaigne's reflective spirit, imagination, and originality, but like so many Montaigne commentators of the eighteenth century, he laments Montaigne's lack of method, the disconnected quality of his thoughts, and the absence of definitive conclusions in many of his essays. Montaigne is absent from the list of the "véritablement grands hommes parmi l'élite qui doivent servir d'exemple à la postérité" in Voltaire's *Temple du Goût* of 1731.[73] Yet Voltaire was a warm admirer of Montaigne, especially of his skepticism: "toujours original dans la manière dont il présente les objets, toujours plein d'imagination, toujours peintre, et, ce que j'aime, toujours sachant douter";[74] of his penchant toward free thought (Voltaire called him "le plus sage et le plus aimable des philosophes"[75]); and of his self-portraiture: "Le charmant projet que Montaigne a eu de se peindre naïvement comme il a fait! car il a peint la nature humaine; si Nicole et Malebranche avaient toujours parlé d'eux-mêmes, ils n'auraient pas réussi!"[76] Voltaire, like Diderot, used Montaigne for his own devices, portraying him as a "philosophe complet,"[77] thus establishing a stereotyped freethinking Montaigne, an image that would have widespread popularity until the nineteenth century. Although he admired his skepticism, Voltaire was condescending toward what he considered Montaigne's lack of clear purpose in his philosophical inquiries. In many ways, this was the primary attitude of intellectuals of the time and Voltaire's description of Montaigne's style is typical: "Le style de Montaigne n'est ni pur, ni correct, ni précis, ni noble. Il est énergique et familier; il exprime naïvement de grandes choses. C'est cette naïveté qui plaît."[78] Voltaire's understanding of Montaigne was superficial and was accused of being so by Clément, who attacked what he believed were Voltaire's erroneous accounts of Montaigne. What Voltaire lamented in Montaigne's style as naive incoherence, Clément praised as "une richesse et une énergie inimitables."[79] We see the *Essais* appropriated again to support conflicting positions and continuing to inspire heterogeneous interpretations of their significance. In Voltaire's case, he used Montaigne in his efforts to oppose intolerant religious dogma and fanaticism (as seen in the famous battlecry of freethinkers "écrasons l'infâme"), making the latter into an ally to further his own causes, yet scorning Montaigne's textual idiosyncrasies.[80]

Montesquieu's references are brief, and for the most part, appreciative. He ranks Montaigne along with Plato, Malebranche, and Shaftsbury as one of "les quatre grands poètes."[81] Yet Montesquieu remained for the most part silent about the *Essais*. There were however certain circumstances shared by the two Bordelais landed gentry: they were both magistrates in the *Parlement de Bordeaux* (positions of which they both tired at a relatively early age), both read, reflected, and wrote in the comfort of their private libraries, and both traveled throughout Germany, Switzerland, and Italy (about which they kept important journals). These experiences inevitably helped to produce parallel temperaments, characterized by enlightened humanism, wit and irony, fascination with antiquity and the history of social institutions, the profound study of humans and society, a tolerant, relativistic outlook, moderate tone, deistic beliefs (veiled by a Catholic exterior), and universal wisdom drawn from the particularities of life.[82] Montesquieu scholar Albert Sorel claims that Montesquieu was clearly indebted to Montaigne's humanist project of commenting on the writing of others to generate one's own work: "Montesquieu aime Montaigne: il le range parmi les grands poètes, il s'en délecte, il s'en nourrit et par moments, il le ressuscite." Yet Sorel is quick to point out the fundamental difference in their life and work: "Montaigne a dispersé sa pensée; Montesquieu a besoin de rassembler la sienne."[83] It is the recent work of John M. Bomer that provides a useful analysis of the presence of Montaigne in the *Lettres Persanes*, showing where the works of both writers intersect and where they contrast.[84] In the *Lettres*, Montesquieu's device of using the foreign observer to expose the social inequalities and political and religious abuses of France has its antecedents in Montaigne's "Des cannibales" and "Des coches." Bomer demonstrates that Montaigne was a significant presence in much of Montesquieu's writing (along with the many other authors on which Montesquieu draws); we can see how Montesquieu learned from Montaigne yet at the same time filtered him through a scientific rationalism — although essayistic in thought, Montesquieu's work has none of the diffuse imagery or discontinuity of the *Essais.*

Montesquieu can thus be considered as a descendant rather than a disciple of Montaigne, adopting him into his writing in a calculated manner of precise intentions and recasting Montaigne's discourse in a mode of philosophic rationalism and enlightenment. Among Montesquieu's "four greatest poets" is not only Montaigne, but also his adversary, Malebranche. From this tension Montesquieu produces a contradictory notion of humankind as "divers and ondoyants" and as a Malbranchean "l'homme de la raison divine"[85] that nevertheless resolves itself in firm decisions. Regularized, yet at the same time part of a vibrant new *oeuvre,* the *Essais* are regenerated by Montesquieu in his reproduction of Montaigne's espousal of the common welfare of society, yet in a mode of thought and presentation commensurate with Montesquieu's own time. With the vast expanse of the *Grand Siècle* between them, Montesquieu emulated the life of Montaigne, yet renewed his thought in a more absolute way.

Diderot commented on Montaigne and his work in many places in his writing, at greatest length in the article "Pyrrhonisme" from the *Encyclopédie.* Diderot's comments on Montaigne's work are often contradictory, although a relatively clear affirmation of the *Essais* can be discerned in his commentary. The most important instance of his explicit admiration for Montaigne is contained in his comparison of the latter with his friend and colleague Helvétius:

> Je ne sais quel cas Helvétius faisait de Montaigne et si la lecture lui en était bien familière, mais il y a beaucoup de rapport entre leur manière de voir et de dire. *Montaigne est cynique,* Helvétius l'est aussi; ils ont l'un et l'autre les pédants en horreur, la science des moeurs est pour tous deux la science par excellence, ils accordent beaucoup aux circonstances et aux hasards, ils ont de l'imagination, beaucoup de familiarité dans le style, de la hardiesse et de la simplicité dans l'expression, des métaphores qui leur sont propres.[86] (emphasis added)

Diderot thus draws a parallel between one of the leading *philosophes* of the day and Montaigne, but not himself. At times Diderot claims that Montaigne's skepticism (read cynicism, something with which Montaigne would not agree) is too extreme and that he "nous croit incapables de rien savoir et de rien connaître" (IV, 90). Diderot, editor of the *Encyclopédie,* had unbound faith in reason and knowledge, and could not therefore adhere to Montaigne's "que sçay-je?" In Diderot's references to him, Montaigne's independence of thought is much admired, yet as seen in the above comparison of Montaigne and Helvétius, Diderot needed to constitute Montaigne as a *philosophe.* He offered no detailed analyses of Montaigne's work; his greatest explicit contribution to the legacy of the *Essais* is to have brought them to the attention of a larger circle of readers. The *Essais* were nevertheless a singularly significant work in the shaping of his thought and writing; Diderot's relationship to them is more complex than Montesquieu's and demands some attention.[87]

Diderot's enthusiasm for Montaigne arose from their shared desire for a liberation from Aristotelianism (the confines of rigorous scholastic method), a sharpened definition of personality, and an enhanced critical perspective. There were of course significant differences between the two. Although Diderot shared Montaigne's conviction that human knowledge should be founded on the understanding of oneself, Montaigne's descent into self-analysis led him to a Pyrrhonian skepticism, which Diderot refused. In Diderot's *Pensées philosophiques,* written during an early skepticist phase while he was formulating his own mode of materialist aestheticism, he distinguished himself from Montaigne by remaining convinced, despite the diversity and undulation of the human condition, of the rational demonstrability of truth: "Qu'est-ce qu'un sceptique? C'est un philosophe qui a douté de tout ce qu'il croit, et qui croit ce qu'un usage légitime de sa raison et de ses sens lui a démontré vrai. Voulez-vous quelque chose de plus précis? Rendez sincère le pyrrhonien, et vous aurez le sceptique" ("*Pensée* XXX," I, 140). Diderot responded to the "Apologie" by maintaining a flexible yet nevertheless unwavering rationalism. Montaigne and Diderot both opposed systematic reductions, equating single-minded formulations with dogmatism. They sought to maintain a flexibility of thought that corresponds to the fleeting and mutable character of human nature. Yet Diderot's intellectual dynamism, although inspired in part from his reception of the *Essais,* maintained that everything is not ultimately "divers et ondoyant," but rather related in a universal way, and that to understand cultural phenomena, "il faudrait posséder la science universelle" ("Sur la diversité de nos jugements," IV, 22). Despite this penchant for teleological resolution, Diderot still supported the open form of the essay: "Cependant à tout prendre, j'aime mieux laisser courir mon homme à toutes jambes que de l'arrêter par une interruption qui le détourne de sa route. J'aime mieux un essai qu'un traité; un essai où l'on me jette quelques idées presque isolées, qu'un traité où ces germes précieux sont étouffés sous un amas de redites" ("Sur la diversité," IV, 23-24). The suppleness of the essay allows for an open inquiry into reality. Diderot realized its value, yet as he became more actively engaged in the intellectual debates of his time as a professional writer, he was required to produce more definitive positions than did Montaigne, whose independence from the literary establishment afforded him a much greater degree of freedom.

Diderot maintained a Montaignean dimension in many of his philosophical treatises. He begins "De l'Interprétation de la nature," for example, with a very Montaignean declaration of his free and natural compositional method: "Je laisserai les pensées se succéder sous ma plume, dans l'ordre même selon lequel les objets se sont offerts à ma réflexion; parce qu'elles n'en représenteront que mieux *les mouvements et la marche de mon esprit*" (II, 9 — emphasis added). Yet the essay is divided numerically and is a more systematic inquiry than Montaigne would have ever attempted, producing a scientific regularity far from the essayist's affection for a more disorderly order. Montaigne's aesthetic is subjective, dynamic, and open, rather than objective, static, and closed. Diderot appropriates and fosters it to a certain degree. Montaigne often reminds us of the improvisational quality of his writing: "J'ayme l'alleure poétique, à sauts et à gambades ... Je vais au change, indiscrettement et tumultuairement. Mon stile et mon esprit vont vagabondant de mesmes" (III, ix, 994-95). Diderot praises Montaigne's essayistic manner of presentation, which can best capture the mind's movement: "c'est le grand art de Montaigne, qui ne veut jamais prouver, et qui va toujours prouvant, en se ballotant du blanc au noir et du noir au blanc" ("Réflexions sur le livre de l'esprit," II, 272). They shared a like temperament, yet were responding to different historical moments from different social positions. Montaigne's was a private enterprise with of course marked, yet surreptitious, public intentions; Diderot was a cosmopolitan man of letters who earned a living from his ideas and writing.

There are other points in common between Montaigne and Diderot that help us to understand their differences. Obvious points of departure for Diderot's "Supplément du voyage de Bougainville," for instance, would be Montaigne's "Des cannibales" and "Des coches." Although the essays have similar themes and ideas, the authors had different purposes. In "Les Adieux du vieillard," Diderot glorifies Tahitian values over European ones, much in the manner of Montaigne in "Des cannibales," with the similar goal of promoting a non-Eurocentric culture as a vehicle for the criticism of existing European institutions and practices. The telling differences between Montaigne's and Diderot's treatment of a similar subject are to be found in the equivocating contours and shifting meanings of Montaigne's arguments, which in the end not only indict European civilization, but all forms of ethnocentrism, whether civilized or "barbare." This is one reason why "Des cannibales" is the most interpreted text in Montaigne's *oeuvre* — it radically problematizes the very concepts of ethnocentrism and cultural relativism, thereby provoking readers into an active production of meaning of the text for themselves.[88] Diderot, on the other hand, remakes this topos into a caricatural presentation of *le bon sauvage* in order to make his point about the shortcomings of European social, religious, and political intolerance. Diderot's use of the Montaignean intertext is thus a springboard for the promotion of his own more definitive agenda. What Montaigne leaves suspended in tantalizing paradox for the reader to unravel, Diderot pushes to a clearer conclusion while attempting to avoid dogmatism. Diderot's work is thus saturated with Montaigne's thought, as Schwarz has meticulously documented. The *Essais* were again given new life after the fifty-year eclipse of the censure; they became firmly rooted in major works, yet with important modifications. It was thus an ambivalent discipleship that perpetuated the life of the *Essais*; it is the very tension of such a reception as Diderot's, accepting while rejecting, manipulating the difficulty of Montaigne's writing to adapt to his own writing project, that underscores the protean nature of the *Essais* and their capacity to generate engaged response and innovative reduplication of their discursive challenges in different times and circumstances.

It is Rousseau who would go beyond the affinities of Montesquieu and even the ambivalent appropriations of Diderot in his reception of the *Essais*. In his work, there is a more pronounced yet equally equivocal set of relations to Montaigne's life and writing. Near the end of his life, Rousseau made the following tribute to him:

> Ce premier philosophe français fut notre maître à tous; sans lui peut-être nous n'aurions jamais eu ni Bayle, ni Montesquieu. Quel homme que ce Michel de Montaigne! Outre la naïveté, la grace et l'énergie de son style inimitable, il avait des vues longues, et, comme il l'a dit, l'esprit *primesautier*.[89]

Rousseau's is the most demonstrable and perhaps symbiotic reception of Montaigne's work in the eighteenth century. In contrast to Voltaire and Diderot, who presented Montaigne as a *philosophe* and hence a partisan of progress, science, and reason, Rousseau admired a very different Montaigne: a natural confessional writer, one whose concerns were often akin to his own and therefore useful to his writing project. There are several major areas of affinity between Montaigne and Rousseau: attitudes on education, epicureanism, and the study of the self all played a central role in their writing. Yet as we have seen with other writers, Rousseau's reception of Montaigne is ambiguous and difficult to clearly ascertain. Intertextual evidence of Rousseau's appropriation of Montaigne can be established to a certain degree, yet his attitudes toward Montaigne are often conflicting and paradoxical. Rousseau sometimes praises, sometimes attacks Montaigne, sometimes quotes him, and sometimes thoroughly assimilates his work. There is a pronounced presence of Montaigne throughout the work of Rousseau, which has been best detailed in Silber's study. Yet Silber, as well as Villey and Dréano, admit to the impossibility of determining where Montaigne's influence leaves off and where Rousseau's originality begins. More recently, it is Colette Fleury who has accomplished the most helpful comparison of the two writers:

> Ces rapports entre les deux auteurs, et leur évolution, ne relevant proprement ni de l'imitation, ni de l'influence, ni de la ressemblance ou de l'opposition, mais de tout cela à la fois, ils ressemblent beaucoup, dans leur ambiguité, aux rapports du père et du fils, et c'est pourquoi j'ai avancé pour caractériser la relation de Rousseau à Montaigne le mot de filiation.[90]

Yet even this successful study of their affiliation claims that the true nature of their relationship is perhaps unresolvable. A perusal of Rousseau's reception of the *Essais* is nevertheless useful to see how Montaigne became involved in an even wider spectrum of literary history.

In Rousseau's first two major works, *Discours sur les sciences et les arts* and *Discours sur l'origine de l'inégalité*, he depends heavily on Montaigne's ideas to support his arguments. In the *Discours sur les sciences et les arts* Rousseau draws on Montaigne's "Du pedantisme" (in which Montaigne berates the emphasis placed on knowledge rather than on virtue) to denounce French eighteenth-century society. Yet in Rousseau's desire to appear original and avoid reference to authority, he never mentions Montaigne in the main body of the text (and only five times in the footnotes). He uses Montaigne to suit his purpose, portraying him as a social critic respectful of pure virtue and sharing his own point of view as he attacks the *philosophes'* presumption that definitive knowledge is both possible and desirable. We can most clearly see Montaigne's early impact on Rousseau in the following passage from the latter's defense of the first *Discours*, "Observations de Jean-Jacques Rousseau de Genève sur la réponse qui a été faite à son *Discours*":

> Le philosophe, qui se flatte de pénétrer dans les secrets de Dieu, ose associer sa prétendue sagesse à la sagesse éternelle: il approuve, il blame, il corrige, il préscrit des loix à la nature, et les bornes à la divinité.[91]

Both the theme and tone of Rousseau's criticism of the "philosophe" resemble Montaigne's recognition of philosophy's inadequacy to comprehend divine wisdom:

> Toutefois, nous luy [Dieu] prescrivons des bornes, nous tenons sa puissance assiégée par nos raisons (j'appelle raison resveries et nos songes, avec la dispense de la philosophie, qui dit le fol mesme et le meschant forcener par raison, mais que c'est une raison de particulière forme); nous le voulons asservir aux apparences vaines et foibles de nostre entendement, luy qui a fait et nous et nostre cognoissance ... . (II, xii, 523)

This is only the first instance of Rousseau's adaptation of Montaigne. In his second major work, *Discours sur l'origine de l'inégalité*, Rousseau depends even more on the *Essais* and especially on

Montaigne's attack on human reason (using examples of animals' superiority to bolster his arguments) in the "Apologie de Raymond Sebond," and his praise for humankind's *état sauvage* in "Des cannibales." Rousseau's position throughout the second *Discours,* in which he valorizes the "natural" over the "civilized," is akin to Montaigne's, yet once again Rousseau hides his debt, mentioning Montaigne only once. In his critique of what he considered the artificial values of society, Rousseau used Montaigne's arguments to support his own. Montaigne was, thus, throughout most of Rousseau's career, a constant presence, though in a harmonious *and* a conflictual manner. Rousseau identified with Montaigne's assault on the false values of society, his defense of the "primitive," and his attack on scholastic philosophy. In later works, as Rousseau became more assured of his own arguments, he was less dependent on the *Essais,* and diverged from them on several points.

Rousseau's *Lettres Morales* are an important turning point in his attitude toward Montaigne. In this work and in Montaigne's "Apologie," both writers attack intellectual presumption, demonstrating the folly of the quest for intellectual certainty through rationalist inquiry. Yet in the *Lettres Morales,* Montaigne becomes for Rousseau the prime representative of a negative skeptical strain in French literature. Rousseau henceforth considers him an erroneous judge of human nature and does not hesitate to attack him on moral grounds and for his insincerity: "O Montagne, toi qui te piques de franchise et de vérité, sois sincère et vrai si un philosophe peut être et dis-moi s'il est quelque climat sur la terre où ce soit un crime de garder sa foi ..." (IV, 1109). Rousseau himself abandoned skepticism in favor of a quest for absolute spiritual values. From this point on, Montaigne was less of an ally to Rousseau, and more of an opponent. Yet, although there were significant differences between the two, Rousseau appealed to the authority of Montaigne concerning education and human behavior, especially in *Emile.* Rousseau seemed to have certain of the *Essais* constantly in mind as he wrote *Emile,* yet although Fleuret and Silber have demonstrated the many similarities in content and style between them, Rousseau's overall attitude toward Montaigne in *Emile* remains ambiguous.

In the areas of education, both intellectual and physical, Rousseau was often in accord with Montaigne, freely borrowing his ideas and even paraphrasing him when useful.[92] Yet Rousseau also frequently opposed Montaigne and attacked the latter's skepticism and what he saw as his insincerity in the refusal to acknowledge conscience and repentance. According to Dréano: "Pour ce qui touche à l'éducation, sur ce qu'il faut enseigner et la manière de l'enseigner, Rousseau répète souvent Montaigne et il l'approuve toujours. En matière de religion, il le juge trop sceptique."[93] The principal inspiration for *Emile* is Rousseau's reaction against what he considered the social corruption of his time and France's flawed educational system. Montaigne, too, was writing against the educational norms of his day; taking issue with French pedagogical practices in "Du pedantisme" and attacking the harsh scholastic methods practiced in French schools in "De l'institution des enfans." Rousseau went much further in attempting to reform society, whereas Montaigne ultimately accepted the prevailing social order and critiqued it in a more subtle manner in order to avoid being censored, ostracized, and perhaps even persecuted. Montaigne seemed to largely accept the dominant political, moral, and religious tenets of his time, while simultaneously embedding more radical, heterodox formulations in his text, accessible to those who read him with persistence and insight. Montaigne often concealed his true beliefs in order to avoid persecution, yet also to keep dangerous truths from the people who were likely to misunderstand them and produce disastrous consequences. Montaigne certainly needed to protect his most radical notions with a surface of conformity. Later, such close readers of the *Essais* as Gournay and Rousseau flushed out and developed Montaigne's more suggestive notions in ways that would not been possible for him to consider in his historical milieu. Gide, Nietzsche, and later Woolf continued this practice of reconstituting what Montaigne only hinted at into more fully developed, explicit notions.[94]

With regard to Rousseau's autobiography, the *Confessions*, Marcel Raymond, in the introduction to Rousseau's *Oeuvres complètes*, has stated: "Le prédécesseur immédiat de Rousseau, c'est Montaigne" (xii). There are of course great differences between Rousseau's autobiography and Montaigne's self-portraiture. The former is a historical account of a life, the latter a documentation of change: "Je veux représenter le progrez de mes humeurs, et qu'on voye chaque pièce en sa naissance. Je prendrois plaisir d'avoir commencé plustost et à reconnoistre le trein de mes mutations" (II, xxxvii, 758). Moreover, Rousseau's principal motive for writing the *Confessions* was self-justification, whereas Montaigne needed to communicate with others through his self-portrait: "Nul plaisir n'a goust pour moi sans communication. Il ne me vient pas seulement une gaillarde pensée en l'ame qu'il ne me fáche de l'avoir produit seul, et n'ayant à qui l'offrir" (III, ix, 986). Rousseau desired to surpass Montaigne in the art of self-portraiture, by being more truthful, revealing, and sincere: "J'avois toujours ri de la fausse naïveté de Montaigne qui faisant semblant d'avouer ses défauts à grand soin de ne s'en donner que d'aimables" (I, 517). Rousseau's project of open confession and avowal of his imperfections embodies the very qualities he attacks in Montaigne. Although Rousseau expressed his reservations about Montaigne, he continued to strongly identify with him, measuring his work against his predecessor's. The basic temperamental differences between them (Rousseau was an outsider seeking explicitly to radically transform society, whereas Montaigne wished to remain within its traditional order while carefully suggesting appeals for political and social reform) may account for the basic differences in their writing. Rousseau, like Gournay, Pascal, and Diderot, owed much to Montaigne's work. He alternated, like Pascal, between praise and blame for the essayist, sometimes borrowing, sometimes rejecting. His reception of Montaigne highlights the question of the paradoxical presentation of the self in its "sincerity."

Rousseau's reception of the *Essais* raises again the question of hermeneutic inconclusiveness. Rousseau's inability or unwillingness to conclude unequivocally his attitude toward Montaigne, coupled with his capacity to accept the self-problematization of his own opinions, is another important instance of the contradictory heritage of the *Essais*. The many scattered and veiled references to the *Essais* in Rousseau's work show his concern for them as a precursive text to be dealt with to some degree. He uses elements of the *Essais* to support his own writing in various places, but never in a systematic or programmatic manner. Like Montaigne's self-professed compositional irregularity, Rousseau's borrowings are a "fagotage de tant de diverses pieces" (II, xxxvii, 758) having no cohesive identity; yet like Montaigne's free use of quotation, they are of a productive nature, around which Rousseau inscribes his own text. Rousseau, at once a *philosophe des lumières* and an opponent of unconditional enlightenment enthusiasm, attempted to produce a revolutionary personalization of authentic being; his impulse toward a Montaignean self-portraiture, coupled with a clear program of autobiographical self-analysis, surpasses Montaigne's less systematic notion of self-expression. Hence the ambiguity of Rousseau's attitude. As Fleuret points out:

> D'une part il l'admire, le lit, s'en pénètre, le copie, l'imite constamment. D'autre part il se sépare de lui, le renie, lui reproche d'être insincère, tiède, accomodant, "comme les autres," ou plus souvent le passe sous silence. Cependant toute son oeuvre atteste qu'il n'a jamais cessé de fréquenter les *Essais* et qu'il est sans doute au 18e siècle le lecteur le plus attentif de Montaigne. (12)

On one level, Rousseau appears to reactivate several of the themes and oppositional tensions of the *Essais* such as nature vs. civilization, the self vs. society, and sincerity vs. dissimulation. Although he rejected Montaigne as a negative influence as he became more confident in his own status as a writer, yet again, late in his career, he depended on the work of Montaigne to draw conclusions on his own life, literary career, and humanity in general.

In the *Rêveries du promeneur solitaire,* Rousseau borrowed Montaigne's themes and phrasing on the instability of the human condition:

> Tout est dans un flux continuel sur la terre. Rien n'y garde une forme constante et arrêtée et nos affections qui s'attachent aux choses extérieures passent et changent nécessairement comme elles. Toujours en avant ou en arrière de nous, elles rappelent le passé, qui n'est plus, ou préviennent l'avenir, qui souvent ne doit point être: il n'y a rien de solide à quoi le coeur se puisse attacher. Aussi n'a-t-on guère ici-bas que du plaisir qui passe; pour le bonheur qui dure, je doute qu'il y soit connu. A peine est-il, dans nos plus vives jouissances, un instant où le coeur puisse véritablement nous dire: *Je voudrais que cet instant durât toujours.* (I, 1046)

Rousseau was searching for the perpetual presence of self-being, a theme developed in Montaigne's "Nos affections s'emportent au delà de nous": "Nous ne sommes jamais chez nous, nous sommes toujours au delà. La crainte, le désir, l'esperance nous eslancent vers l'advenir et nous desrobent le sentiment et la consideration de ce qui est, pour nous amuser à ce qui sera, voire quand nous ne serons plus" (I, iii, 15). Montaigne's continual attempt was to achieve the still-point of self-understanding and stability: "Outre cette diversité et division infinie, par le trouble que nostre jugement nous donne à nous mesmes, et l'incertitude que chacun sent à soy, il est aysé à voir qu'il a *son assiete bien mal assurée* (II, xii, 563 — emphasis added). Yet even in "De l'experience," as Montaigne attempts to conclude the *Essais* by accepting the foibles of the human condition, he remains unsatisfied and condemns his writing project, admitting that it has failed to achieve a final understanding of the world and of himself: "toute cette fricassée que je barbouille n'est qu'un registre des essais de ma vie, qui est, pour l'interne santé, exemplaire assez à prendre *l'instruction à contre-poil*" (III, xiii, 1079 — emphasis added). While considering the same issues, Rousseau maintains that a state of being, solid and durable enough to collect the permanence of one's worth, can be achieved: "un état où l'âme trouve *une assiette assez solide* pour s'y reposer tout entière et rassembler là tout son être" (I, 1047 — emphasis added). Rousseau also suffered from the realization of human inconstancy, yet maintained a greater belief in the possibility that this inconstancy can be stabilized. Rousseau valorizes his own example of this presentation of the self while Montaigne paradoxically veils his project, claiming that he offers himself as an anti-example ("l'instruction à contre-poil"). Rousseau's persona in the "Cinquième Promenade" is the human soul detached from the past, indifferent to the future, occupied only by the present, suffering yet glorying in the experience. Montaigne never freed himself from the past; he relied on the constancy of the ancients to support his own attempts, which he considered to be of a far lesser caliber and which do not achieve Rousseau's putative plenitude of self-being.

Montaigne never accepted that he had a solid ground on which to base a stable self. He could not escape the belief that writing his work was like constructing a "muraille sans *pierre*" (III, iii, 805 — emphasis added), lacking a fundamental solidity on which to establish a stable identity. He admitted that his work is only provisional. Yet Rousseau, in the "Cinquième Promenade," spiritualized this tangible and stable present into pronouncements that later became the centerpiece of his contribution to the romantic aesthetic, achieving "un bonheur suffisant, parfait et plein, qui ne laisse dans l'âme aucun vide qu'elle sente le besoin de remplir" (I, 1046). Rousseau found his "assiette assez solide" during his solitary revery on the island of "Sainte-*Pierre* "(emphasis added), even while floating on the movement of the river that surrounds it. He thus arrived at his final haven of understanding. Yet even in the *Rêveries,* Rousseau proposed a dualistically dynamic system, attempting to produce stability *and* movement: "un mouvement uniforme *et* modéré" (I, 1047 — emphasis added). Rousseau attempted to close himself in his personality in order to block out the world's flux. In the river of signification, Rousseau at once found the solid rock (*pierre*) on which to stabilize his inner movement of thought, which however continued to permutate. In the "Cinquième Promenade," Rousseau strove to resolve at the end of his life what Montaigne chose to leave unresolved; he sought a way out of the impasse set up by Montaigne through the affirmation of self-presence.

What is an irreconcilable tension in the *Essais* resurfaces in the work of Rousseau as it engages the *Essais* sporadically, yet continues important aspects of them with different results, in this case concluding more definitively on the issue of the stability of self-understanding. Yet Rousseau's belief in an "assiette" is only "assez solide," and much of his work, like his reception of the *Essais,* is an enigmatic intertextual field in quest of an elusive self-satisfaction. He continued the diversity and undulancy of Montaigne's essayistic dynamism by embedding it in his own work. Such liquid imagery as Rousseau's recurs in the work of Emerson, Nietzsche, Pater, and Woolf, who use it to express their attitudes toward the instability of language and the human experience, as inspired by their receptions of the *Essais.*

Montaigne's notion of the inconsistency of human experience ("toutes choses y branlent sans cesse" — III, iii, 805) is characteristic of Rousseau's reception of his work. Rousseau's explicit references to Montaigne are not as frequent as Pascal's, his appropriation of the *Essais* is not as visible, yet his ambivalence is equally pronounced, and the *Essais* play an underlying and uncertain role in his writing. Rousseau could not clearly decide on his relationship to the *Essais,* yet nevertheless extended their life considerably by using them as he formulated his own work. His widespread impact was perpetuated in great part by his appropriation of the *Essais*. Rousseau was of course endeared to the romantic left in the early nineteenth century as an incendiary hero of revolutionary proportions, in contrast to Montaigne who was at times considered a revolutionary precursor, but regarded principally as an indifferent conservative bourgeois. Admired for his personal style, he was nevertheless critiqued for his conformism — as Fleuret reminds us: "Et comment pourrait-on comparer au 'Jean-Baptiste' de la révolution française un humaniste qui a passé la St.-Barthélemy sous silence?" (15). Here is ths central paradox of Rousseau's Montaigne: there is a certain parallel between two extreme points — Rousseau's protosocialism and Montaigne's single-minded individualism. The political works of Rousseau, so advanced for his time, are constantly supported by the *Essais*. Yet as Rousseau becomes more confident of his own project, Montaigne begins to fade from view. There are many references in *Discours sur les sciences et les arts*, but in *Discours sur l'inégalité* Montaigne virtually disappears. When Rousseau was struggling to formulate his own version of personal revolt and shaking off the chains of social alienation, Montaigne was there to help. Yet as Rousseau came to construct his social contract, Montaigne was wiped away, at least in appearance; the latter would not have taken seriously such social advances in a time when the horrendous effects of civil war were causing the political instability in which he lived. Rousseau distanced himself from Montaigne in order to actualize what Montaigne left in embryonic form. It was only in his last work, the *Rêveries*, that Rousseau felt comfortable in reaffirming his alliance with Montaigne, although he would never relinquish his claim that he went beyond Montaigne in terms of commitment to the sincerity of self-analysis: "Je fais la même entreprise que Montaigne mais avec un but tout contraire au sien: car il n'écrivait ses essais que pour les autres, et je n'écris mes rêveries que pour moi" (I, 1001).

It is perhaps one of the first commentators on Rousseau's reception of Montaigne who best characterized the former's complex involvement with the *Essais*: "on ne rapprochera jamais assez Rousseau de Montaigne. On épuisera Montaigne à le mettre en notes sous les textes de Rousseau. Rousseau est un homme qui, en représentant Montaigne, fait des idées générales avec les boutades de Montaigne, et les pousse avec passion et éloquence jusqu'au paradoxe."[95] What is already paradoxical in Montaigne, Rousseau reduces to "boutades" in his work, then regenerates new paradoxes from them in order to fulfill his own needs. Montaigne was for Rousseau the initiator of lay humanism, modern skepticism, a *connaisseur* of the human heart, as well as an enlightened teacher and enemy of the prejudice and intolerance that corrupt human nature and close the path to happiness and truth.

Montesquieu and Diderot are distant runners-up to Rousseau's rearticulation of the Essais. In most other receptions of the *Essais* in the eighteenth century, we have seen that Montaigne was most often appreciated as an amusing author, a good friend, and a provocative thinker who stimulates reflection, but whose irregularities impede serious consideration. Through all of this reverence there was little understanding of the audacious implications of many of his essays. Rousseau took him so seriously as to absorb him into his own work; the *Essais* became an organic part of it, much the same way in which Montaigne absorbed his models Seneca, Plutarch, and Plato. Montaigne's impulse toward inner freedom and social tolerance helped Rousseau to construct his model citizen — master and subject of the self, engaged in the collective effort toward a healthy society. This is less of a contradiction than it is a testimony to the surprising ways in which the *Essais* operate — almost in a negative manner, yet with a positive outcome. As in the case of Gournay, Rousseau had to transform Montaigne in order to demarcate his own space. He was thus Montaigne's student *par excellence*, and along with Gournay, redeveloped the *Essais*' implications in the most unexpected ways — in this case, into a program of egalitarian politics and romantic sensibility that Montaigne may not have been able to fathom. Montaigne represented for Rousseau a person who was totally free yet fully integrated into the social fabric, and if Rousseau was the filial descendant of Montaigne, then he overcame his spectre as did Gournay, accepted the unavoidable presence of his ideas into his own work yet conquered them at Montaigne's expense ("à mes dépens"). The conflictual tension in both Rousseau's and Gournay's receptions of the *Essais* opened the doors of social emancipation for groups that had been previously marginalized in French society — first women, then the Third Estate.

Montaigne's surreptitious progressive politics, which lurk in his conservative armarture, were actualized and more fully developed by Rousseau and Gournay.

Outside of Montesquieu, Diderot, and Rousseau, Montaigne's receptions in the eighteenth century happened more quietly. There was a general lack of critical respect for the *Essais.* They were sold on the market in disfigured shapes and simplified versions to the *honnête publique.* Commentaries of a plethora of minor writers — editors, journalists, publishers, and essayists — focused on Montaigne solely as a popular moralist. New editions of the *Essais* were not even based on the original manuscripts, but on previous, and most often erroneous editions. The *Journal de voyage,* discovered and published in 1774, was for the most part ignored. Considered poorly composed, archaic, and impious, Montaigne's writing was accepted as a literary curiosity, outside the canon. The history of Montaigne's time was still being sorted out, his biography was little known, and there were few attempts at any thorough evaluation of his work. Writers made Montaigne into a *libertin,* a *philosophe,* or a revolutionary.[96] He remained the charming, naive, free-thinking, skeptical sage, but in no way a writer worthy of serious consideration. For this, the *Essais* would have to await the nineteenth century, when Montaigne would finally, after Rousseau's reception, be considered "un maître de liberté intérieure."[97] No longer would the depiction of the self be rejected as "haïssable" in the terms of Pascal. If the eighteenth century considered him too idiosyncratic to represent the universality of human nature, in the nineteenth century, this idiosyncracy was admired and the *Essais* were read as a work of "une personnalité unique et singulière."[98]

The central work on Montaigne's reception in the nineteenth century is Frame's.[99] 1812 was chosen as his starting point, since it marks the date when ten *Eloges de Montaigne* were presented to the *Académie Française* for its *concours d'éloquence.* Frame insists upon the romantic period's emphasis on individuality, its acceptance of autobiography, and its espousal of new literary values, elements that quickly generated greater enthusiasm toward and acceptance of the *Essais*: "In his freedom and naturalness of style and vocabulary, in the fact that he dares to write about himself, and in his concept of man as 'divers et ondoyant,' he is far closer to the

Romantics than to the Classicists."[100] There was great admiration for Montaigne's friendship with La Boétie and a shift of focus away from his inconsistent thinking and disorderly writing and toward his profound moral philosophy and mastery of style. The organic, non-systematic order of the *Essais*, along with Montaigne's penchant for a natural over an artificial mode of writing, his nonchalance, and preference for the tangible over the abstract now made him less of a capricious curiosity and more of a significant writer to be studied as such. In 1856, Cuvillier-Fleury attested to Montaigne's achievement of a solid place in literary history: "Aujourd'hui on peut assurer que notre grand Montaigne est plus lu, plus aimé, plus demandé, et pour tout dire en un mot, 'plus à la mode' qu'il n'y fut jamais."[101] Even Napoléon left for the Russian campaign with a copy of the *Essais* in his baggage.[102] Montaigne and Rousseau thus set the stage for the modern paradoxical self that obsessed generations of writers.

It was particularly Sainte-Beuve who paid the most critical attention to the *Essais* and helped to raise Montaigne into the pantheon of French culture. The renewed interest in Montaigne's self-portraiture and lay morality during the early nineteenth century, a trend inspired by the romantic period's concern with personality, self-analysis, and independence of intellectual spirit, provoked Sainte-Beuve to come to terms with Montaigne. Montaigne's presence in the work of Sainte-Beuve is dispersed and irregular (as it is in that of Pascal and Rousseau), with the exception of the chapters devoted to Montaigne in *Port Royal*, which portray Montaigne as a writer to be seriously reckoned with.

There is a creative dimension in Sainte-Beuve's reception of the *Essais* — he freely develops his interpretation of Montaigne's work, yet is often unfaithful to the essayist, distorting the latter's positions in order to represent his own opinions and develop his own arguments. His portrait of Montaigne is not always accurate, nor is it always flattering; yet he went to greater lengths than any other writer in the nineteenth century in France to devote serious critical attention to the *Essais*. His remarks are more critically oriented than Gournay's, Pascal's, Diderot's, or Rousseau's receptions, all of which nevertheless prepared the context in which Sainte-Beuve addressed Montaigne's work. Like the others, he does not escape inconstancy and diversity in his evaluation of the *Essais*. In several digressions from his series of lectures, *Port-Royal,* he says that all Montaigne's readers see something of themselves in him: "Il y a du Montaigne en chacun de nous. Tout goût, toute humeur et passion, toute diversion, amusement, fantaisie."[103] This reiterates Pascal ("Ce n'est pas dans Montaigne, mais dans moi, que je vois tout ce que j'y vois"), again pointing to the adaptability of the *Essais* by other writers. Sainte-Beuve creates his own Montaigne, yet follows the lead of the *Essais,* by formulating a critical approach based on "l'homme *et* l'oeuvre," which generations of critics have since come to practice. Sainte-Beuve's historicist doctrine of considering the historical context to explain the work and writer, which is inextricably related to Taine's *la race, le milieu, et le moment,* was founded upon Montaigne's insistence that we consider not just the writer, but the whole person in his or her cultural and historical circumstances.

Yet Sainte-Beuve's position on the *Essais,* although he attempted to come to a clear understanding, remained in some ways unresolved, thereby reinforcing Montaigne's claim of the "naturelle instabilité de nos meurs et opinions" (II, i, 332). This is what allows him and other readers of Montaigne to filter their own concerns through the latter's writing. The *Essais* are a text that makes extensive demands on readers, first making them submit their own personality to Montaigne's brilliance, leading them to overcome him by interjecting personalized arguments into their receptions. Sainte-Beuve, ironically, was faithful to the *Essais,* thus becoming an ally, even while grafting his own ideas onto Montaigne's. His manner of creative criticism was in the spirit of Montaigne's hybrid genre of the essay: an interdisciplinary exploration of universal human problems throughout history, an analytical creative evaluation of the self and the world. In this sense, the newness of the projects of Gournay, Pascal, Diderot, Rousseau, and Sainte-Beuve, the way they found a place in the *Essais* to fuse their thought with his, is an essential element of a personalized response to literary history that began to appear with greater frequency in the late nineteenth and early twentieth centuries. The "dangerous" elements of Montaigne's writing as codified in the seventeenth century later came to life in reactivations of his most innovative characteristics: the constant movement between the self, the world, and the text, idiosyncratic use of sources, suggestive ideas, and the ability to defer closure while saying something significant are the qualities of the *Essais* that interest their most attentive readers. The *Essais* thus produced a modernist dynamism and inspired the work of subsequent writers who, as they attempted to analytically comprehend the *Essais*, participated in their methods and concerns and reproduced Montaigne's most controversial and disconcerting qualities.

Sainte-Beuve most often appropriated whatever portions of the *Essais* best suited his arguments, fleshing them out with his own thoughts, overlooking or ignoring other parts that conflicted with his positions. He often accepted Montaigne's value as a writer, but just as often rejected him, for example in accusing him of being a religious hypocrite. There are echoes of Sainte-Beuve's reception of Montaigne in the work of Emerson, whose intertextual relationship to the *Essais*, as we will see in Chapter Two, also frequently frustrates definitive critical certainty. One of the major common denominators of the history of Montaigne commentary is, in fact, the ability of the *Essais* to assume various identities in the eyes of different interpreters. It is the shifting nature of the *Essais'* textuality that makes this possible. The notion of flux and change is perhaps the quintessential characteristic of Montaigne's writing project:

> Finalement, il n'y a aucune constante existence, ny de nostre estre, ny de celuy des objets. Et nous, et nostre jugement, et toutes choses mortelles, vont coulant et roulant sans cesse. Ainsin il ne se peut establir rien de certain de l'un à l'autre, et le jugeant et le jugé estans en continuelle mutation et branle. (II, xii, 601)

It is also important for Sainte-Beuve's notions of living and of writing: "Ne nous figeons pas; tenons nos esprits vivants et fluides."[104] It is this fluid dynamism that produces shift and instability, qualities widely accepted as "modernist," and which play an important role in Sainte-Beuve's reception of the *Essais*. Sainte-Beuve, like Montaigne, was a writer "divers and ondoyant;" their intertextual relationship, as Frame has discussed at length, is intricate and difficult to clarify. This critical undecideability is in fact a recurring problem for many critics as they constantly admit to the impossibility of determining fixed relationships between the *Essais* and their most attentive readers (witness Dezon-Jones on Gournay, Schwartz on Diderot, Fleuret on Rousseau — Croquette avoids the problem by limiting his venture to a positivist study of Pascal's reception). The

Essais thus problematize the very concept of reception. Yet critical response based on the reciprocal nature of literary affiliation does seem to make this less of a barrier, by accepting the impossibility of finalized interpretation and by admitting this factor to be a dominant quality of the *Essais,* a text that in turn generates similar interpretations. In France, it was Sainte-Beuve who brought Montaigne into the center of literary activity during the nineteenth century by demonstrating the *Essais*' heterogeneous identity. His characterization of Montaigne's style emphasized how quintessential the imagistic, rhapsodic, metamorphic mode of thinking and writing as developed in the *Essais* is to modernist concerns:

> Montaigne a eu, plus qu'aucun peut-être, ce don d'exprimer et de peindre; son style est une figure perpétuelle, et à chaque pas renouvelée; on n'y reçoit les idées qu'en images ... son heureuse rhapsodie d'images, d'un bout à l'autre, jusque dans ses reliefs les plus divers, est tout d'un pan; on marche avec lui de pensée en pensée dans les métamorphoses. (I, 863-5)

After Sainte-Beuve's reception, the *Essais* played an increasingly important role in French literary history.

Chapters II and III of Sainte-Beuve's "Livre Troisième" in *Port Royal* form the centerpiece of his reception of Montaigne. He begins by recounting the history of Montaigne's suppression in the seventeenth century and gradually digresses to his own judgments on the *Essais.* Sainte-Beuve saw Montaigne as the most "natural" of writers: "Montaigne, ce n'est pas un système de philosophie, ce n'est pas même avant tout un sceptique, un pyrrhonien; non, Montaigne, c'est tout simplement la nature ..." (836). He goes to great lengths to develop Montaigne as *"la Nature au complet sans la Grâce"* (836), and as the quintessential unrepentant skeptic: "le démon de l'incrédulité" (817). Concerning Montaigne as a moralist, however, Sainte-Beuve accuses him of ideological treachery, maintaining that he is a demonic fatalist laughing at human misery:

> Il n'y a de riant que l'apparence. Montaigne, en ce chapitre et dans tout son livre, a fait comme un démon malin, un enchanteur maudit, qui, vous prenant par la main, et vous introduisant avec mille discours séduisants dans le labyrinthe des opinions, vous dit à chaque pas, à chaque marque que vous voulez faire pour vous retrouver: "Tout ceci n'est qu'erreur ou doute, n'y comptez pas, ne regardez pas trop, en espoir de vous diriger au retour; la seule chose sûre est cette lampe que voici; jetez le reste: cette lampée sacrée nous suffit." (861)

This critique in the Jansenist manner shows Sainte-Beuve entangled in an ambivalent relationship with the *Essais*. It is significant that he came to Montaigne by way of Pascal, and indeed was smitten by the Port Royalists as he himself went through an examination of his own religious conscience.[105] It would appear then that Sainte-Beuve was eventually seduced by the *Essais* to adopt Montaigne rather than Pascal as his guide; later in his career, he demonstrated a greater appreciation for Montaigne, accepted his philosophical skepticism, and even went as far as to proclaim him "le Français le plus sage qui ait jamais existé."[106]

As with Pascal and Rousseau, we can witness in Sainte-Beuve's reception a conflictual attitude toward Montaigne, one alternating between praise and blame, as well as an impulse to sometimes borrow from, sometimes denigrate the *Essais*. Frame attempts to clearly establish Montaigne's influence on Sainte-Beuve, yet cannot decide whether it is true influence or coincidental similarity that produces the many resemblances between the two. Sainte-Beuve, like Pascal and Rousseau, shifts his points of view, and Frame's attempt at an empirical understanding of Sainte-Beuve's Montaigne is inconclusive, again demonstrating Montaigne's belief that "nous ne faisons que nous entregloser" (III, xiii, 1069), and that the critical enterprise is in its very nature equivocal and interminable. The ability of the *Essais* to problematize the commentaries of reader after reader is closer to the project of Montaigne's impulse to refuse dogmatic certainty: "je prononce ma sentence par articles descousus, ainsi que de chose qui ne se peut dire à la fois et en bloc. La relation et la conformité ne se trouvent poinct en telles ames que les nostres, basses et communes" (III, xiii, 1076). The unity of the *Essais* and of their receptions is thus the disunity of response that they engender. This is the "forme maistresse" (III, ii, 811) of receptions of the *Essais*: the recurring interpretive ambiguity that is also an act of liberation toward the freedom of interpretation. It is this hermeneutic undecideability that can be seen in part as Montaigne's modernist identity. Sainte-Beuve, more than anyone else at this time, engaged the problematics posed by the *Essais* and produced undulating commentary, seeing Montaigne both as a positive influence in French literary history and also a negative one in terms of religion and morality. Sainte-Beuve sees some of Montaigne in everyone, yet as his enchantment with the *Essais* dissipates, Montaigne becomes quickly associated with Machiavelism and Faustian satanism, and ultimately a hypocrite: "je ne vois pas ce qu'on gagnerait à toute force, à faire conclure qu'il peut bien avoir paru très-bon catholique, sauf à n'avoir guère été chrétien" (851). Yet in the art of living calmly and naturally amid personal and social strife, Sainte-Beuve valued Montaigne as the intellectual precursor of his own situation.

Montaigne would not have been surprised at the discordance of these writers' opinions on his work, as diversity was for him one of the basic principles of existence, and an issue that recurs as a leitmotif throughout the *Essais*.[107] Indeed, "diversité," "varieté," and "dissimilitude," qualities fundamental to almost every page of the *Essais*, seem to permeate their receptions throughout history. Jauss's concept of the "horizon-of experience" proves to be essential in considering the evolving fortunes of the *Essais* — each age reflects itself in its interpretations of the *Essais* and generates its own version of them — yet these acts further problematize the quest for the "true" identity of Montaigne and his work, a problem that subsequent generations attempt to solve. The perpetual problematic is that major writers in every century expose their inability to establish harmonious relationships with Montaigne's work, producing inconsistency and contradiction, thereby reactivating the dynamic indeterminability of the *Essais*. Michael Baraz, in his discussion of the contradictory nature of such critical apprehensions of the *Essais*, rightfully claims: "Ceci est paradoxal et contradictoire, mais l'intuition fondamentale de Montaigne n'est-elle pas précisément celle de la coexistence des contraires?"[108] The aesthetics of reception is thus an essential vantage point from which we can attempt to understand how these coexistences of contrarieties operate. The notion of reception is in itself prepared in some ways by the *Essais*, one of the first works in the Western tradition that seeks to develop an interactive critical understanding with the world, what we will see in Chapter Two as Nietzsche's "critical" (*kritische*) relationship with history and the self.

Along with Montaigne's uncanny ability to provoke readers to see something of themselves in the *Essais*, the capacity to produce contradictions and interpretive inconsistencies in these readers' conclusions is one of the essential aspects of Montaigne's influence. The notion of fluidity contained in the very etymology of "influence" (L. *influo,* "to flow in") sheds light on the history of Montaigne's receptions, in which commentators are unable to escape the flux of the *Essais'* swirling discourse, which undermines either their admiration or their abnegation of them. The imposition of one's "horizon of experience" onto the critical process is inevitable. Even with determined critical effort, there will always be some degree of inconsistency in one's arguments. This is what Montaigne attempted to produce in his writing: a nexus of relationships whose final resolution is virtually indeterminable, opening the possibility for further readers to engage them in the production of their own points of view. A reader can attempt to continue articulating the *Essais* even with the awareness of being caught in the undecidable flux that makes absolute critical articulation of their diversity difficult to achieve. There is no escaping *aporia* without a certain dogmatic reductionism — and herein lurks a crucial aspect of Montaigne's modernism: the refusal of a totalization of meaning, both in the *Essais* themselves and in their receptions. Instead of achieving closure and some ultimate understanding, critical receptions seem to move in the opposite direction, becoming more complex, opening up more issues, and generating a greater complexity as they become involved in wider ranges of problematics through the centuries.

After the commentary of Sainte-Beuve, there was no important critical work done on Montaigne in France until the end of the century. The efforts of Dr. Jean-François Payen, however, deserve mention. Payen, whose name is linked to Montaigne's in the nineteenth century as was Gournay's in the seventeenth, published an edition of the *Essais* in 1837 and until his death in 1870 was a tireless champion of Montaigne, carrying out historical research on his life and times, publishing articles, and especially gathering the many documents and books that have come to constitute the *fonds Payen* of the Bibliothèque Nationale. Rare editions of the *Essais,* books from Montaigne's personal library, letters, testimonies of friends and family members, and business documents are today essential materials for an understanding of the daily realities of Montaigne.[109]

Later in the century, as Montaigne gained official status in the French literary canon, several important critical and historical studies appeared. Paul Bonnefon's work, *Montaigne, l'homme et l'oeuvre,* published in 1893, did a great deal to stimulate interest in Montaigne's life and work. Edouard Ruel, in his work *Montaigne,* published in 1901, was one of the first to insist on the stylistic worthiness of the *Essais*. Edmé Champion's *Introduction aux "Essais" de Montaigne,* published in 1900, points out that Montaigne did not write an autobiography, but rather a general picture of the permutations of his inner life. Champion's innovative thesis is that Montaigne's opinions evolved through the years and that the text's accretions coincided with the development of his thought. This was a glimpse of what would become the "evolutionary" Montaigne, the quintessential contribution of historicist scholarship to Montaigne studies in the early twentieth century. Thus in the nineteenth century, Montaigne became for the first time a master of style as well as of thought. In the previous three centuries, his style, when liked, was most often regarded as charming and captivating, but almost always criticized for its lack of correctness, regularity, and order. Montaigne's work was either superficially praised, ruthlessly edited, banished, or in the case of Gournay, Pascal, Montesquieu, Diderot, Rousseau, and Sainte-Beuve, drawn into the literary and philosophical issues with which they were dealing in their own work.

Nineteenth-century commentators thus gradually abandoned the idea of Montaigne as a naive and disorderly writer, accepted his unique style, and proclaimed him a master of French literary language. As Frame summarizes:

> In the matter of style, the old view stresses the *naïveté,* energy, freedom, and boldness of his writing, but adds that it is impure and incorrect; the new view stresses the richness, color, charm, and capriciousness of his prose and sees him as a great and fully conscious stylist.[110]

As we have seen, Sainte-Beuve himself admired Montaigne, not only as a thinker, but also as a stylist of merit. Sainte-Beuve's reception, while continuing to concern itself with Montaigne's ideas, also freed the *Essais* from classicist strictures of composition, appreciated the essayist's stylistic innovation, and thereby allowed him to be seen in a more judicious light, an event that fueled the popularity of the *Essais* — which thenceforth played a central role in the receptions of writers contemporary with and subsequent to Sainte-Beuve's formulation, inside and outside of France. Perpetual, renewable, and imagistic, in Sainte-Beuve's terms — these are the qualities of

Montaigne's writing that projected the *Essais* into ever widening spheres of appropriation — his innovative qualities become more and more recognizable in the dawn of the modernist "horizon-of-experience." A paradoxical moment thus arose in the late nineteenth and early twentieth centuries. During the "modernist" period, a time in which such writers as Woolf and Gide adapted Montaigne into their own innovative writing projects, there was a countercurrent historicist antiquarianism that appropriated the *Essais* and defended them against any radical notions as to their identity by regularizing them in a very positivistic, sophisticated, and what proved to be for some time convincing way.

At the turn of the twentieth century, there was a flourishing of academic interest and an accompanying series of significant works on Montaigne's life and writing. They were carried out by a group of French professor-critics, a generation of scholars trained under the influence of Ferdinand Brunetière, who took his cue from Sainte-Beuve and promoted an historicist approach to literary studies. Brunetière's contribution was to seek objectivity in criticism, centering on the ascertainable questions of the chronology of the composition of an *oeuvre,* on the facts of the author's life, on the sources and origins of a text, on the intellectual climate contemporary with its composition, and on its critical editions, thereby achieving unambiguous certainties about literary works. Brunetière, the self-appointed successor of Taine, was a literary Darwinist combatting critical impressionism and insisting on scientific objectivity in literary studies:

> Nier la possibilité de la critique objective, c'est nier la possibilité d'une science quelconque. S'il n'y a pas de critique objective, il n'y a non plus d'histoire naturelle, ni de chimie, ni de physique objective.[111]

Villey, Gustave Lanson, and Fortunat Strowski all came under Brunetière's influence and produced works in general accord with his historicist doctrine. Lanson, Brunetière's most accomplished student, published *Les "Essais" de Michel de Montaigne* in 1930. In it, he set himself the task of regularizing the disorderly, archaic *Essais* in order to make them, according to him, more palatable to the reading public:

> Ce livre est une introduction à la lecture des *Essais.* Il a pour objet d'initier ses lecteurs au mouvement et à la couleur de la pensée de

> Montaigne, et d'atténuer la difficulté de la première rencontre, qui résulte autant de la liberté d'allure de l'écrivain, du passage perpétuel et brusque d'un thème à l'autre que de l'archaïsme de la langue. *J'ai essayé d'ordonner ce désordre* et de faire l'inventaire de cette richesse. J'ai pratiqué sur les *Essais* une opération assez analogue à celle qu'il y a un peu plus de trois siècles de Pierre Charron.[112] (emphasis added)

Lanson freely admitted to distorting the text, deeming it necessary for a clear understanding of its meaning. He continued to feel it necessary to remove discrepancies from the *Essais* in order to make them more readable. His work supports a belief in literary history as the path to literary criticism. He begins by discussing Montaigne's life, moves to the intellectual and political climate of his time in the Tainean mode ("Le Milieu et le Moment") and, finally, examines the *Essais* thematically (skepticism, religion, morality, humanism, and philosophy of life). His final, short chapter on the language, composition, and style of the *Essais* for the most part quotes Montaigne on these subjects and accomplishes little textual analysis. Lanson remained squarely in the tradition of Brunetière, relying on biography, intellectual climate, sources, and origins to explain the text.

Another of Brunetière's students, Strowski, discovered Montaigne, as did Sainte-Beuve, by way of Pascal. In the preface to his work *Montaigne*, Strowski claims his method to be that of scientific historicism: "Je crois être le premier à publier un livre ou la méthode historique et génétique soit appliquée à la pensée de Montaigne."[113] In this work, Strowski is rigorous in his systematic division of the *Essais* into three periods representing the changing state of mind of its author: stoicism, skepticism, and "dilettantisme" (read epicureanism). Strowski leans heavily on biographical material to support his theory, and tries to methodize the *Essais* into a coherent evolutionary scheme. Strowski seeks to regularize the *Essais* by either overlooking, disregarding, or suppressing Montaigne's own admission of his lack of methodical procedure:

> Je prends de la fortune le premier argument. Ils me sont également bons. Et ne desseigne jamais de les produire entiers. Car je ne vois le tout de rien. Ne font pas, ceux qui promettent de nous le faire veoir. De cent membres et visages qu'a chaque chose, j'en prens un tantost à lecher seulement, tantost à effleurer et parfois à pincer jusqu'à l'os. (I, i, 302)

Strowski thereby thwarted the *Essais*' impulse toward a freer process of textual production and commentary. His work added, however, an important dimension to Montaigne studies: a more precise textual documentation of the *Essais*; yet it attempted little examination of them beyond the drawing of parallels between Montaigne's life and his work.

Whereas Strowski's focus was on the *Essais*' chronology, additions and variants, and Montaigne's biography, Pierre Villey, Lanson's student, was more interested in the text's sources and believed that by establishing what Montaigne read, and at what point in his career he read it, one could achieve an enhanced understanding of his work. In the "Avant Propos" to his monumental study *Les Sources et l'Evolution des "Essais" de Montaigne*, Villey outlines this project:

> Mon but n'est pas donc de donner une étude complète sur les *Essais*. J'ai simplement cherché à reconnaître les transformations de la pensée de Montaigne, de sa méthode de travail, du genre littéraire qu'il a créé, à expliquer ces transformations par ses lectures, par sa biographie, par son milieu que la lecture des ouvrages contemporains m'a permis de mieux connaître.[114]

Like Strowski, Villey was more interested in the "histoire de la pensée," and less in textual analysis. Villey's contribution to Montaigne scholarship is to have determined the sources and chronology of the *Essais* and to have developed, in a more complete and convincing manner than Strowski, the idea of an evolving Montaigne. More recently Floyd Gray, among others, has objected to such a systematized reconstruction of the evolution of Montaigne's thought, criticizing the intentional fallacy inherent in the work of Strowski and Villey, in the belief that the book does not equal the author's life.[115]

Albert Thibaudet's reception of Montaigne is a special case. Not strictly an academic, Thibaudet was an erudite journalist writing literary criticism and must ultimately be classified as a "creative critic" in the manner of Sainte-Beuve. Thibaudet saw Montaigne as a precursor to Bergsonian philosophy: movement, the fundamental principle of Montaigne's style, is also that of Bergson's thought, as well as of Thibaudet's own work. For Thibaudet, Montaigne is "l'homme du passage et du mouvement. Se peignant lui-même dans les *Essais*, il peint ce qu'il sent particulièrement en lui-même, et ce que la plupart des hommes connaissent mais ne sentent pas: l'instabilité et le changement."[116] His six hundred-page work on Montaigne is as labyrinthine and asystematic as are the *Essais* themselves. He believed critical engagement to be less of an exact science and more of an artistic collaboration with the writer under consideration. The critic for Thibaudet should have an empathetic identification with the author under critical scrutiny: "Le meilleur de la critique réside dans cette sympathie de sentiment ... la critique devient créatrice dans la mesure où elle s'incorpore des puissances de sympathie."[117] In one sense, Thibaudet's criticism is similar to that of Villey and Strowski: he also seeks to give unity to the *Essais*, yet his version of their unity is found in the Bergsonian philosophical principle of intuition over intellect.

According to Thibaudet, movement in the *Essais*, which characterizes Montaigne's inner life, is the *ordre moteur* that produces the reality and the unity of the work. In considering Bergsonian mobility as the essence of reality, Thibaudet rightly claims that Bergson's thought can be seen as an extension of Montaigne's notions of self-analysis. Bergson, in fact, could not have better described the Montaignean principle of movement as one of the keys to self-discovery: "... la vérité est que notre esprit ... peut s'installer dans la réalité mobile, en adopter la direction sans cesse changeante, enfin la saisir intuitivement ... il aboutira ainsi à des concepts fluides, capables de suivre la réalité dans toutes ses sinuosités et d'adopter le mouvement même de la vie intérieure.[118] In contrast to his more positivist contemporaries, Thibaudet did not see a segmented "evolutionary" text, but rather one of flux, not a flux that coalesces into a chronological order, but one of constant diversity that forms a mobile whole. Although Thibaudet depended on the historicist apparatus as the foundation for his critical approach, he went beyond the scientific method, entered into the creative spirit of the *Essais*, and rewrote them, thereby following Montaigne's suggestion that subsequent authors should continue the writing of the *Essais*. Thibaudet in fact made a claim for the *Essais* as a *productive* text: "la grandeur du rôle de Montaigne est faite de bonne partie de tout ce qu'on a pensé au-dessus de lui et contre lui."[119]

Thibaudet's creative identification with the *Essais* moved in a direction opposite to that of the academic critics of more exacting temperaments. Refusing to reduce the *Essais* to a formulaic identity, and taking them in an opposite direction, is Thibaudet's achievement; by generating an empathetic response in the spirit of Montaigne, he enlarges the *Essais'* innovative scope and productive capacity. Montaigne the dualist would perhaps call for a balance between flexibility toward the issues (in the manner of Thibaudet) and an accompanying rigor of critical judgment (the efforts of the *universitaire* critics). However, his very own text makes a final harmonious stasis of the conflicting forces they generate perhaps unachievable. The missing unity of the *Essais* is found in the concerns of readers' receptions of them in different times and places. In this way, reading the *Essais* can trap readers into interpretive writing for as long as (in Montaigne's terms) there is ink and paper in the world.

The work of the *universitaire* critics at the turn of the twentieth century greatly enhanced Montaigne's popularity. The *Essais* became on the one hand codified by the academy, and on the other valorized as a textual muse. In the work of Lanson, Villey, and Strowski, we have seen the impulse toward the positivist search for concrete facts about the *Essais* and the organicist desire to posit the work as a coherent whole. These critics are, for the most part, rooted in a common purpose: using biography, sources, chronology, and evolution to interpret the *Essais*. Thibaudet and, as we will see, Gide took a different approach, and as an alternative to the historicist critics, engaged in intuitive dialogs with Montaigne's work. Although Thibaudet and Gide were editors for, and published by, the academic press "La Nouvelle Revue Française," they stand apart in their less empirical approaches. Thibaudet wrote creative criticism in the spirit of the *Essais*, and is more in line with Sainte-Beuve than with Rousseau or Pascal; he was both an objective critic and a creative collaborator. His rewriting of the *Essais* in a freer manner reaches back to Jean-Pierre Camus's *Diversitez*. It is the same type of response to the *Essais* as produced by Pater, as will be discussed in Chapter Three.

Writers and critics of the seventeenth century most often focused on Montaigne's position (actual or putative) concerning religious matters. They also opposed his style, preferring a less disorderly arrangement, and vehemently attacked his ideas on fideism and self-portraiture. In the eighteenth century his philosophical skepticism was used to propound attacks on religious dogmatism; yet there was no great admiration of the *Essais'* compositional qualities, and Montaigne's ideas were interpreted according to individual temperament and mood. The appreciation of Montaigne's skepticism, however, may have been greatly exaggerated, since he is a writer who stood behind many definite opinions, especially on education, ethics, government, dogmatism, rationalism, love, marriage, and the value of the self-portrait, to name a few. In both of these centuries, the tendency was to decry Montaigne's compositional irregularity and issue neatly tailored editions of the *Essais*. The early nineteenth century was unique in its recognition of several issues central to the *Essais* to which little or no consideration had been previously given. Montaigne's project of self-portraiture and his highly personal style were now looked at in a positive light as the *Essais* became accepted into the pantheon of French literature thanks to the efforts of Sainte-Beuve and Payen. At the turn of the twentieth century, the *universitaire* critics looked at the *Essais* from a textual, historical, and biographical point of view, more closely than ever before, calling atention to them as a text that henceforth merited close critical consideration. Thus began the systematic evaluations toward an enhanced understanding of Montaigne's project. Yet the screen through which these latter critics examined the *Essais* also distorted them — each interpretive attempt sought to methodize their unmethodical qualities while ignoring or explaining away idiosyncracies and inconsistencies in the positivist zeal to ascertain the unequivocal facts, consistent themes, and stylistic contours underlying Montaigne's irregularities. Writers and critics of four centuries have thus examined the *Essais* through the horizon of their own particular predilections, each creating his or her own Montaigne.

The *Essais*' chameleon-like quality, changing color to match the surrounding environment, allows them to adapt to diverse climates of opinion, yet at the same time to remain constant, as readings of successive periods produce versions of Montaigne to fulfill their own concerns, readings that are nevertheless interrelated: "There have been almost as many different Montaignes as there have been readers of him. For the pious, he was a man of piety, and for the free-thinkers, a free-thinker, for the pagan, a pagan."[120] The various critical attempts at explicating the *Essais* expose how Montaigne's more eccentric (Gk. *ex-centros*, "outside of the center") elements produce open and indeterminate responses. In light of the French etymology of *essayer* ("to try, "to test," and by extension "to assay," "to assess," in English), we can see that the *Essais* and their receptions are experimental assessments ("essais"). The diachronic approach to receptions of the *Essais* clarifies their place in literary history yet also demonstrates that the problematics involved in reading the *Essais* throughout several centuries are not so dissimilar. Successive "horizons-of-experience" share reactions to the *Essais*. There is a similarity as well as a divergence of response, diversity in the unified consensus that the *Essais* are worthy of appropriation and interpretation. The receptive approach pursues the diversity of response with an enhanced degree of awareness since it concurs with the interactive *Essais* — a text demanding active reading in order to apprehend its implications on its own terms.

There are two other important Montaigne commentators in France during the first half of the twentieth century who helped to develop the *Essais*' modernist identity. The first is Gide, the second is Merleau-Ponty. Gide did much to disseminate Montaigne's popularity in the early part of the century. He combined both the academic and the creative attitudes, publishing popular and authoritative editions of the *Essais*, yet doing so in a totally personalized way — presenting the *Essais* nearly as if they were his own writing. Gide's edition of the *Essais* is divided according to themes of his choice and followed by excerpts from the *Essais* to give Montaigne's position on particular subjects. Gide was thus another purveyor in the long tradition of simplified and neatly packaged *Essais*.[121] Yet more central to an understanding of Gide's reception of Montaigne are his two essays "Essai sur Montaigne" and "Suivant Montaigne."[122] Neither piece makes an attempt at critical evaluation of style and both are overtly personal interpretations of Montaigne's life and work. Gide insists on Montaigne's affirmation of individualism and sees his greatest contribution to be the freedom from self-constraint and the discovery of a human-centered universe: "L'individualisme s'est-il jamais exprimé en termes plus exprès et plus forts?" (10). Both essays discuss the importance of Montaigne's "autobiography," the contradictory nature of humanity, and the affirmation of life in its fullest. Gide makes the distinction between the nonchalant Montaigne and the ascetic Pascal, preferring of course the former. He did not falsify Montaigne, yet he chose to see in him, as do many others, that which best suits his own temperament: he sometimes had a "rather free and easy way ... of bending Montaigne's thought to his own."[123]

In Gide's "Essai sur Montaigne," the fluctuation and inconstancy of the world is a central concern: "Car Montaigne reste préoccupé du perpétuel écoulement de toutes choses, la non-stabilité de la personnalité humaine ... un insaisissable devenir" (17-18). Gide valued the heterodox, unstable, and questing personality, so important to many of his fictional protagonists.[124] He saw the idiosyncratic as a prerequisite for achieving a certain level of genuineness. Yet Gide proposed an amoral attitude whereas Montaigne adhered to a certain ethical constancy in order to find a harmonious balance between himself and the world. Gide was not the first to recognize himself in Montaigne, but he went even further than Sainte-Beuve or Thibaudet in his highly subjective interpretation of the *Essais*, while concurrently playing an official role in their dissemination. Motivated by the zeal to prove an affinity that he wanted to exist between himself and Montaigne, Gide attempted to tip the scale too much in favor of the essayist's skepticism and use it in the service of his valorization of an uncompromising individualism. It was not skepticism in itself that Gide admired, but rather the attempt to move beyond doubt and continual inquiry. Indeed, in his desire to relish conflict and revolt, Gide developed Montaigne's claim that human existence is a paradoxical harmony of contradictions and ambiguities:

> Nostre vie est composée, comme l'harmonie du monde, de choses contraires, aussi de divers tons, douz et aspres, aigus et plats, mols et graves ... Et nous aussi, les biens et les maux, qui sont consubstantiels à nostre vie. Nostre estre ne peut sans ce mélange, et y l'une bande non moins nécessaire que l'autre. (III, xiii, 1068)

Montaigne had no desire to reconcile all of the contradictions in the *Essais* — he often produced irreconcilable elements and used their conflict to generate more inquiry. Gide followed him by nurturing such conflicts without explicit attempts at reconciliation in order to stimulate his best efforts in living and writing: "C'est que je suis resté malgré tout très amoureux de ce qui m'a le plus gêné, et que je ne puis jurer que cette gêne même n'ait pas obtenu de moi le meilleur."[125] In Gide's desire to see Montaigne as a precursor of himself, he selected from the *Essais* that which served to help him in the development of his own personality. In Lanson's opinion, "Gide le lit à la lumière de sa propre sensibilité, à la lumière de la sensibilité des hommes d'aujourd'hui."[126] Lanson's comment again points out (while perhaps failing to see his own implication in the process) that this is the recurring fact in most attentive receptions of Montaigne's work. Gide wanted to assimilate elements from the *Essais* "comme les abeilles de Montaigne ... de préférence ce qui convenait à [son] miel" (XI, 283) and he took Montaigne's bee metaphor so seriously that he attempted to appropriate the *Essais* by transforming them into his own thought, thereby succeeding in believing that Montaigne's personality and work were an extension of his own. Yet Gide flirted with the danger pointed out by Montaigne of not adequately assimilating one's sources:

> C'est tesmoinage de crudité et indigestion que de regorger la viande, comme on l'a avallée. L'estomac n'a pas faict son opération, s'il n'a faict changer la façon et la forme à ce qu'on luy avait donné à cuire. (I, xxvi, 151)

Gide struggled with Montaigne and finally produced his own personalized edition of the *Essais*, a streamlined version of aspects of Montaigne's writing most important to him. Like previous editors, Gide ignored or omitted what did not suit his predilections. He did not continue Montaigne's writing so much as direct it into his own flourishing impulse toward self-understanding.

Gide went so far as to counteract the "official" versions of Montaigne's life and work in his reception of the *Essais*. It is particularly on the question of religion that Gide attempted to bring to light the modern identity of Montaigne's work. In the words of Braak: "la plus belle conquête du protestantisme, celle que Gide admire le plus, c'est d'avoir opposé à l'immobilité catholique l'idée du libre examen."[127] The desire that seems to truly motivate Gide in his two essays on Montaigne is to establish the latter as an avatar of the modernist spirit. After his presentation of the general dimensions of the *Essais*, Gide begins to focus on Montaigne's putative conservatism in religious matters. Gide proposes that Montaigne is prudent in his attitude toward the Catholic church, but not passionate, and marvels at the fact that he never bothers to speak of Christ: "Montaigne est le premier de ces catholiques non chrétiens, qui font profession de se rattacher à Rome et qui pourtant ignore le

Christ" (43), and even guardedly attacks Catholicism: "chaque fois que Montaigne parle du christianisme, c'est avec la plus étrange impertinence" (18). Montaigne was aware of the potential difficulties that he could have with the Papal authorities (was not his travel to Rome primarily to obtain the Vatican's acceptance of his work?) and consequently maintained a certain religious conservatism in his writing that Gide regards more as wariness than faith. Gide claims that what Montaigne perceived as the order of antiquity and the stability of the Catholic religion, though not unconditionally good, were better left alone.

Gide thus developed the idea that readers have ignored the true nature of Montaigne's antipathies, not only concerning the official religion of his time, but also concerning politics, the family, and women — Gide maintained that Montaigne really didn't care for any of them. In trying to call attention to Montaigne's less admirable qualities, Gide strove to counter the efforts of academic criticism to monumentalize Montaigne by putting him on a pedestal and sanitizing the *Essais*: "vis à vis des auteurs hardis, néanmoins devenus classiques, la grande occupation des pédagogues, c'est de les rendre inoffensifs" (31). Gide wanted to restore a hardy and offensive Montaigne to the foreground, and Montaigne's putative aversion to "nouvelletez," which would contradict the claim that he was an innovative modernist, was seen by Gide as a smokescreen, and a very weak one at that, to obscure his ideological audacity and discursive liberty — making the required overtures to political and ecclesiastic authorities, while craftily maintaining his intellectual and spiritual independence. He quotes Montaigne's own version of this ironic movement between freedom of the self and conformity to authority: "'Toute inclination & soubmission leur est deuë, sauf celle de l'entendement. Ma raison n'est pas duite à se courber & fléchir, ce sont mes genoux'" (61). Gide saw the ironic dimensions of Montaigne's outward submission to the hegemonic powers of his time, coupled with the totally unique and revolutionary dimensions of his work as the key to understanding Montaigne's importance to his own work. Exploring alternatives to the established and conventional, Gide's restless temperament renovated Montaigne as an ally in his own attempts to shake readers out of their complacency and motivate them to revise their conventional attitudes toward religion, education, science, culture, sexuality, and society in general. It was his reception that brought Montaigne more into the foreground of high modernism as a divided being struggling to promote that which is most unique in a conformist world.

Merleau-Ponty's reception of Montaigne occurred more quietly in "Lecture de Montaigne," his only explicit work on the *Essais*, which focuses on Montaigne's skepticism and how the *Essais* were the first text to fully develop a philosophy of subjectivity: "La conscience de soi est sa constante, la mesure pour lui de toutes les doctrines."[128] Merleau-Ponty maintained that Montaigne refused commitment except to his personal self and, as an opponent of Cartesian rationalism, constituted Montaigne as a disciple of phenomenological existentialism *avant la lettre.* Merleau-Ponty's position of an oxymoronic *skeptical engagement* (somewhere between the polarities of Husserlian phenomenological perception and Sartrean commitment), as well as his valorization of textual mobility, dominate his essay on Montaigne.[129] Merleau-Ponty was writing against the Cartesian tradition and the critical idealism emanating from the work of critics such as Brunschvicg. Such idealism produced a harmonious systematization of human experience, yet, as Merleau-Ponty saw it, did not do justice to the fundamental discontinuity between consciousness and the world and between one consciousness and another.[130] He saw in the life and work of Montaigne not only the exploration of his unique consciousness, but also an affirmation of the world's reality. Montaigne's attempt to conceptualize the world was dependent on his perceptual milieu — it is because the *Essais* participate fully in the world around them that Merleau-Ponty posited Montaigne as an essential example of the mediation between individual subjectivity and the inescapable tangibility of quotidian experience. The paradoxical quality of both Montaigne's and Merleau-Ponty's work, in which polar qualities can be valid at the same time, has been summarized by Rosalie Colie: "The negative and positive meanings are so balanced that one meaning can never outweigh the other. The paradox is literally speculative, its meaning infinitely mirrored, infinitely reflected in each other."[131] In Merleau-Ponty's terms, the goal of philosophical speculation for Montaigne and for himself was not "résoudre le problème de l'homme," but rather, "décrire l'homme comme problème" (1049).

This is what Montaigne demands of his readers — not the establishment of dogmatic conclusions, but an evaluation of how the *Essais* problematize the very concept of conclusion — provoking awareness of one's interpretive strategies, ideological predilections, and especially of the very problem of how to understand oneself conclusively.

Merleau-Ponty's notion of the discontinuity between consciousness and the world as fundamental to an understanding of human subjectivity provoked him to read Montaigne's work as a dialogue between involvement with society and intellectual freedom. He posited the mediation between self and the world as central to the understanding of Montaigne's thought. It is also a key to the understanding of Merleau-Ponty's:

> Le monde n'est pas pour lui un système d'objets dont il ait par devers soi l'idée, le moi n'est pas pour lui la pureté d'une conscience intellectuelle. Pour lui, comme plus tard pour Pascal, nous sommes intéressés à un monde dont nous n'avons pas la clef, également incapables de demeurer en nous-mêmes et dans les choses, renvoyés d'elles à nous et de nous à elles. (1045)

Montaigne was, for Merleau-Ponty, the modern founder of the philosophy of subjectivity, a perennial quality of much literature and philosophy, but in the life and work of Montaigne, a central and determining factor. In his insistence on Montaigne's creative skepticism and philosophy of the self, Merleau-Ponty was another of Montaigne's commentators who projected their own preoccupations into their understanding of the *Essais*. In his reception, we can discern another pronounced instance of the *Essais*' impact on the concept of literary self-expression in the twentieth century in terms of subjectivity, paradox, and innovative discourse. Montaigne is looked to again and again as an essential precursor to, and a catalyst of, new trends of thought. His "modernism" is embodied in his production of a textual dynamic from which unfolds newer and newer essayistic strategies toward the understanding of the Western intellectual tradition as well as of the human condition.

♦ ♦ ♦

The *Essais* introduced a new form of writing and inquiry into French literature — one so unique that the genre could never be imitated *per se*, but nevertheless became an extremely reproduceable set of textual configurations in the intellectual concepts of European culture as seen in the many receptions since the 1580s. Montaigne's impact was widespread and, as we have seen, has generated numerous responses by many writers. His style was disarming to his first readers and disorienting to two centuries of commentators — the *Essais'* disorderly order, paradoxical certainties, sinuous composition, and unbridled intertextuality generated in many of their receptions attempts to regularize them, as in the seventeenth and eighteenth centuries, to discover their hidden unity, as in the early twentieth century, or to simply decry them as unworthy writing. Montaigne himself claims that his writing is in no way the polished work of a professional writer: "Au demeurant, mon langage n'a rien de facile et poly: il est aspre et dédaigneux, ayant ses dispositions libres et desreglées, si non par mon jugement, par mon inclination" (II, xvii, 638), yet we have seen many commentators attempting to remedy this situation rather than to pursue its implications. The *Essais'* "modernism," their ability to problematize regularizing tendencies while generating inconsistency in their receptions, can be witnessed throughout the history of Montaigne commentary. On the other hand, there have been more empathetic receptions of the *Essais*, suggestive commentaries, and reactivations of various aspects of his thought and writing. The most pronounced are the receptions of Gournay, Rousseau, Sainte-Beuve, Thibaudet, Gide, and Merleau-Ponty. These writers struggled with the innovative dimensions of the *Essais* and attempted to regenerate them in their own work. This chapter's inquiry has been by no means comprehensive, yet it has discussed the writers in France who have done the most to perpetuate the innovative dimensions of the *Essais* as well as their evolving role in European literature, which will come into fuller light in other contexts in the following chapters.

The three essential problematics that arise in a reading of a sequence of Montaigne commentators show the *Essais* playing a role in many of the works and problematics of writers from the late sixteenth century up to the middle of the twentieth. The first problematic results in the impulse to legitimize the *Essais* and reduce them to some type of unity, whether through editorial surgery or through their reduction into a critically coherent framework. The second is that many interpretations of the *Essais* are rich in contradictions. Montaigne himself realized that interpretations, rather than establishing some final truths about a text, only inspire new ones: "Ce n'est rien que foiblesse particuliere qui nous faict contenter de ce que d'autres ou que nous-mesmes avons trouvé en cette chasse de cognoissance; un plus habile ne s'en contentera pas. Il y a tousjours place pour un suyvant, ouy et pour nous mesmes, et route par ailleurs. Il n'y a point de fin en nos inquisitions; nostre fin est en l'autre monde" (III, xiii, 1068). This appears to be particularly true of many receptions of the *Essais*, which, like the *Essais* themselves, are characterized by their restless inquiry, having no end. Many of the writers examined here unwittingly admit uncertainty and defer the authority of a fixed and present meaning in their pursuit of the best implementation of the *Essais*' to suit their individual needs. In this sense, the *Essais* anticipate a Derridean attitude in which meaning is never absolutely present outside of a play of differences, a position that puts systematic thought into question, often leaving interpreters in the realm of the undecidable, forcing them to continue the active quest for meaning and fulfilling Montaigne's belief that our critical judgments will always be fraught with varying degrees of uncertainty ("en continuelle mutation et branle"). The proper critical response to the *Essais* is to face the problem of considering them at all — and the more one attempts to examine the diversity of their receptions, the more difficult the *Essais* are to read. If Montaigne's "chasse de cognoissance" is never final, the most difficult thing to accept is the demand for an intellectual fluidity while continuing to engage the critical pluralism surrounding them without despairing — one only need to consider the four centuries of commentary, which increasingly outweigh Montaigne's *oeuvre*; witness Pierre Bonnet's and H. Peter Clive's voluminous bibliographical compilations.[132]

The third problematic witnessed in studying receptions of the *Essais* is that they are often adapted to reflect a writer's own concerns, exposing the paradoxical dynamics encountered and responses offered when confronting the *Essais*. In this sense, the *Essais* are like any other text whose history of reception reveals the critical "horizon-of-experience" of a given historical moment. Most commentators tend to see the *Essais* as a mirror of themselves and use whatever elements of the *Essais* they please in order to develop their own arguments. The shifting historical identities of the *Essais* as well as their heterogeneous qualities defy any dogmatically coherent set of ideological or literary expectations and most often produce more difference than consensus of opinion, sometimes even in the same writer. Most readers submit to this experience in one way or the other while engaging Montaigne's writing. This study is also drawn into the web of the *Essais'* ability to problematize critical closure and must likewise struggle against both relativism and reductionism, qualities that are, on the other hand, necessary to conduct research between disciplinary and national boundaries. This is the exfoliating capacity of the *Essais*: their appropriated elements generate new extensions of their discourse, which attempt ("essayer") to articulate the contours of Montaigne's thought. This very act of positing *discourse* as a dynamic engagement of cultural situations, and not as a teleotic means to a predetermined goal (L. *discursus*, "conversation" — *dis*, "in different directions" + *currere*, "to run"), is Montaigne's gesture of accepting that which is *other* (books, people, cultures, opinions, ideas) in his essayistic manner of verbal expression — a relativistic notion perhaps, yet one nevertheless seeking to counteract hermeneutic dogmatism, thereby providing for a more tolerant dimension in human interaction, whether religious, political, social, or cultural.

It is in the context of these three problematics that we can begin to gather together some aspects of Montaigne's modernism. The *Essais* defy facile categorization and their textuality rejects authoritarian strictures of discourse. They either escape the embrace of reductive "unifying" interpretation or contrarily adapt themselves to any interpretation that encompasses a small part of their scope suitably developed to conform to the borrower. A fragment can thus be transformed into a new whole, supporting Montaigne's claim that "chaque lopin y face son corps" (I, xxvi, 172). Because Montaigne's writing is provisional, and since the *Essais* are by definition tentative gestures at understanding, he calls upon the reader as an ally in the production of meaning. The displacement of the authority of author-work over a text's meaning and the valorization of the triadic relationship of author-reader-text, where the reader becomes, not just a consumer of an artistic product, but the producer of an aesthetic object, is a central "modernist" quality of the *Essais*. Montaigne often disowns the responsibility of his text, telling us "je jette le plus souvent la plume au vent, comme on dict, et m'abandonne à la mercy de la fortune" (II, xvii, 654). He unravels the truth-telling function of language, disclaims authority over his writing, and in comparing the communicative process to a game of tennis, places the responsibility for the status of the text's meaning on the interaction between reader and text: "La parole est moitié à celuy qui parle, moitié à celuy qui l'escoute. Cettuy-cy se doibt préparer à la recevoir selon le branle qu'elle prend. Comme entre ceux qui jouent à la paume, celuy qui soustient se desmarche et s'apreste selon qu'il voit remuer celuy qui luy jette le coup et selon la forme du coup" (III, xiii, 1088). A reception study of the *Essais* must attempt to face this challenge and engage Montaigne's problematization of issues while striving to produce a flexible yet equitable demarcation of their configurations.

Montaigne's penchant for paradox, textual dispersion, and plural enunciation necessitates the reader's participation to an intensified degree. This activity, a concept important to much literary modernism as well as to the practice of participatory reading, demands the reciprocal involvement of text and reader in which the latter is no longer a consumer but a producer of the text thereby defining the *Essais* as a *scriptible* work that requires greater involvement on the part of the reader to give it meaning.[133] Montaigne is thus an important antecedent to the notion of readerly reception present in, for example, Mallarmé's revolutionary theory of suggestion: "Trouver un objet et en dégage un état d'âme, par une série de déchiffrements, donnant aux lecteurs cette joie délicieuse de croire qu'ils créent."[134] A similar idea is present in the writing of Joyce, who claimed in a conversation with Frank Budgen: "I've created enough problems in my work to keep the professors busy for five hundred years."[135] It is also found in Proust's *A la recherche du temps perdu,* a work whose reading "is completed in incompletion, forever in suspense, forever to be taken up again, since the object of that reading is constantly thrown into a dizzy rotation."[136] This latter evaluation may also be applied to Montaigne's *Essais,* a text whose *scriptible* quality has generated a myriad of conflicting, contrasting, and sometimes confluent interpretations. This is the interpretive problematic presented by the *Essais* that is inescapable for critics who inevitably read their own experience into a response to Montaigne's writing, attempting to mediate between its horizon and their own. The *Essais* constantly produce this empathetic identification by virtue of their characteristics that can be provisionally qualified as "modern," that is, their open and discontinuous use of historical materials toward the development of an alternately tentative and assertive textual progression in a mobile expressive style, demanding of individuals a personal account of their own thoughts and activities while engaging the *Essais*.

The chain of reception and influence is complex, each interpretation giving rise to the necessity for others. In Montaigne's own terms: "Nos opinions s'entent les uns sur les autres, la premiere sert de tige à la seconde, la seconde à la tierce. Nous eschellons ainsi de degré en degré" (III, xiii, 1069). The abundance of receptions of the *Essais* make the task of delineating clear trends of interpretation difficult, and the results somewhat diverse and undulating. Yet within the diversity of the attempt to understand the role of Montaigne's intellectual descendants is a constancy: a constant inconstancy that is demonstrated by the ability of the *Essais* to generate new and problematic receptions of their significance. The *Essais* in turn are "influenced" by various receptions and will be reread in new ways as they are regenerated in other times and contexts. The *Essais* are innovatively modern in the sense that Montaigne is one of the first whose development of this reciprocal process of literary production engenders centuries of attempts at critically understanding, misunderstanding, and extending his essaying. We will now turn to more detailed analyses of receptions of the *Essais* outside of France, which will help to particularize the problematics as seen in this chapter as well as to expand the notion of Montaigne's impact on the modernist temperament.

Notes to Chapter One

1. For the history of Montaigne's reception and interpretation, from the appearance of the first edition in 1580 to the middle of the nineteenth century, the essential works are: Alan Boase, *The Fortunes of Montaigne: A History of the "Essais" in France: 1580-1669* (New York: Octagon Books, 1970), Mathurin Dréano, *La Renommée de Montaigne en France au XVIIIe siècle: 1677-1802* (Angers: Editions de l'Ouest, 1952), Donald Frame, *Montaigne in France: 1812-1852* (New York: Columbia University Press, 1940). Other useful works are: Pierre Villey, *Montaigne devant la postérité* (Paris: Boivin Editeurs, 1935), and Arthur Tilley, "Montaigne's Interpreters," *Studies in the French Renaissance* (New York: Barnes and Noble, 1968), 259-293. More recently, Yvonne Bellenger has perhaps achieved the most popular historical contextualization of the *Essais* in France. See *Montaigne: Une fête pour l'esprit* (Paris: Editions Balland, 1987).
2. Dominique Baudier, "Lettre à Van Blijenburgh," quoted in Villey, 57.
3. Jauss, 21.
4. Gustave Lanson, *Les "Essais" de Michel de Montaigne* (Paris: Méllottée Editeur, 1930), 325.
5. Dréano considers the most important work on Montaigne to be that of the major writers such as Pascal, Diderot, Voltaire, Rousseau, and Sainte-Beuve. Yet a host of lesser writers also play an important role in the history of Montaigne's receptions, and help enrich the *Essais'* evolving historical identity. Covering over three centuries of Montaigne interpretation, Boase, Dréano, and Frame have evaluated their individual contributions as well as the myriad of connections between innumerable writers' commentaries on Montaigne. I wish neither to repeat nor to paraphrase their work, but to develop the several issues I have delineated above, which they may have touched upon, but without fully exposing their implications.
6. La Croix du Maine, *Bibliothèque française* (Paris: Rigolet de Juvigny, 1772), 20.
7. Boase, 19.
8. Villey, 62.
9. Etienne Pasquier, "À M. de Pelgé, conseiller du roi et maître en sa chambre des comptes de Paris," *Oeuvres choisies*, ed. Léon Feugère (Geneva: Slatkine Reprints, 1968), 389-398.
10. Villey, 5.
11. In this light it is useful to peruse the photographic reproduction of the 1580 edition of the *Essais* compiled by Daniel Martin (Paris: Librairie Honoré Champion, 1976).
12. See Donald Frame, *Montaigne: A Biography* (New York: Harcourt, Brace & World, 1965): "In general, then, the first reception of the *Essays* was fairly good, though probably better in 1580 than in 1588, the plaudits varying in inverse proportion to the originality of the book" (312).
13. Daniel Ménager, "Jugements sur Montaigne et sur les *Essais*," *Montaigne: "Essais"* (Paris: Librairie Larousse, 1973), 121.

14. See Géralde Nakam, "Navarre entre la Ligue et la Réforme," *Montaigne et son temps: les événements et les "Essais"* (Paris: Librairie A.-G. Nizet, 1982), 13-38.

15. Marie de Gournay, "Préfaces sur les *Essais* de Michel, Seigneur de Montaigne," *"Essais" de Michel de Montaigne* (Paris: Abel l'Angelier, 1595), iii. The preface has recently been edited by François Rigolot and republished in *Montaigne Studies* I, 1 (1989): 7-60.

16. Dominique Baudier, "Lettre à Van Blijenburgh," quoted in Villey, 57.

17. Gournay, "Préfaces," vii-vii.

18. Hugo Friedrich, *Montaigne* (Paris: Editions Gallimard, 1968), 351.

19. Villey, 66.

20. Quoted in Villey, 61.

21. Villey, 166.

22. In this vein, essential readings are Cecile Insdorf, *Montaigne and Feminism* (Chapel Hill: North Carolina Studies in the Romance Languages and Literatures, 1977) and especially Pierre Leschemelle's "Montaigne et les femmes," *Montaigne et la révolution philosophique du XVIe siècle*, ed. Jacques Lemaire (Brussels: Editions de l'Université de Bruxelles, 1992), 75-92, as well his "La Passion des femmes," *Montaigne, ou le mal à l'âme* (Paris: Editions d'Images, 1991), 83-134. For a more general view of the status of women at this time, see Ian Maclean, *The Renaissance Notion of Women* (Cambridge: Cambridge UP, 1980).

23. Leschemelle, "Montaigne et les femmes," 78.

24. See Cathleen Bauschatz, "'Leur plus universelle qualité, c'est la diversité': Women as Ideal Readers in Montaigne's *Essais*," *Journal of Medieval and Renaissance Studies* 19 (1989): 83-101. See also Bauschatz's "The Gender of Genre," *Montaigne Studies* II, 1 (1990): 26-47, a particularly informative article on the specific historical conditions of Montaigne's relationships to women readers and writers, and Robert D. Cottrell's, "Gender Imprinting in Montaigne's *Essais*," *L'Esprit Créateur* XXX, 4 (1990): 85-95. Cottrell rightly claims: "Misogynistic discourse is, however, always already problematized in the *Essais*" (93).

25. The pertinent passages in II, X expressing Montaigne's interest in these three "feminine" genres are: poetry (410-12); moral philosophy, "par où j'apprens à renger mes humeurs et mes conditions" (413); and history, "Les Historiens sont ma droitte bale" (416).

26. Two essential works on the life and works of Gournay are by Elyane Dezon-Jones, *Fragments d'un discours féminin* (Paris: José Corti, 1988) and Marjorie Isley, *A Daughter of the Renaissance: Marie le Jars de Gournay* (La Haye: Mouton, 1963).

27. See Dorothy Gabe Coleman, "Montaigne: The Living Text," *French Studies* 40, 4 (1986): 393-400. The passage in question is the following:

    J'ay pris plaisir à publier en plusieurs lieux l'esperance que j'ay de Marie de Gournay le Jars, ma fille d'alliance: et certes aymée de moy beaucoup plus que paternellement, et envelopée en ma retraitte et solitude, comme l'une des meilleures parties de mon propre estre. Je ne regarde plus qu'elle au monde. Si l'adolescence peut donner presage, cette ame sera quelque jour capable des plus belles choses ... . Le jugement qu'elle fit des premiers Essays, et femme, et en ce siecle, et si jeune, et seule en son quartier, et la vehemence fameuse dont elle m'ayma et me desira long temps sur la seule estime qu'elle en print pour moy, avant de m'avoir veu, c'est un accident de tres-digne consideration. (II, xvii, 661-62)

28. Marie de Gournay, "Quatrains pour la maison de Montaigne," in Alexandre Nicolaï, *Les Belles amies de Montaigne* (Paris: Editions Dumas, 1950), 195-198. In "A Madame de Montaigne" Gournay praises Montaigne's wife Françoise for her conjugal love: "Tu ressembles Alceste en amour conjugale, / La Tyndaride Graecque, en grâce et en beauté. / Mais soit de notre siècle ou de l'antiquité, / En l'heur d'un grand mary nulle autre ne t'égalle" (195).

29. Dezon-Jones, 31.

30. Dezon-Jones, 67.

31. *Grief des dames* in Dezon-Jones, 129.

32. "Discours sur ce livre, A Sophrosine," *Les Advis ou les presens de la Demoiselle de Gournay* (Paris: Toussainct Du-Bray, 1624), 1.

33. See R. Fromillage, *La Vie de Malherbe* (Paris: Armand Colin, 1954), II, 42.

34. Marie de Gournay, "Préface sur les *Essais* de Michel, Seigneur de Montaigne," ed. Philippe Desan, *Montaigne Studies* II, 2 (1990): 92.

35. Another instance of how Montaigne's slippery conservatism can give rise to innovative events is the fact that his niece Jeanne de Lestonnac, daughter of his Calvinist sister Jeanne d'Eyquem, ultimately became a devout Catholic with Montaigne's support. Jeanne the younger, having been brought up in a humanist, protestant milieu, learned that the reformers were more concerned about educating their children than Catholics and would eventually translate this knowledge into the founding of the *Compagnie de Notre-Dame* in 1605, one of the first schools for women in France. Bordeaux thus "apparaît comme la première capitale d'*une nouvelle forme d'éducation relativement démocratisée*" (emphasis added). This quote is taken from a recent television documentary, "La nièce de Montaigne se voue à l'éducation des filles," *Raconte* (France 2: 25 July 1993). Montaigne's life and work again unexpectedly provides for the unfolding of egalitarian principles. I am indebted to Louisette Halioua of Toulouse, France for having called my attention to this program.

36. Tilley, 259.

37. Boase, 103.

38. Pierre Charron, *De la Sagesse*, ed. Barbara de Negroni (Paris: Librairie Arthème Fayard, 1986), 46.

39. Villey, 106.

40. Bellenger, 267.

41. Boase, xv.

42. Quoted in Boase, 421.

43. Quoted in Boase, 422.

44. Villey, 303.

45. Villey, 303.

46. Pierre Daniel Huët, *Huëtiana*, quoted in Boase, 104.

47. See H. Busson, *La Pensée religieuse française de Charron à Pascal* (Paris: Librairie Philosophique, 1933).

48. Chapter V, "La Vie posthume" of Mathurin Dréano's *La Religion de Montaigne* (Paris: A.-G. Nizet, 1969) is perhaps the best source for a useful detailing of the specific writers who either opposed or supported the *Essais*, as well as for understanding the trends of thought emanating from them and the debates they incited throughout the seventeenth century. As for the repression of the *libres penseurs* of the time, many of whom rallied around the epicureanism of the *Essais*, see Antoine Adam, *Histoire de la littérature française au XVIIe siècle* (Paris: Editions Mondiales, 1962).

49. Several studies have considered the relationship of Pascal's work to Montaigne's. See especially Frank M. Chambers, "Pascal's Montaigne," *PMLA* 65 (1950): 790-804; Kyriaki Christodoulou, "Pascal critique de Montaigne," *Montaigne et les "Essais" 1580-1980* (Paris: Librairie Champion, 1983), 336-345; Léon Brunschvicg, *Pascal et Descartes: Lecteurs de Montaigne* (Neuchâtel: Baconnière, 1945); and Bernard Croquette, *Pascal et Montaigne: Etude des réminiscences des "Essais" dans l'oeuvre de Pascal* (Genève: Librairie Droz, 1974).

50. The text and accompanying commentary used here is that of Pierre Courcelle, *L'Entretien de Pascal et Sacy* (Paris: Librairie Philosophique J. Virin, 1960).

51. Léon Brunschvicg, "Introduction aux *Pensées* de Pascal," *Grands écrivains de la France* (Paris: Librairie de la Hachette, 1904).

52. Blaise Pascal, *Oeuvres Complètes*, eds. Léon Brunschvicg and Pierre Boutroux (Paris: Librairie de la Hachette, 1904), XII, 63. All further references appear in text with indication of *pensée*, section, and page.

53. For a systematic account of Pascal's use of the *Essais*, see Chambers and Croquette.

54. Most recently, Emmanuelle Baillon in "Montaigne et Pascal: deux esprits si proches par les prémisses et si distant par les conclusions," *Montaigne et la révolution philosophique au XVIe siècle* (Brussels: Editions de l'Université de Bruxelles, 1992) sees Pascal's reception of the *Essais* as an attempt to remedy what he considered as Montaigne's mistaken acceptance of human imperfection: "Les faits que Montaigne décrivait, Pascal les présente comme des fautes" (100).

55. Courcelle, 20-21.

56. Lanson, 336.

57. Antoine Arnauld and Pierre Nicole, *La Logique ou l'art de penser* (Paris: Garnier Flammarion, 1970), 331. This work is commonly referred to as *La Logique de Port Royal*. All further references appear in text.

58. Jacques-Bénigne Bossuet, "Troisième sermon pour la fête de tous les saints," *Oeuvres Complètes* (Paris: J. A. Lebel, 1815), 365.

59. Villey's *Montaigne devant la postérité* discusses the profusion of such negative reactions to the "Apologie" at length in Chapter V.

60. Nicolas Malebranche, *La Recherche de la vérité* (Paris: Boivin et Compagnie, 1938), 365. All further references appear in text.

61. Villey, 302.

62. Quoted in Dréano, 15.

63. Boase has dedicated individual chapters to Montaigne's importance for these writers. The presence of Montaigne in their works, as demonstrated by Boase, lies in the realm of themes and ideas and not of style or motifs. It is thus difficult to distinguish between where Montaigne's work actually had an impact and where these writers may have assimilated ideas from elsewhere.

64. Dréano, 552.

65. Dréano, 552.

66. Dréano's work is the most important study of Montaigne's reception in the eighteenth century. Dréano is more interested however in the minute documentation of numerous writers, editors, and personalities who commented on Montaigne or brought forth editions of, and articles on, his work rather than examining how Montaigne's work was rearticulated. There is also a certain imbalance in the space he gives to some of his chapters. There is a lengthy discussion of Voltaire's relation to Montaigne (the latter's influence on the former is negligible), whereas only a short and superficial chapter is dedicated to Rousseau, who owed a great deal to Montaigne.

67. L'Abbé Trublet, "Les *Essais*," *Mercure de France*, June 1733, quoted in Dréano, 173.

68. M. Pessalier, *L'esprit de Montaigne*, quoted in Dréano, 173.

69. This is widely considered as Montaigne's starting point. The first *Essais* were writings in the manner of the *exempla* or *leçon* (collections of quotations with accompanying commentary and reflections) except that Montaigne continued to add to them, embellishing them with anecdotes and digressions, until they had swollen to a new genre, that of the essay. Friedrich discusses this at length. See also André Tournon, *La glose et l'essai* (Lyon: Presses Universitaires de Lyon, 1983).

70. Dréano documents the various editions of the *Essais* in the eighteenth century, and how each differed from the other. The common denominator of these editions was their highly condensed quality, which varied according to the individual editor's desires.

71. Dréano, 149.

72. The latter, drawing the most from Montaigne in the eighteenth century, has inspired important studies on the relation of his work to the *Essais*. See Ellen Silber's "Rousseau and Montaigne: The Evolution of a Literary Relationship," Ph.D. diss., Columbia University, 1968, and Pierre Villey's *L'Influence de Montaigne sur les idées pédagogiques de Locke et de Rousseau* (Paris: Librairie de la Hachette, 1911).

73. François-Marie Arouet Voltaire, *Oeuvres Complètes* (Paris: Chez Lefèvre, 1834), XII, 315. All further references appear in text and refer to this edition with accompanying indications of volume and page number.

74. Voltaire, "Lettre à Tressan, 1746," LV, 136-37.

75. Voltaire, "Doutes sur le testament de Cardinal Richelieu," XLII, 74.

76. Voltaire, "Remarques sur les pensées de Pascal," XXXVII, 69.

77. Dréano, 323.

78. Voltaire, "Siècle de Louis XIV," XX, 251.

79. Quoted in Dréano, 332.

80. "When Voltaire defends his [Montaigne's] self-portrayal he is less concerned to praise Montaigne than to discredit Pascal." Frame, *Montaigne: A Biography*, 316.

81. Charles de Secondat Montesquieu, "Mes Pensées," *Oeuvres complètes*, ed. André Masson (Paris: Les Editions Nagel, 1950), 296.

82. Two works provide the general outlines: Jean-Eugène Bimbenet, "Montaigne-Montesquieu," *Société d'agriculture, sciences, belles-lettres et arts d'Orléans* 54 (1882): 1-12 and *Entre Montaigne et Montesquieu: les écrivains bordelais et la vie intellectuelle au XVIIe siècle*, ed. Guy Turbet-Delof (Bordeaux: L'Imprimerie Biscaye, 1985).

83. Albert Sorel, *Montesquieu* (Paris: Hachette et Compagnie, 1887), 11-12.

84. John M. Bomer, *The Presence of Montaigne in the "Lettres Persanes"* (Birmingham, AL: Summa Publications, Inc., 1988).

85. Fortunat Strowski, *Montaigne* (Paris: Champion, 1906), 310.

86. Denis Diderot, "Réfutation de l'ouvrage d'Helvétius," *Oeuvres complètes*, eds., J. Assézat and M. Tourneux (Nendeln, Liechtenstein: Kraus Reprint Ltd., 1966), II, 290. All further references appear in text.

87. See Jean Thomas, *L'Humanisme de Diderot* (Paris: Société d'Edition "Les Belles Lettres," 1938) and especially Jérome Schwartz, *Diderot and Montaigne: The Shaping of Diderot's Humanism* (Genève: Librairie Droz, 1966).

88. See Edwin M. Duval, "Lessons of the New World: Design and Meaning in Montaigne's 'Des Cannibales' (I:31) and 'Des Coches' (III:6)," *Yale French Studies* 64 (1983): 95-122.

89. J. Dusaulx, *De mes rapports avec J. J. Rousseau* (Paris: Didot, 1978), 100.

90. Colette Fleury, *Rousseau et Montaigne* (Paris: A.-G. Nizet, 1980), 188.

91. Jean-Jacques Rousseau, *Oeuvres Complètes*, eds. B. Gagnebin and M. Raymond (Paris: Editions Gallimard, 1959-69), III, 41. All further references appear in text.

92. See Fleuret, Chapter IV, "La Révolution culturelle: de Montaigne à l'*Emile*," 83-121.

93. Dréano 314. In Chapter IV of her dissertation, Silber takes the same position, but she does a more thorough job than Dréano in analyzing what Rousseau owes to, and where he detracts from Montaigne concerning these issues. Fleuret surpasses both Dréano and Silber in critical acumen.

94. For a more detailed account of Montaigne's surreptitious social and political agenda, see David Schaefer's highly suggestive *The Political Philosophy of Montaigne* (Ithaca: Cornell University Press, 1990) as well as his "Montaigne and Leo Strauss," *Montaigne Studies* II, 2 (1990): 34-57.

95. Emile Faguet, *Rousseau penseur* (Paris: Boivin et Compagnie, 1910), 27.

96. He even appears as one of the saints of the Convention in the "Almanach des Républicains pour servir à l'instruction publique" of 1793. See Dréano's *La Renommé de Montaigne*, 539-540.

97. Lanson, 350.

98. Lanson, 354.

99. Frame, *Montaigne in France.*

100. Frame, *Montaigne in France,* 113.

101. Alfred-Auguste Cuvillier-Fleury, *Dernières études historiques et littéraires* (Paris: M. Lévy, 1859), 196.

102. Pierre Michel, *Montaigne* (Bordeaux: Ducros, 1969), 83.

103. Charles Augustin Sainte-Beuve, *Port Royal,* ed. Maxime Leroy (Paris: Librairie Gallimard, 1952), I, 838. All further references appear in text.

104. Charles Augustin Sainte-Beuve, *Nouveaux Lundis* (Paris: M. Lévy, 1883), VII, 50.

105. Richard M. Chadbourne, in *Sainte-Beuve* (Boston: G.K. Hall & Co., 1977), has remarked: "His own search for a religious solution to his problems, furthermore, attracted him to what is both a great literary and a great religious era in French history. He had not yet settled into what he later called his 'definitely skeptical frame of mind,' and still hoped to find in seventeenth-century spirituality, as Amaury had found, a 'moral authority' that might provide him with the inner peace and stability which he lacked" (107).

106. Sainte-Beuve, *Nouveaux Lundis,* VII, 177.

107. See R. A. Sayce, *The "Essays" of Montaigne: A Critical Exploration* (London: Weidenfeld and Nicholson, 1972), especially Chapter 8, "Diversity and Skepticism."

108. Michael Baraz, *L'être et la connaissance selon Montaigne* (Paris: Librairie Josi Corti, 1965), 176.

109. Jean-François Payen, *Recherches et documents inédits ou peu connus sur Montaigne* (Genève: Slatkine Reprints, 1970).

110. Frame, *Montaigne in France,* 201.

111. Ferdinand Brunetière, *Essais sur la littérature contemporaine* (Paris: Calmann-Lévy, 1892), 21.

112. Lanson, ii.

113. Strowski, vii.

114. Pierre Villey, "Avant-Propos," *Les Sources et l'Evolution des "Essais" de Montaigne* (Paris: Librairie de la Hachette, 1933), viii.

115. Floyd Gray, *Le Style de Montaigne* (Paris: Librairie Nizet, 1958).

116. Albert Thibaudet, *Montaigne* (Paris: Editions Gallimard, 1963), 363.

117. Albert Thibaudet, *Physiologie de la critique* (Paris: Editions de la Nouvelle Revue Critique, 1930), 188.

118. Henri Bergson, *Matière et mémoire: essai sur la relation du corps à l'esprit* (Paris: Presses Universitaires de France, 1982), 7.

119. Thibaudet, *Montaigne,* 570.

120. Hubert Luthy, "Montaigne on the Art of Being Truthful," *Encounter* 1, 2 (1953): 12.

121. André Gide, *Les pages immortelles de Montaigne choisies et expliquées par André Gide* (Paris: Gallimard, 1948).

122. André Gide, "Essai sur Montaigne," *Oeuvres Complètes*, 15 vols. (Paris: Nouvelle Revue Française, 1939), XV, 3-31 and "Suivant Montaigne," XV, 35-63. References to both essays appear in text.

123. Michel Guggenheim, "Gide and Montaigne," *Yale French Studies* 7 (1951): 107.

124. See Sybrandi Braak, *André Gide et l'âme moderne* (Amsterdam: Firma A.H. Kruyt, 1923).

125. André Gide, "9 Septembre, 1940," *Les Journaux d'André Gide* (Paris: Editions Gallimard 1948), 53.

126. Lanson, 352.

127. Braak, 171.

128. Maurice Merleau-Ponty, "Lecture de Montaigne," *Les Temps Modernes* 3 (1947): 1045. All further references appear in text.

129. Jane Couchman has discussed in detail the relation of Montaigne and Merleau-Ponty in "Twentieth-Century Responses to Montaigne."

130. See Rémy C. Kwant, *The Phenomenological Philosophy of Maurice Merleau-Ponty* (Pittsburgh: Duquesne UP, 1963).

131. Colie, 7.

132. Pierre Bonnet, *Bibliographie méthodique et analytique des ouvrages et documents relatifs à Montaigne* (Genève: Editions Slatkine, 1983) and H. Peter Clive, *Bibliographie annotée des ouvrages relatifs à Montaigne: 1976-1985* (Paris: Librairie Honoré Champion, 1986).

133. Roland Barthes, *S/Z* (Paris: Editions du Seuil, 1970). Is Barthes' definition not in some ways an apt summary of Montaigne's method of literary production?: "Pourquoi le scriptible est-il notre valeur? Parce que l'enjeu du travail littéraire (de la littérature comme travail) c'est de faire du lecteur, non plus un consommateur, mais un producteur du texte" (10). Montaigne is an important antecedent to the notion of readerly reception as seen in his penchant for a paradoxical textual polyvocalism that demands a reciprocal involvement of text and reader in order to respond to his challenge.

134. Stéphane Mallarmé, "Sur l'évolution littéraire," *Oeuvres Complètes* (Paris: Editions Gallimard, 1945), 866.

135. Quoted in David Hayman, *Mallarmé et Joyce* (Paris: Hachette, 1947), 109.

136. Gérard Genette, "Proust Palimpsest," *Figures of Literary Discourse* (New York: Columbia UP, 1982), 222.

Chapter Two

Emerson and Nietzsche: Between Innovation and Repetition

He that can compose himself is wiser
than he that composes books.

— Benjamin Franklin, *Poor Richard's Almanac*, April, 1737.

In the nineteenth century, Ralph Waldo Emerson and Friedrich Nietzsche were the two most significant thinkers outside of France who approached Montaigne from a philosophical and aesthetic perspective. They adapted many elements of the *Essais* and articulated them in their own work while making numerous references to Montaigne. The question of his impact on their writing raises a network of problems — including that of justifying the methods of comparison to be used in examining their relationship to the *Essais*. Emerson's and Nietzsche's connections to the work of Montaigne are for the most part fragmentary, yet we can find important recurring patterns in their various points of contact with the *Essais*. In the work of all three, mediation between the author's writing-self and the deployment of cultural tradition produces a myriad of intertextual relationships. This mode of literary production is active in all writers concerned about the role of textual precursors in their own work. Yet Montaigne, Emerson, and Nietzsche are linked in the explicitness of their discussions of the problematic relationship of reading the past and writing in the present. Montaigne was an important source of these concerns for Emerson and Nietzsche, yet it was Emerson's and Nietzsche's readings of the *Essais* that brought these qualities of Montaigne's work into greater prominence. The most constant theme in the work of all three is the mission of self-cultivation that must endlessly struggle against the influx of established cultures and texts, which are capable of overwhelming individual productivity. Such problematic engagement of the past was undertaken on almost every page of the *Essais*. Emerson and Nietzsche reactivate this problematic to varying degrees in their works, in ways that demonstrate their debt to Montaigne's writing. The attempt to assert vital, dynamic subjectivity under the spectre of the authoritative past is older than literature and civilization itself. Yet in the work of Montaigne, Emerson, and Nietzsche it plays a central role in their respective and interrelated efforts at revitalizing their particular historical and cultural situations.

A dialog between the unique self and cultural tradition is foregrounded in the work of all three, as Montaigne puts it: "La matiere de l'histoire, nue et informe; chacun en peut faire son profit autant qu'il a d'entendement" (II, x, 417), thus giving license to tamper with the past according to one's personal understanding of it. Emerson and Nietzsche generated this same spirit of modernity embodied in Montaigne's conception of the free use of tradition. Both admired Montaigne's level-headed capriciousness and often used it to justify their own writing, emulating it to suit their needs. In this sense, they participated in the same dynamics of reception as the writers discussed in Chapter One. Yet insofar as Emerson was an American modernist and Nietzsche was an indisputable avatar of modernist and postmodernist writing, both writers' receptions of the *Essais* moved Montaigne's presence into a wider cross-cultural, ideological, and textual spectrum.[1]

Montaigne develops arguments for what he considers the most beneficial use of one's historical and cultural tradition in "Du pedantisme" and "De l'institution des enfans." Emerson's "Quotation and Originality" discusses the most fruitful ways in which writers can assimilate their readings into an original work. Nietzsche's "Vom Nutzen und Nachteil der Historie für das Leben" berates an overly insistent historicist approach to education, which imposes more accumulated information of the past than an individual or a culture can healthily digest. These will be several of the texts considered in a comparative examination of what is a substantial intertextual field: the opposition between the renovation and rejection of cultural tradition, an issue particularly important to Montaigne, Emerson, and Nietzsche, and one that informs a wide range of modernist literature. The comparisons undertaken here will thus serve as a prime example of what Paul de Man has referred to as "the complications that ensue when a genuine impulse toward modernity collides with the demands of a historical consciousness or a culture based on the disciplines of history."[2] Montaigne's work was obviously not the only source for the respective works of Emerson and Nietzsche, both of whom incorporated a wide range of learning into their writings; but the *Essais* play such an active role in the development of several of their literary and philosophical perspectives that it can be instructive to explore their confluential relationship.

♦ ♦ ♦

In 1825, Ralph Waldo Emerson wrote in his journal: "I read Cotton's translation of Montaigne. It seemed to me as if I had written the book myself so sincerely it spoke my thought and experience. No book before or since was ever so much to me as that."[3] Elsewhere in his journals Emerson freely admits to his dependence on Montaigne: "Books are apt to turn reason out of doors. You find men talking everywhere from their memories, instead of from their understanding. If I stole this from Montaigne, as is very likely, I don't care, I should have said the same myself" (II, 441). Emerson justified his attitude of free appropriation of the *Essais* by claiming complete identification with them. In this sense, he was close to Montaigne's attitude of adapting of textual material to express his own opinions, as discussed in "Des livres": "je fay dire les autres ce que je ne puis si bien dire" (II, x, 408). By assuming the authority to freely adapt Montaigne's work as he pleases, Emerson echoes Pascal's and Sainte-Beuve's receptions and further asserts the *Essais*' ability to interrelate with the beliefs of a wide range of readers.

Emerson's work contains frequent references to Montaigne, beginning in 1820 and extending throughout his career; he acknowledges several times the importance of Montaigne's work for his own.[4] Emerson's empathetic appropriation of the *Essais* reaches back to the response of Pascal and foreshadows Gide's. He believed that the *Essais* were representative of his own "thought and experience," and thus felt justified in using them as his own. This seductive power of Montaigne's writing caused Emerson, after letting himself be guided awhile by the *Essais,* to depart on his own course and rewrite them into his own work. Most of his explicit valorization of the *Essais* occurs in his journals, not in his own essays (with the exception of "Montaigne; Or, the Skeptic"), yet his implicit use of them, although indirect, forms an essential intertextual web vitally connecting the *Essais* to his thought and writing. Although he saw Montaigne as somewhat of an ally, Emerson seemed somewhat unsure of what to do with him:

> A gross, semisavage indecency debases his book, and ought doubtless to turn it out of doors; but the robustness of his sentiments, the generosity of his judgements, the downright truth without fear or favor, I do embrace them with both arms. It is wild and savory as sweet fern ... and it is exhilarating, once in a while, to come across a genuine Saxon stump, a wild, virtuous man who knows books, but gives them their right place in his mind, lower than his reason. (II, 440-41)

Emerson saw Montaigne's textuality as a somewhat transgressive yet useful source for his own work, yet only intermittently ("once in awhile"). In a moment of cultural slippage Emerson even anglicized Montaigne, putting his quintessential hardiness to use as catalyst for the primordial vivacity he believed was needed in shaping the future of an American literary culture. Montaigne himself proclaimed his uniqueness in terms that stress the ferocious extravagance of his work: "C'est le seul livre au monde de son espece d'un *dessein farouche* et *extravagant*" (II, viii, 385–emphasis added) — this quality seemed both to fascinate and to worry Emerson.

The most obvious point of Emerson's contact with Montaigne is in *Representative Men,* "Montaigne; Or, the Skeptic." Discussing the skeptical attitude in his *Journals,* Emerson states: "[The] value of the Skeptic is the resistance to premature conclusions. If he prematurely conclude, his conclusion will be shattered, and he will become malignant. But he must limit himself with the anticipation of law in the mutations — *flowing law*" (VII, 112 — emphasis added). The position of opposing the certainty of truth, an attitude by no means limited to Montaigne and Emerson, is most fully stated in the former's case, in the "Apologie," the centerpiece of skepticism in the *Essais* in which Montaigne demonstrates how ignorant humans really are in the face of the diversity and complexity of the world. Montaigne goes much further than Emerson in his dismantling of the certainty of empirical conclusions, and of the inconstancy of human existence, often using liquid metaphors to help conceptualize his skepticism ("Et nous, nostre jugement, et toutes choses mortelles, vont *coulant et roulant sans cesse,*" being one of the most primordial as it appears in the first essay of Book I and serves as a leitmotif throughout the *Essais*). In his journals, Emerson constantly echoes Montaigne's notion of the fluidity of life and how to best confront it: "The philosophy we want is one of fluxions and mobility; not a house but a ship in these billows we inhabit" (VII, 61). Yet despite Emerson's interest in Montaigne's skeptical attitude, nowhere in his work does he make reference to the "Apologie," the cornerstone of Montaigne's pyrrhonist attitude. Young maintains that Emerson never read this essay and believes that in his attraction to Montaigne, equally as a man, writer, moralist, and "skeptic," he tended toward vague comprehensive definitions of his life and work. There is in fact little specific discussion of Montaigne's skepticism in the essay "Montaigne." There is a brillant seven-page introduction that discusses the conflict of materialism and idealism, in which Montaigne is nowhere to be found. After a few pages on the general characteristics of Montaigne's life and writing, Emerson digresses from him for the last nine pages, generally taking to task Montaigne's "que sçay-je" and finally denying skepticism as a worthy philosophical position. What Emerson pursues most in the essay is a certain conception of skepticism (his own), in which he calls for the temporary suspension of judgemnt in order to attain an expanded nature of truth that will finally be resolved in a higher understanding. He thus uses Montaigne in a gratuitous way to support his own position, and claims he is doing so with good intentions.

What Emerson admired most in the skeptical attitude is that it periodically interrogates the exisiting order by availing itself of "the checks and balances in nature, as a natural weapon against the exaggeration and formalism of bigots and blockheads" ("Montaigne," IV, 171). Yet Emerson's purpose in "Montaigne" was to use Montaigne as a symbol of the skeptical state of mind without any definite examination of his actual position, which was a more complex issue than Emerson chose to admit. Unlike Montaigne, Emerson generally strove for a dialectical resolution in his writing in the belief that the skeptical temperament should be maintained only temporarily toward the formulation of solid judgments: "Every superior mind *will pass through* this domain of equilibration" ("Montaigne," IV, 171 — emphasis added). Emerson's casualness toward his appropriation of Montaigne is thus related to Montaigne's attitude toward his own *auctoritates*. Emerson relied on Montaigne, but only to help him arrive at his own intellectual independence. Emerson's "representative" thinkers and writers thus provided focal points around which he developed his own perspectives; in this sense, Emerson was very a Montaignean writer. The "Apologie" is one of the best examples of Montaigne's penchant to establish a subject for discussion in his title, then deviate from it for most of the essay. Emerson turns this trick on Montaigne, using him in the title to frame the discussion of own ideas, yet discussing him only briefly.

In "Montaigne," Emerson prefers to examine his own doubts about thought and experience and finally shows himself to be a thinker of affirmation, not one of suspended judgment, and ultimately takes on a preacherly tone to refute skepticism:

> The final solution in which skepticism is lost, is in the moral sentiment, which never forfeits its supremacy. All moods may be safely tried, and their weight allowed to all objections: the moral sentiment as easily outweighs them all, as any one. This is the drop which balances the sea. I play with the miscellany of facts, and take those superficial views which we call skepticism; but I know that they will presently appear to me in that order which makes skepticism impossible. ("Montaigne," IV, 183)

Emerson thus decided on moral deliverance from skepticism. Montaigne, in his later essays, also went beyond the suspension of judgment to affirm moderation and self-knowledge as valuable undertakings beyond doubt. He attempted to move toward the resolution of contradiction, but realized the difficulty of finalistic conclusion, as seen in one of his later additions: "Si mon ame pouvoit prendre pied, je ne m'essaierois pas, je me resoudrois: elle est toujours en apprentissage et en espreuve" (III, ii, 805). Montaigne's writing often displays this provisional attempt toward truth, a dialectical movement without final synthesis, whereas Emerson demanded a more finalized understanding of issues. The latter could never have embraced Montaigne's adoption in the "Apologie" of the pyrrhonist assertion that there are no final answers: "Car cela, d'establir la mesure de nostre puissance, de connoistre et juger la difficulté des choses, c'est une grande et extreme science, de laquelle ils doubtent que l'homme soit capable" (II, xii, 502). The question of skepticism is the most obvious place to begin a comparison of Emerson and Montaigne, since "Montaigne" is the only specific work Emerson wrote on the essayist. Yet the issue of skepticism is more revealing of differences than of similarities between the two. According to Young, Emerson seems little interested in adhering to Montaigne's often bewildering skepticism: "And this apparent indifference to it, compared with his lively interest in Montaigne as a man, writer, or moralist, seems to be confirmed by Emerson's letters and journals, as well as by his published works."[5] Montaigne's pyrrhonism, his suspended judgment in the service of dismantling dogmatic presumption, goes well beyond what Edward Dowden has called Emerson's "prudential agnosticism — admitting his limitations and accepting them."[6]

To speak of Emerson's critical reception of Montaigne, which is at once obvious and problematic, is thus a tenuous undertaking. Although Emerson made frequent references to Montaigne throughout a long career — his journals and letters are sprinkled with references to the *Essais* — there is very little attempt at sustained critical apprehension. Young addresses this very question, yet never engages the issue:

> And so, for the best part of a lifetime, Emerson had more or less acquaintance with the great sixteenth-century essayist. Yet one cannot determine the extent of Emerson's reading in the *Essays*. Emerson's Montaigne, at any rate, would seem to be a middle term between what Emerson really knew of the *Essays*, and what came of that knowledge. No answer to these questions can be definitive. It would be folly to pass judgement on Emerson's interpretation of Montaigne.[7]

Young thus undertakes to establish the "rapports de fait" between Emerson and Montaigne in order to determine a foundation of factual reference, but his work does not go much further than this.[8] Establishing a more vital connection between the two writers, going beyond factual relations (which serve however as a useful foundation), and considering the question of influence in light of intertextual correlation, both comparative and contrastive, can produce an enhanced perspective on their relationship. What then are some other points of contact between Emerson and Montaigne? In a previous inquiry, W. L. Ustick chose to examine the similarities and differences between them from two points of view: style and intellectual temperament.[9] Ustick sees stylistic similarities, since they both developed idiosyncratic literary forms to suit their habits of mind: the *essai* in the case of Montaigne, and the "card-catalog" method of composition and oratorical style in the case of Emerson. There are, in fact, important stylistic parallels between the two: the mosaic-like quality of their writing based on the juxtaposition of disparate elements, the disruption of linear argument, a desultory style, the use of abundant illustration and quotation, and liberated variation of literary precursors. Both writers also praise the value of plain and vigorous speech. Emerson calls for writing "with sinew and vivacity comparable to Plutarch and Montaigne" and "not only the low style, but the lowest classifying words outvalue arguments" (V, 420). Both passages could very well have been written with the following passage of Montaigne in mind: "Le parler que j'ayme, c'est un parler simple et naïf, tel sur le papier qu'à la bouche; un parler succulent et nerveux, court et serré, non tant delicat comme vehement et brusque ..." (I, xxvi, 171). Yet both writers' putative admiration of a plain style is suspect since they often wrote highly rhetorical sentences of sinuous complexity.

Emerson is in the general line of the Anglo-American tradition of the "essay," developed by such writers as Browne, Lamb, Hazlitt, and Carlyle and adopted by many subsequent writers. It is a mode of writing characterized by personal and associative observation, intimacy and familiarity, tortuous yet effective style, skepticism, and humor.[10] Emerson's reception of Montaigne is thus colored by many other sources. Yet Montaigne is perhaps the most important source of the essay tradition in Anglo-American literature of which Emerson was a part. Although Emerson and Montaigne may share general similarities in style, a position difficult to verify even in the light of detailed comparison since Emerson's work contains so many intertextual points of contact with such a wide range of writers, (it must be added that Emerson never read Montaigne in the original but in Hazlitt's edition of Cotton's translation), there may be other ways to evaluate their affiliation.[11] There is in fact a good deal of material that would justify evaluating Emerson's debt to the *Essais*.

Outside of the studies cited, there is a surprising paucity of comparison of these two writers. Yet a perusal of Emerson's titles demonstrates a strong contextual affinity with the work of Montaigne. Emerson's essays "Books," "Experience," "Education," "Friendship," "On Socrates," and "Plutarch" invite discussion in the context of Montaigne's "Des livres," "De l'experience," "De l'institution des enfans," and "De l'amitié." Montaigne expresses recurring admiration for Socrates, on whom Emerson wrote his Harvard dissertation; both similarly praise him for his ability to accept the foibles of human nature. Furthermore, Emerson often uses Montaigne as an authority to support his preferences. He says for example that Plutarch "perpetually suggests Montaigne, who was the best reader he has ever found, though Montaigne excelled his master in the point and surprise of his sentences" ("Plutarch," X, 299). Montaigne played an important role in Emerson's thought, and beyond Emerson's explicit references to Montaigne, which are not frequent in the context of his overall work, there is a significant relationship between the two writers that suggests Emerson's continual appropriation of the *Essais* to a greater extent than he admitted to. As Montaigne "excelled his master," so did Emerson attempt to exceed Montaigne, complementing the *Essais* with his own experience.

Charles Dédéyan's work on Emerson and Montaigne has delineated some structural similarities between their work:

> En tout cas le plis est pris; que ce soient les *Essais* ou les *Hommes Représentatifs,* la démarche adoptée nous rappelle celle du Périgourdin, avec ses illusions contemporaines, ses anecdotes, ses références constantes à l'antiquité, et ses expressions tirées du vieux modèle.[12]

Yet beyond these stylistic generalities, there is a more essential common denominator between Emerson's and Montaigne's writing in their attitude toward the cultivation of the self, beginning with their attitudes on education, where Emerson's ideal pupil is related to Montaigne's and to Rousseau's. In "Education," Emerson calls for an instruction that is not merely a matter of memorizing but rather of learning how to judge and to do:

> We exercise their understandings to the apprehension and comparison of some facts, to a skill in numbers, in words; we aim to make accountants, attorneys, engineers; but not to make able, earnest, great-hearted men. The great object of Education should be commensurate with the object of life. ("Education," X, 135)

Emerson redevelops Montaigne's argument for a more liberal and practical education in "De l'institution des enfans" ("Qu'il ne luy demande compte des mots de sa leçon, mais du sens et de la substance, et qu'il juge du profit qu'il aura fait, non par le tesmoinage de sa memoire, mais de sa vie").The individual must have the benefit of information but only so far as it serves the development of his or her rounded self ("life" and "vie"): "Or nous qui cerchons icy, au rebours, de former non un grammarien ou logicien, mais un gentil'homme" (I, xxvi, 169). A more developed example concerning this issue will serve to demonstrate the extent of Emerson's interest in the same concerns as Montaigne and how he may have incorporated elements of the *Essais* into his work toward the development of his own thought.

Reading Emerson's essay "Quotation and Originality" reveals an important problematic in interpreting Emerson, the *Essais*, and many modernist works as well: how do writers assimilate a wide range of ideas and quotations of other writers into the fabric of an original work, thereby achieving a personalized renovation of the literary tradition? In the case of Montaigne, it is a "creative" method of quotation since he sometimes quotes directly, yet often translates a potential quotation without documentation, assimilating it into the fabric of his own text. He frequently paraphrases without reference to the original source, generally does not name the author quoted, and avoids transitional phrases to introduce the quotation.[13] Clements, in his discussion of influence, has gone as far as to call Montaigne an "archplagiarist."[14] The appropriation of tradition and its incorporation into an original work is, of course, an issue not limited to Montaigne and Emerson. Indeed, if one agrees with Eliot, then every writer rewrites the tradition in the production of new literary works of art.[15] André Malraux expressed a more radical formulation of the problem: "... every civilization is like the Renaissance, and creates its own heritage out of everything in the past that helps it to surpass itself."[16] Yet in the case of Montaigne, and to a substantial degree Emerson, the issue of quotation and originality is radically problematized. According to Young: "An initial deposit of tradition is not as apparent in his work as in Montaigne's, yet Emerson abounds, increasingly, as the creative impulse declines, in the gathered wisdom of life. Their work assimilated to itself, each in its own way, much wisdom from the past."[17] Young's commentary is rooted in the concept of creativity springing from the inner impulse of the artist vs. a less original appropriation of external models. But it is intertextual contact that stimulated Emerson and Montaigne to write in the first place. The developmental binarism of Young's scheme is more reductive than Montaigne or even Emerson would have accepted in their desire for a continually mobile reception and development of past literary models. Young's unitary approach attempts to normalize the dynamics of intertextual reception operating in their work, thereby obscuring the very points Montaigne and Emerson are trying to develop.

How is it possible to reconcile this reliance on tradition with the notion of, in Montaigne's case, his unique self as the subject of his work ("je suis la matiere de mon livre"), and in Emerson's, the insistence on "self-reliance?": "Insist on yourself; never imitate. Your own gift you can present every moment with the cumulative force of a whole life's cultivation; but of the adopted talent of another, you can only have extemporaneous, half-possession" ("Self-Reliance," II, 83). The substratum of tradition in the work of both writers provides in fact a foundation on which they build their literary personalities. Yet it is neither the "creativity" of Young, nor Villey's evolutionary demarcation of Montaigne's sources that best characterizes the *Essais,* and in turn Emerson's use of them. It is the perpetual tension between the self and previously written texts in the *Essais* that helps to produce Emerson's positioning of what he considered the correct relationship between historical learning and literary self-development. This tension often produces a current of undecidability in the work of both writers. This issue is further complicated when considering that Emerson's American "renaissance" is a repetition, a renaissance of a renaissance, the latter of which already contains, in the case of the *Essais,* a problematized articulation of the relationship between tradition and innovation.[18] Emerson's "renaissance," the attempt to propagate a movement of secularism and preeminent individuality in American intellectual life, are qualities dear to Montaigne; yet Emerson also adheres to a notion of cultural progress, not to Montaigne's more pragmatically pessimistic agenda, thereby exposing the incompatibility of the two writers.

In Emerson's discussion of the interplay between knowledge of the world and its use in developing the self, he often uses agricultural or botanical metaphors to describe the process:

> There is a time in every man's education when he arrives at the conviction that envy is ignorance; that imitation is suicide; that he must take himself for better, for worse, as his portion; that though the wide universe is full of good, no kernel of nourishing corn can come to him but through his toil bestowed on that plot of ground which is given him to till. ("Self-Reliance," II, 46)

In a similar manner, Montaigne mediates between the storehouse of classical antiquity and self-portraiture. The earlier *Essais* are distinguished by the abundance of examples with interspersed commentary by the author. As the *Essais* progress, Montaigne's personal experience plays a much greater role, his opinions rely less on ancient tradition. Yet the substructure of tradition remains intact and provides the springboard for self-portraiture. Montaigne attempts to use the texts of others as pretexts for his personal variations: "Je ne dis les autres, sinon pour d'autant plus me dire" (I, xxvi, 148). This characteristic of the *Essais* has been best demonstrated by Friedrich, who traces Montaigne's literary development as it progressed from commentary on the models of antiquity to a fuller self-expression. The binary model is useful in considering the development of both writers but does not allow for the open intertextual relationship between self and history that both continually developed and demonstrated throughout their work. It is this conflictual dynamism between past and present that produces the rich ambiguities of their writing. The difference between Montaigne and Emerson on this point is that the movement between tradition and self-expression is reversed. This reversal exposes both the compatibility and divergence of Emerson and Montaigne. Emerson began his writing career with an impulse toward novelty, then progressed to a more conservative aesthetic mode. Montaigne, always relying on his models, only became more "new" and "original" as his literary personality developed and his text gradually assumed more self-assured and innovative dimensions. His establishment of the genre of essayistic self-portraiture prepared the way for Emerson to begin his writing project by being "original." Yet Emerson eventually produced a more historical perspective in his work as he came to understand the value of a culturally charged mode of literary production.

A good example of Montaigne's understanding of how one is to use the tradition of literature, history, and philosophy to the best advantage is contained in the following passage from "De l'institution des enfans":

> Les abeilles pillotent decà et delà les fleurs, mais elles en font apres le miel, qui est tout leur; ce n'est plus thin ny marjolaine: ainsi les pieces empruntées d'autruy, il les transformera et confondera, pour en faire un ouvrage tout sien, à sçavoir son jugement. Son institution, son travail et estude ne vise qu'à le former. (I, xxvi, 152)

The notion that the reader must make the material his own is also the crux of Emerson's "Quotation and Originality":

> It is inevitable that you are indebted to the past. You are fed and formed by it. The old forest is decomposed for the composition of the new forest. The old animals have given their bodies to the earth to furnish through chemistry the forming face, and every individual is only a momentary fixation of what was yesterday another's, is today his, and will belong to a third tomorrow. So it is in thought. Our knowledge is the amassed thought and experience of innumerous minds. ("Quotation," VIII, 200)

Emerson used Montaigne as he did many "innumerous minds." A good deal of his work, like Montaigne's, is a vast mosaic of the thoughts of other writers. Yet despite the patchwork quality of the *Essais*, "ce fagotage de tant de diverses pieces" (II, xxxvii, 758), Montaigne attempted to bind them together by the coherence of his individuality. Emerson also sought to demonstrate the unity of his project while confronting the diversity and undulancy of intertextual appropriation:

> Everyone of my writings has been furnished to me by a thousand different persons ... a thousand things. But there remains the indefeasible persistency of the individual to be himself. One leaf, one blade of grass, one meridian, does not resemble another. Every mind is different; and the more it is unfolded, the more pronounced is that difference. He must draw the elements into him for food, and if they be granite and silex, will prefer them cooked by sun and rain, by time and art, to his hand. But, however received, these elements pass into the substance of his constitution. ("Quotation," VIII, 200-201)

For Emerson, learning should not be alien to the self, but consubstantial with it. In *The Cornucopian Text,* Terence Cave discusses the importance of assimilation, digestion, and redevelopment of one's cultural tradition in textual production during the European Renaissance. The ways a text naturalizes its materials, by digesting them so to speak, is essential for the perpetuation of new writing.[19]

The alimentary metaphor is not unique to Emerson; it can be found in significant places in French literary history of the sixteenth century. It occurs in Rabelais' *Tiers Livre*: "car nature n'a créé l'homme que pour prêter et emprunter ... chacun membre s'alimente à sa guise"[20] and in Du Bellay's *La deffence et illustration de la langue francoyse,* where he encourages readers to ingest Latin authors, then digest and transform them as the Romans had the Greeks: "Imitant les meilleurs auteurs Grecz, se transformant en eux, les devorant et apres les avoir bien digerez, les convertissant en sang et nourriture."[21] Montaigne, in "De l'institution des enfants," expresses a related notion in a similar manner, maintaining that in appropriating another writer's work into one's own, it is necessary to digest and absorb in order not to regurgitate ("C'est tesmoinage de crudité et indigestion que de regorger la viande comme on l'a avallée"). This dynamic, which permeates Montaigne's writing practice throughout the *Essais* is put into explicit play in "Des cannibales" in the context of Montaigne's discussion of anthropophagy as practiced by the Amerindian tribe, the Tupinamba. Montaigne's intense amplification of materials, his use of otherness, his incorporation and regeneration of other texts is characteristic of his method of composing the *Essais.* In Cave's terms: "The paper on which the text of the *Essais* appears is, indeed, a place of difference: it allows the rewriting and naturalization of foreign texts; it permits the search for the identity of a *moi* in contra-distinction from what is 'other' ..." (272).

Montaigne went beyond his predecessors and prepared the way for the modernist notion of recreating the past in oneself. He *became* the past and the past became him; his idiosyncratic appropriation of cultural precedents, his intellectual ingestion and textual digestion reproduced cultural traditions by physically absorbing them into his work. Montaigne, in "De l'institution des enfans," expressed a notion similar to Emerson's, and strove to solve the problem of how not to simply write within the tradition but to become it by making the knowledge of others our own:

> Pour revenir à mon propos, il n'y a tel que d'allécher l'appétit et l'affection, autrement on ne faict que des asnes chargés de livres. On

> leur donne à coups de fouet en garde leur pochette pleine de science, laquelle, pour bien faire, il ne faut pas seulement loger chez soi, il faut espouser. (I, xxvi, 177)

Montaigne would thus have agreed with Emerson's final definition: "This vast memory is only the raw material. The divine gift is ever the instant life, which receives and uses and creates, and can well bury the old in the omnipotency with which Nature decomposes all her harvest for recomposition" ("Quotation," VIII, 204). The importance of the notion of assimilation and originality makes it very difficult — Young goes as far to say impossible — to give a critically rigorous account of Emerson's Montaigne. Yet the conjunction of the two writer's thoughts on the question of textual assimilation raises questions central to the concept of literary modernism. It is particularly Emerson's ability to weave Montaigne's work into his own textual structures, without direct reference, that allowed the *Essais* to play a catalytic role in the development of his thought and writing whereby the infinitude of Montaignean privatism provided him a context in which to work out his idealism in a socio-historical formulation of its importance.

In "Traditional and the Individual Talent," T. S. Eliot states a position that has become one of the more pervasive phenomena of modernist studies:

> No poet, no artist of any art, has his complete meaning alone. His significance, his appreciation is the appreciation of his relation to the dead poets and artists. You cannot value him alone; you must set him, for contrast and comparison, among the dead. (38)

A writer thus participates simultaneously in the past and in the present. Eliot's conclusion, that the introduction of a new work into the pantheon of existing monuments results in the alteration of the complete existing order, takes a leap beyond Emerson and Montaigne yet underscores an important characteristic of much of modernist literature: its attempt to deploy the past in an effort to produce new textual configurations. The cultivation of the past is as old as any literary activity, yet in the case of modernist practice "the materials exploited were old, yet the style of exploitation was new."[22] On the other hand, a conspicuous element of the modernist paradigm is the rejection or dismantling of the past: "In cosmic terms, nothing new is under the sun; but modernism gives us a sense of an entire cultural heritage being ploughed up and turned over."[23] Herein exists an important oppositional characteristic of modernism: the simultaneous rejection and adaptation of literary and cultural traditions. It was particularly innovative for Emerson and Montaigne to develop such an approach in the context of their historical moments. In Montaigne's case, he was countering a codified educational system in France, as well as problematizing stratified norms of literary discourse. Emerson was challenging the cherished romanticist notion of the writer's personal inspiration and originality. Their concern for the authority of tradition (both Emerson and Montaigne rely on quotation in the extreme to substantiate their arguments), accompanied by an obsession with the unique self, produce a creative tension in their writing. The opposition between assertion of the new (a quintessential modernist gesture) and the assimilation of tradition (a more neoclassical impulse) plays an important role in the work of Montaigne, Emerson and, as we will see, Nietzsche, and thus serves as an essential criterion in the comparison of their work. Montaigne, in his pact of self-referentiality ("il ne faut pas seulement loger chez soi, il faut *espouser*"), sought to remain outside of discursive and ideological constraints while pursuing the essayistic freedom of expression in his writing. For many years he kept his work private and finally published it himself to insure its independence of purpose. Emerson, however, moved in the opposite direction, seeking to temper an over-developed insistence on self-development as seen in the work of Thoreau and Whitman by appropriating literary models on which to ground his self-expression, as Matthiessen has pointed out: "Emerson knew that each age turns to particular authors of the past, not because of the authors but because of its own needs and preoccupations that those authors help make articulate."[24]

Montaigne was one of the first Western thinkers to challenge the precepts of a humanistic education that united a normative view of the world with a free mode of analytical inquiry. Yet faced with the growing complexity and diversity of the social order, he reacted skeptically to the intellectual system in which he had been educated.[25] At the prestigious Collège de Guyenne, as he recounts in "Du pedantisme" and "De l'institution des enfants," students were required to analyze the classics minutely and not encouraged to search for knowledge, but rather to present the texts effectively.[26]

Montaigne reacted against this experience throughout the *Essais* as seen in his efforts to develop a natural and spontanous style, free of affected eloquence. He also wished his writing to inspire the reader's pursuit of his or her own personal understanding of the world. The innovative gesture embodied in Montaigne's free use of tradition, as well as his rejection of Ciceronian humanism and pedagogical scholasticism, made him a nemesis to the neoclassical hegemony in France, and later in England; yet it is this very characteristic of his work that made him so interesting to the modernists of the nineteenth and twentieth centuries. He was wary of systematic speculation and thus an important critic of the early renaissance for his "deidealization of the Humanist manifesto."[27]

Emerson initially professed a more ego-centered notion of the sovereignty of original self-expression and evolved to a more tempered adherence to the security of past models. His relationship to the paradigm of quotation and originality, being inverse to Montaigne's, exposes a nuanced difference in both authors' notions of cultural reformation. Montaigne's "renovation" of the past is carried out in his efforts at self-understanding (although he certainly wrote to influence his contemporaries). Emerson wrote many of his essays as public lectures by which he earned his living; they are for the most part revised addresses first made to public audiences. The latter believed in the possibility of cultural renewal in contrast to the former's wariness of change, an attitude precipitated by the religious wars and political instability of his time. In his desire to perpetuate a new and vibrant American culture, Emerson maintained a romanticist notion of inspired creativity that ultimately reshapes the past in a new and vital presentness. Montaigne, although he proposed a creative redeployment of the past, remained commited to the view that present effort, although essential, cannot exceed the greatness of earlier times: the inverse symmetry of their projects led them both to establish a middle-ground of mediation between tradition and originality, yet with a different awareness of the problem.

For both writers, the desire for synthetic harmony remained heuristic — a provisional attempt in the face of a dynamic conjunction of forces that refuse final closure (although Emerson demonstrated a greater belief than Montaigne in definitive certainty). Like Montaigne, Emerson constantly defered to past authority even while being original. The work of Montaigne, already innovative in its use of tradition, thus became one of the key members of Emerson's canon. The *Essais* play an active role in the interactive process of tradition and originality and complicate the matter in that their originality becomes part of a new tradition. On this issue of cultural reformation, Emerson both affirmed and denied his debt to Montaigne. On one hand, the writer is trapped by chronological circumstance: "he that comes second must needs quote him that come first" ("Quotation," VIII, 203), on the other, this reverence for the past must be redeveloped in response to present exigency: "We cannot overstate our debt to the Past, but the moment has the supreme claim. The Past is for us; but the sole terms on which it can become ours are its subordination to the Present" ("Quotation," VIII, 204). Montaigne explicitly glorified the past through copious quotation while implicitly valorizing the present in his unprecedented self-portraiture. Emerson redeveloped Montaigne's doubleness in his ambivalent acceptance of innovation: "Only an inventor knows how to borrow, and every man is or should be an inventor" ("Quotation," VIII, 204), by claiming, on the other hand, that our debt to the past is so overwhelming that "one would say there is no pure originality" ("Quotation, VIII, 178). The circular movement between a reliance on the cultural past and an attempt at self-realization, between the individual as creator and as a function of the tradition within which he or she writes was problematized by Emerson after his contact with the work of Montaigne. In neither writer is this circular movement resolved; it was further problematized by Nietzsche. Emerson's Montaignean skepticism appears not in his explicit references to the *Essais*, but in his manner of essayistically developing arguments on subjects important to Montaigne.

There are important implications in Emerson's reception of Montaigne for an understanding of American modernity. But how can we best characterize the ways in which Montaigne's work helped Emerson to become the "genius of democracy," especially since Montaigne would in no way have accepted being labeled a progressive liberal?[28] Emerson, like Montaigne, was a writer with a double consciousness — the problem he seems to have dealt with throughout his life is how to best formulate the relationship between the subjective individual and the collective action needed in a healthy society, how to reconcile self-sufficiency with social solidarity. Emerson's embrace of the Heraclitean doctrine (*"flowing law"*) is diametrically opposed to a certain degree of dogmatism that he saw as necessary in maintaining a social bond of laws, business practices, customs, politics, etc. Emersonian privatism was in a sense antipolitical; yet, arising as it did in an atmosphere of religious crisis, a time in which the authoritative structures of religious belief were coming apart in New England (in parallel to the religious discord of Montaigne's time), Emerson's distanciated engagement of socio-political questions was an appropriate response. His doctrine of individuation, like Montaigne's project of self-portraiture, is very much an embodiment of what Herbert Marcuse has formulated as "affirmative culture":

> By affirmative culture is meant that culture of the bourgeois epoch which led in the course of its development to the segregation from civilization of the mental and spiritual world as an independent realm of value that is also considered superior to civilization. Its decisive characteristic is the assertion of a universally obligatory, eternally better and more valuable world that must be unconditionally affirmed: a world essentially different from the factual world of the daily struggle for existence, yet realizable by every individual for himself "from within," without any transformation of the state of fact. It is only in this culture that cultural activities and objects gain that value which elevates them above the everyday sphere. Their reception becomes and act of celebration and exaltation.[29]

Has not the perennial problem of American culture and politics been how to reconcile extravagant interiority with the "daily struggle for existence?" Montaigne posed no clear solution to this impasse — he was not a dialectical thinker and saw no direct transformative possibilities between the life of the inner self and the world of political events — he seemed to be satisfied with the attempt to stimulate the self-understanding of his *suffisants lecteurs*, who one day would hopefully give rise to a more enlightened populace capable of equitable and informed decision-making. Emerson's writing project, like Montaigne's, is not one of a sentimental humanism; his social ontology is reciprocal, yet he is more adamant in formulating the correct balance between subjectivity and objectivity — the successful citizen for him is he or she "whose inward and outward senses are truly adjusted to each other" ("Nature," I, 9).

Emerson's notion of an American intellectual tradition is most clearly expressed in "The American Scholar," in which intellectual speculation is considered to be not inferior to the world of concrete social activity. The Scholar's mode of being in the world is one of interactive movement — the intellectual is neither a self-referential transcendentalist nor a political actor seeking to force the social will to conform to a particular set of dogmatic axioms, but rather, "In the right state, he is Man Thinking. In the degenerate state, when the victim of society, he tends to become a mere thinker, or still worse, the parrot of other men's thinking" ("The American Scholar," I, 84). Writing and thinking are thus experiences that must precede lived experience, whose unfolding will be enhanced by this informative intellectual inquiry. Emerson's notion of individual expression balanced by public duty is essential for the well-being of the political body ("the right state"). Montaigne's insistence on himself was likewise balanced by his political activities and very public concerns; his conception of the citizen as an individual founded on sociability and tolerance (the "gentilhomme"), rather than on honor and piety, is very much Emerson's whole citizen (in line with his admiration for Montaigne's hearty naturalness and dialectical living) and what Tocqueville saw as the "natural, frank and open" character of social intercourse in America.[30]

America's political independence having been secured, Emerson in the 1830s was seeking to develop a democracy of intellect and conscience whereby true subjectivity, understanding one's own worthiness as well as limitations, would serve to perpetuate an enhanced social fabric in which individualism could open onto the vista of the collective: "Another sign of our times also marked by an analagous political movement, is the new importance given to the single person. Every thing that tends to insulate the individual, — to surround him with barriers of natural respect, so that each man shall feel the world is his, and man shall treat man as a sovereign state, — tends to true union as well as greatness" ("The American Scholar," I, 113). Inwardness is thus not a refusal of social interaction but, paradoxically, an activity that will bond a nation of citizens to one another, each their own microcosmic fragment of the whole. Montaigne's reception of antiquity, his self-informed writing project, and his participation in the political events of his time provided Emerson with this useful model of a responsible thinker-citizen: "The scholar is that man who must take into himself all the ability of the time, all the contributions of the past, all the hopes of the future" ("The American Scholar," I, 113). Montaigne of course had no great hopes for the future and did not necessarily anticipate Emerson's work, but he did oblige the latter to formulate his own positions in relation to the *Essais*.

The reciprocal movement between reliance on the cultural past and self-realization, as developed in "Quotation and Originality," is played out in a different context in "The American Scholar" whereby self-realization acts as the foundation from which a social contract can be constructed. Emerson, like Montaigne, developed a flexible working philosophy rather than one of systematic consistency. His own essayistic *scriptibilité* is essential in his attempt to create the possibility for future readers to engage his work in a fructifying manner. The human experience for Emerson is always in a state of becoming and is, like nature itself, founded upon polarity and metamorphosis. The attempt to integrate the individual into the collective, the ability to synthesize differences within a composite sameness, the effort to produce a diverse unity is the experiment (essay) of American democracy — it has never reached its potential but has shown increasingly how problematic and perhaps impossible this social ideal is. Emerson's configuration of individuated collectiveness manifests a much greater faith in human goodness than Montaigne or most people today would accept. He promoted a social equality emanating from the innate divinity of the human spirit: "A nation of men will for the first time exist, because each believes himself *inspired by the Divine Soul* which also inspires all men" ("The American Scholar," I, 115 — emphasis added). Montaigne (Catholic and monarchic) did not promote, and could never have imagined a collectivist system of political governance and the notion of a citizenry empowered by knowledge, based on a direct apprehension of divinity. Yet he did not trust that the highest truths should necessarily be mediated by ecclesiastics or academics and thus provided an opening for a humane and progressive educational system, extended by Emerson into the political and cultural realms, in terms that curiously foreshadow the latter: "qu'il faut colloquer les enfans non selon les facultez de leur pere, mais *selon les facultez de leur ame*" (I, xxvi, 163 — emphasis added). Montaigne finally became what was so feared in seventeenth-century France: a progessive Unitarian. Whitman's development of the epitome of Emerson's personal autonomy that embraces at the same the variegated whole of American society, *Leaves of Grass,* has a first subtitle and opening passage, "Song of Myself," that recalls Montaigne's *sine qua non* of focusing on the world through his own experience: "I celebrate myself, and sing myself, / And what I assume you shall assume, / For every atom belonging to me as good belongs to you."[31] Whitman's essayistic appropriation of the human landscape of America, the most culturally and ethnically intertextual country the world has yet seen, is a distant yet significant instance of Montaigne's legacy outside of France. It was Emerson who first assimilated the *Essais* into his agenda of American cultural development, which perhaps owes more allegiance to the *Essais* than previously believed.

Emerson read Montaigne before Nietzsche and in a more attentive and explicit way. The presence of Montaigne is only incidental to Nietzsche's work; the latter made no sustained effort to appropriate the *Essais.* Yet his contact with Montaigne, both directly and through the intermediary of Emerson, produced an active intertextual Montaignean dimension, which plays a pronounced role in his thought and writing. Nietzsche's reception of Montaigne through Emerson is important and complicates the already complex relationship of Nietzsche and Montaigne. Nietzsche came into contact with Emerson before encountering Montaigne and made important appropriations of the former's work, evening translating several of his essays. He appropriated Emerson's exaltation of the self, skeptical individualism, and revolt against an unreflective attitude toward the past into his work.[32] He often adopted, however, the same qualities from the work of Montaigne and the lines of demarcation of this appropriation, when Nietzsche draws on Montaigne and when from Emerson, would inevitably lead one closer to Nietzsche's Emerson rather than Nietzsche's Montaigne. Yet in general terms it is probable that Emerson's discussions of Montaigne prepared Nietzsche's subsequent interaction with the *Essais* and his production of the second significant crosscultural reception of Montaigne's writing during the nineteenth century in the generation following Emerson's.

There is much circumstantial evidence in considering Emerson's importance to Nietzsche. They were a nation and a generation apart, yet there are suggestive correlations of their ancestry, milieu, and work. Both were descended from several generations of theologians; both lost their fathers at an early age and were raised by mothers and aunts; the orthodox Puritanism of New England in the nineteenth century was not unlike the provincial orthodox Lutherism of Nietzsche's Germany. Beyond the language difference, both would have equally felt at home at Emerson's Harvard of 1825 or Nietzsche's Schulpforta of 1860. Both were by instinct intellectually independent, skeptical of moral, religious, political, philosophical, and literary dogmatism; both were likewise antagonistic toward a slavish attitude to custom and tradition. Yet there are significant dissimilarities in their thinking and work: Emerson's optimism opposed to Nietzsche's pessimism, his Christian humanism opposed to Nietzsche's dionysian paganism. Emerson, however problematic the positions he took, continued on his equananimous way until old age; Nietzsche reached the limits of his sanity and became silent — the sage of Concord and the dithyrambic persona of *Ecce Homo* are thus extremely incompatible. Yet it is this incompatibility that makes possible such promiscuous comparison. The harmfulness of truth and the use of error, the use and abuse of history, even the indispensability of error as an important conflictual dynamic that perpetuates the intellectual life, produced circular dialectics in the work of Montaigne, Emerson, and Nietzsche. There is in fact a marked unsystematic impetus in the thinking of Emerson, and in Nietzsche's work, as prepared by Montaigne's. Nietzsche's aphoristic style is not that far from Montaigne's essaying or from Emerson's disseminate textuality, especially in his journals, which are fundamentally series of affirmations and digressions with a minimum of logical sequentiality, very much in the Montaignean mode. Emerson's writing, slow and sure, Nietzsche's, fast and furious, with Montaigne somewhere in between, constitute an intercultural trinity whose significance to the modern age is distinctive.

♦ ♦ ♦

The explicit presence of Montaigne's work in Nietzsche's is minimal, yet its impact is substantial. In *Ecce Homo*, Nietzsche claims a close identity to Montaigne: "dass ich etwas von Montaignes Muthwillen im Geiste, wer weiss? vielleicht auch im Leibe habe."[33] Nietzsche's comparison of himself and Montaigne is not gratuitous. *Ecce Homo* is in a sense Nietzsche's Montaignean self-portrait: his own version of the development and significance of his life and work. In several other places in his work Nietzsche attempts to identify himself with Montaigne and especially with what he considers the essayist's triumphant self-discovery. Self-cultivation, appreciation of the contemplative life, confessional sincerity, and radical skepticism are aspects of the *Essais* held in esteem by Nietzsche.[34] This is the general range of Nietzsche's attraction to Montaigne. He often used Montaigne's concrete insights to temper abstract metaphysics and drew elements from the *Essais* to help him analyze the individual in relation to his or her cultural context.

Nietzsche's actual contact with and interest in Montaigne's work has been best documented by Andler, who considers Cosima Wagner's Christmas gift in 1870 "d'une belle édition de Montaigne" to be a major event in Nietzsche's reading of French authors.[35] Williams documents how Nietzsche was "deeply acquainted with French literature" and more importantly that his "most consistent admiration was given to Montaigne, whom he read continually."[36] Nietzsche's work is sprinkled with references to Montaigne and, as we shall see, the *Essais* were important for his intellectual development on several key points. Although Nietzsche had been interested in the *Essais* before 1870, Andler demonstrates that his intense cultivation of them stems from this time. Williams's position is similar; he posits a difference in Nietzsche's work from before 1870, as in *Die Geburt der Tragödie,* which he sees marked by an enthusiasm and clear formulations, and after 1870, as in "Über Wahrheit und Lüge im aussermoralischen Sinne," in which a more pronounced anti-dogmatic, disillusioned attitude began to assert itself. In 1874, Nietzsche himself singled out Montaigne's importance for his work, and established him as a positive countering agent against the pessimistic dimensions of Schopenhauer's work:

> Ich weiss nur noch einen Schriftsteller, den ich in Betreff der Ehrlichkeit Schopenhauer gleich, ja höher noch stelle: das ist Montaigne. Dass ein solcher Mensch geschrieben hat, dadurch ist wahrlich die Lust, auf dieser Erde zu leben, vermehrt worden. Mir wenigstens geht es seit dem Bekanntmachen mit dieser freiesten und kräftigsten Seele so, dass ich sagen muss, was er von Plutarch sagt: 'kaum habe ich einen Blick auf ihn geworfen, so ist mir Bein oder ein Flügel gewachsen.' Schopenhauer hat

> mit Montaigne noch eine zweite Eigenschaft, ausser der Ehrlichkeit, gemein: eine wirkliche erheiternde Heiterkeit. (I, 296-7)

The *Essais* were thus for Nietzsche a text that gave him more reason to live and one that exfoliates in the context of his own work ("so ist mir Bein oder ein Flügel gewachsen"). In 1875, Nietzsche made another important admission concerning Montaigne, drawing a connection between the essayist and the "modern spirit," in terms of qualities he himself seeks to embody:

> Was der einzelne Montaigne in der Bewegtheit des Reformations-Geistes bedeutet, ein In-sich-zur-Ruhe-Kommen, ein friedliches Für-sich-Sein und Ausatmen — und so empfand ihn gewiss sein bester Leser Shakespeare — das ist jetzt die Historie für den modernen Geist. (I, 378)

As Pater also did, Nietzsche posited Montaigne's mode of subjectivist expression as one of the originary events of a modernist attitude. Nietzsche liked Emerson for the same reasons he liked Montaigne: because he could order the flux of his experience and find a solid ground for affirming life: "Emerson hat jene gütige und geistreiche Heiterkeit, welche allen Ernst entmutig ... sein Geist findet immer Gründe, zufrieden und selbst dankbar zu sein" ("Streifzüge eines Unzeitgemässen," *Götzen-Dämmerung,* II, 998). These specific instances of Nietzsche's commentary on Montaigne thus show his concern for the *Essais,* yet it is important to inquire further and examine what transformative role Nietzsche's reception of Montaigne's work may have played in the development of his thought and writing. It is possible that the affinities and contrasts between their work are coincidental. If so, then what are the reasons for such coincidences? If not, then how can we better understand the work of both authors when read in conjunction? Emerson is always lurking in the background.

In the work of both Nietzsche and Montaigne, there is a conception of the instability of language and a concern for what they posit as a crisis of representation. In "Über Wahrheit und Lüge im aussermoralischen Sinne," Nietzsche presents a notion of language that operates, according to him, not as an objective tool deployed to represent the world, but a metaphoric creation of the users of that tool. Truth is therefore inaccessible to human reason: "Was ist also Wahrheit? Ein bewegliches Heer von Metaphern, Metonymien,

Anthropomorphismen, kurz eine Summe von menschlichen Relationen ... die Wahrheiten sind Illusionen, von denen man vergessen hat, dass sie solche sind ..." (III, 314). Nietzsche maintains that we are locked in a prison of blind faith in our trust of language and that through it we can never achieve a true understanding of things in themselves: "Wir glauben etwas von den Dingen selbst zu wissen, wenn wir von Bäumen, Farben, Schnee und Blumen reden und besitzen doch nichts als Metaphern der Dinge, die den ursprünglichen Wesenheiten ganz und gar nicht entsprechen" (III, 312-313). Nietzsche's question, "ist die Sprache der adäquate Ausdruck aller Realitäten ...?" (III, 311), has similarities to Montaigne's own mistrust of the linguistic sign: "Il y a le nom et la chose, ce n'est pas une partie de la chose ny de la substance, c'est une piece estrangere joincte à la chose, et hors d'elle" (II, xvi, 618).[37] How do we achieve an understanding of truth if we are imprisoned in a language that is unable to attain substantial knowledge? — "Nous sommes tous creux et vuides: ce n'est pas de vent et de voix que nous avons à nous remplir; il nous faut de la substance plus solide à nous reparer" (II, xvi, 618). Montaigne posited a nominalist attitude toward language, where only individual entities exist and where linguistic structures are unable to embody universal principles. His suspicion of *verba* and his faith in *res* informs many issues in the *Essais*. He sought to place matter (*inventio*) over manner (*dispositio*), maintaining that language should be based on a natural and not artificial expression: "Mais que nostre disciple soit bien pourveu de choses, les parolles ne suivront que trop; il les entrainera, si elles ne veulent suivre" (I, xxvi, 169). Montaigne was attempting to counteract a system of rhetorical education that had developed to the point of ossification in its emphasis on speaking well yet saying little of substance. He cites Cicero's dictum from "De Finibus" to counteract what he considered a debilitating state of affairs: "'Ipsae res verba rapiunt'" (I, xxvi, 169). This raises the question of the natural or artificial status of language as discussed in Plato's "Cratylus" where words' natural origin (*physei*) is opposed to their conventional character *(thesei)*.[38]

Montaigne wrote in a transitional moment of history when discursive structures were shifting from a mode of resemblance to one of representation. He lamented the fact that words had been wrested free of things and reduced to the arbitrary relation of representation. There were no longer kinships, affinities, and similitudes, only an order of things inadequately paralleled and represented by an order of words.[39] Because of the "artificial" nature of language, Montaigne's attitude in the *Essais* is that there is never full apprehension of the truth; we are forever lost in discursive Babel: "La diversité d'ydiomes et de langues, dequoy il troubla cet ouvrage, qu'est-ce autre chose que cette infinie et perpetuelle altercation et discordance d'opinions et de raisons qui accompaigne et embrouille le vain bastiment de l'humaine science" (II, xii, 553). Nietzsche was also uncertain of achieving final knowledge, and in the following passage from "Menschliches, Allzumenschliches" expresses his mistrust of truth:

> Macht man jemandem klar, dass er, streng verstanden, nie von Wahrheit, sondern immer nur von Wahrscheinlichkeit und deren Graden reden könne, so entdeckt man gewöhnlich an der unverhohlenen Freude des also Belehrten, wie viel lieber den Menschen die Unsicherheit des geistigen Horizontes ist und wie sie die Wahrheit im Grunde ihrer Seele wegen Bestimmheit *hassen*. (I, 746-7)

This is an important notion shared by Nietzsche and Montaigne: the explicit rejection of inherited dogma and skepticism toward rigid intellectual evaluations, and along with this, an aversion to reductive conclusions. They were also wary of the possibility of firmly grounded meaning and used metaphors of mutability to evoke perpetual strife and instability in their arguments. This led to a skeptical independence in both writers, who continually berated dogmatic assertion as an enemy of the search for truth even while they were themselves dogmatic on many issues.

Along with the concerns of the auto-portrait and skepticism in the work of Nietzsche and Montaigne, there is another important affinity: the valorization of a Heraclitean view of the world and an accompanying awareness of the world's instability. Montaigne often expresses this inconstancy of the world through liquid metaphors in the spirit of Heraclitus's Fragment LI: "One cannot step twice into the same river, nor can one grasp any mortal substance in a stable condition, but it scatters and again gathers; it forms and dissolves, and approaches and departs."[40] This would be an apt characterization of much of the writing in the *Essais*. It is of a pre-Socratic orientation: often proposing no resolution of opposing entities, producing a precarious balance of polarities that rebel against final solution and keep open new potentialities of their relationship. Montaigne was of course wary of such hermeneutic instability and preferred a margin of safety by not getting overly intoxicated with pre-Socratism, keeping to the riverbank when the water is too deep: "je l'essaye, sondant le gué de bien loing; et puis, le trouvant trop profond pour ma taille, je me tiens à la rive" (I, L, 301). Montaigne's writing thus involves itself in a dynamic of nominalization and its undermining, leaving behind the responsibility for the reader to undertake a fluid and mobile replication of sense needed to constitute meaning. This aspect of the *Essais* offers an important clue toward the understanding of how they are adapted to suit so many different points of view.

Nietzsche also acknowledges the importance of the conception of the mutability of all things, and draws on Heraclitus's acceptance of ontological paradox in "Die Philosophie im tragischen Zeitalter der Griechen":

> Das ewige und alleinige Werden, die gänzliche Unbeständigkeit alles Wirklichen, das fortwährend nur wirkt und wird und nicht ist, wie dies Heraklit lehrt, ist eine furchtbare und betäubende Vorstellung und in ihrem Einflusse am nächsten der Empfindung verwandt, mit der jemand bei einem Erdbeben das Zutrauen zu der festgegründeten Erde verliert. (III, 371)

The instability of the physical world, and an untrustworthy language system that is incapable of permanently stabilizing our understanding of that world were notions of primary importance for Nietzsche and Montaigne. Embodied in this conception of language that valorizes movement and paradox is a philosophy of uncertainty that asks how stable understanding can be achieved if the system by which thought is expressed is mutable and unstable. Montaigne raised paradoxical questions in the *Essais* that often refuse resolution; he produced a text in movement to invoke the impermanence of the world and problematized confidence in firmly grounded interpretation. For both, the world and the individual can never be definitely comprehended since they never cease to change. Their belief in the perpetual dialectical strife between opposites shakes faith in certainty ("das Zutrauen zu der festgegründeten Erde verliert"). Yet for both writers, this assertion of diversity and instability of the language system is somewhat overstated. Neither was so uncertain of the fact that it prevented him from writing prolifically. Although Nietzsche expressed his concern for the problem of the elusiveness of a firmly grounded earth ("fesgegründeten *Erde*"), it is Montaigne's writing that helped him to accept this unstable quality of human experience and understanding ("dass ein solcher Mensch geschrieben hat, dadurch ist wahrlich die Lust, auf dieser *Erde* zu leben, vermehrt worden"). Montaigne thus provided Nietzsche a ground from which he could examine the bases of understanding; the latter marveled at the former's ability to remain somehow assured of himself even when faced with the overwhelming predicaments of human experience.

How then do these issues sketched above — self-portraiture, skepticism toward language, and Heracliteanism — contribute, first, to the comparison and contrast of Nietzsche and Montaigne, and second, to their "modernism"? How do certain of Montaigne's conceptions infuse modernist dynamics through Nietzsche's adaptation of them? What are the degrees of directness and indirectness of this transmission? On the other hand, in considering the differences between Montaigne and Nietzsche, there are glaring incongruities between their positions. Nietzsche's tragic vision and self-denial conflicts with Montaigne's acceptance of human limitations and his own moderate self-indulgence. Secondly, Nietzsche's radical distrust of continuity and his suspicion of history motivate him to call for its total revaluation in the service of innovation: "Die Neuheit, der *Mut* der Neuerung ist wirklich ersten Ranges" ("Briefe, 30 Oktober, 1888," III, 1327). This position appears to contrast with Montaigne's desire to write himself through the authority of his models of classical antiquity and his suspicion of *nouvelletez*, which generally has a pejorative sense in the *Essais*, as opposed to custom and tradition, which are typically accorded a more positive value. Yet the conflictual tension between the past and its use in the present is a key intertextual correlation between several of the *Essais* and Nietzsche's "Vom Nutzen und Nachteil der Historie für das Leben." Although Montaigne and Nietzsche appear at first glance to be at opposite ends of the spectrum on the question of the use of cultural tradition, it is an issue that provides a dynamic point of contact and contrast between their work, provoking and demanding clarification through comparative examination, whose attention to the problematics shared by Nietzsche and Montaigne will unsettle Bouillier's proscriptive judgment:

> Tout compte fait, il n'apparaît nullement que Nietzsche serait autre ou moindre s'il avait ignoré ou négligé les *Essais*. Montaigne a été simplement pour lui un ami, qui distrait, console, qui excite l'esprit et lui procure parfois quelques suggestions.[41]

Nietzsche picked up on these "suggestions" and developed them in original ways. The *Essais* are not always immediately recognizable in his work, yet they played an underlying, often catalytic role. Nietzsche thus pursued an active redevelopment of what he learned from the *Essais* in a manner that Montaigne himself promoted: "ce n'est pas un livre à lire, c'est un livre à estudier et apprendre" (III, viii, 941).

Any underlying conclusions that may arise from readings of Montaigne's and Nietzsche's attitudes toward the relationship of history and the self must first be qualified by both writers' adherence to the position that there will always be uncertainty in human understanding. Montaigne strikingly presented his mistrust in systematic certainty in an unsystematic way and in a non-professional idiom — thus sometimes mirroring, sometimes undermining the content of his text with its signifying structure. Although maintaining that pure truth is unattainable, he still concluded that there is no more important quest than the attempt to attain it: "Car nous sommes nais à quester la verité" (III, viii, 928). Nietzsche also lamented the impossibility of fully understanding reality, yet likewise maintained the importance of the search for better understanding.

Nietzsche opens "Vom Nutzen und Nachteil der Historie für das Leben," a text that demonstrates many affinities with the *Essais*, by quoting Goethe: "Übrigens ist mir alles verhasst, was mich bloss belehrt, ohne meine Tätigkeit zu vermehren oder unmittelbar zu beleben" (I, 209). This quote could equally characterize Montaigne's conception of education in "De l'institution des enfans," in which he calls not for the simple accumulation of historical information by his student, but for the development of the student's own mind in relation to that material: "Qu'il ne luy apprenne pas tant les histoires, qu'à en juger" (I, xxvi, 156). Nietzsche goes on to say that history limited to knowledge must be rejected, and be used instead in the service of life and action: "Dass heisst, wir brauchen sie zum Leben und zur Tat, nicht zur bequemen Abkehr vom Leben und von der Tat, oder gar zur Beschönigung des selbstsüchtigen Lebens und der feigen und schlechten Tat. Nur soweit die Historie Leben dient, wollen wir ihr dienen" (I, 209). History must *serve* life in action, and not simply remain a "Garten des Wissens" (I, 209). In order for a culture to flourish, there must be vital interplay between past memory and greatness of present effort. Montaigne likewise calls for an active engagement with historical precursors: "Il practiquera, par le moyen des histoires, ces grandes ames des meilleurs siecles" (I, xxvi, 156).

In "Vom Nutzen und Nachteil," Nietzsche develops a tripartite scheme of history: "monumentalische" history (the quest for heros), "antiquarische" history (the consolidation of the knowledge of the past), and "kritische" history (one must be a judge of, not a slave of history). The general opposition is what Nietzsche calls elsewhere the historical ("das Historische") versus the unhistorical ("das Unhistorische"). He initially makes a plea for the latter, rejecting the empirical accumulation of history and promoting the harmonization of the chaos of historical information into a new and healthy existence. He maintains that the dynamic interrelationship of the historical and the unhistorical is essential for the survival and well-being of a people and its culture and should not be allowed to fossilize into the systematic reductions of pedagogical paradigms: "Dies gerade ist der Satz, zu dessen Betrachtung der Leser eingeladen ist: *das Unhistorische und das Historische ist gleichermassen für die Gesundheit eines einzelnen, eines Volkes und einer Kultur nötig*" (I, 214). He goes to great lengths in "Vom Nutzen und Nachteil" to berate the historical attitude, by which he means the penchant for intellectual excess and an ossified knowledge of the past, qualities which he believes dominate his historical moment. What his age takes the most pride in, historical education ("ihre historische Bildung," I, 210), Nietzsche considers to be overwhelmingly debilitating, depriving society of the possibility of living a fruitful life in the present: "so unterschlägt er doch zugleich dabei die Gegenwart und das Dasein" (I, 212). It is blind dependence on historical knowledge that impedes living more instinctually and less deliberately in the present. Nietzsche wants present effort to overcome an overdeveloped historical consciousness, preserve subjectivity while communing with the past, and experience the relationship between history and life in fuller immediacy:

> Wer sich nicht auf der Schwelle des Augenblicks, alle Vergangenheiten vergessend, niederlassen kann, wer nicht auf einem Punkte wie eine Siegesgöttin ohne Schwindel und Furcht zu stehen vermag, der wird nie wissen; was Glück ist, und noch schlimmer: er wird nie etwas tun, was andre glücklich macht. (I, 212)

The development of a fruitful dialog with the cultural tradition is also an important element in Montaigne's writing project. He often expresses his desire to avoid blind pedagogy and uses his learning for self-enlightenment: "si j'estudie, je n'y cherche que la science qui traicte de la connoissance de moy mesmes, et qui m'instruise à bien mourir et à bien vivre" (II, x, 409).

When Montaigne discusses the use of tradition in "De l'institution des enfans," it is usually in the context of instruction ("si j'estudie"). Although the *Essais* are an intertextual labyrinth of ancient and modern learning, Montaigne's literary project is essentially an attempt (*un essai*) at the education of an individual in his quest to learn about himself: "Je m'estudie plus qu'autre subject. C'est ma metaphisique, c'est ma phisique" (III, xii, 1072). In "Du pedantisme" and "De l'institution des enfans," Montaigne most clearly develops his position on the shortcomings of scholastic pedagogy and the changes that he would like to see. Nietzsche's "Vom Nutzen und Nachteil" has more profound implications, yet there is a significant recurrence of themes and terms in his text to warrant comparison with Montaigne's related discussions. Nietzsche proposes a radical revision of the cultural education of his age: "Für mich aber gewinne ich etwas, was mir noch mehr wert ist als die Wohlanständigkeit — öffentlich über unsere Zeit belehrt und zurechtgewiesen zu werden" (I, 210). As Montaigne develops his system of "nourriture et institution" for his "petit homme" (I, xxvi, 146), so Nietzsche proposes a new "historische Bildung" for the "Kind dieser jetzigen Zeit" (I, 210). In their conceptions of the best use of history, Nietzsche and Montaigne propose radical societal revisions for their respective historical moments. Montaigne's basic premise in "Du pedantisme" (one redeveloped by Nietzsche) is that human understanding is debilitated with too much history, as minds become saturated with too many other minds and consequently cannot think for themselves:

> Je dirois volontiers que, comme les plantes s'estouffent de trop d'humeur, et les lampes de trop d'huile: aussi l'action de l'esprit, par trop d'estude et de matiere, lequel, saisi et embarassé d'une grande diversité de choses, perde le moyen de se desmesler; et que cette charge le tienne courbe et croupi. (I, xxv, 134)

Both writers often denigrate a system of education that generates more information than one can assimilate and use in an original manner.

In the pedagogical notions of both, a crisis of information is at hand. Montaigne suffered from a growing awareness of the impossibility of knowing all that there was to be known by a well-informed individual (a trend created by printing as well as the humanist project). For Nietzsche, in late nineteenth-century Germany, as a result of an overdeveloped historicist sensibility, the past had become an overwhelming shadow that could no longer be sifted through adequately to achieve comprehensive understanding. Nietzsche maintained that an overdeveloped sense of history chokes healthy self-assertiveness: "Oder, um mich noch einfacher über mein Thema zu erklären: *es gibt einen Grad von Schlaflosigkeit, von Wiederkäuen, von historischem Sinne, bei dem das Lebendige zu Schaden kommt und zuletzt zugrunde geht, sei es nun ein Mensch oder ein Volk oder eine Kultur*" (I, 213). At the same time, life also requires the service of history: "In dreierlei Hinsicht gehört die Historie dem Lebendigen: sie gehört ihm als dem Tätigen und Strebenden, ihm als dem Bewahrenden und Verehrenden, ihm als dem Leidenden und der Befreiung Bedürftigen" (I, 219). Montaigne also presents a point of view contradictory to his first proposition about the burden of learning: "Mais il en va autrement: car nostre ame s'eslargit d'autant plus qu'elle se remplit" (I, xxv, 134).

Nietzsche attacked the blind absorption of masses of dead knowledge that suffocate the intellect instead of stimulating it in the service of a healthy life. He participated in Montaigne's undermining of the rigidity and abstraction of the academic attitude. Nietzsche's tripartite historical scheme concerning the relation of the self to history displays discursive characteristics similar to those of Montaigne. Nietzsche first argues that monumental history is an object worthy of study. His *monumentalische* history is the study of past heros who lived the great moments in the earlier struggles of human existence and embody humanity's highest achievements:

> Dass die grossen Momente im Kampfe der einzelnen eine Kette bilden, dass in ihnen ein Höhenzug der Menschheit durch Jahrtausende hin sich verbinde, dass für mich das Höchste eines solchen längstvergangenen Momentes noch lebendig, hell und gross sei — das ist der Grundgedanke im Glauben an die Humanität, der sich in der Forderung einer *monumentalischen* Historie ausspricht. (I, 220)

Montaigne proposed that his student learn from the great monuments of history, extracting lessons from magnanimous writers, the best of whom not only transmit their knowledge, but also demonstrate their wisdom and superiority through the examples of their worthy lives. Montaigne insisted on the important educational value of such examples. His student "practiquera, par le moyen des histoires, ces grandes ames des meilleurs siecles" (I, xxvi, 157). The study of the monumental should not be a "vain estude" but rather "une estude de fruit inestimable" (I, xxvi, 157). It is less of an exact appraisal of what happened than a moral lesson whereby the student learns to judge and use reading in the service of life: "qu'ils s'amusent plus aux conseils qu'aux evenemens, plus a ce qui part du dedans qu'à ce qui arrive du dehors" (II, x, 416). Historical authority for Montaigne must be transformed into usefulness in the present. Montaigne uses the word "utile," which is close to Nietzsche's sense of "Nutzen."

Montaigne began the *Essais* by compiling *exempla* in the form of sayings (the practice of the *leçon* or *florilège*). He eventually abandoned the practice of compilation and surpassed the accumulation of factual material in order to extract their nourishment as fuel for his own intellectual development: "Je ne compte pas mes emprunts, je les poise" (II, x, 408). "Poise," the modern French "peser," is etymologically related to Latin "exagium" — "essai." The *Essais* are in fact attempts at weighing the balance of past authority and present uniqueness. Montaigne's attempts do not always seek to tip the scale in favor of one conclusion over another. He was less interested in exhaustive comprehension than in capturing the spirit of his readings and transplanting them into his own mobile understanding of the world: "raisons et inventions que je transplante en mon solage" (II, x, 408). History must be used in the service of life in the present. Following Montaigne, Nietzsche posits an active confrontation with history: "Dass das Leben aber den Dienst der Historie brauche, muss ebenso deutlich begriffen werden als der Satz, der später zu beweisen sein wird — dass ein Übermass der Historie dem Lebendigen schade"

(I, 219). Nietzsche's useful history will belong to the thinker powerful enough to confront the past, engage it, and cultivate its lessons in order to combat contemporary mediocrity: "Die Geschichte gehört vor allem dem Tätigen und Mächtigen, dem, der einen grossen Kampf kämpfte, der Vorbilder, Lehrer, Tröster braucht und sie unter seinen Genossen und in der Gegenwart nicht zu finden vermag" (I, 219). There is danger involved in the cultivation of monumental greatness, but it is an important weapon in the face of present banality. In the shadow of the belief in the continual superiority of past ages, people, and events, positive change in the present becomes difficult if not impossible.

The conflictual relationship of innovation and tradition occurs no more clearly in the *Essais* than in "De la coustume et de ne changer aisément une loy receüe." The essay begins by underscoring the danger of habit and how it tyrannizes personal freedom:

> Car c'est à la verité une violente et traistresse maistresse d'escole que la coustume. Elle establit en nous, peu à peu, à la desrobée, le pied de son autorité: mais par ce doux et humble commencement, l'ayant rassis et planté avec l'ayde du temps, elle nous descouvre tantost un furieux et tyrannique visage, contre lequel nous n'avons plus la liberté de hausser seulement les yeux. Nous luy voyons forcer, tous les corps, les reigles de nature. "*Usus efficacissimus rerum omnium magister.*" (I, xxiii, 109)

Yet Montaigne's concluding quotation of Pliny contradicts his initial assertion, and habit quickly changes from a furious and tyrannical mistress into a benevolent master. In the following paragraphs, Montaigne counters Pliny's opinion, telling us how much habit stupefies the senses: "combien l'accoustumance hebete nos sens" (I, xxiii, 109). Elsewhere in the same essay Montaigne opposes "accoustumance" (habit or custom) to "nouvelletez" (novelty or innovation) telling us that "Je suis desgousté de la nouvelleté, quelque visage qu'elle porte, et ay raison, car j'en ay veu des effets tres-dommageables" (I, xxiii, 119). Montaigne thus simultaneously valorizes two opposing entities. He admits to the detrimental effect of habit ("L'assuefaction endort la veuë de nostre jugement"–I, xxiii, 112), yet seeks to avoid the dangers of innovation. Although the principal effect of custom is to "nous saisir et empieter" (I, xxiii, 115), one should obey "l'empire de la coustume" (I, xxiii, 116) since, as he claims in "De la vanité," it is far more dangerous to upset a current system than to conform to its values and exigencies, as well as its imperfections: "le plus viel et mieux cogneu est tousjours plus supportable que le mal récent et inexperimenté" (III, ix, 959). Montaigne thus proposes an equivocal attitude as a means of confronting the interaction of innovation and habit: "le sage doit au dedans retirer son ame de la presse, et la tenir en liberté et puissance de juger librement des choses; mais, quant au dehors, qu'il doit suivre entierement les façons et les forms receues" (I, xxiii, 118). He posits reciprocal movement between inner freedom and outward conformity and seeks to maintain, in Friedrich's terms, "cette position double vis-à-vis de la tradition ... respect et distance, amour et indépendance."[42] The context of Montaigne's argument is, in this instance, political and religious, yet its implications can be extended to his writing project.

Beneath the authority of classical antiquity, Montaigne pursued his own idiosyncratic ruminations, conformed outwardly (as seen in his practice of copious quotation and in the founding of his arguments on ancient authority), yet at the same time took great liberties to create an original persona embodied in an unprecedented genre of eclectic dimensions. He attempted to be simultaneously faithful to both internal and external demands. In "De la coustume," habit is harmful yet innovation dangerous. Montaigne outwardly adhered to the former, yet preserved his inner space and subjective sovreignty by putting into practice the latter. He attempted to clearly define "coustume," yet endowed it with various and shifting meanings, thus failing to integrate his argument on both the level of signifier and signified. This contradictory nature of Montaigne's project is a central aspect of his modernism. He generates a nexus of conflicting currents that often render his writing indeterminate.

In Nietzsche's reference to deadening habit ("die dumpfe Gewöhnung" — I, 220), he was berating an overdependence on monumental history. Once it becomes a habitual study, it impedes the change and development of generations ("den Wechsel der Geschlechter" — I, 220). Blind adherence to belief in earlier greatness ("dem Klassichen und Seltenen früherer Zeiten" — I, 221) prevents striving in the present toward self-improvement. The second downfall of monumental history for Nietzsche is that in focusing solely on the greatest cultural monuments, great portions of history are neglected: "ganze grosse Teile derselben werden vergessen, verachtet, und fliessen fort wie eine graue ununterbrochene Flut, und nur einzelne geschmückte Fakta heben sich als Inseln heraus" (I, 223). Montaigne also wanted to surmount this exclusionist view of history and go beyond the study of the "grandes ames des meilleurs siecles" to allow the past to speak in a fuller multiplicity:

> Il y a dans Plutarch beaucoup de discours estandus, tres dignes d'estre sceus ... mais il y en a mille qu'il n'a que touché simplement: il guigne seulement du doigt par où nous irons, s'il nous plaist, et se contente quelquefois de ne donner qu'une attainte dans le vif d'un propos. Il les faut arracher de là et mettre en place marchande. (I, xxvi, 156)

Montaigne demanded that the vicissitudes of history be unleashed to live in their fullness, thereby allowing the reader to creatively interact with them, and arrange their lessons into his or her own life. Likewise, out of the dispersed directions that Montaigne's writing takes, the reader will display them ("mettre en place marchande") according to his or her own vision. The interactive drama of the past (the *Essais*) and the present (new readings of them) plays itself out as the reader, in engaging the movement of Montaigne's text, demonstrates the participation needed to come to an understanding of the *Essais'* importance to literary and philosophical modernism. To work for example through the problematic of "coutume" and "nouvelletez," one must adopt Montaigne's strategy of using history. Theory is thus put into practice toward a tentative hermeneutic elucidation, an interpretive attempt that is both "gefährlich" and "une branloire perenne." Both Nietzsche and Emerson adopted to varying degrees Montaigne's method of confronting history, yet it is Nietzsche who drew the more radical implications from his Montaignean experience.

For Montaigne, a history given solely to the high points is both useless and useful: "C'est un vain estude, qui veut; mais qui veut aussi, c'est un estude de fruit inestimable" (I, xxvi, 156). Nietzsche also presents the case paradoxically: the blind veneration of the monumental is harmful to the creation of life, yet it is needed if profitably used: "Gegen ihre Erbfeinde, die starken Kunstgeister, also gegen die, welche allein aus jener Historie wahrhaft, das heisst zum Leben hin, zu lernen und das Erlernte in eine erhöhte Praxis umzusetzen vermögen" (I, 224). The tradition of monumental art, "der Kanon der monumentalen Künste" (I, 224), must be assimilated, transcended, and transformed into a new and vital creation. Yet the novelty of this creation makes it a volatile gesture. In the context of using and abusing the past, both Montaigne and Nietzsche berate the academy for its suppression of the personal judgment and original creation of its students. Nietzsche attacks the academic specialists ("die Kunstkenner") who attempt to stifle attempts at present greatness, comparing them to physicians who poison young minds instead of helping them toward self-cultivation: "Denn sie wollen nicht, dass das Grosse entstehe: ihr Mittel ist, zu sagen, 'seht, das Grosse ist schon da!'" (I, 224). Montaigne also berates teachers who saturate students with monumental information rather than teach them how to regenerate this material into the development of a better soul:

> On ne cesse de criailler à nos oreilles, comme qui verseroit dans un antonnoir, et nostre charge ce n'est que redire ce qu'on nous a dict. Je voudrois qu'il corrigeast cette partie, et que, de belle arrivée, selon la portée de l'ame qu'il a en main, il commençast à la mettre sur la montre, luy faisant gouster les choses, les choisir et discerner d'elle mesme: quelquefois luy ouvrant chemin, quelque fois le luy laissant ouvrir. (I, xxvi, 150)

Instead of transferring the powerful lessons of the monumental into the productive activity of life in the present, Montaigne's professors suppressed energetic subjectivity. Instead of allowing the living past to vitalize the moribund present, the shroud of the dead past smothers the living present: "... in welchem verkappt sie den eigentlichen Sinn jener historischen Betrachtungsart in den entgegengesetzten umkehren; ob sie es deutlich wissen oder nicht, sie handeln jedenfalls so, als ob ihr Wahlspruch wäre: lasst die Toten die Lebendigen begraben" (I, 225). In conversing with the past, the danger is to bury the self and extinguish subjectivity.

Nietzsche also accepted the paradoxical nature of historical confrontation, maintaining that the monumental or antiquarian abuse of history is debilitating, but that all three kinds of history are necessary and must be used confluentially. The monumental and the antiquarian, which Nietzsche collapses at times into one category — the historical ("das Historische") must be judged by critical history ("die *kritische* Geschichte"), which he also calls the unhistorical ("das Unhistorische"). Critical history embodies a conflictual impulse toward the past, the desire to interrogate, condemn, and dissolve history, the motivation to cut cultural roots in order to live more fully in the present. It is a mode of creation that destructs while it constructs and produces a dangerous ("gefährlich") process. Yet in judging and banishing its own past, a society condemns itself since it is part of that past: "Denn da wir nun die Resultate früherer Geschlechter sind, sind wir auch die Resultate ihrer Verirungen, Leidenschaften und Irrtümer, ja Verbrechen; es ist nicht möglich, sich ganz von dieser Kette zu lösen" (I, 229-230). Nietzsche's shifting attitudes toward history shake the solid ground of interpretive certainty. Habit and custom will preserve inherited innate knowledge necessary for the culture's stability, yet critical history must arise in the form of innovative actions to establish present identity. The danger of disseminating "[den] Garten des Wissens" into a new unique configuration is that it will inevitably be weaker than the original:

> Wir bringen es im besten Falle zu einem Widerstreit der ererbten, angestammten Natur und unserer Erkenntnis, auch wohl zu einem Kampfe einer neuen strengen Zucht gegen das von alters her Angezogene und Angeborene, wir pflanzen eine neue Gewöhnung, einen neuen Instinkt, eine zweite Natur an, so dass die erste Natur abdorrt ... immer ein gefährlicher Versuch, weil es so schwer ist, eine Grenze im Verneinen des Vergangen zu finden, und weil die zweiten Naturen meistens schwächlicher als die ersten sind. (I, 230)

There is, however, negative affirmation in the process of critical history since the new identity created out of the destruction of the old itself becomes part of the monumental and the antiquarian: "dass jede siegende zweite Natur zu einer ersten wird" (I, 230). If repetition of the past prevents the assertion of a new beginning, then surmounting it through the struggle of critical history allows for culture's self-perpetuation. Yet the later accomplishment ("eine zweite Natur") itself becomes a first nature ("die erste Natur"). De Man summarizes this predicament in the following manner: "If history is not to become sheer regression or paralysis, it depends on modernity for its duration and renewal, but modernity cannot assert itself without being swallowed up into a regressive historical process."[43]

As demonstrated by de Man, this contradictory nature of Nietzsche's position concerning the relationship between past stability and present change is a prevalent one in modernist literature. Ambivalent toward the spectre of the past, yet skeptical about new beginnings, Nietzsche's modernism can only be posed as a problematic: how does self-assertion come into full being while tied to the past's claims to enforce the present? His articulation of the problem is prepared in part by his reception of Montaigne. But Nietzsche was also thinking of Pascal's interplay of binary opposition, which is likewise caught up in this problematic, as can be seen in *Pensée* 93: "la coutume est une seconde nature qui détruit la première. Mais qu'est-ce que nature? pourquoi la coutume n'est-elle pas naturelle? J'ai grand'peur que cette nature ne soit elle-même qu'une première coutume, comme la coutume est une seconde nature" (XIII, 20-21). Yet Pascal's ultimate way of reading is in diametrical opposition to Nietzche's and Montaigne's, as seen in his attitude toward contradiction: "*Contradiction* — On ne peut faire une bonne physionomie qu'en accordant toutes nos contrariétés, et il ne suffit pas de suivre une suite de qualités accordantes sans accorder les contraires. *Pour entendre le sens d'un auteur il faut accorder tous les passages contraires*" (*Pensée* 684, XIV, 121-22 — emphasis added). The need to harmonize the contradictions is something lacking in Pascal's reception of Montaigne and in Nietzsche's reception of almost anyone. Pascal often configured chiasmic patterns of binary oppositions that may never be reconciled, but his primary impulse was nevertheless to attempt to totalize them. This is a principle of understanding opposed to Montaigne's less severe teleology and the reason why Nietzsche ultimately moved away from Pascal, while ever emulating his notion of asceticism. Pascal, Montaigne's nemesis, yet also his contrapuntal companion, resurfaced again, after Sainte-Beuve's reception, in the ethics of interpretation.[44]

As we've seen, Montaigne, Nietzsche, and Emerson often use digestive metaphors to describe the process of assimilating one's cultural tradition. In his discussion of the modernist predicament, de Man reverses this process. Instead of taking sustenance from the past, the past "swallows up" the present and thus the attempt at assertion of the new fails since the newest new will itself become the tradition from which a future "modernism" can be initiated. Eating sustains a life that is eaten in its own turn. In "Des cannibales," Montaigne demonstrates how the Amerindian Tupinamba alternately eat and are eaten by their enemies. They consume the enemy flesh, not for physical sustenance, but in order to absorb spiritual energy. Eventually, the one who has eaten will be eaten, and can even enjoy the prospect as he taunts his enemies with the fact that the flesh they ingest was once nourished on their own ancestors. Montaigne discusses this valor in the face of death as a triumphant loss, "des pertes triomphantes" (I, xxxi, 211) in the tradition of Leonidas and the Spartans who sacrificed themselves at Thermopylae. The notion of triumphant loss is the ethical foundation on which the Tupinamba community depends. Sacrificing one's life becomes a victory by preserving self-integrity. As de Man maintains, the new is ultimately absorbed into the historical process, yet defiance (the gesture of self-assertion) produces victory in the face of impending death.

In the work of Nietzsche and Montaigne, historical reading involves self-sacrifice: one surrenders the unity of subjectivity to commune with dead spirits and this dialog with cultural tradition leads to a triumphant loss that is also hope for regeneration. Modernist textuality, as practiced by Nietzsche and Montaigne, is an uncertain process with which the reader must interact in his or her critical enterprise. Nietzsche and Montaigne saw no way out of the impasse and produced tantalizing paradoxes that call forth the procreative potential for the future engagement of the problem where readers must undertake their own struggles to harmonize past (previous writings and cultural traditions) and present (new readings and critical responses). Montaigne and Nietzsche lose in the sense that their arguments are not definitively finalized. The victory is embodied in their ability to ensure a perpetual engagement of the problems by future readers who continue the life of the texts and actively create new meaning in their own particular historical circumstances. It is useful to remember that both Montaigne and Nietzsche often wrote with pedagogical purposes in mind — they were concerned with how their ideas could be extended to the problem of how citizens (and not only the specialized readers of the academy) should best study history, philosophy, and literature, and then make positive use of that learning. Montaigne's essaying sacrificed a coherent dogmatic identity. This loss of unequivocal certainty is however a paradoxical victory in that new readers are urged to approach culture as an open-ended dialog. He proposed a mode of conjectural interplay in order to overcome monological perspectives inadequate in responding to the diversity of a multivocal world.

Montaigne deals most explicitly with the predicament of past and present, with custom and innovation in a political and religious context — yet the issues also surreptitiously play themselves out in his discursive structures. In "De la coustume," he first develops the theme that habit creates absurd conventions and enslaves judgment. For Montaigne, the present (Nietzsche's "zweite Natur") *should be* infused with the past (Nietzsche's "erste Natur") and whatever deviates from officially recognized culture is generally condemned as unacceptable: "Par où il advient que ce qui est hors de gonds de coustume, on le croid hors des gonds de raison" (I, xxiii, 116). An individual must respect custom as society's universal law, yet concurrently preserve inner freedom: "La societé publique n'a que faire de nos penseés; mais le demeurant, comme nos actions, nostre travail, nos fortunes et nostre vie propre, il la faut préter et abandonner à son service et aux opinions communes ..." (I, xxiii, 118). The individual must assert freedom of judgment while remaining within the confines of custom. Montaigne proposes that the self live in the present yet that the second nature remain true to the first. Present uniqueness is preferred yet past habit is respected. Montaigne goes on to say that any innovation of the old fashion must be avoided at all costs ("Je suis desgousté de la nouvelleté"). Montaigne is referring specifically to the religious wars of his time. He compares the Protestants to "inventeurs" and the Catholics to "imitateurs" (I, xxiii, 119). In preserving past custom, the imitators have been guilty of evil, yet the inventors have the potential to do greater harm. Yet if the dynamic of innovation and repetition is extended to Montaigne's writing project, we can see a textual manifestation of the problematic — his quotations are less traditional authorities than places where he can seek refuge and develop his self-portraiture gradually — it is precisely this active intertextual relationship of the *Essais* to the literary past that provides Montaigne with a sense of his own innovative identity. Yet a simultaneous attitude of resistance to the past counterbalances his aversion to "nouvelleté" in an essay appropriately entitled "Des menteurs," in which he claims that his penchant to forget books and places, and then later to remember them, acts as a catalyst in the formation of new dimensions of understanding: "... et que les lieux et les livres que je revoy me rient tousjours d'une *fresche nouvelleté*" (I, ix, 35 — emphasis added).

Elsewhere he makes a claim for the newness of his writing project: "Et est un amusement *nouveau et extraordinaire* qui nous retire des occupations communes du monde" (II, vi, 378 — emphasis added). Which of Montaigne's formulations of repetition and innovation should one believe? Outwardly, Montaigne played a politically conservative role, yet he was discursively on the side of the "inventeurs," generating a discourse endowed with innovation and instability. In this sense he weaved surreptitiously into the *Essais* potentially radical aesthetics and politics.

Such innovation arises from a dependence on critical history: "Toutes sortes de nouvelle desbauche puisent hereusement en cette premiere et foeconde source, les images et patrons à troubler nostre police. On lict en nos loix mesmes, faites pour le remede de ce premier mal, l'apprentissage et l'excuse" (I, xxiii, 120). Innovative reading of the past in the service of reform is harmful: "Mais le meilleur pretexte de nouvelleté est tres-dangereux" (I, xxiii, 120). Montaigne proposes that respect of custom and tradition, although imperfect, is preferable to novelty, whose uncertainty can only bring on inevitable evil: "Si me semble-il, à le dire franchement, qu'il y a grand amour de soy de presomption, d'estimer ses opinions jusque-là que, pour les establir, il faille renverser une paix publique, et introduire tant de maux inevitables et une si horrible corruption" (I, xxiii, 120). As Montaigne's argument in "De la coustume" revolves around the kernel words "coustume" and "nouvelleté," he calls for respect to old ways, yet his argument deviates from traditional dogmatic lessons. His terms, criteria, and values shift; his judgments are caught in inevitable flux and "vont coulant et roulant sans cesse." The reader who attempts to become his competent reader ("un suffisant lecteur") cannot be passive or inattentive and must attempt to work through the labyrinth of conflictual meanings, using them as subject-matter for further critical engagement and development, and thereby becoming his ideal student: "Un suffisant lecteur descouvre souvant és escrits d'autruy des perfections autres que celles que l'autheur y a mises et apperceües, et y preste des sens et des visages plus riches" (I, xxiv, 127). The *Essais*' heterogeneous structure produces diverse meanings that increase the reader's participatory role by demanding engaged readings. Montaigne undermines authorial tyranny and provides readers an enhanced role in the discursive contract between text and audience. This quality, characteristic of many modernist and postmodernist texts, has as well determined many varieties of reader-response criticism.[45] Nietzsche was such a *suffisant lecteur*; he appropriated the problematics generated by Montaigne concerning conflictual engagement of the past and redeveloped them in an overtly more radical enterprise. He picked up on Montaigne's suggestion by enhancing the *Essais* with new and enriched dimensions ("des sens et des visages plus riches").

Montaigne first charges "coustume" with negative connotations, slowly strips them away, then restores to it a positive sense. Thus the "warring forces of signification" that Montaigne arranges make unequivocal domination of one term over the other problematic.[46] The movement of Montaigne's text resembles the subject he treats: an innovative "modern" writer who is eventually absorbed into the official literary canon. Is he still a "dangerous writer in need of censorship" in the nineteenth century as he was in the several preceding centuries? In opposing innovation and custom, Montaigne develops textual incompatibilities that circulate in the realm of the undecidable. He finds his way out of the circle through paradox and irony, whereas Nietzsche does so through apocalyptic vision. Montaigne refuses to disturb the laws and structures, which bind society together, through innovative change which could potentially endanger society's coherence. He forbids critical history to be practiced on the political body and rejects dissolution of the latter for the sake of the former's desire to modify. Yet Montaigne's reasoning and his signifying structures are eclectic and innovative. He creates a new genre by being totally himself and by releasing for the first time a radically divided consciousness into the literary canon. Although outwardly valorizing the immutable institutions ("les constitutions et observances publiques et immobiles") he pursues the instability of a private fancy ("l'instabilité d'une privée fantasie"). Thus, after conforming to "observation et obeissance," he concludes equivocally and begins to recharge innovation with positive value: "C'est ce dequoy Plutarque loüe Philopaemen, qu'estant né pour commander, il sçavoit non seulement commander selon les loix, mais aux lois mesme, quand la necessité publique le requeroit" (I, xxiii, 123). In considering the relationship of the historical and unhistorical, Montaigne modulates and produces the problematic of modernity and history. The writer is free yet chained, as Nietzsche puts it: "es ist nicht möglich, sich ganz von dieser Kette zu lösen" (I, 230). More than a period code or a paradigm, modernism in Montaigne and Nietzsche is an impulse that carries the seed of its own upheaval in order to create the possibility for anticlassical *scriptible* interaction.

Nietzsche encourages yet discourages the effort of creating one's own private space at the expense of the customary attitude toward the past: "Es ist ein Versuch, sich gleichsam *a posteriori* eine Vergangenheit zu geben, aus der man stammen möchte, im Gegensatz zu der, aus der man stammt" (I, 230). The attempt is dangerous, but in the battle of decision-making the struggling ones or fighters ("die Kämpfenden") can find remarkable consolation ("merkwürdigen Trost"). Montaigne's and Nietzsche's reception of historical models demonstrates another aspect of Jauss's "horizon-of-experience." Both writers constantly mediated between their selves, their own cultural moments, and their respective cultural traditions. They used what they need of history, discarded the rest, and weaved what remained into their personal visions. Nietzsche maintained that a culture must at times forget its past in order not to repeat the same mistakes. Montaigne's use of the past was more systematic than Nietzsche's. Although he moved into the unhistorical, which allowed him a personalized discourse, he did not fully adopt Nietzsche's solutions of forgetting and producing anew in order to heal cultural decadence. He attempted to bolster his text with the comfort of cherished writers and, while doing so, emptied it of reassuring coherence by demonstrating the disturbing inconsistencies of thought, language, culture, and civilization. His answer to what he saw as the cultural decline of his time was to demand of his readers to engage themselves in greater individual effort in face of the incongruities of human existence. By offering problematic formulations of a modernist vision, and equivocal responses to the questions it raises, Montaigne produced newness ("nouvelletez") while not explicitly admitting that he did so. The flux he set up in the various polarities in his text is of course a characterization of only one aspect of a modernist literary impulse; it is central to his relationship with Nietzsche, who used the *Essais* not so much to reflect his own concerns, as seen with other writers, but audaciously, in order to radically redevelop issues as prepared by Montaigne.

Both writers developed important pronouncements on modernism and history in the context of education. This perspective provides several other intertextual correlations between their work. Nietzsche considered an educated person to be one who can make cultural decisions, using his or her learned information in a productive way. Yet this educated individual can also be very historically uneducated: "es kann einer sehr gebildet und doch historisch gar nicht gebildet sein" (I, 232). If knowledge is not properly digested, one is overfilled and sluggish, may perish of indigestion ("dass eine solche Bildung nicht an Unverdaulichkeit zugrunde gehe" — I, 232), and become a walking encyclopedia, unable to transfer what is needed for a healthy individual or cultural life. Montaigne used the digestive metaphor, yet in his case the over-eater is not just overfilled with history, but regurgitates it and is left empty ("C'est tesmoinage de crudité et indigestion que de regorger la viande comme on l'a avallée"). In both cases, inner being must be developed through a dynamic interchange with culture. For Nietzsche it is the will to power that must effect this change. Montaigne was less aggressive yet no less tenacious and effective in his quest for a fruitful dialog with historical culture. The "unhistorical" use of the "historical" produces a circular, self-destructive yet self-generating process, continuing the life of the past while enlarging its existence through the development of the self in the present.

For Nietzsche, inner being ("unser Inneres") must be strong enough to develop influential models into personal response; a culture is weakened when it absorbs too much of its history: "der moderne Mensch leidet an einer geschwächten Personlichkeit" (I, 236). Too much non-subjectivity turns modern citizens into Montaigne's laughable pedants ("les lourdes testes"). Nietzsche complains about the mechanized attitudes of his intellectual contemporaries: "Sind das noch Menschen, fragt man sich dann, oder vielleicht nur Denk/, Schreib/, und Redemachinen" (I, 240)? Both writers berate dogmatic academics and call for the strong expansive personality to overcome the "kalten Dämon der Erkenntnis" (I, 244): "Qu'il cele tout ce dequoy il a esté secouru, et ne produise que ce qu'il en a faict" (I, xxvi, 152). Both go beyond the confines of the educational context and extend their positions to society in general. In Montaigne's school of life ("cette eschole du commerce des hommes"), it is the heroic individual, strong enough to absorb the past and regenerate its power through wisdom, who is to be admired: "Comme il n'affiert qu'aux grands poetes d'user les licences de l'art, aussi n'est-il supportable qu'aux grandes ames et illustres de se privilegier au dessus de la coustume" (I, xxvi 154). The most responsible deployment of monumental history makes possible the heroic expansion of the soul, transcends the paralyzing historical constraints of one's age and develops a mature understanding of ourselves through our past.

The immediate engagement of existential experience is what Montaigne recommends over the school of historical knowledge: "Au nostre, un cabinet, un jardin, la table et le lit, la solitude, la compaignie, le matin et le vespre, toutes heures luy seront unes, toutes places luy seront estude" (I, xxvi, 164). Nietzsche counsels his student to follow nature; he should pursue his course of studies in "die einzige Werkstätte der einzigen Meisterin Natur" (I, 278). Montaigne is known for his adherence to the natural in order to preserve intellectual, physical and moral health. Both writers propose to follow *nature* as the way out of what they see as the political strife and pedagogical nonsense of their times. Both are seeking a way out of this cultural decadence by proposing revisions. Yet the status of this *natural* is ironic since Montaigne and Nietzsche often cultivated a highly stylized, baroque, or manneristic mode in their writing.[47] Their own critical history has produced discursive structures that are less coherent and stable than more traditional academic argumentative procedures would allow.

In order to remedy the historical impasse in which culture is trapped, the patient must drink a natural remedy to regain health. Nietzsche's invocation of a hygienic aesthetic, a "*Gesundheitslehre des Lebens*" (I, 282), needed to provoke his student to forget and create his own new and improved culture ("der Begriff der Kultur als einer neuen und verbesserten Physis" — I, 285), is an affirmation of innovation, yet also a gesture needed for survival. It is a position shared by Montaigne, who, on the other hand, derides medical cures in "De la ressemblance des enfans aux peres." This is Montaigne's and Nietzsche's paradoxical practicality in the service of radical institutional revision. In the face of cultural crisis, both attempted to regenerate new life into the disorganized sensibilities of their contemporaries through individual potentiality. In accordance with the Delphic teaching, the new heroic student "muss das Chaos in sich organisieren, dadurch, dass er sich auf seine echten Bedurfnisse zurückbesinnt" (I, 284). In the advancement of authentic culture, the student must organize the chaos of the historical and produce culture in harmony with life. Although Nietzsche did not entirely depend on the *Essais* for his ideas, he developed similar concepts in a dynamic way and put his theory of the creative use of history into practice. In "Vom Nutzen und Nachteil," he maintains that when society consists of non-reflective historical learning, it threatens its own existence and will perish unless it brings itself closer to forming a balance of self-developed culture and dynamic historical understanding. Yet the attempt to pursue such an individualistic path deviates dangerously from customary practice. Both Montaigne and Nietzsche remain cognizant of this paradox throughout their arguments and propose that *natural* inclinations should be strengthened by learning and not dominated by it: "Les inclinations naturelles s'aident et fortifient par institution; mais elles ne changent gueire et surmontent" (III, 2, 810). Yet the beneficial *natural* as opposed to the harmful *cultured* is continually reversed and puts binary opposition into conflictual play.

Montaigne's writing project thus revolves around the opposition of historical conformity and contemporary individualism. This reciprocal relationship is one central quality of what can be called his particular development of a modernist textuality. It is an original attitude in the sense of Eliot's concept of the active relationship between "the old and the new." Montaigne is less interested in antiquarian or monumental historical appropriation in and of itself and does not valorize the critical attitude toward history over the other two. He is however concerned with the relationship between the lives and writings of past writers and how their lessons, not only epistemological but also ontological, can be developed into new configurations by subsequent writers. Montaigne's mediation between the age of antiquity and his own demonstrates this cultural conservatism. He strives to preserve custom and tradition in order to counteract the negative effects of "nouvelletez," which he claims to reject, not only in its political and religious manifestations, but in any of its forms: "quelque visage qu'elle porte" (I, xxiii, 119). Yet Montaigne's conservatism was ritualistic: he produced the outward activities necessary for political and religious conformity and well-being (he was a privileged landowner, successful politician, and regular churchgoer), yet maintained his inner freedom by producing the open text which, as seen in the variegated receptions of Chapter One, escapes interpretive finalization and defers dogmatic and reductive conclusion. De Man refers to this aspect of Montaigne's "modernism": "l'avenir, cela va sans dire, demeure toujours ouvert; aucune conclusion n'est définitive et la contradiction est loi de l'esprit."[48] Montaigne thus proposed the use of history yet refused to let historical finality be imposed on his text. He attempted both to continue and to transcend history. His reactivation of cultural models, and his concomitant ability to extend his own formulations indefinitely through new undulating and diverse readings of the *Essais*, comprise his paradoxical "nouvelletez." His incessant undertakings exceed each subsequent attempt at delimiting their radical instability in one systematizing interpretation after another. The configuration of a normative Montaigne is difficult to achieve. The *Essais* create new values in their revaluation of historical predecessors in the context of their author's self-exploration. They are thus the new beginning for a series of receptions on the nature of the relationship between historical continuity and the pursuit of the new. In Montaigne's simultaneous pursuit of an antiquarian, monumental, and critical positioning of his writing project, the *Essais* become an important text in the Western canon that explicitly exposes this modernist conflict in process — the continual reshaping of the past in original formulations, the very process of which undermines its own integrity (L. *integritas*, "completeness").

Montaigne's description of the relationship between history and modernity ("nouvelletez") produces the essence of a modernist predicament as delineated by Nietzsche in "Vom Nutzen und Nachteil." Yet Montaigne and Nietzsche approach the problem from opposite ends: the former desiring the repetition of the monumental past and the putative avoidance of newness, the latter seeking to avoid repetition in the production of modernity. Both writers ultimately produce the opposite term in the dual configuration that they are explicitly seeking to overcome. In the attitudes of both, the predicament is left in hermeneutic suspension. The relationship of repetition and originality is posited in the work of both writers *as a problematic* and their respective "solutions" remain necessarily ambivalent. Their belief in speculative intelligence provokes them to observe a kaleidoscope of contradictory positions and maintain an acceptance of conflictual movement in their texts. What Montaigne and Nietzsche share is a dynamic and adventurous attitude toward critical thinking. They produce a fruitful tension in their work where the resolution of metaphysical certainty is rarely permanent.

In Montaigne's development of the problematic, the terms are "sçavoir" vs. its "usage;" Nietzsche pits "die Wissenden" against the "die Könnenden." In both cases, the active refiguration of historical material is set against its stagnant accumulation. This correlation in their discussions of the issues, beyond Nietzsche's dispersed quotations on Montaigne and his admiration of the essayist's skepticism, originality, and individualism, is the most fundamental aspect of Nietzsche's adaptation of elements from the *Essais*: it is also an appropriation that has important implications for literary modernism. What Nietzsche fears as the chaos that the abuse of historical education has instigated ("Das rasend-unbedachte Zersplittern und Zerfasern aller Fundamente, ihre Auflösung in ein immer fliessendes und zerfliessendes Werden, das unermüdliche Zerspinnen und Historisieren alles Gewordenen durch den modernen Menschen" — I, 267) echoes Montaigne's similar attack on the chaos that thoughtless learning and education produce:

> Or qui n'entre en deffiance des sciences, et n'est en doubte s'il s'en peut tirer quelque solide fruict au besoin de la vie, à considerer l'usage que nous en avons: "*nihil sanantibus litteris*?" Qui a pris de l'entendement en la logique? ou sont ses belles promesses? "*Nec ad melius vivendum nec ad commodius disserendum.*" Voit-on plus de barbouillage au caquet des harengeres qu'aux disputes publiques des hommes de cette profession? (III, viii, 926)

What Nietzsche worries about as "Jene erschreckende Verknöcherung der Zeit" (I, 268), Montaigne likewise berates as the stagnancy that historical education has imposed on his age and his country: "En mon pays, et de mon temps, la doctrine amande assez les bourses, rarement les ames. Si elle les rencontre mousses, elle les aggrave et suffoque, masse crue et indigeste; si desliées, elle les purifie volontiers, clarifie et subtilise jusques à l'exinanition" (III, viii, 927). Either ossification ("Verknöcherung" in Nietzsche's terms) or inanition ("exinanition" in Montaigne's) are the results of a dogmatic adherence to historical education, which produce, in both writers' eyes, attitudes detrimental to the spontaneous vitality needed for the survival of their respective cultures.

Both the prepositional qualifier in Nietzsche's title "Vom Nutzen und Nachteil der Historie *für das Leben*" and Montaigne's belief that from learning should be extracted a lesson applicable to "la vie" direct both writers' reflections on the opposition of past and present. Yet the antitheses that both establish are never absolute: Nietzsche qualifies his claim for the unhistorical by maintaining that life must be experienced unhistorically, yet only *to a certain degree* ("bis zu einem bestimmten Grade," I, 214) and Montaigne, as has been demonstrated, wishes to preserve history, yet only dynamically reformulated. The conjunction of incompatible entities — in de Man's terms, history and modernity — is an irresolvable paradox since "modernity discovers itself to be a generative power that not only engenders history but is part of a generative scheme that extends back into the past."[49] Both Nietzsche and Montaigne define the relationship between history and the modernist impulse as ultimately unresolvable. As Montaigne claims, there are no objective facts, only interpretations: "Il y a plus affaire à interpreter les interpretations qu'à interpreter les choses" (III, xiii, 1069). Nietzsche adheres to the attitude that it is impossible to understand a *Welt an sich*: "Gegen den Positivismus, welcher bei den Phänomenen stehn bleibt 'es gibt nur Tatsachen' würde ich sagen: nein, gerade Tatsachen gibt es nicht, nur *Interpretationen*. Wir können kein Faktum 'an sich' feststellen" ("Aus dem Nachlass der Achtzigerjahre," III, 903). Both writers direct their readers to cautiously evaluate the variegated issues presented in their writings in order to arrive at a new, yet provisional understanding. The reactivation of the historical in a critical mode should only be taken in this open, interactive sense, and Nietzsche uses Montaigne to insist upon this modernist notion of the certainty of uncertainty. In this way he displays Montaigne's most essential importance for his work: as a purveyor of the provisional nature of truth: "Ja! und Nein! — das geht ihm [the skeptic] wider die Moral; umgekehrt liebt er es, seiner Tugend mit der edlen Enthaltung ein Fest zu machen, etwa indem er mit Montaigne spricht: 'was weiss ich'" ("Jenseits von Gut und Böse," II, 670). Nietzsche uses Montaigne, however indirectly, to develop his metaphysical pursuits, especially in "Vom Nutzen und Nachteil." He goes beyond Montaigne's notions and thus exposes the conflict between their respective positions and the impossibility of the convergence of their thought. Yet this conflict highlights how Nietzsche's reception of the *Essais* projects Montaigne's thought into the modernist landscape.

The contradictory relationship between history and innovation has come to be understood as one of the essential predicaments of literary modernism. The pursuit to resolve this opposition is not necessarily the modernist impulse. It is perhaps the *impossibility* of overcoming this obstacle that is the primary notion shared by Nietzsche and Montaigne, one that plays a role in subsequent writing that explicitly poses itself as a problematic. Montaigne and Nietzsche were writers who thought and wrote not only about themselves but against themselves, struggling with the perhaps unresolvable problem of history and modernity and responding to it with ambivalence in the belief that it is the pursuit of ineluctable truth that is the *raison d'être* of their existence and of their attempts ("essais") toward mobile, anti-dogmatic understanding. This same dynamic played an important role in the work of Pater and Woolf, whose receptions of the *Essais* and of Nietzsche's legacy helped to direct of their thought. Yet there is a fundamental difference between Nietzsche's and Montaigne's respective conceptions of the predicament posed by the opposition of history and modernity. Nietzsche ends "Vom Nutzen und Nachteil" with an affirmation of the possibility of a new and revitalized culture. He believed that German civilization had the ability to organize the chaos of historical learning appropriated from other cultures into a new and healthy beginning:

> Dies ist ein Gleichnis für jeden einzelnen von uns: er muss das Chaos in sich organisieren, dadurch, dass er sich auf seine echten Bedürfnisse zurückbesinnt. Seine Ehrlichkeit, sein tüchtiger und wahrhaftiger Charakter muss sich irgendwann einmal dagegen sträuben, dass immer nur nachgesprochen, nachgelernt, nachgeahmt werde; er beginnt dann zu begreifen, dass Kultur noch etwas andres sein kann als *Dekoration des Lebens*. (I, 284-285)

Nietzsche's modernist attitude is the belief in the necessity, and the possibility, of cultural renewal through the superior effort of extraordinary individuals. It is this aspect of his thought that influenced writers of the following generation. Nietzsche's valorization of the terms "Neuheit" and "Neurung" — newness and innovation — was an attempt to create new forms of cultural production to offset the historicist attitude and to radically question accepted orthodoxies. In this sense he was important to the "emerging modernist sensibility in literature."[50] Nietzsche sought to break with the past, or at least with existing ways of thinking about the past, in order to create new cultural possibilities. Yet his approach in "Vom Nutzen und Nachteil," a central, almost programmatic text for much of the literature of the modernist period, is constantly paradoxical and radical in its shifting of terms and ideas. Montaigne is present through Nietzsche's dynamic reception of the *Essais* and his transformation and modification of their implications function within his own work.

In this context, Nietzsche's radically aggressive approach to the predicament of history and modernity goes beyond Montaigne's more serene mission of personal development and cultural integrity. Montaigne is equivocal concerning the opposition of history and modernity, yet he ultimately achieves a more harmonious acceptance of the conflict embodied in his overall project of submitting all inquiries to the pursuit of self-expression and personal understanding. Here exist the incompatibilities between the work of Montaigne and Nietzsche. Montaigne proposes no fixed agenda for the progress of culture. He would rather maintain the cultural paradigm as it is, however imperfect, in order to avoid political and social upheaval and new attitudes that may produce more harm than is already present:

> Mais le meilleur pretexte de nouvelleté est tres-dangereux: "*adeo nihil motum ex antiquo probabile est.*" Si me semble-il, à le dire franchement, qu'il y a grand amour de soi et presomption, d'estimer ses opinions jusque-là que, pour les establir, il faille renverser une paix publique ... . Est ce pas mal mesnagé, d'avancer tant de vices certains et cognus, pour combattre des erreurs contestées et debatables? (I, xxiii, 120)

This discussion is in a political context, yet it helps to demonstrate Montaigne's pragmatic approach to change and innovation. He explicitly promotes historical continuity to help individuals to live better and to make clear judgments in their lives: "Il ne fut jamais tant d'historiens. Bon est-il tousjours et utile de les ouyr, car il nous fournissent tout plain de belles instructions et louables du magasin de leur memoire; grande partie, certes, au secours de la vie" (III, viii, 931). Montaigne's greatest paradox is that he often conforms to, yet often deviates from, what he proposes.

Nietzsche offers no criticism of Montaigne as he does with most of the other writers dealt with in his work, whom he alternately praises and blames. The range of contradictions in his writing, in their radically aggressive problematization of issues, goes beyond Montaigne's humanistic paradoxes and putative striving for dynamic harmony in his work. Montaigne's conclusory acceptance of himself in "De l'experience": "les plus belles vies sont celles qui se rangent au modelle commun et humain avec ordre, mais sans miracle et sans extravagance" (III, xiii, 1116) is far from Nietzsche's own self-presentation in *Ecce Homo,* with its self-congratulatory and hysterical tone: "Wo ich nicht mehr mit Worten, sondern mit Blitzen rede" (II, 1116). Nietzsche's more tragic vision of cultural crisis and aggressive search for new beginnings exceeds Montaigne's acceptance of humanity's imperfections and the skeptical ability to live with such knowledge. Yet Montaigne offered Nietzsche a useful model for the development of his own essayistic exploration of the striving for self-expression in the face of historical culture, as seen in "Vom Nutzen und Nachteil." Nietzsche appropriates freely from Montaigne, and his use of the *Essais* has important implications for the twentieth century. Both attack "modern" man as corrupt and decadent and both seek the cure in the embrace of an "authentic" individual consciousness. For Montaigne, the saving grace is to become himself, for Nietzsche, to transcend himself. Both, in their distrust of logical analysis, reason, and scholarly dogmatism, maintain that the individual can only realize his or her potential by rejecting the moribund imitation of conventional values. Individuals vitally aware of their own personalities will create new values based on active learning and the production of vital self-awareness. They will avoid being passive links of the historical chain and embody the superhistorical creator who lives and writes for the moment, transcends the burden of the past, and produces an eternal superiority. Even in Montaigne's numerous claims against "nouvelletez," and in his abundant dependence upon the authority of ancient writers, his originality as a writer is to have produced this unique individualism in his own work: "Moi qui m'espie de plus prèz qui ay les yeux incessamment tendus sur moy" (II, xii, 565).

In this restless movement between past and present, between self-assertion and conformity to the exigency of cultural repetition, dynamic constructs that motivate many issues in "Vom Nutzen und Nachteil" and in the *Essais*, another important oppositional relationship is that of *remembering* (adherence to the "Historische") versus *forgetting* (the adventure of the "kritische" enterprise). The act of critical history depends on the ability to forget — to rid oneself of cultural residue and to participate in a fuller and more immediate present. A comparison of these terms uncovers thematic concurrences, topical similarities, and lexical choices that further demonstrate the Montaignean dimensions of Nietzsche's attempts to explain the confrontation of self-cultivation with historical learning. Nietzsche uses the example of a grazing herd of animals who enjoy the immediacy of the present moment, oblivious to any consciousness of the past: "sie weiss nicht, was Gestern, was Heute ist, springt umher, frisst, ruht, verdaut, springt wieder, und so vom Morgen bis zur Nacht und von Tage zu Tage, kurz angebunden mit ihrer Lust und Unlust, nämlich an den Pflock des Augenblicks, und deshalb weder schwermütig noch überdrüssig" (I, 211). Humans, unlike animals, are condemned to live with the memory of past events. Even when humans attempt to live in the present, they inevitably remember ("ich erinnere mich" — I, 211) and are forced to live with the burden of the past ("die grosse und immer grössere Last des Vergangenen" — I, 212), forever wishing for the bliss of the elusive presentness enjoyed by the animals ("in überseliger Blindheit" — I, 212). In "Vom Nutzen und Nachteil," the impossibility of living in an eternal immediacy of experience as do animals must be counteracted by the efforts of creative individuals to forget: "zu allem Handeln gehört vergessen" (I, 213). Forgetting is what Nietzsche sees as the key for the production of innovative configurations of creative life: "das Fundament liegt auf dem überhaupt erst etwas Rechtes, Gesundes und Grosses, etwas wahrhaft Menschliches wachsen kann" (I, 215). In order not to be overwhelmed and rendered creatively impotent by what is foreign and what is past ("Überschwemmung durch das

Fremde und Vergangne" — I, 284), Nietzsche exhorts his contemporaries to assimilate and subordinate historical knowledge to their genuine individual needs ("seine echten Bedürfnisse" — I, 284), and thereby create a true culture ("der *wahren* Bildung sein muss" — I, 285). Bearing in mind Nietzsche's proclaimed wariness of "truth," such absolute adjectival qualifiers as "echten" and "wahren" ("genuine," "true," "pure," "authentic") make Nietzsche's claims suspect. Even the most essential points of his argument are rendered uncertain by virtue of the instability of his chosen terms. It is an instability that he established elsewhere in his work and now uses against himself, knowingly or unknowingly. He "forgets" his own textual history, in the form of what he previously wrote ("Über Wahrheit," written in 1873 — "Vom Nutzen," in 1874) thereby allowing himself to say something new, which, however, is a paradoxical utterance exposing his ultimate skepticism even as he is passionately engaged in articulating a philosophical position.

Montaigne also enlists the example of animals in his attempt to subordinate the multiplicity of cultural material necessary for the sovereignty of his project of self-expression. He likewise valorizes forgetting as one of the keys to the integrity of one's project of individual cultivation and creativity. In the "Apologie," he uses examples of animals' many admirable qualities to attack human vanity and to show how all of our philosophy, history, and reason has rendered us inferior to them in many ways. His numerous examples are often hyperbolic and even surpass Nietzsche in humoristic exaggeration. Yet as his strategies shift from demonstrating the excessive claims of human superiority over animals to a discussion of the limits of human knowledge, he uses animals one final time and offers his own remedy for a more authentic mode of living: "Voulez-vous un homme sain, le voulez-vous reglé et en forme et seure posture? affublez le de tenebres, d'oisiveté, et de pesanteur. Il nous faut abestir pour nous assagir, et nous esblouir pour nous guider" (II, xii, 492). The similar choice of lexicon employed by Nietzsche and Montaigne to describe their attitudes toward self-cultivation is striking. In order for one to be healthy ("Gesundheit" and "sain et en forme"), one must achieve the superior historical "blindness" of animals ("Blindheit" and "esblouir"), and thereby obliterate the harmful effects of an overly developed dependence on knowledge and historical understanding. As with Nietzsche, however, Montaigne's inability to find his convincing "assiete" betrays his claim by proposing the very possibility of achieving a true stability ("seure posture"). Even as Nietzsche and Montaigne propose solutions, the terms with which they do so, having been problematized elsewhere in their work, betray the essayistic quality of their propositions. In their attempts to say something unique about what is truly good, they produce triumphant losses since they make great claims but fail to do so unequivocally. They are trapped by their own metaphors and subvert their own positions even as they are victorious in producing an enhanced understanding of the difficulty involved in developing a formula for individual creativity.

Both the "Apologie" and "Vom Nutzen und Nachteil" function on at least one level as indictments of human presumption. Montaigne slowly dismantles all human claims to superiority based on knowledge and arrives at his celebrated pyrrhonist suspension of judgment: "que sçay-je?" He forgets absolutes, condemns reason, and accepts his ignorance as the best position from which to confront all philosophical discussions whose diverse approaches have yet to produce stable and certain knowledge of the human experience. In a handwritten addition to "De l'institution des enfans," Montaigne finally abnegates all understanding and claims to have achieved a state of bestial, yet informed quietude: "Nous ne sommes, croy-je, scavantes de la science presente, non de la passée, aussi peu que de la future" (I, xxvi, 136). Nietzsche also derides all systematic exclusionist approaches at understanding: neither the historical, unhistorical, or critical, nor the kinds of philosophical consciousness prevalent in Germany at the time (variations of the Hegelian, Darwinian, and Hartmannian) have provided adequate answers to the best way in which individuals should learn, think, and write.[51] Yet neither do Nietzsche and Montaigne escape the problem of finding a certain understanding of the problems with which they are dealing. Nietzsche's terminology to describe historical processes, like Montaigne's permutating opposition of custom and innovation, fails to achieve stable conceptualization. Montaigne's presence in "Vom Nutzen und Nachteil," though not explicit, can thus help us to better understand a text that is extremely "divers et ondoyant," and one that continues to pose interpretive difficulties.

In Montaigne's pyrrhonist strategy in the "Apologie," he condemns his own discourse, since doubt, as embodied in his refusal of affirmation, is itself an affirmation. In "Vom Nutzen und Nachteil," Nietzsche also practices a form of suspension of judgment (Montaigne's *epoché*) by never stating exactly what his system of a "history in the service of life" would be, only what it should not be. If, as he claims, all acting requires forgetting ("zu allem Handeln gehört vergessen"), then he has deployed this premise in his own textual practice by forgetting to tell us what he initially wished to achieve in the essay: the development of a paradigm for the amelioration of the particular historical predicament in which he found himself. As Montaigne does not escape his own circular paradox in the "Apologie" in his proposition of a pyrrhonist solution which by definition can only be a non-solution, so Nietzsche attempts to resolve the problematic paradoxically since he sees no way out of the circle. He proposes as his "solution" for an "abusive" attitude toward history, history. Yet it is the "Unhistorische," the ability to forget, and the "Überhistorische," the search for a stabilizing mode of creativity, that are the best antidotes for the moribund "Historische." This homeopathic remedy has its dangers: just as one suffers from the dangers of the historical, one will also have to suffer from its antidote, the unhistorical, and make heroic efforts toward a new beginning. As Nietzsche poses as a cultural doctor in "Vom Nutzen und Nachteil," (there is medical terminology used throughout: "health," "malady," "remedy") it appears that he allows the text's usefulness to rely on his multiple diagnoses rather than on any specific prescriptions or cures. He nevertheless claims that the open and indeterminate quality of his text will be understood by the "suffisant lecteur" and developed in a manner that answers to their personal needs: "Von diesen *Hoffenden* weiss ich, dass sie alle diese Allgemeinheiten aus der Nähe verstehn und mit ihrer eigensten Erfahrung in eine persönlich gemeinte Lehre sich übersetzen werden" (I, 283 — emphasis added). Like Montaigne, he calls for his attentive readers ("diesen Hoffenden") to continue reproducing his suggestive arguments in quest of their own self-understanding. This gesture also allows him to abdicate responsibility for the closure of his arguments.

The concept of the dualistic remedy of unhistorical and superhistorical helps to expose an essential relation between Nietzsche and Montaigne. Nietzsche's final definitions of the unhistorical: "die Kunst und Kraft *vergessen* zu können und sich in einen begrenzten *Horizont* einzuschliessen" and the superhistorical: "die Mächte, die den Blick von dem Werden ablenken, hin zu dem, was dem Dasein den Charakter des Ewigen und Gleichbedeutenden gibt, zu *Kunst* und *Religionen*" (I, 282) represent one polaristic construct toward which Montaigne's writing project often gravitates. In numerous instances in the *Essais*, Montaigne complains about his poor memory: "Il n'est homme à qui il siese si mal de ... parler de memoire. Car je n'en reconnoy quasi trasse en moy, et ne pense qu'il y en ay ... une autre si monstrueuse en defaillance" (I, ix, 34). Montaigne claims that he constantly forgets things, admits that he loses track of what he read and where he read it, often to the extent that he develops others' writings as if they were his own. This "forgetting," whether putative or actual, is what allows him to generate his own unique textuality. In order to overcome the accumulation of the historical knowledge amassed in his book, he must "forget" it in order to structure his own productivity: "à faute de memoire naturelle j'en forge de papier et ... je l'escris" (III, xiii, 1092). Montaigne's impulse toward the unhistorical, his forgetting, is what allows him to produce superhistorical configurations — those of understanding himself and of creating the "stability" of his writing, which, however provisionally, orders his existence:

> Autant que je m'en rapporte à elle [memory], je me mets hors de moy, jusques à essaier ma contenance; et me suis veu quelque jour en peine de celer la servitude en laquelle j'estois entravé, là où mon dessein est de representer en parlant une profonde nonchalance et des mouvemens fortuites et impremeditez, comme naissans des occasions presentes. (III, ix, 963)

Too much memory stifles his efforts at self-expression, puts him outside of his inner essentiality. As he forgets, he can live and express himself in the vital present of his writing project, which has no precedent ("impremeditez") and is a spontaneous production of "nouvelletez." It is Montaigne's ability to mediate between the unhistorical and the superhistorical that helps him to "organize the chaos" of his learning and thinking, yet in a manner that allows him to let his lived experience rule over his knowledge ("soll nun das Leben über das Erkennen herrschen" — I, 282). What Nietzsche insists on near the end of "Vom Nutzen und Nachteil" as this ability to produce a personal doctrine of historical understanding ("eine persönlich gemeinte Lehre"), is very much a mode of textual production as first carried out by Montaigne in the *Essais*.

In response to the academic presumption of his age, Nietzsche's categories are so diverse (for even as he proposes the unhistorical and the superhistorical as remedies, he soon returns to the monumental, antiquarian, and critical as the best methods for engaging history) that one cannot say he has concluded the essay, rather, he has left it in suspension to be further developed by his true readership, the "hopeful ones" ("diesen Hoffenden"). Nietzsche maintains that all of his propositions may be teeming with important implications for the study of history ("gefüllt sind" — I, 283) yet that they also may be totally devoid of value ("die wohl auch leer sein können" — I, 283). His calling into question the worthiness of his own discourse renders his efforts at publicizing his personal feelings devoid of any definitive value: "Ich habe mich bestrebt, eine Empfindung zu schildern, die mich oft genug gequält hat; ich räche mich an ihr, indem ich sie der Öffentlichkeit preisgebe" (I, 209). There is no normative system of historical education that Nietzsche can adequately develop as an alternative; for even as he searches for a legitimate mode of historical apprehension toward the amelioration of the sickness of German culture, his categories (though they admirably draw attention to important intellectual and social problems), reach the point of undecideability. Nietzsche's response to the impasse is to revert to the "Historische" by citing the timeless wisdom of the Delphic Oracle:

> Und wie kommen wir zu jenem Ziele? werdet ihr fragen. Der delphische Gott ruft euch, gleich am Anfange einer Wanderung nach jenem Ziele, seinen Spruch entgegen: "Erkenne dich selbst." Es ist ein schwerer Spruch: denn jener Gott "verbirgt nicht und verkündet nicht, sondern zeigt nur hin", wie Heraklit gesagt hat. Worauf weist er euch hin? (I, 284)

Nietzsche's Heraclitean qualification of the oracle ("sondern zeigt nur hin") points to his belief in the suggestive quality of his arguments as well as to the participatory engagement needed to understand them. He backs out of the issues, throwing the ultimate responsibility for their conclusion onto the reader.

What Montaigne sees in his examination of the Delphic Oracle, which he also offers as a remedy for the sickness of his historical moment ("un temps malade comme cettuy-cy" — III, ix, 993) is also paradoxical:

> C'estoit un commandement paradoxe que nous fasoit anciennement ce Dieu à Delphes: Regardez dans vous, reconnoissez-vous, tenez-vous à vous ... c'est toujours vanité pour toi, il n'en est une seule si vuide et necessiteuse que toy ... tu es le scrutateur sans connoissance. (III, ix, 1001)

More self-knowledge as proposed by the oracle leads only to greater futility in understanding since humankind is basically devoid of any positive qualities except the realization of the very emptiness that self-knowledge brings about. Nietzsche's discourse thus empties itself out in "Vom Nutzen und Nachteil" (it is both "gefüllt" and "leer") as he becomes the investigator without ultimate knowledge (Montaigne's "scrutateur sans connoissance"). The more he probes and develops his terms, the further he moves away from the "instruction of the age" that he had initially hoped to achieve. He is finally forced to equivocate on his concluding remarks and thus fails to firm up his position. In Nietzsche's own vanity of looking into himself and exploring his personal attitudes on the value and function of historical knowledge ("dass ich mich mit der Naturbeschreibung meiner Empfindung hervorwage–" I, 210), he finds that his discourse, as Montaigne warned in "De la vanité," is "vuide et *necessiteuse*." It is "needy" in the sense that, even today, intense critical engagement is required to understand its importance for our own time.[52]

How then does Nietzsche, even if he can't find a way out of the paradox, end the essay? He does so, further problematizing his previous claims, by reverting to the categories of the monumental and the antiquarian as solutions. His final paragraph turns to the example of ancient Greece, which he considers to have dealt with the same problematic of how not to perish through too much dependence on the "Historische." Nietzsche fills the void created by "kritische" inquiry with the monumental example of the Greeks' success at subordinating other cultures and traditions to their own needs. He seemingly "forgets" his previous categories and relies on a return to a Hellenic notion of culture as an answer to the problems of his own. The Greeks' ability to organize the chaos ("das Chaos zu organisieren") is what Nietzsche himself fails to achieve in "Vom Nutzen und Nachteil," as seen in his continual evaluation and revaluation of concepts, which always circle back on themselves in contradiction. What the strong personality must do is to overcome historical models and actively reproduce them in accord with the dynamically creative self: "Seine Ehrlichkeit, sein tüchtiger und wahrhaftiger Charakter muss sich irgendwann einmal dagegen sträuben" (I, 285). Is this not what Nietzsche so admired in Montaigne? It is his honesty ("Erlichkeit" — I, 296) and integral self-sufficiency ("friedliches Für-sich-Sein und Ausatmen" — I, 378) to which Nietzsche turns to find his way out of the argument. Montaigne thus serves as a philosophical bridge over which Nietzsche finds the way back to ancient greatness.

However, Nietzsche does not use Montaigne directly in "Vom Nutzen und Nachteil," perhaps because Montaigne's success in producing the *Essais* as he overcame the "burden of the past" bothered Nietzsche, since the latter could not achieve what Montaigne had first developed: a self-sufficient, autonomous, yet integrated personality. It is possible that Nietzsche, in his own attempts to reproduce Montaigne's "Muthwillen im Geiste" ("wantonness," mischievousness," "sportiveness") does so in the *body* of his text ("wer weiss? vielleicht auch im *Leibe*") and therefore must intentionally "forget" him in order to produce his own attempt at the explanation of the value and function of the past. One could object that Montaigne plays no role whatsoever in Nietzsche's work since he is almost always explicitly absent from the text. On the other hand, Nietzsche's paradoxical essaying of issues important to Montaigne, the concurrence of thematic concerns, topical similarities (education, habit, innovation, presumption, self-knowledge), and lexical choice point again and again to the Montaignean dimensions of Nietzsche's efforts in explaining the confrontation of self-cultivation and historical knowledge. Nietzsche far exceeds Montaigne's hesitant modernism, yet his reception of the *Essais* brings into greater prominence Montaigne's importance to contemporary discussions of philosophy, history, and literature.

Nietzsche's contradictory reception of Montaigne, on the one hand admiring his equanimity, calmness, and tolerance, on the other his mischievousness, wantonness, and playful excess, exposes the schismatic identity of Montaigne's modernity as well as of Nietzche's own work. For it is here in this realm of irreconcilable opposites that we can perhaps begin to see the significance of Nietzsche's Montaigne. Nietzsche's "modernism," his perpetual pursuit of new values, is perhaps the essence of a postmodern problematic — that of attempting to overcome one's own past, present, and future. The postmodern is perhaps the modern in a perpetual *kritische* mode, and by extension the postmodern is thus the failure of the modern — in Nietzsche's work it manifests an "anti-totalizing, affirmative, melancholic perspective, challenging the totalizing excelsior intimacy of modernity."[53] Nietzsche's position in the relatively early essay "Vom Nutzen und Nachteil" changed through his writing over the years, culminating in *Zarathrustra,* in which he showed how the *kritische* spirit can be used against itself again and again to transform society for the better, an event that will in turn go through the same process, always being caught up in a doubtful repetition of the same.

The two sides of Nietzche's reception of Montaigne, Socratic optimism vs. libertine transgression, are the polaristic Apollonian and Dionysisan impulses that must work together in order to produce a unified, healthy culture. Near the end of *Die Geburt der Tragödie,* Nietzsche berates contemporary German culture for its reified modes of being: "in dem abstrakten Charakter unseres mythenlosen Daseins, in einer zur Ergötzlichkeit herabsgesunkenen Kunst wie in einem vom Begriff geleiteten Leben, hatte sich uns jene gleich unkünstlerische, als am Leben zehrende Natur des sokratischen Optimismus enthüllt " (I, 133). In contrast, he proposes a radically existential, cultural self-transformation, endlessly destructing as it constructs anew, as a child does a sandcastle: "das spielende Aufbauen und Zertrümmern der Individualwelt als den Ausfluss einer Urlust offenbart, in einer ähnlichen Weise, wie wenn von Heraklit dem Dunklen die weltbildende Kraft einem Kinde verglichen wird, das spielend Steine hin und her setz und Sandhaufen aufbaut und wieder einwirft" (I, 133). Montaigne's, Emerson's, and Nietzsche's desire for immediate engagement in the present leads to the postmodern impasse of radical individuality lost in the morass of fragmented, non-integrated social reality, condemned to organize the chaos by seeking some totalizing form (Montaigne's "forme maistresse") that can gather the fragmentary into a coherent context. For Nietzsche goes beyond *Die Geburt der Tragödie* and "Vom

Nutzen und Nachteil," where the unhistorical impulse attempts to forget all and enclose oneself in a limited, subjective horizon, and creates in *Zur Genealogie der Moral* the notion of the "superhistorical" — the desire to achieve some stability of character and immutability of reality. Culture must get beyond mere resistance to the literary, cultural, or historical past, refuse speculation on the future, and escape the limitations of subjective oblivion in the present by making difficult choices. In the second essay of the *Genealogie*, Nietzsche recapitulates the question he never really got around to answering in "Vom Nutzen und Nachteil": how to create memory for the human animal? Seeing the present clearly is not enough; we must also understand our temporality subjectively, look at the self less as a construction of consciousness and more as an ontological subject in order to overcome the obligations of past and future, and choose that which helps us concretely and personally. In White's terms: "Creative forgetting, Nietzsche held, is at the same time creative remembering. For creative forgetting is nothing but a remembering of one's own will, one's own powers and talents. And it is with whole generations as it is with the individual."[54]

Montaigne's and Nietzsche's condition of doubleness and split consciousness motivated them to write throughout their lives on questions they knew to be unanswerable. The existential engagement of these two writers who sought cures, not only physical ones in their own literal travels throughout Europe, but psychic ones in their textual quests for the sickness of dogmatism, vulgar skepticism, ignorance, and cruelty, are models toward the creation of improved societal relations. Neither maintained the illusion of ever being able to find a satisfying epistemological stasis; their innovative modernity was to seek refuge in the obligations of tradition, in which they discovered their own unprecedented identities. Yet the constant reciprocity of their projects does not allow these identities to remain untouched for long; more *kritische* interrogation will inevitably turn against one's own newly produced selfhood. This is perhaps their postmodernism, which is perhaps an antimodernism: the perpetual interrogation of the relationship of tradition and innovation in a seriously playful perspective. The principles of denying the totalizing character of one's own discourse and of refusing the hegemonic embezzlement of individual presence and being, are perhaps two ways in which traditionalists and innovators can begin to work toward some dissonant harmonies.

♦ ♦ ♦

The commentary of Paul de Man has been put into service several times in the interpretation of the relationship of Montaigne and Nietzsche. He has been a highly visible commentator of Nietzsche's work in the past two decades yet almost unknown as a commentator of Montaigne. Yet an examination of his little-known article "Montaigne et la transcendance" helps to gather the issues generated by the oppositional categories of innovation/tradition and remembering/forgetting in a context that helps to demonstrate how Nietzsche's Montaigne continues to have important implications for current literary and critical discussions.

De Man's strategy in "Montaigne et la transcendance" is another example of a Montaignean approach in its radical digressiveness from a proposed topic; it is written under the rubric of its sub-heading "Hugo Friedrich: *Montaigne*." Yet in this eleven-page "review," Friedrich's work is quoted merely twice and referred to only briefly as de Man pursues his own understanding of Montaigne's importance to the opposition of "la transcendence" and "l'immanence pure." De Man examines the status of Montaigne's subjectivism ("le reflet d'une subjectivité absolue," — "Montaigne," 1012) as promoted by Friedrich, yet uses Friedrich's position as a springboard for his own inquiry into the question of Montaigne's status as a writer. De Man is wary of the normative systematizing of Montaigne's work in the manner of Friedrich and strives to examine the issues in an open manner: "on doit toujours se méfier quand on pense pouvoir enfermer dans une formule tranchante" ("Montaigne," 1012). De Man posits that Montaigne's writing is best understood as a dialectical movement between stability, "un équilibre statique" and restless productivity, "réflexions infinies" ("Montaigne," 1012) and sees that the only solution to the opposing of entities in the *Essais* is to accept problematic ambiguity as such. De Man uses the example of the "Apologie" to demonstrate Montaigne's complex encounter of literary, philosophical, religious, and political history as he attempts to develop his own subjective response to the *Essais*. Since the spectre of ancient learning ("l'immense masse de sagesse de nos ancêtres," — "Montaigne," 1014) is teeming with paradox and ambiguity ("fourmille de contradictions et de contresens" — "Montaigne," 1014), de Man sees Montaigne as a protomodernist in his efforts to expose the limits of the rationalist confrontation of absolute understanding. Montaigne's struggle to comprehend immutable truths (whether divine or historical) is an heroic attempt, "un acte dangereux" ("Montaigne," 1015), since he risks the loss of self-identity in carrying out the enterprise. De Man therefore sees Montaigne's undertaking as double and diverse; it is not simply subjectivist, but also a demonstration of the failures of subjectivity: "Montaigne parlant de l'impossibilité de se connaître est en plein dans la transcendance" ("Montaigne," 1017). On the other hand, Montaigne's ability to confront the problem of the impossibility of subjectivity is carried out in a subjective mode of discourse — his writing is both transcendent (overcoming both the past and the difficulty of being true to himself) and immanent (he is truly himself).

De Man considers this mobile status of Montaigne's engagement of the past, and his ability to personally express this activity in his writing, as a dynamic and self-referential modernist force in literature, which "s'y nourrit et s'y revitalise, s'élançant de là vers de nouvelles et incessantes démarches que rien ne soutient, hors de sa propre énergie" ("Montaigne," 1018) — yet he also realizes the danger of constituting a "modernist" Montaigne in the face of the essayist's impulse to maintain the status quo in religion and politics. De Man again pursues a dualist's solution and claims that Montaigne's conservatism is ritualistic, outwardly conforming to his age while ensuring that this ritualistic orthodoxy conforms to his notion of the "exigences de subjectivité" ("Montaigne," 1019). De Man's argument abruptly shifts to a discussion of the paradigm of conformity and subjectivity in the context of the specific political events of Montaigne's time. It is particularly Montaigne's relation to *La Ligue*, the coalition of ultraconservative Catholics most responsible for the persecution of French Protestants that poses a problem for him. Although a moderate Catholic who adhered to a position of tolerance on the question of religious reformation, Montaigne's diatribes against religious and political "nouvelletez" as well as his active role as an advisor and friend of Catherine de Medici and Charles IX (who designed and implemented the massacre of thousands of Protestants on 24 August 1572, in which men, women, and children were butchered in their homes and on the streets), implicate him in the excesses of the political authorities of his time. Montaigne's silence on the Saint Bartholemew's Day Massacre is bothersome; he was so candid on most of the important political events pertinent to his life, yet for some reason decided to remain silent about this one.[55] Montaigne was certainly not responsible, nor even a participant in the atrocities of the massacre, which killed 30,000 Protestants in all during a six-week period, yet his silence on such an important event of his time, which roughly coincides with the inception of his writing of the *Essais*, does call into question his moral complicity. According to eyewitnesses, Charles IX, who had less than a year before named Montaigne a *gentilhomme ordinaire de la chambre du roi* indulged in all of the bloodthirsty excesses of a madman and gleefully shot Protestants with his crossbow from a window of the Louvre and had their naked corpses piled high before him.[56] Montaigne seemed to be able to somehow emotionally distance himself in his writing from such an event.

One can only speculate on the reasons for Montaigne's silence. His religious background was mixed: his mother was of Jewish descent, and although his family remained predominantly Catholic, he had siblings and other extended family members who converted to Calvinism. His father was open-minded enough to tolerate these converts in his family. Montaigne's silence could thus be attributed to a sense of mortification at the massacres, respecting the individuals close to him in his multidenominational family. On the other hand, he was perhaps wary of critiquing too harshly either side in the religious/political conflicts out of a sense of personal expediency — his refusal to adhere fanatically to either side in the religious wars is in line with his tolerant temperament. Yet this act could also be construed as a refusal of collective action — not taking a polaristic stand allowed him the opportunity to be a confidant of the leaders on both sides and thus a valued advisor and intermediary. This also placed him in the precarious position of being considered someone who could perhaps not be trusted: he was as a result once imprisoned, once accosted while on a journey, and on many occasions felt his life threatened, as he tells us himself: "j'avois d'une part les ennemys à ma porte … et essoyais toute sorte d'injures militaires à la fois" (III, xii, 1041). Whether it was for familial or political reasons, Montaigne nevertheless repressed the Saint Bartholemew's event from his writing. 1572, the year of the massacre, was also the year in which Montaigne began to write the *Essais.* It is perhaps coincidental, but Montaigne retired in 1571, as he tells us in "De l'oisiveté," with the intention of spending his life in distanciated repose, secure and pleasurable retreat. This idleness soon gave rise to the appearance of "chimeres et monstres fantasques, les uns sur les autres, sans ordre, et sans propos" (I, viii, 33). Such neurosis is the genesis of his writing of the *Essais* — the "monstres fantasques" of his unbridled imagination, which needed a discursive outlet, are also the nightmarish circumstances in which he lived and which would not allow him to exist in isolated tranquillity. Armed with Plutarch, whose *Oeuvres morales* (translated by Amyot) also appeared in 1572, he spent the next twenty years inquiring into the enigmatic nature of the human experience. The Saint Bartholemew's Day Massacre, although explicitly absent from his work, must nevertheless be considered one possible catalyst for Montaigne's decision to write the *Essais* — his diverse and undulating answer to the excesses of overzealous dogmatism. Montaigne's attempt to stimulate people to look inside themselves and around themselves with a judicious eye was a response to the extreme fanaticisms that created political and cultural havoc throughout most of his life. The *Essais* can certainly be seen in part as a response to such atrocities as carried out on "La Saint Barthélemy."

Montaigne's penchant for tolerance was very much influenced by La Boétie's *Discours de la servitude volontaire,* a work that is above all a defense of political freedom. The Calvinist reformers misconstrued La Boétie's positions to be outright declarations of radical religious reform.[57] The Montaigne of 1561, an adherent to La Boétie's notion of social harmony based on judicious concessions (perhaps related to Montaigne's notion of "des pertes triomphantes") was a very different one from the 1588 advisor to both Henri de Navarre, the Protestant heir to the throne, and Henri III. At the later date he saw the quest for unity as perhaps illusory: religious harmony and political utopia did not exist and Montaigne's enigmatic engagement of religious and political questions as well as his refusal to adhere to either side of the conflict or to promote some clear formula toward resolution point to his belief that the only possibility was that of the coexistence of contraries. This could be construed as a relativistic escapism but it is also possibly the only informed response to such unresolvable tensions as those in which Montaigne found himself involved.

De Man's discussion of Montaigne's ambivalent relationship to the *Ligue* then shifts to events contemporaneous to his own life: "les misérables mythes" and "les loyautés les plus factices — celles du nationalisme et de la race" ("Montaigne," 1020). How to remain true to oneself while answering to the political exigencies of the historical moment is the question with which de Man struggles as he analyzes Montaigne's manner of dealing with the problem. In light of the recent controversy on de Man's implication in the fascist ideologies prevalent during the Second World War (by virtue of his articles published in the collaborationist paper *Le Soir* in Belgium between 1940 and 1942), his choice of discussing Montaigne's struggle with the problematic relationship of political alliance and intellectual self-expression is a significant moment in understanding how Montaignean textuality continues to play a role in contemporary discussions of literature, history, and politics. De Man's "Montaigne et la transcendance" was first published in 1953, at which time de Man was at Harvard University, undoubtedly struggling with the securing of a livelihood, with the creation of his personal identity, and with the drama of the relation of his past actions to his role as an emerging scholar in the American academy. Just as we cannot know what de Man suffered after World War II in dealing with his own moral conscience as he ignored his past activities and created a new life in the United States, so he tells us that we cannot know what Montaigne may have experienced at this difficult juncture in his life when he was retiring from public service and beginning to write the *Essais*: "quoique nous ne sachions évidemment pas quelles impulsions aient pu tourmenter Montaigne jeune avant qu'il se fût mis à écrire les *Essais*" ("Montaigne," 1016). There is a striking correspondence between this statement of de Man on Montaigne and Derrida's recent one on de Man: "What could the ordeal of this mutism have been for him? I can only imagine it."[58] De Man uses Montaigne's example to justify his own difficult attempts at a balancing act between past and present, between self and history, in de Man's terms "entre la stabilité sereine des objets et la fluidité de la conscience subjective" ("Montaigne," 1021).

The temporal perspective, whether that of the read past or of the lived past, can lead to the immobility of the writing subject unless it is overcome in some way. What was Montaigne's solution of overcoming the past in order to write the *Essais* in de Man's terms? It was that of *forgetting*: "le passé tombe aussitôt dans l'oubli, parce qu'il se décolle de la subjectivité de l'immédiat; a-t-on assez songé au fait extraordinaire que Montaigne ne se réfère jamais à ses déclarations précédentes? Littéralement, il les a oubliées" ("Montaigne," 1021). Nietzsche's exhortation to forget in order to create anew is an essential generative dynamic in modernist literary production — one must confront the past yet negate it through forgetting in order to produce textual articulation. Yet another facet of the will to "forget" has a more problematic, perhaps subversive quality as seen in its more literal application to the question of de Man's Montaigne. Did Montaigne "forget" to write about the fact that he exercised more caution than courage by refusing to enter the city of which he was mayor during the time of a devastating plague that killed half of the population of Bordeaux in 1585, or that he was a confidant of Catherine de Medici and Charles IX, the principal orchestrators of the Saint Bartholomew's Day Massacre, which was equally violent in Bordeaux as it was in Paris? Is it not an "extraordinary fact" that de Man never referred to his "déclarations précédentes," his now controversial wartime articles from the preacademic period of his life, thereby "forgetting" what it was professionally expedient to supress from the autobiographical details of his life? Does de Man essay the life and writing of Montaigne at a crucial point in his own life, and to his advantage, to perhaps ease his conscience as he constitutes what he chooses to see as the essayist's similar predicament? Are de Man's silence and ability to overcome "history" not founded on the very "tranquille ironie" that he sees as the quality that allows our discussions of Montaigne's work and of his to continue? As he puts it: "C'est avec la même ironie qu'il doit considérer nos efforts incessants pour le saisir" ("Montaigne," 1022).

The radical impulse that lurks within the *Essais* comes into greater prominence as we read the juncture of Montaigne, Nietzsche, and de Man. Montaigne slowly forgot his *florilège* as he produced his own writing and also edited the historical events contemporaneous with his life in order to present himself in an advantageous light.

Nietzsche willfully attempted to negate through "forgetting" the whole panorama of stratified concepts and traditions provided him by the historicist hegemony of nineteenth-century Germany. Years later his insanity would be a literal manifestation of the annihilation of personal and cultural historicity. De Man shunned the historical dimensions of literature, valorized its hermeneutic uncertainty, and "forgot" his own personal history in the production of a critical enterprise purged of explicit ideological engagement. In all three writers' ambivalence toward history and concomitant embrace of idiosyncratic discourse, there is a productive and perhaps underhanded identity in the modernist enterprise. De Man's commentary on Nietzsche insists on this predicament shared by all three writers: "Modernity exists in the form of a desire to wipe out whatever came earlier, in the hope of reading at last a point that could be called a true present, a point of origin that marks a new departure." [59] The forgetting of history is also the production of more history whose implications demand to be confronted from a new perspective in the attempt, not to "wipe out the past," but to engage it critically, no matter how unresolvable the predicament. De Man sees Montaigne as the earlier proponent of the "subjectivité de l'immédiat" a quality produced by paradoxically engaging and often abnegating the past in the formulation of a unique textuality of the present moment. Yet even as this "new" is produced, it is never freed from Nietzsche's historical chain: it engenders more history and inevitably produces more problematic efforts toward an understanding of what is at stake in the encounter of cultural foundations and the new identities conflictually generated from them. In Montaigne's terms: "le centiesme commentaire le renvoye à son suivant, plus espineux et plus scabreux que le premier ne l'avoit trouvé. Quand est-il convenu entre nous: ce livre en a assez, il n'y a meshuy plus que dire?" (III, xiii, 1067).

One of de Man's lessons concerning the question of modernity, embedded as it is in the work of Montaigne and Nietzsche, provokes us to consider not only the difficulty in coming to terms with the dynamics of repetition and innovation in modernist and postmodernist literary production, but also the way in which surreptitious historical and political dimensions may be generated from their encounter. Do Montaigne, Nietzsche, and de Man "abuse" history? Does Montaigne's impulse to hide significant aspects of his personal life undermine the presumably impeccable ethics of his sincere humanism? Do Nietzsche's multivocalism and concept of "forgetting" provide an opening for nefarious misreadings such as the Nazi appropriations of his work, or in post-1945 Germany's desire to obliterate the memory of its own atrocities? Is de Man's "silence" emblematic of an academic attitude that seems to condone the separation of the worthy public scholar and the private person who may not be so admirable? In such collective efforts at deciphering de Man's predicament, as seen in *Responses* or *Diacritics* (Fall, 1990), his life and writing have been scrutinized and rehistoricized. In this light, one can no longer read innocently de Man's opening remarks in *Blindness and Insight*: "I am not given to retrospective self-examination and mercifully forget what I have written with the same alacrity I forget bad movies — although, as with bad movies, certain scenes or phrases return at times to embarrass and haunt me like a guilty conscience" (xii).

How do we then read such events in their intertextual context? Although Nietzsche was writing for his *suffisant lecteurs* ("diesen Hoffenden"), of which there were few in his lifetime, he also anticipated his worst readers, eventually seen in the Nazi interpretations of his work as inspired by his sister Elisabeth Foerster Nietzsche and other extremist advocates of imperialism and racialism, who constituted Niezsche as the apostle of the National Socialism.[60] Although there may be "Hoffenden," there are also "the worst readers" who would behave in a manner that eerily prognosticates his reception by the Nazi party: "*Die schlechtesten Leser sind die, welche wie plündernde Soldaten* verfahren: sie nehmen sich einiges, was sie brauchen können, heraus, beschmutzen und verwirren das übrige und lästern auf das Ganze" ("Vermischte Meinungen und Sprüche," I, 789 — emphasis added). The lack of understanding of his contemporaries suggested to Nietzsche a disturbing future exemplified in Hitler having himself photographed beside a bust of Nietzsche, interpreting his manuscripts (bequeathed to him personally by Elisabeth), and appropriating "morceaux choisis" from which he developed the incarnation of the Aryan "superman" to be loudly proclaimed at the ceremonies of the budding Third Reich. This sinister side of Montaigne's *scriptibilité* ("par ces traits de ma confession, on en peut imaginer d'autres à mes dépens") is used against

Nietzsche; his sister's appropriation and dissemination of his work in the late nineteenth and early twentieth centuries is a sinister complement to Gournay's feminist reception three hundred years before. Nietzsche falls victim, as we saw Montaigne did in Chapter One, to a negative register of *scriptibilité*, read to suit an ideology that he perhaps unintentionally anticipated, but would most likely not have adhered to.

In de Man's case, what is important is that the ephemeral juvenalia written under the Nazi occupation of Belgium should perhaps not be judged too harshly; in a mode of Montaignean subservient innovation, de Man made the necessary homage to the inevitable powers of his time and even reproduced their ideological motifs in his writing, yet he did so in a way that was enigmatic enough to protect him from unequivocal criticism from either side. He equivocates, perhaps like Montaigne, but to characterize his whole *oeuvre* as a pretext for disavowing the guilt for his wartime articles, to assert that his theoretical and critical writings are a hidden allegorical defense of his repressed collaboration, is perhaps too contrived. For there are readings and there are readings and who determines which ones are informed or which ones are like the "sacking soldiers?" Montaigne's "nous sommes doubles en nous-mesmes" is de Man's "blindness and insight"; the split subject in search of authentic selfhood will most likely never achieve a self-satisfying state of consciousness: "The best that we can hope for, it seems, is the kind of rigorously undeceiving knowledge — the remorseless dialectic of 'blindness' and 'insight' — that eschews all appeals to authentic selfhood and thus, at very most, achieves the kind of negative 'authenticity' which comes of not falling prey to such naïve illusions."[61] This "negative 'authenticity'" is the "pertes triomphantes," with which we must now struggle as Montaigne comes of age.

♦ ♦ ♦

Analyzing the interrelationship of Montaigne, Emerson, Nietzsche, and de Man has served to contextualize the opposition of innovation and repetition over a wide historical and cultural spectrum and helped us to better understand Montaigne's role in the modernist phenomenon. Montaigne's relationship to history is interactive and constructive, and we have seen how he sometimes conceals potentially revolutionary projects under the mask of a skeptical conservatism. Montaigne's refusal of textual absolutism points to the essentially mobile character of the confrontation of innovation and repetition. Emerson, Nietzsche and de Man are, indeed, three of Montaigne's *suffisant lecteurs* — they engage his surreptitious modernity in their receptions of the *Essais* and reproduce it in their own problematic formulations of the relationship between tradition and innovation. Emerson, Nietzsche and de Man have rearticulated Montaigne's work, and even gone beyond it ("à mes despens"), by developing more explicitly what was only suggested in the *Essais* as a response to their own situations.

As seen with the writers examined in Chapter One, Nietzsche and Emerson use Montaigne idiosyncratically and open his ideas up, instead of delimiting coherent structures toward the interpretation of the *Essais*. They pick up on directions indicated by Montaigne and redevelop them in radical ways. Montaigne is an important determinant in the formulation of Emerson's and Nietzsche's attitudes on the relationship between past and present. Although there are currents of the thoughts of many other writers in their work, we've seen that their writing is vitally connected to Montaigne's in their deployment of his essayistic method, which was to avoid reductive conclusions, keep an understanding of the issues open and dynamic, and thereby problematize totalization of meaning. The *Essais* attempt to achieve a balance between reason and unreason, yet they also produce recurring polar tensions that supersede resolution. In this sense Nietzsche's thought is clearly indebted to the *Essais*. He adopts Montaigne's premise that the way to truth is to know oneself and that the knowledge one attains through learning and tradition is only important if it affects the ability to live better. Yet these premises cannot always be definitively categorized and often produce the recurrence of reciprocally paradoxical assertions. Through Nietzsche's reception of Montaigne, the transmission of the *Essais* into important problematics of writing in the twentieth century can now be seen as a definite intertextual field that could be further explored.

Nietzsche generated a more radical appropriation of Montaigne's writing in his own work than did Emerson and extended the presence of the *Essais* into several important problematics of twentieth-century thought and writing. Nietzsche, who learned important lessons from contact with the work of both writers, developed a radical reappraisal of the question of "quotation and originality." What manifests itself as dialectical tension, ultimately resolvable in Emerson's work, is more problematized in that of Nietzsche and Montaigne, who share a greater penchant for paradox than Emerson. They present what at first appear to be coherent theses yet gradually unravel their arguments in a dismantling process that creates dynamic paradoxes exceeding Emerson's writing project of developing antithetical ideas in a more constructive manner. In his moral pragmatism and democratic progressivism, Emerson does not wholly reproduce Montaigne's paradoxical stature, nor fully anticipate Nietzsche's tragic one. Emerson aims more toward absolute truth and away from the skeptical independence of Montaigne and the iconoclasm of Nietzsche. Yet both help to bring the *Essais* into a wider crosscultural field of inquiry with far-reaching implications for the twentieth century.

Emerson and Nietzsche are thus two of the most important points of contact in Montaigne's relationship to nineteenth-century intellectual history. The intertextual field constructed here between the three writers, and de Man, produces an enhanced nexus of connections between their work in the context of which one can not only better understand their interrelationship, but also better appreciate a fundamental modernist strain in the work Montaigne. All three writers depend on their learning, yet attempt to temper it, with varying degrees of success, through insistence on personal achievement, self-education, and successful living; they share a greater desire to encompass a wide spectrum of unresolvable issues, recognizing them as such and willing to suspend their closure. In focusing on their similar and contrasting positions, we have seen strategies unfold in the attempt to write the self in the present as it rises out of the past. The possibility of new cultural beginnings is precarious, but necessary. Caught in the dialectics of the undecidable, interpretation must surpass itself and initiate renewal. Montaigne is an earlier instance of this dynamic force —outward use of the past and inward development of the self is fundamental to a significant modernist impulse in literature. The dynamics of remembering and forgetting continue to operate as an impetus in current literary and theoretical practice. As writers triangulate between the writing self, the past, and their "horizons-of-experience," so must a commentator who in participating in the mobility of Montaigne's propositions attempts to produce new related configurations. In Chapter Three, Pater's adoption of this strategy in his work, and Woolf's more innovative production of it in hers, will establish even further Montaigne's notable role among the moderns.

Notes to Chapter Two

1. John Burt Foster's work best demonstrates the central role of Nietzsche's work in literary developments of the twentieth century. One should also consider the neo-Nietzschean dimensions of French intellectual thought over the last 30 years — in much of Michel Foucault's work, in Gilles Deleuze's *Nietzsche et la philosophie* (Paris: Presses Universitaires de France, 1962), and in Jacques Derrida's *Spurs: Nietzche's Styles/Eperons: Les styles de Nietzsche* (Chicago: The University of Chicago Press, 1978) as discussed by Vincent Descombes in *Le même et l'autre* (Paris: Les Editions de Minuit, 1979). More recently, Erich Heller's *The Importance of Nietzsche* (Chicago: The University of Chicago Press, 1988), as well as Richard Schact's "Nietzsche's Coming of Age" in the *German Book Review* (Munich: Goethe Institute, 1991): 45-46, have convincingly reiterated Nietzsche's pervasive role in intellectual history and literary sensibility in the twentieth century. In the case of Emerson, critics continue to assert his important influential role in modern American culture. See for example *Modern Critical Views: Ralph Waldo Emerson*, ed. Harold Bloom (New York: Chelsea House Publishers, 1985) and especially several recent studies that have asserted the primacy of Emerson's role in American literary and political traditions: Irving Howe, *The American Newness: Culture and Politics in the Age of Emerson* (Cambridge: Harvard University Press, 1986), David Marr, *American Worlds Since Emerson* (Amherst: The University of Massachusetts Press, 1988), and Gustaaf Van Cromphout, *Emerson's Modernity and the Example of Goethe* (Columbia: University of Missouri Press, 1990).

2. Paul de Man, "Literary History and Literary Modernity," *Blindness and Insight* (Minneapolis: University of Minnesota Press, 1983), 145.

3. Ralph Waldo Emerson, *Journals of Ralph Waldo Emerson,* 10 vols. (Boston: Houghton Mifflin Company, 1911), VI, 371-72. All further references appear in text with accompanying indications of volume and page number. The edition used for Emerson's works is Ralph Waldo Emerson, *Complete Works,* 11 vols. (Boston: Houghton Mifflin Company, 1903). All references include title, volume, and page number.

4. Charles Lowell Young, *Emerson's Montaigne* (New York: The MacMillan Company, 1941). Young's study on the contours of Emerson's relationship to Montaigne documents Emerson's numerous comments on the *Essais.* It is the most complete work written on the relationship of Emerson and Montaigne but is, as we will see, unsatisfying for important reasons.

5. Young, 16.

6. Edward Dowden, *Montaigne* (London: J. B. Lipincott, 1905), 156.

7. Young, Chapter 4, "Emerson's Acquaintance with Montaigne," 82.

8. An important aspect of earlier work in the field of comparative literature, established by such critics as J. M. Carré and F. M. Guyard, sought verifiable factual information (*rapports de fait*) concerning the interrelationships of writers of different nationalities and linguistic backgrounds as the only acceptable domain of

comparatism. Young's "comparative study" seems to adhere to this approach of literary hide and seek in his positivistic pursuit of specific references to Montaigne in Emerson's work with little or no comparative evaluation of this material. In general, the same may be said for the existing work on the other writers considered in this study and their relationships to Montaigne. A full discussion of the methods of Carré and Guyard, and of the uses and limitations of such criteria for comparison, is found in Chapter Two, "Influence and Imitation" of Ulrich Weisstein's *Comparative Literature and Literary Theory* (Bloomington: Indiana UP, 1968). See also Robert J. Clements, *Comparative Literature as Academic Discipline* (New York: The Modern Language Association of America, 1978).

9. W. L. Ustick, "Emerson's Debt to Montaigne," *Washington University Studies* 9 (1922): 245-62.

10. See Graham Good, *The Observing Self: Rediscovering the Essay* (New York: Routledge, 1988) for his succinct yet encompassing delineation of the history of the English essay.

11. The question of the editions read by various Montaigne readers and especially the translations of such editions raises an enormous problem which should in itself be the subject of another book on the history of the receptions of the *Essais.*

12. Charles Dédéyan, *Montaigne chez ses amis Anglo-Saxons* (Paris: Editeurs Boivin, 1943), 282.

13. Mary McKinley, in *Words in a Corner* (Lexington, Kentucky: French Forum, 1981), posits the use of an "echo technique" in Montaigne's use of quotation, which gives the *Essais* a secondary form of coherence, a necessary undertaking since Montaigne believes in the limited communicative power of the word. He thus uses the tradition as an element of structuration "to create a new form that is uniquely personal" (111).

14. Clements, 155.

15. T. S. Eliot, "Tradition and the Individual Talent," *Selected Prose of T. S. Eliot,* ed. Frank Kermode (New York: Harcourt Brace Jovanovich, 1975): "What happens when a new work of art is created is something that happens simultaneously to all the works of art which preceded it. The existing monuments form an ideal order among themselves, which is modified by the introduction of the new (the really new) work of art among them. The existing order is complete before the new work arrives; for order to persist after the supervention of novelty, the *whole* existing order must be, if ever so slightly, altered; and so the relations, proportions, values of each work of art toward the whole are readjusted; and this is the conformity between the old and the new" (38-39). All further references appear in text.

16. André Malraux, "The Cultural Heritage," *Yale French Studies* 18 (1957): 31-38.

17. Young, 209.

18. For a discussion of the problematic notion of a "renaissance of a renaissance" see Jonathan Arac, "F.O. Matthiessen: Authorizing an American Renaissance," *The American Renaissance Reconsidered,* eds. Walter Benn Michaels and Donald E. Pease (Baltimore: The Johns Hopkins UP, 1985), 90-112 as well as Matthiessen's *American Renaissance* (New York: Oxford UP, 1941).

19. Terence Cave, *The Cornucopian Text* (Oxford: Oxford UP, 1979).

20. François Rabelais, *Pages choisies*, eds. Chappon et Pons (Paris: Classiques Larousse, 1955), 19.

21. Joachim Du Bellay, *La Deffence et illustration de la langue francoyse*, ed. Henri Chamard (Paris: Classiques Larousse, 1966), 42.

22. Robert Martin Adams, "What Was Modernism?" *Hudson Review* 5 (1978): 21.

23. Adams, 28.

24. Matthiessen, 101-102.

25. See Zachary S. Schiffman, "Montaigne and the Rise of Skepticism in Early Modern Europe: A Reappraisal," *Journal of the History of Ideas* 3 (1984): 499-516.

26. See Paul Porteau, *Montaigne et la vie pédagogique de son temps* (Paris: Librairie Droz, 1935).

27. Harold Bloom, "Introduction," *Modern Critical Views: Montaigne*, ed. Harold Bloom (New York: Chelsea House, 1987), 5. On this point see also Hiram Hayden, *The Counter-Renaissance* (New York: Scribner, 1950): "He [Montaigne] represents the culmination and terminus of the Counter-Renaissance — a movement born of men's weariness with the pretensions of the speculative intellect and the systematizing mind" (76).

28. The term is Perry Miller's from "Emersonian Genius and American Democracy," *The New England Quarterly* XXVI, 1 (1953): 27-44.

29. Herbert Marcuse, *Negations: Essays in Critical Theory* (Boston: Beacon Press, 1968), 95.

30. Alexis de Tocqueville, *Democracy in America*, ed. Phillips Bradley (New York: Alfred A. Knopf, 1985), II, 169.

31. Walt Whitman, *Leaves of Grass*, eds. Harold W. Blodgett and Sculley Bradley (New York: New York University Press, 1965), 28.

32. See Frederick Ives Carpenter, "Emerson and World Literature," *Emerson Handbook* (New York: Hendrick House, 1953), 209-254 and Hermann Hummel's particularly suggestive piece, "Emerson and Nietzsche," *New England Quarterly* XIX, 84 (1946): 60-82.

33. Friedrich Nietzsche, *Ecce Homo, Werke in drei Bänden*, ed. Karl Schlechta (Munich: Carl Hanser, 1956), II, 1088. All further references to Nietzsche's works appear in text with indications of title, volume and page number.

34. Four essential studies on Nietzsche's relation to Montaigne are Charles Andler, *Nietzsche: sa vie et sa pensée* (Paris: Nouvelle Revue Française, 1920), one of the first to address the subject; Victor Bouillier, *La Renommée de Montaigne en Allemagne* (Paris: Librairie Ancienne Edouard Champion, 1921); Brendan Donellan, "Nietzsche and Montaigne," *Colloquia Germanica* 19 (1986): 1-20; and W. D. Williams, *Nietzsche and the French: A Study of the Influence of Nietzsche's French Reading on his Thought and Writing* (Oxford: Basil Blackwell and Mott Limited, 1952). Jean Starobinski, in *Montaigne en mouvement* (Paris: Editions Gallimard, 1982), goes so far as to claim that "On ne s'étonnera sans doute pas qu'en restituant ainsi à l'apparance la primauté que Montaigne lui avait déjà

consentie, Nietzsche, avec son 'éternel retour,' retrouve presque du même coup les 'roues' selon lesquelles Montaigne voyait tourner le cours des histoires" (363).

35. Andler, 107.

36. Williams, xix.

37. See Guy Mermier, "Inconstance et relativité, pieces maîtresses de la modernité de Montaigne," *Bulletin de la Société des Amis de Montaigne* 25 (1978): 51-56. In his discussion of Montaigne's "modernité," Mermier develops "l'idée que les choses de la foi et les choses du siècle peuvent être distinctes, mais c'est le nominalisme qui fera triompher la notion de relativité en affirmant l'incapacité de la raison à atteindre la preuve de l'existence de Dieu" (51). The secular version of nominalism proposes the disparity between words and things and maintains that universal names (*nomina*) or concepts have no objective reality outside the mind, and that only individual things and events exist objectively. The metaphoric quality of language, elsewhere considered as a rational tool used to represent reality, is fundamental to the skeptical attitude toward language held by Montaigne and Nietzsche; in the former case, through the dismantling of medieval realism, and in the latter, from opposition to later developments of the same issues in a different guise, that of empiricism, and in the case of both, in rejection of Platonic idealism.

38. Speaking of Cratylus's position that words should function naturally and not solely as predetermined signs, Hermogenes states: "I should explain to you Socrates that our friend Cratylus has been arguing about names. He says that they are natural and not conventional." *The Collected Dialogues of Plato*, eds. E. Hamilton and H. Cairns (Princeton: Princeton University Press, 1961), 422.

39. Michel Foucault, *Les Mots et les choses* (Paris: Gallimard, 1966): "A la limite, on pourrait dire que le langage classique n'existe pas. Mais qu'il fonctionne: toute son existence prend place dans son role représentatif, s'y limite avec exactitude et finit par s'épuiser. Le langage n'a plus d'autre lieu que la représentation, ni d'autre valeur qu'en elle: en ce creux qu'elle a pouvoir d'aménager" (93).

40. Heraclitus, *The Art and Thought of Heraclitus*, ed. and trans. Charles H. Kahn (Cambridge: Cambridge UP, 1979), 53.

41. Bouillier, 45.

42. Friedrich, 52.

43. De Man, 148.

44. For a detailed discussion of the complexities of Pascal's intelligibility see de Man's "Pascal's Allegory of Persuasion," *Allegory and Representation: Selected Papers from the English Institute*, ed. Stephen Greenblatt (Baltimore: The Johns Hopkins UP, 1981), 1-25. Pascal's influence on Nietzsche has been discussed by Andler and delineated in James Robert Dionne's *Pascal et Nietzsche: Etude historique et comparée* (New York: Burt Franklin and Co., 1965).

45. See Cathleen M. Bauschatz, "Montaigne's Conception of Reading in the Context of Renaissance Poetics and Modern Criticism," *The Reader in the Text*, eds. Susan R. Suleiman and Inge Crosman (Princeton: Princeton University Press, 1980), 264-292. One could also consider the many other writers who develop the notions of participatory reading and of the open or *scriptible* text in the wake of

the *Essais*. Montaigne's importance to writers such as Barthes, Kristeva, and others has been admirably discussed by Réda Bensmaïa in *The Barthes Effect: The Essay as Reflective Text* (Minneapolis: The University of Minnesota Press, 1987).

46. The term is Barbara Johnson's in her introduction to Jacques Derrida's *Disseminations* (Chicago, University of Chicago Press, 1981), xiv. It is very useful in considering Montaigne's frequent deconstructive moods.

47. See Morris Croll, *"Attic" and Baroque Prose Style* (Princeton: Princeton UP, 1966). Croll helped to "modernize" the baroque and mannerist qualities of Montaigne's writing and thereby open a wider spectrum in which to consider Montaigne as a more central stylistic force in European writing than previously considered.

48. Paul de Man, "Montaigne et la transcendance," *Critique* IX, 79 (1953): 1019. All further references appear in text.

49. De Man, "Literary History and Literary Modernity," 150.

50. Foster, 417.

51. Hayden White for example has commented in "Nietzsche: The Poetic Defense of History in the Metaphorical Mode" in *Metahistory: The Historical Imagination in Nineteenth-Century Europe* (Baltimore: The Johns Hopkins UP, 1973): "Hartmann's doctrine of the sovereignty of the unconscious is, then, just as dangerous as Hegel's doctrine of the 'World Spirit' and Darwin's apotheosized Nature. It represents a hardening of the will to form to the detriment of the will to life. All general schemata must be eschewed, Nietzsche repeated, if history is to serve the needs of living men" (354).

52. J. P. Stern contends that we are still trying to understand the implications of "Vom Nutzen und Nachteil" for our own age: "But the help we receive is limited to his insistence that a major problem awaits solution." "Introduction," *Friedrich Nietzsche, Untimely Meditations*, trans. R. J. Hollingdale (Cambridge: Cambridge UP, 1983), xx.

53. Babette Babiche, "Nietzsche and the Condition of Postmodern Thought: Post-Nietzschean Postmodernism," *Nietzsche as Postmodernist: Essays Pro and Contra*, ed. Clayton Koelb (Albany: State University Press of New York, 1990), 256.

54. White, 360.

55. See Nakam, 13-38.

56. See Henri Noguères, *La Saint Barthélemy* (Paris: Editions Robert Laffont, 1959), for a descriptive account.

57. See Malcolm Smith, *Montaigne and Religious Freedom: The Dawn of Pluralism* (Geneva: Librairie Droz, 1991) for his excellent historical analysis of Montaigne's life and thought in the context of the religious and political events of sixteenth-century France.

58. Jacques Derrida, "Like the Sound of the Sea Deep Within a Shell: Paul de Man's War," *Responses* (Lincoln: University of Nebraska Press, 1989), 150.

59. De Man, *Blindness and Insight*, 148.

60. See Marius Paul Nicolas, *From Nietzsche Down to Hitler* (New York: Kennikat Press, 1938) and "Self-Denial, Self-Affirmation" in David Hayman, *Nietzsche: A Critical Life* (New York: Oxford UP, 1980), 351-361.

61. Christopher Norris, "Settling Accounts: Heidegger, de Man and the Ends of Philosophy," *What's Wrong with Postmodernism: Critical Theory and the Ends of Philosophy* (Baltimore: The Johns Hopkins UP, 1990), 261.

Chapter Three

Pater and Woolf: A Modernist Renaissance?

But if a writer should be quite consistent,
How could he show things existent?

— Lord Byron, *Don Juan*, Canto 15.

No other modernist writers in England redeveloped the *Essais* more than Walter Pater and Virginia Woolf, nor brought them more into the mainstream of recognition. Both wrote critical material on Montaigne and transformed components of the *Essais* in their own writing. Aesthetic dimensions and thematic elements of the *Essais* can be seen playing a substantial role in Pater's and Woolf's critical as well as creative work. Montaigne's relationship to Pater is more explicit and somewhat less problematic than his relationship to Woolf. It is the latter's reception of the *Essais*, less obvious and more suggestive, that raises several issues important to modernist literary practice as well as to feminism. The lives of all three were very much struggles in their individual experiences as writers under somewhat unique circumstances: maverick feminist author, Victorian professor/aesthete, and Renaissance gentleman/essayist. We will see, however, striking correspondences between their divergent, yet related, attitudes and works.

Pater's and Woolf's receptions of Montaigne produce an intertextual field characterized by skepticism and sincerity, innovation and conformity. These elements produce similar notions in the thought and prose of all three in their attempts to establish personalized aesthetic systems while producing a mannerist style generated by a pyrrhonist attitude. Pater's and Woolf's readings of Montaigne converge in their correlative approaches to philosophical and aesthetic problems as worked out in the *Essais*. Pater constituted Montaigne as a protomodernist and the *Essais* consequently played an important in the work of Woolf who would become a less obvious yet far-reaching disseminator of the *Essais* in the twentieth century. Montaigne's role in Woolf's writing is a less certain area of inquiry, but her work nevertheless demonstrates enough essential points of contact with the *Essais* to develop hypotheses about how their writing operates interactively.

Pater and Woolf read Montaigne in the context of their respective "horizons-of-experience." Yet it is important to consider to what degree they fused the target text, their own visions, and their specific historical moments in their own unique manners. This is what distinguishes Montaigne's readers from each other. In the case of Pater and Woolf, essential elements of the *Essais* are distributed throughout their work and are closely related to some of their most fundamental perspectives on literature, history, and philosophy. Pater for instance began reading Montaigne at an early age and assimilated the *Essais* into his own work throughout his life.[1] Montaigne's work is sprinkled throughout Pater's writing and has its fullest development in Chapters IV and V of *Gaston de Latour*. It is most likely that Woolf was first exposed to Montaigne in 1898 when her father, Sir Leslie Stephen, allowed her unlimited access to his library, at which time she came across Montaigne's work first through Pater, and then directly.[2] Their receptions of Montaigne are also unique in that they were the first to extend aspects of the *Essais* in narrative works since Marie de Gournay. Yet one could also argue that Woolf and Pater influence Montaigne, that they analyze the *Essais* through the looking glass of their own predilections, thereby constituting a modernist Montaigne by insisting on the qualities of his textuality most akin to their own. We will see numerous examples of this contact throughout their work. The reciprocal, self-perpetuating attitude toward the literary experience as produced in the *Essais* is thus reformulated by Pater and Woolf.

Woolf's writing generates so many different perspectives: it is radically dynamic, mixing past and present, lyricism and philosophy, history and fictive biography, often in the same work. Pater struggles between religion and aesthetics, decadence and moralism, and whether to commit to himself or to cultural traditions. Both writers deal uniquely with the problematics seen in Montaigne's receptions thus far. In the waters of unstable signifiers and systems of thought, Montaigne, Pater, and Woolf build their textual arcs even while they are caught in the whirlpool of a Nietzschean triad of multiply dynamic connections of historical forces. This is non-illusory modernism: newness caught in the vortex of historical fatalism and death. There is no escape from the historical chain, yet recognition of this fact leads to a gesture of literary self-sacrifice in the production of new aesthetic configurations, which ultimately fail to break the historical shackles they inadvertently perpetuate. Pater, and Woolf to a lesser degree, infuse their writing with the intertexts of a great deal of dead writers, yet do so only with the larger intention of expressing their own predilections and concerns. This is very pronounced in their respective receptions of the *Essais*; as we will see, the liquid metaphors are not gratuitous.

Although Pater and Woolf borrowed explicitly from the *Essais* only occasionally in the context of their overall work, much of what they touch upon is central to Montaigne's theory and practice of writing, and to their own. They often amplify their versions of the *Essais* in their own texts, seeking to understand them through the historical haze — translations, different editions, commentaries, and *Zeitgeist* — and to incorporate them into their own textual formulations. This is the problem many readers face when thinking critically about texts: how to be faithful to oneself and to the work under scrutiny. The reader is private and is invaded by the publicity of the text. He or she surrenders to it, becomes absorbed in its body in order to conform publicly, yet strives to maintain an element of inner freedom by revolting against the text even while captured and, by doing so, fuses the text with self-producing integrity (L. *integritas*, "completeness"), between existing text and new analysis (Gk. *analuein*, "to dissolve"). This process of idiosyncratic reception was first produced in the *Essais* — a work grounded on a close reading of the past, which nevertheless dissolves and absorbs cultural tradition into its own discourse, thereby regenerating history through personalized vision. Montaigne wished this process to remain heuristic (Gk. *heurisko*, "to find"), and encouraged his readers to use him as he used others, thereby enabling them to learn through trial and error as they interpret his "experiment" of personal interpretation of previous texts that were, in their time, interpretations.

On the other hand, the reader is public; his or her cultural concepts are developed before the reading of a text, which is a locus of private signification to be discovered and explored. This is the dilemma posed by the *Essais*: the doubleness of the literary enterprise ("nous sommes doubles en nous-mesmes"), of the interplay between self and world, of Nietzsche's historical and unhistorical. Pater and Woolf thus appropriated the three-hundred-year-old *Essais* in innovative literary works within a new cultural space. They read and judged while modulating their personal aesthetic systems on elements of *Essais* most useful to them. Both writers treated Montaigne's work as "classic" (an exemplary member in the European canon of great literature, and to be respected as such) and as "modern" (a daring and original text to be actively engaged). Montaigne was thus concurrently a monumental, antiquarian, and critical writer in their respective and correlative receptions. It is a confrontation of triadic historical vision that constitutes the modernist attitude active in their work — neither exclusively expressive nor mimetic, but grappling with the interrelationship of past and present to produce an intertextual tension that is perhaps a key to understanding their modernist identities. Pater and Woolf complicated an already complex intertextual field by innovatively rethinking a text that was quietly innovative three hundred years before their receptions and, as we've seen, often suppressed accordingly. The status of the *Essais* assumed radically new dimensions after being reformulated by Pater and Woolf as they used the *Essais* in significantly different ways in order to give them a new existence, producing many Montaignean resonances in their own work, and generally helping to perpetuate a rich intertextual field between Montaigne and the English-speaking world.

Pater and Woolf would probably have been innovative modernists had they never heard of Montaigne. Yet the current of the *Essais* in their work, what Pater terms the "under-texture" in his essay on Pascal, is significant. Pater's reformulation of the *Essais*, in the wake of Carlyle's and Arnold's, caps off the English fascination with Montaigne in the nineteenth century. He embodies the conflicting tendencies of Montaigne's reception in England, summarizing the various positions into his own complex formulation of Montaigne's modernity.[3] Pater's reception of the *Essais* occurred soon after Emerson's, contemporaneously with Nietzsche's, and is in some ways indebted to theirs.[4] Woolf responded to the *Essais* at the same time that Villey, Lanson, and Thibaudet were formulating what became the official academic interpretations of the *Essais* and while Gide was using them for self-discovery and the development of his own work. Pater and Woolf ultimately developed what Pater called the "*Montaignesque* element in literature"[5] in another language, and did so in a more free-spirited yet focused way than was attempted by their French contemporaries, or by either Emerson or Nietzsche. They went beyond the philosophical essaying of Emerson and Nietzsche and developed Montaigne's work in intentionally particularized ways. Their freer yet more concrete adaptations of the *Essais* promote the innovative dimensions of Montaigne's writing and highlight the convergences as well as the divergences between Montaigne's work and their own. Pater and Woolf thus continued the hybrid genre of philosophy and literature in a subjectively skeptical mode, as carried out in the *Essais*. Montaigne's writing thus assumes a new identity in a context more or less overlooked in previous scholarship.

Pater's notion of "under-texture" is a useful one in analyzing his reception of Montaigne. He develops the notion in his essay "Pascal," an important text toward the understanding of Pater's reception of the *Essais*, considering that Pater discusses Montaigne in the final parts of the essay in order to clarify his position on Pascal — something he never completely does. In the last essay that Pater worked on in his life, he was still vitally concerned with Montaigne, searching for a comforting Pascalian solution, but thwarted by Montaignean skepticism. All texts, argued Pater, carry with them a trace or an "under-texture;" he understood that Pascal redeveloped Montaigne on important points even while simultaneously rejecting those points ("Pascal," *Miscellaneous Studies*, VIII, 68). He also recognized that any original text is only a repetition of something else already written. Even in moments of inner freedom and self-expression, the writer is still caught in the vortex of historical influence: "There are moment's of one's own life, aspects of the life of others, of which the conclusion that the will is free seems to be the only —

is the natural or reasonable — account. Yet those very moments of reflection, on second thoughts, present themselves again, as but links in a chain, in an all-embracing network of chains" ("Pascal," VIII, 55). The privileged moments of the private self are already permeated with previous texts. It is their residue that fuels the development of perception, personality, and artistic creation, thereby making these moments possible. Writing was thus for Pater an interdependent network of coherent chains moving forward and backward, vertically and horizontally. Pater was more comfortable with the implications of the chain metaphor than was Nietzsche, who suffered from the knowledge that we are inevitably trapped in the tyranny of historical continuity. Pater found a certain comfort and security in seeing himself as part of a vast historical continuum. Yet he never reconciled the religion of Pascal and the aesthetics of Montaigne — the very receptions of Pater's own work, the radical one of Wilde (an unbridled hedonism) and the conservative one of Eliot (a rigid neoclassicism), attest to the problematic doubleness of his own identity. Pater's ellipses ("… ") at the end of the Pascal essay act as ideogrammatic links of the chain, underscoring the need for the continued redevelopment of the issues by future readers (Gk. *elleipsis,* "a falling short, a defect"). The *Essais* thus provide an important "under-texture" for Pater's work as well as for his and Woolf's attempts to add new links to the chain as they generate narrative experiments that highlight the opposition between innovation and custom, and consequently produce obsessed encounters of old and new.

The *Essais* were written near the end of a historical period of increased intellectual interest and reactivation of ancient literature. Montaigne was not as important a pioneering thinker within this phenomenon as he was its most idiosyncratic and paradoxical practitioner. Although he revered ancient greatness and pragmatic stability, his writing manifests innovation, contradiction, and mobility. Pater revived these latter qualities of Montaigne's work in the service of his eccentric literary renaissance. He emulated several qualities of the ideal student that were discussed in the context of Montaigne's and Nietzsche's social pedagogy. He did his historical homework — reading and writing on a wide range of Western literature, philosophy, and criticism while striving to reach beyond these models in order to use them in unique ways. By embedding past texts in his own, he prepared the expression of new ideas in the contexts of past ones, making his debts explicit, then using the chosen models in a free manner. As Montaigne did in the *Essais,* he compiled an intertextual garland, a *florilège* of historical authority, then improvised themes around and often beyond their parameters. Eventually his own notions developed in response to historical models and literary predecessors become his primary focus — a practice emanating in great part from his understanding of the *Essais.* He may thus be considered the Victorian modernist, a label as incongruous as is Montaigne's innovative conservative. Textual absorption and modulation of Montaigne's writing helped Pater to develop his own literary practice. Much the same can be claimed for Woolf in her reception of Montaigne, and also for her reception Pater.

Woolf's main points of contact with Montaigne arise from her reading of the *Essais* and from her reading of Pater reading Montaigne. Complicating the process is Woolf's own ambivalent reception of Pater, perhaps her most important literary and critical precursor. Meisel has demonstrated how Woolf concurrently adopted and rejected Pater, overcoming his "paternal" authority while developing intertextual traces of his work in her own. By reading Pater, Meisel seeks to understand better the sensibility of Woolf: "... a close reading of Pater contributes immensely to a close reading of Woolf."[6] Pater's development of the aesthetic personality, the concept of the privileged moment, and an accompanying vivid expressiveness to concretize these notions, are elements learned in part from his study of the *Essais*; they also play an important part in Woolf's work. Reading Woolf's Pater helps to clarify these qualities. Considering reception based on reciprocal interchange, either a former or a later writer may be analyzed in order to shed light on an understanding of the other.

Woolf and Pater thus reactivated the *Essais* in a creative manner, producing narratives with a pronounced Montaignean under-texture, modulating his ideas and strategies in their own, thereby establishing him as an earlier practitioner of the type of textuality they eventually developed. Yet Woolf attempted either to reject the lessons of cultural tyranny as in *A Room of One's Own,* to interact with it as in *The Common Reader,* or to satirize it as in *Orlando.* She used tyranny's lessons even as she turned against them. She was a more *kritische* writer than either Montaigne or Pater and took from them exactly what she needed to counteract that with which she disagreed. She assimilated Pater more thoroughly than Pater did Montaigne, thereby achieving an intimate knowledge of both writers' work. She in fact acknowledges Pater's importance to her own work in the preface to *Orlando*; she was also tutored in Greek by Pater's sister Clara and was therefore extremely familiar with his life and work.[7] Yet Woolf's innovative moves take a leap beyond her textual *pater*, whereas Pater maintained a more *monumentalische* attitude in his commentary on the work of Montaigne. She became herself in defiance to the authority of either Pater or Montaigne, even while they provided her with working models whose potential she redeveloped. Much like Gournay's simultaneous assimilation and transcendence of Montaigne, she moves beyond her *pères d'alliance* in order to develop a writing project independent of them. Both Gournay and Woolf came into their own as writers at the beginning of new centuries, three hundred years apart, inheriting male traditions that they renovated into unique feminist positions. Woolf's essay "Montaigne" is the only place she dealt explicitly with Montaigne's life and work, yet a good deal of her writing is permeated with a Montaignean under-texture.[8] There are also more oblique, yet perhaps fundamental connections to the *Essais* in other places in her work. Woolf's greatness was to approach the concordances but especially the discordances between her male predecessors' notions and her own as a resource for her writing project, not as a threat to it.

Pater's and Woolf's actual commentary on Montaigne and his writing provides a clear framework in whose context the writers' interrelationship can be demarcated and examined. Yet it must also be considered that in light of a Montaignean outlook, it is difficult to establish firm and immutable evaluations between the work of any two writers. The unexpected correlation of Montaigne, Pater, and Woolf as well as the confluential complexity of the work of the three, renders its study inevitably partial and tentative. Yet we will see certain preoccupations emerge in the comparative analysis of their lives and writing, which will particularize our understanding of Montaigne's role in modernist literature.

♦ ♦ ♦

In *Shakespeare and Montaigne,* John Robertson, literary critic and contemporary of Pater, commented on Montaigne as a precursor of modernist literature:

> I would put it that Montaigne is really, for the civilized world at this day, what Petrarch has too enthusiastically been declared to be, the first of the moderns. Montaigne was not only a new literary phenomenon in his own day: he remains so still; for his impressionism, which he carried to such lengths in originating, is the most modern of literary inspirations; and all our successive literary and artistic developments are either phases of the same inspiration or transient reactions against it.[9]

Pater would have concurred with Robertson, whose favorable characterization of Montaigne's "impressionism" certainly stands in contrast to the many previous criticisms of Montaigne as an overly subjective writer. At this time critical response colored by personal temperament was regarded in a more positive light. The subjectivity of knowledge and understanding, an essential aspect of Montaigne's work, became characteristic of a good deal of Pater's. Montaigne's descent into the self and attempt to express its significance strongly influenced Pater. Faithfulness to the inner vision and the development of an expressive language to best produce its dimensions are essential to both writers' work.

By virtue of Montaigne's dispersed presence throughout his work, Pater is one of the most visible disseminators of the *Essais* in England. There was something of a vogue of Montaigne in nineteenth-century English letters, in which Pater actively participated and helped to produce. In the 1820s, there was a newly revived enthusiasm for Montaigne in England, for many of the same reasons as there was in France, although there was also disapproval. Walter Landor for example praised Montaigne as a worthy Epicurean of great wit and tolerance.[10] Yet at about the same time, Thomas Carlyle expressed a certain ambivalence toward the *Essais,* claiming that Montaigne, "patient, good-natured, though exuberant," was too egotistical, too skeptical on matters of religion, and guilty of a certain "coarseness and obscenity" in discussing love.[11] There was always this contrast in the English reception of Montaigne in the nineteenth century: he was admired as a freethinker in an age of bigotry, yet also subjected to moral criticism. In the middle of the century, Matthew Arnold's response to Montaigne was to consider him as one of the ideal critics of all time and "one of the excellent markers and recorders of the traits of human life."[12] Arnold's unequivocal approval offsets Carlyle's moralistic reservations and it is thus that Pater found himself caught in between this praise and blame for Montaigne. He seemed somewhat unsure of what to think; he praised him for his "fineness of sensation" (*Gaston*, VI, 136) yet was hesitant to fully embrace his relativism, which he nevertheless admitted was the "proper intellectual equivalent to the infinite impossibility of things" (*Gaston*, VI, 130-31). What makes Pater's reception of Montaigne both interesting and problematic is the fact that he never succeeded in presenting a unified attitude, nor did he arbitrarily systematize the *Essais*; he used them strategically at certain points in his thought and writing in paradoxical reformulations. He developed his attitude toward Montaigne's work most often while developing his ideas on skepticism and on what he often referred to as "the personal style." By incorporating many of Montaigne's tendencies into his own writing, and by virtue of his wide influence as critic and novelist, Pater regenerated the *Essais* into an essential modernist activity: dynamic, provisional writing in the service of relative understanding. Montaigne's work, due to the unique redevelopments of Pater, took on less systematic and unified features, and their more innovative qualities were allowed to develop without their reduction into fixed interpretive models.

Montaigne claimed that his thoughts became so infused with those of his quotations that often he did not bother to distinguish between them: "Es raisons et inventions que je transplante en mon solage et confons aux miennes, j'ay à escient omnis parfois d'en marquer l'autheur, pour tenir en bride la temerité de ces sentences hastives qui se jettent sur toute sorte d'escrits ..." (II, x, 408). He thus set up the possibility of a freer interplay between past and present. Active reception and regeneration accomplished in an unique stylistic manner, the personalizing of tradition, is also what Pater saw as a Montaignean strain in literary history. Pater strove to develop his aesthetic vision through carefully chosen models. His integration of Montaigne's ideas into his writing touches upon at least several extensive issues: the subjectivity and limits of knowledge, epistemological skepticism, and the dynamic relationship between self-expression, ambivalence toward cultural authority, and idiosyncratic style.[13] His relativistic attitude toward Montaigne is symptomatic of the latter's ability to generate uncertainty into receptions of his work. Pater wanted to embrace Montaigne's skeptical exuberance but was disturbed by it, which is why he had his protagonist Gaston gradually shy away from Montaigne's relativism and grow fonder of Giordano Bruno's more absolute notions; Pater also looked for his "pierre" and his "assiete" concerning his relationship to the *Essais*, but never found them.

Dédéyan has documented the many instances in which Pater commented on Montaigne.[14] Yet his discussion of Pater and Montaigne, like Young's of Emerson and Montaigne, stops at factual documentation and avoids the examination of intertextual contact. The role of the *Essais* in Pater's writing is most visible in *Gaston* and plays a quieter but no less important role in several key notions within his conceptual apparatus. As with any reader's reception of the *Essais*, Pater's critical evaluation was only partial — it was an attempt to particularize a textual abundance that produces too many signifying possibilities to be fully explored in any commentators' interpretive lifetime. Pater thus modulated on his *morceaux choisis* of the *Essais* and entered into the canon of readers who inevitably developed Montaigne within their respective "horizons-of-experience" and personal predilections. As we've seen with Pascal, Sainte-Beuve, Emerson, and Gide, Pater believed that Montaigne's thoughts expressed his own and were written especially for his use.

Pater often referred to the "essay" as the most effective form for communicating what he considered quintessential "modern" gestures: the suspension of dogmatic judgment and subjective textuality (*Plato and Platonism*, IX, 175). In Pater's work, the individual, whether a writer under critical scrutiny or a protagonist in a novel, is most often at the center of attention and is presented in a complex and problematic manner. Individual consciousness is allowed to develop, yet the decisive aspects of passionate, intense existence, a quality of life most explicitly valorized by Pater in his "Conclusion," are generated through a rigorous absorption of historical experience. This can be seen especially in *Marius the Epicurean* and more idiosyncratically in *Gaston*. The individual's self-conscious landscape in its adventurous movements is an active element in Pater's work; yet the writer's unique sensibility develops only through the dynamic engagement of cultural tradition. It is again the problematic tension between selfhood and history that is the modernist Montaignean element, itself another permutation of what is generally called the late renaissance: an attempt to give rebirth to the cultural past through a personalized vision, yet with an accompanying skepticism toward the undertaking of such an enterprise.

The *Essais* became a breviary of learned wisdom from a personal point of view in Montaigne's time, as did *The Renaissance* and *Marius* in Pater's. Yet, like Montaigne, Pater was also castigated for his eccentric manners of thought and style by (among others), Woolf's father Sir Leslie Stephen and by educational and religious authorities, who were suspicious of Pater's morality.[15] He was considered in some ways a dangerous writer for what he said and, as with Montaigne, for the innovative identity that shows through his neoconservative persona. Pater's critical evaluation, cast in the mold of creative response, and his method of personalized revaluation of culture became a paradigm for subsequent writers such as Woolf, and even Joyce, Eliot, Pound, Proust, and others. This particular mode of historical renovation as developed by Pater is vitally related to his reception of the *Essais*.

Pater's work demonstrates a fascination with human character in the visionary moments of its particularity and diversity, as well as with the sources of monumental greatness and faith. He sees these as the apexes of activity, which allow human existence to flourish. Yet, like Montaigne, he was partial toward equilibrium and valued self-discovery in writing, whether "critical" or "creative" (terms that become more problematic in the Paterian practice of what is often called "aesthetic criticism"). Pater was a writer of Montaigne's temperament, regenerating what he saw as the essayist's most important contribution, "the fruit of a quickened multiplied consciousness" (*The Renaissance*, I, 190). Pater's choice of metaphor is appropriate in light of Cave's characterization of Montaigne's "cornucopian" textuality that produces a many-faceted verbal proliferation and at the same time frustrates any apprehension of definitive finality.[16] Cave's demonstration that literary production in the *Essais* is a superabundant overflowing of the writing subject complements Pater's belief in the *Essais* as a self-centered text. The latter often referred to the *Essais* as a characteristically "modern" work — laden with learning and tradition even while it produced, in an unprecedented style, innovative assessments of the inconsistency of human experience.

In *The Renaissance,* Pater traces an important source of modern individuality back to Du Bellay and Montaigne and praises "that intensely modern sort of poetry in which the writer has for his aim the portraiture of his own most intimate moods, and to take the reader in his confidence. That age has other instances of this intimacy: Montaigne's *Essays* are full of it" (*The Renaissance,* I, 137). According to Pater's expressionistic aesthetic of literary and critical writing, the self constitutes a microcosm of humanity. Yet, like Montaigne, Pater expresses the inner world of his thought through vital interconnections with historical vision based on his reading. Individual temperament thus shines through the matrix of cultural awareness and erudition. Both Montaigne and Pater seek a harmonious balance of these competing forces, but it is often a Nietzschean triumph of the new production of vital personality that wins out. It is the assertion of the self in its autonomous presentness that Pater proclaims as the artistic triumph of the creative individual: "for art comes to you proposing frankly to give nothing but the highest quality to your moments as they pass, and simply for these moments' sake" (*The Renaissance,* I, 190). Montaigne, who liked to revel in the immediacy of experience, would have perhaps agreed.

Pater's attraction to Montaigne's method of self-portraiture and analysis of the flux of human experience is thus an important component of his premodernism. Another instance of it arises in his discussion of Charles Lamb:

> With him, as with Montaigne, the desire of self-portraiture is, below all more superficial tendencies, the real motive in writing at all — a desire closely connected with that intimacy, that modern subjectivity, which may be called the *Montaignesque* element in literature. ("Charles Lamb," *Appreciations,* V, 116-117)

To most efficiently express this "modern subjectivity," the desire to intimately portray one's subjectivity as it unfolds, Pater proposes the essay as the most effective genre for writers and considers Montaigne to be at the origin of this modernist mode of writing: "and as the best instance of it in French literature in the century preceding Browne is Montaigne, from whom indeed, in a great measure, all those tentative writers or essayists derive" ("Sir Thomas Browne," *Appreciations*, V, 124). An opponent of rigorous method, Pater sees Montaigne as the founder of the essay as well as of the modern spirit, and the essay as the form of writing best able to embody personal experience, the provisional nature of truth, and the suspension of definitive judgment:

> The poem, the treatise, the essay ... are necessities of literary form. The form of the essay, as we have it towards the end of the sixteenth century, most significantly in Montaigne, representative essayist because the representative doubter, inventor of the name as, in essence of the thing — of the essay, in its seemingly modest aim, its really large and adventurous possibilities — is indicative of Montaigne's peculiar function in regard to his age, as in truth the commencement of our own. It provided him with precisely the literary form necessary to a mind for which truth itself is but a possibility, realizable not as general conclusion, but rather as the elusive effect of a particular personal experience; to a mind which, noting faithfully those random lights that meet it by the way, must need content itself with suspension of judgement, at the end of the intellectual journey, to the very last asking: "Que sçais-je?" Who knows? in the very spirit of that old Socratic contention that all true philosophy is but a refined sense of one's ignorance. (*Plato and Platonism*, IX, 175)

Pater thus sets up a parallel between the late sixteenth and late nineteenth centuries. He perceives the subjectivity of knowledge, relativism, and skepticism as shared elements between these two historical moments and revises them into an expanded notion of the modern age. These are several of the characteristics absorbed from the literary and philosophical past into his own work. They constitute an important strain of the "*Montaignesque* element" in the work of one of the most important precursors of the modernist period, who articulated a new context in which to consider the *Essais*.

Pater reactivated the *Essais* in the manner of others — in a supporting role to help formulate his own positions. His reception of Montaigne generated fragments ("random lights that it meets by the way") of their significance in his own writing and according to his own needs ("a particular personal experience"). Pater used the *Essais* in his own work and to his advantage as a more modern exemplar of the "old Socratic contention." He reproduced the *Essais*' "peculiar function" by extending their historical horizons in a new form. Innovative deployment of the *Essais* thus occurred in

Pater's construction of a network of Montaignean *florilège* around which he constructed the narrative journey of *Gaston*. Explicit appropriation of Montaigne's work helped Pater to write his most open and exploratory text. In *Gaston*, Pater produces the same irresolvable tensions in Gaston's thoughts that the protagonist reads in Montaigne's writing. Mediating between custom and innovation, classic and modern, mobile thought becomes a key factor for Pater in this problematic of tradition and its renovation. Around it is the essayistic journey of Gaston, a protagonist who attempts to capture his thoughts on the run, responding to questions that defy resolution, accepting their unresolvable nature, and perpetuating their existence. This is a narrative of "really large and adventurous possibilities" in that it sets up a dynamic that affects Woolf's writing of *Orlando* — which remains, for any reader, an indisputable literary adventure.

Montaigne is a *kritische* historian, even as he is antiquarian and monumental, when he develops problematic networks of textual knots and retreats into a serenely ironic skepticism. Pater sees such practice as a reaction to the "paradoxical condition of the world, the natural inconsistency of man" ("Pascal," VIII, 69). Pater traces these two tendencies from Montaigne through Pascal, and finally into his own work. The impact of Pascal's Montaigne can be seen in Pater's summary of their importance: "Reading them, so modern are these thoughts, so rich and various in suggestion, that one seems to witness the mental seed-sowing of the next two centuries, and perhaps more ..." ("Pascal," VIII, 66). Pater maintains elsewhere that the essay, in the sense of the Montaignean discursive adventure, is where the innovative impulse finds its most adequate expression. Pater establishes Montaigne as its original and most accomplished practitioner, and considers him the model for all subsequent writing in a modernist mode: "The strictly appropriate form of our modern philosophic literature, the essay, came into use at what was really the relative or modern spirit, in the Renaissance of the sixteenth century" (*Plato and Platonism*, IX, 175). Montaigne is also Pater's prototype for the modern skeptical strategy: "And the skeptical philosopher of Bordeaux does but commence the modern world" (*Plato and Platonism*, IX, 194). The *Essais* thus provide Pater with meticulously wrought examples of strategic doubt and he uses them to begin a new configuration of intellectual history. Pater sees the origins of his own work in that of Montaigne. Truth for the latter, according to Pater, *is only a possibility*; the mind must content itself with the suspension of judgment, the writer must distill his or her own supple medium to express that state of mind. Pater's assessment of the modernist predicament, which he sees as emanating from Montaigne's writing, focuses on the relativity of understanding: "modern thought is distinguished from ancient by its cultivation of the 'relative' spirit in place of the 'absolute'" ("Coleridge," *Appreciations*, V, 68).

Pater was thus essentially connected to Montaigne in his belief that the *Essais* provided him an earlier example of an attitude that he considered very similar to his own. Montaigne offerred Pater a literary model that by definition lends itself to free development. Montaigne's skeptical mannerism occurred in the face of his sense of the decline of civilization and culture and of weakened faith in blind adherence to humanistic ideals.[17] We have seen how threatening his discourse was to the neoclassicizing and politically centralizing forces of the seventeenth and eighteenth centuries, as well as to the enlightenment ideal of rational clarity. Pater, too, was a subtly dangerous figure; his homosexuality, breakdown of genres, stylistic innovation, and hedonistic aesthetics threatened the Victorian cultural hegemony. This can be acutely seen in Sir Leslie Stephen's veiled yet unmistakable attack on Pater in "Art and Morality," in which he characterizes him as immoral and aesthetically irresponsible and refers to him as an "indolent epicurean."[18] In the context of Pater's personalized reception, the *Essais* can be more authoritatively appreciated for what was previously considered aberrant. Montaigne's "modernism" comes into clearer focus as a revised notion of the *Essais* is produced in Pater's reactivation of some of their more innovative characteristics in a different literary tradition.

Outwardly, Montaigne would probably have countered the more rigorous rhetorical exigencies of Pater. He did not adhere closely to systematic models of composition and developed a style with more rough edges than Pater's. Pater was a professor, one of Montaigne's culprits of authority, yet one temperate enough to develop a personalized attitude that Montaigne would have appreciated. Yet he still wrote in a more polished manner of expression than did Montaigne, and developed in general a more accessible, systematic approach to writing, however impressionistic and idiosyncratic his style may be. In seeking the balance between innovation and tradition, Pater thus had much greater faith in philosophical and linguistic systems. Montaigne's tentative belief in the equivalency of words and things, his impulse to write a problematic text with no end ("sans cesse"), which he wished to be extended "autant qu'il y a d'encre et de papier au monde" (III, ix, 945), pushed the *Essais* toward one of their most original qualities: playful undecideability. Pater on the other hand maintained a greater belief in the equivalency of *verba* and *res*, and in the possibility that a writer can fully express thoughts with words:

> The essence of all good style, whatever its accidents may be, is expressiveness. It is mastered in proportion to the justice, the nicety with which words balance or match their meaning, and their writer succeeds in saying what he *wills*, grave or gay, severe or florid, simple or complex. ("Pascal," VIII, 52)

These are in fact the qualities that he admired in the work of Pascal, not Montaigne. Yet even as he praised calculated and well-executed expression in the manner of the *Pensées* ("mastered in proportion"), Pater was unable to offer a clear solution to the problem of good style ("grave or gay, severe or florid, simple or complex"). In an equally inconsistent manner, Montaigne made a concerted effort to emulate Seneca and Plutarch even while he rejected Cicero, thereby producing a highly expressive, rhetorically charged style that he outwardly refused in many places in the *Essais*. The uniqueness of both writers is found in the ability to write inconsistencies into their work that undermine unequivocal resolution and then pursue their implications. It is a structure of constructing and then dismantling, working against oneself in order to allow the free play of paradox to captivate readers and engage the issues in their own understanding of the world and of themselves.

Pater's reception of Montaigne through Pascal, like Sainte-Beuve's, is fraught with contradictions. Pater rightfully insisted on the fact that Pascal, try as he would, could not extract himself from Montaigne's skepticist reasoning. Pater went as far as to consider Montaigne's hold over Pascal inescapable, both sharing a certain "Satanic intimacy" in their understanding of the cruelness of humanity and of "the paradoxical condition of the world, the natural inconsistency of man; his strange blending of meanness with ancient greatness" ("Pascal," VIII, 69). At the end of his life, Pater continued to develop his reciprocal notion of modernist aesthetics in the very encounter of Pascal and Montaigne. Pascal's work was for Pater emblematic of a hypersensitive attitude attempting to come to terms with an unacceptable precursor. His failure to do so was the greatness of his effort. It is perhaps Montaigne's *pertes triomphantes*, recast in Pascal's and in perhaps his own work, which Pater saw as the sublime failure of the attempt to reformulate one's precursors in a satisfying manner. Pater never really resolved the issue. Eliot picked up where he left off and engaged Pascal's accomplishment in order to resolve the impasse from which Pater could not extricate himself. In Eliot's terms, Pascal's Jansenist zeal could only outwardly counteract Montaigne — Eliot went so far as to say that he was Montaigne's greatest adversary since his unflinching spirit of belief needed the foil of Montaigne's skepticism in order to work out his own position; yet, Pascal could not master him. Eliot contends that although Pascal may have set out to destroy Montaigne, Montaigne's enigmatic invincibility triumphs:

> One cannot destroy Pascal, certainly; but of all authors Montaigne is one of the least destructible. You could as well dissipate a fog by flinging hand-grenades into it. For Montaigne is a fog, a gas, a *fluid, insidious element*. He does not reason, he *insinuates, charms, and influences*; or if he reasons, you must be prepared for his having some other design upon you than to convince you by his argument. It is hardly too much to say that Montaigne is *the most essential author to know*, if we would understand the course of French thought during the last three hundred years.[19] (emphasis added)

Echoes of Malebranche's backhanded praise or Bossuet's and Arnauld's diatribes against the *Essais*! Eliot saw Montaigne as the most important writer in the French tradition, but for negative reasons. Eliot extricates himself from Pater's problematic in a reactionary move that sees Montaigne as a "*fluid, insidious* element;" the very mobility of his essayistic project, that which Pater and Woolf promote, is countered by Eliot's reactionary proscription. Like Pater (who refers to Montaigne's "Satanic" persona), Eliot sees in him some ethereal mysticism: a seductive charmer who produces an enveloping skepticism difficult for any intellectual to escape. Eliot thus chooses to wear the gas mask of dogmatism in order to combat Montaigne, an opponent of systematic discursive norms (*Hebrew*: *Satan*, "adversary"). He underscores again, after Sainte-Beuve's and Pater's equivocal engagements of the problem of Pascal's Montaigne, the nature of Montaigne's ubiquitous pyrrhonism, powerful yet dangerous, difficult to escape, impossible to dominate — even the brilliant Pascal fails to do so. It is Montaigne's unsettling qualities that are his most unique, yet also his most threatening, and Eliot, although admiring him, does not hesitate to chastise him for it.

Pater, caught in between Pascal and Montaigne, realized that Montaigne's work virtually coerces one to adapt in some ways to his inescapable pyrrhonist reasoning. He thus chose, it would seem, Montaigne's sanguine acceptance of "poor lovable humanity" ("Pascal," VIII, 69) over Pascal's Jansenist wrath. The polarity of Pascal and Montaigne in Pater's work demonstrates the dual temperament that the latter sees as another aspect of a modernist attitude: the writer's perpetual struggle between two perennial intellectual dispositions, those of absolutism and relativism, without a facile or dogmatic preference of one over the other. This attitude produces of course the problematic of mobile ambivalence, the very quality that frightened Eliot and Pascal and was embraced by Pater as the key to modernist literary production. Pater achieves in fact a suspension of closure in the essay "Pascal." Such tentative phrases as "and the like," "and so forth," or the elliptical ending are invitations to pick up where he left off by the *suffisant lecteur*. Pater attempts to take a stand on Pascal and Montaigne, ambiguously develops the qualities of both writers, and suspends his conclusions in mid-air. It is no coincidence that Pater's last essay before his death was on Pascal (read Montaigne). It was his last attempt to convey his position on the aesthetics of being. Whereas Pascal demanded all or nothing, Pater embraced Montaigne's penchant for "middle terms" ("Pascal," VIII, 87). Autonomous art must always be legitimized by history; neither wholly self-indulgent, nor espousing a nostalgic view of the past, Montaigne offered Pater, in contradiction to Pascal's single-minded quest for religious being, the opportunity to communicate the incompleteness of experience. In this, the *Essais* provide the possibility for a modernist rewriting of the past: "The aesthete lives in contradiction to reality, and herein lies the revolutionary aspect of his attitude, for his approach breaks up existing, solidified forms of life."[20] Montaigne's movement between self and history, stability and its dissolution, and certainty and skepticism helped to create the genre of the essay and the intellectual dynamics it embodies. Pater's insight into Montaigne's work was to have illuminated this condition.

The *Essais* provoked Pater to work out his own type of philosophical skepticism, stylistic expressionism, and relativistic attitude toward past and present, as well as to mix the categories "renaissance" and "modern," and even to use them in places as a single descriptive category. Pater often uses the *Essais* to discuss the two notions as essentially related phenomena, which helps him to establish his concept of modernity in literature. He gives the *Essais* an opportunity to show off their innovative dimensions by valorizing their originality. Montaigne's modernist identity thus becomes tangible in light of Pater's reception of the *Essais*, a work that he considers to be a quintessential catalyst of literary modernism: "Those essays, as happens with epoch-marking books, were themselves a life, the power which makes them what they are, having been accumulated in them, imperceptibly by a thousand repeated modifications, like character in a person: at the moment when Gaston presented himself, to go along with the great 'egotist' for a season, that life had just begun" (*Gaston*, VI, 84).

A further example of Pater's evaluation and adaptation of the *Essais*, in which he responds tentatively yet positively to a potentially pessimistic doctrine (pyrrhonism), can be seen in his description of Marius's consideration of Aristippus's response to skepticism generated by the philosophy of Heraclitus. In this case, Marius values above all "the spectacle of one of the happiest temperaments coming, so to speak, to an understanding with the most depressing of theories, and making the best of it; turning its hard bare truths, with wonderful tact, into precepts of grace, and delicate wisdom, and a delicate sense of honour" (*Marius*, III, 135-36). In the post-Kantian specter of disillusionment in which Pater wrote, he struggled with the difficulty of passing beyond individual experience in order to attain "that sense of large proportion in things, that all-embracing prospect of life as a whole" (*Miscellaneous Studies*, VIII, 12). Thus, Montaigne's epithet "que sçay-je?" becomes a springboard for Pater's optimistic modernist gesture in the face of limitation embodied in the often dismal lessons of nineteenth-century philosophy.[21] Pater's brand of optimistic skepticism and absolute relativism is strongly marked by Montaigne's. He develops the *Essais* in the service both of critical awareness and of an integrated, self-generated vision of the world.

Pater's intellectual quest in relation to the work of Montaigne unfolds most visibly in *Gaston,* in which the protagonist's search for self-understanding is nourished on models of the past (Ronsard, Bruno, and especially Montaigne). Chapters IV and V of *Gaston* contain Pater's most detailed reconstruction of Montaigne's thought. The Montaigne episodes demonstrate the interdependence of Montaigne's skepticism and Pater's aestheticism, in which innate and original predilection is developed through a transformation of monumental history, as seen in Gaston's dialog with his literary and spiritual guide. Gaston, like Pater and Montaigne, is an intuitive, impressionistic critic, coloring his understanding of the past with personal response: "The essential dialogue was that of the mind with itself; but this dialogue throve best with some text shot from a book, the queries and objections of a living voice" (*Gaston,* VI, 109). As Gaston goes on his "haphazard journey" (*Gaston,* VI, 110) through Périgord, he strives to understand the past while monitoring the cultivated expansion of his own abilities. He asserts his individual will while participating in collective historical experience and travels without ever reaching a satisfying destination. He is incapable of making clear decisions, and instead of fully understanding his experiences, remains an uncertain observer in the "shadow of events" (*Gaston,* VII, 203).

Pater's choice of the European renaissance, and of Montaigne's life and work in particular as the centerpiece of Gaston's education, reproduces Montaignean textuality, which thereby begins to play an explicit role in the modernist movement. In *Gaston,* the protagonist journeys through Périgord to Montaigne's estate, and into the imagined life and thought of the essayist while seeking to understand himself through his reflections on the *Essais.* It is difficult not to notice Pater's play on words between *Gaston de Latour* and Montaigne, *the Gascon de la tour* — a correlation that points to the strong affinity Pater felt for Montaigne at this point in his career. The work is in a fragmentary, often unpolished state, another poorly jointed configuration ("une marqueterie mal jointe") in the spirit of the *Essais* that precludes any ultimate solutions to its problems. The protagonist's journey in *Gaston* is representative of Pater's own intellectual adventures through the past and particularly, for two central chapters, of his experiences in reading and reflecting on the *Essais*. It has not been unequivocally determined by critics whether Pater's choice to abandon the completion of *Gaston* was by chance or by necessity. Pater did not, or could not, conclude the narration of Gaston's quest. *Gaston* is an incomplete work; he put the project on hold after writing six chapters and died two years later.[22] Pater thus failed near the end of his life to establish an unequivocal place for Montaigne in his *oeuvre* — the qualities of the *Essais* that he admired most prevented him from establishing the final role they were to play in his work and from concluding on their ultimate importance. The dissemination of Montaigne's work throughout Pater's is very much in line with Montaigne's practice of freely integrating portions of other ideas and texts into his own as he pleased. The unfinished quality of *Gaston* thus exposes a rawer literary attempt, a more *kritische* outlook than developed in *Marius*. Pater was wary of the *Essais*' ability to frustrate critical systematization, and therefore developed in *Gaston* the implications he saw in Montaigne's work in a literary form, thereby giving him fuller freedom of expression while remodulating the "*Montaignesque* element." Like the *Essais, Gaston* is a work of thoughts often needing to be more fully developed. What further changes and additions would Montaigne and Pater have made given more life? The problem of a definitively established text of the *Essais*, because of the various editions and layers of the text, may never be resolved with certainty; the same may be said of *Gaston*.

Pater's protagonist Gaston is one of the prototypes for the uncertain questing mobility of *Orlando*, for even in the chapters that Pater did complete, the protagonist is always groping and never intellectually satisfied. In order to cultivate his personality in the context of Montaigne's essays on various aspects of human existence, Gaston explores the problematic nature of understanding and judgment: "The diversity, the undulancy of human nature! — so deep a sense of it went with Montaigne always that himself too seemed to be ever changing colour sympathetically therewith" (*Gaston*, VI, 91). Recognizing the multiplicity of the universe, Gaston realizes that he must create his own truths, and not rely on externals: "Whatever truth there might be, it must come for each one from within, not from without" (*Gaston,* VI, 136). In accepting that there is "doubt everywhere" and that "a sapient, instructed, shrewdly ascertained ignorance" (*Gaston,* VI, 133) is the only proper response to the uncertainty of existence, Gaston works toward understanding the world and especially himself: "I have no other end in writing but to discover *myself*"(*Gaston,* VI, 135). The function of life for him is the fulfillment of the self, the effort to communicate inner being, directly and instantaneously. Pater uses paradox and ambiguity to entice readers to produce their own immediacy of experience by reading and reflecting on the *Essais* and develop a personalized understanding of their importance. The juncture in Gaston's thought of skepticism and an inward-looking, self-referential relation to the world leads to some recognizable modernist literary techniques: inconclusive arguments, experimental form, creative use of quotation, and psychological instability. Pater distilled these elements from the *Essais* and recast them in *Gaston,* a text that has remained unresolvable and has served as a precursor of modernist narrative practice.

Were it completed, *Gaston* would have been a character study parallel to *Marius the Epicurean.* In both works, the heros live through important transitional moments in history in the search for intellectual development, self-awareness, and spiritual refinement. Marius's reading of ancient philosophy produces in him "a perpetual, inextinguishable thirst after experience" (*Marius,* III, 112). His metaphysical quest is a fundamental constituent of the modernist sensibility that is based on a personalized perception of the public world. D. W. Fokkema's concept of modernism is useful as a summary model of that which Montaigne helps to produce in Gaston's vision: "Modernist narration is explicitly and professedly selective. It allows for the personal view, as expressed in the stream of consciousness. The Modernist *can* focus on the selective personal view since he does not claim general validity for that view."[23] Montaigne is not a "stream-of-consciousness" writer in the generally accepted sense of the term. Yet he does follow the movement of his thoughts and attempt to communicate them dynamically. It is interesting to note the liquid metaphor of a widely accepted critical concept. It is an apt one in light of the Heraclitean production of the *Essais,* prototype for the flux of human consciousness on the page. Montaigne's example in "Des cannibales" of the river Dordogne and the Atlantic Ocean, which constantly wash away firm ground and create new landscapes over a period of years, metaphorically underscores his acceptance of the mutability and instability of reality and language. Likewise, his praise of Plato's *furor poeticus* is carried out in terms of a *flow* of inspired and spontaneous language, much like his own mode of expression: "le poëte ... verse de forme tout ce qui luy vient en la bouche, comme la gargouille d'une fontaine, sans le ruminer et poiser, et luy eschappe des choses de diverse couleur, de contraire substance et d'un cours rompu" (III, ix, 995). In *Gaston*, the Loire river serves as a symbolic reminder that nothing stands still, but constantly moves toward the openness of the unknown: "And in a while the dominant course of the river itself, the animation of its steady, downward flow, even amid the sand-shoals and whispering islets of the dry season, bore his thoughts beyond it, in a sudden irresistible appetite for the sea" (*Gaston*, VI, 78-9). As we've seen, Nietzsche and Emerson also used liquid metaphors to describe their attitudes toward the mutability of language and human understanding. The fluid quality of human experience and expression would become the raging torrent of the swollen Thames, which washes away a whole stage of Orlando's life and pushes him onward to the sea in a journey to understand the world as a literary artist.

Pater was drawn to this fundamental quality of Montaignean textuality: the individualistic exfoliation of writing based on active relationships with cultural tradition. The aesthetic vision is essentially the writer's own, yet it is developed through a parasitic use of historical models. Pater, like Montaigne, read widely and eclectically, integrating bits and pieces of the past into the fabric of his own writing. Gaston, for example, mediates between his self and the subject matter of his literary education. His quest is to solve the problem of understanding the past through the full expansion of his own potential. The literary experience for Gaston, expressed in his own terms and in those taken from the *Essais*, is "a continual journey in thought, 'a continual observation of new and unknown things'" (*Gaston*, VI, 108). Pater embeds quotation in quotation, allowing Montaigne's thought to merge with Gaston's. Gaston's education is developed through Montaigne's apprehension of paradoxical truths, his movement of thought, his suspicion of certain understanding: "Men's minds were like the grotesques which some artists of that day loved to join together, or like one of his own inconstant essays, never true for a page to its proposed subject. 'Nothing is so supple as our understanding; it is double and diverse; and the matters are double and diverse too'" (*Gaston*, VI, 94). Montaigne's sincere ambiguity and relative judgment thus permeate Gaston's pilgrimage: "For so pronounced a lover of sincerity as Monsieur de Montaigne, there was certainly a strange ambiguousness in the result of his lengthy inquiries, on the greatest as well as on the lightest matters, and it was inevitable that a listener should accept the dubious lesson in his own sense" (*Gaston*, VI, 114-115). For Gaston, Montaignean doubt and mobility are the keys to his education. They catalyze his open dialog with life while his experimental adventures develop their "dubious lesson" in idiosyncratic ways ("in his own sense"). The *Essais* provide for the development of a prototype of the uncertain protagonist of the modernist novel.

The Gaston-Montaigne episodes are essentially a critical essay on the *Essais* through the voice of a sympathetic observer. They are new dialogs of "the mind with itself," in the autoreflective mode of the *Essais*. Yet this self is permeated with appreciations of preexisting texts. In considering Montaigne, "the solitary conscience of the age" (*Gaston*, VI, 114), Gaston develops the ability to let his thoughts wander in various directions within the range of his personalizing tendencies and self-cultivation. Montaigne's château provides Gaston with asylum and with the counsel that helps him to continue his intellectual journey. In bringing together an historical and an imaginative character, Pater highlights the interconnectedness of the writer's work and his or her literary precursors. This is his method for demonstrating the relevancy of exemplary persons (Nietzsche's *monumentalische*) to the aesthetic life. It is critical perception put into creative practice.

Perception of the public past and its private deployment are perennial concerns for literary texts that assimilate the work of a large number of writers. In the case of Pater, this critically creative reception of the *Essais* becomes one of the centrifugal forces in his aesthetic system.[24] Much of his work relies on an understanding of Montaigne's ability to mediate between the judging of external events (whether present or past) and the development of the private self in relation to that material. Pater does likewise, conforming publicly (not without being attacked from time to time) as an Oxford academic, yet rebelling privately by becoming an innovative writer. Like Montaigne, Pater often put on a public persona and was efficient in his social tasks; yet he retreated inwardly to create the world of his unique inner experience through writing. Montaigne's tantalizing relativism, along with his mask of learned ignorance, allow Gaston to "keep his soul free and roving" (*Gaston*, VI, 146), liberate his speculations, avoid reductive closure, and always develop himself further in the quest for wisdom. Both Pater and Montaigne ultimately resist authoritative philosophies of presence and work hypothetically in order to better — not completely understand — human experience, thereby fulfilling the Paterian dictum that "not the fruit of experience but the experience itself is the end" (*The Renaissance*, 188). For Gaston, as seen in his frustrated attempt to explain "the terrible Eve of St. Bartholemew, 1572" (*Gaston*, VI, 149), nothing can be definitively understood, ambiguity and contradiction being an all-pervasive condition of human existence. As do the *Essais*, *Gaston* offers a problematic nexus of concerns for critics to develop.

The Saint Bartholemew's Day massacre provides a significant intertextual correlation between the *Essais* and *Gaston*. Neither Montaigne's implication in this event, nor his attitude toward it will ever be fully understood. It is this silence, as we've seen in the context of de Man's dilemma, that links Montaigne to the ethics of modernism. Pater picks up on this absence in Montaigne's self-portraiture and develops Gaston's emotional and intellectual response to the historical circumstances surrounding the event. Pater makes Gaston's thoughts the testing ground for that which Montaigne remained silent about. It is a curious reversal of Montaigne's "forgetting." Pater "remembers," through Gaston's voice, what he could never have known and attempts to provide a response to a circumstance that Montaigne chose not to discuss; he thereby complements the *Essais* by developing a narrative exfoliation of an issue important to Montaigne's life, but missing in his writing. Gaston is in Paris during the time immediately preceding the massacre and has an intimate knowledge of its unfolding. Yet even as he becomes closely involved and reflects upon the event's complex series of intrigues and consequences (his new wife is a victim of the mass killings), he suddenly loses perspective ("he had lost for awhile the exacter view of certain outlines" — *Gaston*, VI, 159), and eventually becomes oblivious to the activities surrounding him. At a moment when it appears that Gaston is finally about to take control of his life and become a fully developed person engaged in historical events, his certainty erodes and a firm grasp of the significance of his life escapes him. It is a Montaignean sense of flux and instability that renders an adequate comprehension of his life and of the historical moment impossible:

> Was the "undulant" philosophy of Monsieur de Montaigne, in collusion with this dislocating time, at work upon him, that, following with only too entire a mobility the experience of the hour, he found himself more than he could have thought possible the toy of external accident? (*Gaston*, VI, 159)

After the massacre, Gaston considers the weakness of Montaigne's position as well as of his own "helplessness amid the obscure forces around him" (*Gaston*, VI, 161). Pater uses Montaigne to produce an equivocating protagonist who is buffeted by both historical personages and circumstances in the search for an elusive stability. The whirlpool of Gaston's uncertainties later helped Woolf to endow Orlando with similar qualities, although with exaggerated emphasis in the continued development of the problematic modernist hero.

The analysis of a passage from *Gaston* helps to demonstrate how Pater's expressive style accentuates the perpetual movement of Gaston's problematic understanding of the *Essais*:

> How many curious moral variations he had to show! — "vices that are lawful" : vices in us which "help to make up the seam in our piecing, as poisons are useful for the conservation of health" : "actions good and excusable that are not lawful in themselves" : "the soul discharging her passions upon false objects where the true are wanting" : men doing more than they propose, or they hardly know what, at immense hazard, or pushed to do well by vice itself, or working for their enemies: "condemnations more criminal than the crimes they condemn" : the excuses that are self-accusations: instances, from his own experience, of a hasty confidence in other men's virtue which "God had favoured" : and how, "even to the worst people, it is sweet, their end once gained by a vicious act, to foist into it some show of justice." In

> the presence of this indefatigable analyst of act and motive all fixed outlines seemed to vanish away. The healthful pleasure of motion, of thoughts in motion! (*Gaston*, VI, 121)

The "fixed outlines" of syntactic order seem to dissolve as Gaston contemplates fragments of Montaigne's pronouncements on human nature. Yet these spontaneous "thoughts in motion" are not Montaigne's but rather Gaston's, as seen in the way he attempts to link together a disparate *florilège* of Montaigne's maxims into a dynamic, yet coherent whole. The series of clauses are loosely linked by colons that would lead a reader to assume causal relations between the semantic groupings. The first series ("vices ... vices ... the soul") appears at first to be a progressive discussion of the variable positions Montaigne maintained on negative and positive human characteristics. Yet after reading the catalog, it is difficult to demarcate clear relations between the various propositions. The following colon seemingly continues the "thoughts in motion" of Montaigne and proposes another philosophical snippet, but as this clause ("men doing") assumes its place in the sequence, it becomes evident that Gaston's own reflection is becoming absorbed into the sequence of quotations from the *Essais*. The next three colons develop a pattern of quotation of Montaigne, Gaston's thought, and quotation of Montaigne. The relation of this pluralistic grouping of quotes out of context appears to revolve around the question of the paradoxical nature of good and bad human actions. Yet it is also about the impossibility of fully ordering one's thoughts while engaging the *Essais*. The paragraph lacks strong punctuating order, which frustrates the reader's ability to sort through the cornucopia of Montaignean clichés as presented through Gaston's irregular efforts to understand their significance. The *morceaux choisis* taken from the *Essais*, in their spontaneous and discontinuous ordering, poses the same problem for the reader as for Gaston in understanding them: "Yes! Gaston felt them, the oldest of them, moving, as he listened, under and away from his feet, as if with the ground he stood on" (*Gaston*, VI, 121). This passage is rendered even more problematic by this concluding qualification. Why are these particular pronouncements "the oldest?" (Montaigne discusses these themes throughout the *Essais* and especially in the later ones of Book III). Who is Gaston "listening" to: Montaigne speaking, his own reading of the text, or his auditory memory? Another textual complication is that Gaston "felt" these thoughts; Pater mixes the tactile and the auditory, moving from Gaston's mental capability (his mind) to a physical one (his feet), using the thoughts as a metaphor for the "ground" on which he stands. Is this "ground" the fixed presence of Montaigne's thought in which Gaston takes comfort? It cannot be so since they are "thoughts in motion." And why is this motion of Montaigne's thought a "healthful pleasure" since these particular thoughts are discussing metaphoric illnesses of the human condition?

If Gaston chooses to admire the position that "poisons are useful for the assertion of health," then his imperfect understanding of Montaigne has a beneficial quality for the development of his personality. Pater picks up on the paradoxical equation of Nietzsche that in order to overcome history one must turn to history. The homeopathic dynamism of the paragraph is flooded with fragments of antiquarian notions that overwhelm Gaston's ability to order them and create anew for himself; this super-abundance impedes his ability to achieve a synthetic understanding of their significance. Yet this impossibility of fully comprehending "history" (Montaigne's paradoxical pronouncements) does lead to a Nietzschean type of "new and healthy culture," namely, Gaston's personally cultivated realization that humans are incapable of absolute knowledge and are to be berated for believing that they can ever achieve it: "and this was the vein of thought which oftenest led the master back contemptuously to emphasize the littleness of man. — 'I think that we can never be despised according to our full desert'" (*Gaston*, VI, 121-22). In this instance, Pater's expressive style leads to a philosophical impasse, which itself is embodied in the refusal of a clear exposition of the paradoxical pluralism of Montaigne's thought. The *Essais* help Pater to produce the equivocating protagonist, a gesture that becomes a model for other uncertain, groping protagonists in works of the modernist period, such as Prufrock, Bloom, Mauberly, and Orlando.

Montaigne's skepticism is not only philosophical but stylistic. His textual structures are most often nonlinear and discontinuous in the refusal to posit an unequivocal mode of representation. Pater's attempt in *Gaston* to put into narrative practice this pluralistic, skeptical style shows this text to be emblematic of his belief in the relativism and instability of literary practice. The playful artifice of modern self-conscious mannerism as developed in *Gaston* anticipates Croll's and even Curtius's discussions of mannerism as a recurrent phenomenon in literature. Pater uses the *Essais* to develop his "crotesques" in playful junctures and imperfect arabesques of Gaston's thought and Montaigne's writing, both of which are very much complex and ornate designs of intertwined figures, both intellectual and textual. As Gaston tries to come to terms with the wisdom, beauty, and paradoxes of the *Essais* and its "double philosophy" (*Gaston*, VI, 146), he is troubled about their irreconcilable aspects. Pater ends Chapter V, "Suspended Judgement," with more questions than answers as well as with an abrupt shift of focus. The "inconsistent or inconsecutive" (*Gaston*, VI, 147) qualities of the *Essais* leave the reader searching for greater certainty: "what might that ground be?" (*Gaston*, VI, 148) is Gaston's final question as he dazedly leaves Montaigne's château, feeling insecure about what he has learned. Pater duplicates Montaigne's writing by producing a discontinuous narrative, meandering through a mental conversation with himself and the *Essais*, yet remaining incapable of making a final decision on how to best understand them. The nature metaphor ("ground") has, as we've seen, its antecedents in Montaigne's "riviere" and Nietzsche's "Erde": all three writers make a paradoxical stylistic choice since they describe with naturalistic imagery that which is not "natural," but "civilized," namely, the imperfections of human understanding. The natural and the conventional, the world and the self, the past and the present are the dynamic polarities that generate a persistent movement between their possible arrangements.

As a politician, churchman, landowner, soldier, aristocrat, diplomat, traveler, husband, and writer, Montaigne was the embodiment of conformity to ancient greatness and contemporary exigency. He approached life with a pragmatist's sagacity and acceptance of the world, yet simultaneously inscribed a radical independence of mind in his text. Pater attempted to rearticulate this latent modernism. *Gaston* begins with the protagonist resisting the historical burden that his illustrious family imposes upon him. He becomes a clerk at the Cathedral of Chartres, but feels the need to escape the "shadow" of the church, which functions as an embodiment of historical tyranny. Ronsard's poetry helps him to live in the immediacy of the present moment, but he then feels uncomfortable at being cut off from a historical past. It is thus his Montaignean experience that helps him to bridge the gap between past and present by helping him to overcome the absolute understandings he had previously sought. Gaston's final experience, an enthusiastic embrace of Bruno's pantheism, provokes him to try to conclude on the sum of his previous experiences. Yet this final attempt to appropriate a model for life becomes another foiled possibility and he is forced into accepting the provisional quality of the past's ability to improve life in the present. Pater tries to "end" Gaston, as Montaigne "concludes" the *Essais*: with an acceptance of the natural condition of the human experience in all its complexity and diversity. Yet, as with Montaigne's "conclusion," underneath Gaston's attempt to establish a stable model for life is an awareness of the impossibility of serene resolution and that the intellectual journey is virtually endless: "The theoretic recognition of that mobile spirit of the world, ever renewing its youth, became the motive of a life as mobile, as ardent, as itself, of a continual journey, the venture and stimulus which would be the occasion of ever new discoveries, of renewed conviction" (*Gaston*, VI, 197). Gaston makes this claim even after he has been involved with Bruno's system of the integration of mind and matter and of body and soul. It is at first an attractive solution to Gaston, bothered as he is by his own apparent indifference and inability to take a clear stand on issues, which he sees as an evasion of moral responsibility. Yet in the end, even Bruno's martyrdom leaves him with an inescapable sense of the irresolvable nature of human experience when looked at honestly and exhaustively.

Pater's reception of the *Essais* activates their most innovative dimensions and reproduces them in his own writing. This is a key event toward the understanding of the modernist identity of the *Essais*. Like the *Essais*, Gaston's life was one of "a thousand repeated modifications" (*Gaston*, VI, 84). This is drawn from Montaigne's conception of the multiple aspects of the human personality that he was trying to communicate: "ainsi je me propose, en mille visages" (III, xiii, 1112). The Montaigne intertexts help Gaston to reach this apex of self-understanding and the accompanying realization of the impossibility of ever fully understanding anything. The evolving Gaston, his thoughts always in movement, develops his evolutionary self through Montaigne's writing. Yet Pater goes beyond mere literary contact and actually has Gaston receive a letter of invitation from Montaigne, travel to Perigord, and converse with him in person. He literalizes contact with the cultural past. In *Orlando,* Woolf redevelops this strategy yet satirizes such spiritual affinities with past writers in one of her efforts to dismantle the patriarchal perpetuation of culture. *Gaston* is generally considered a minor work in Pater's *oeuvre.* We have seen that it is nevertheless a major text toward a revised notion of a Montaignean modernism in its regeneration of the *Essais* in a new context, in which a text like *Orlando* would flourish.

♦ ♦ ♦

Comparison implies contrast, and the question of how to approach the disparities inherent in the confrontation of texts always demands more criteria to articulate the connective tissues between them. At the intersection of the work of Montaigne, Pater, and Woolf is the figure of Sir Thomas Browne. He was at once an adherent to the essayistic method, a generation after Montaigne, and an important literary model for Pater and Woolf. For Pater, Browne was an important appropriator of Montaignean skepticism, style, and textual playfulness and produced an important continuation of what Montaigne founded, the modern essay. For Woolf, the work of Browne was also an important stylistic and philosophical model; she discusses his work in her essays and weaves it into the textual fabric of *Orlando.* Browne's multiple points of contact with the work of Montaigne, Pater, and Woolf forms an under-texture that both links aspects of their work and allows us to see the "*Montaignesque* element" in a broader perspective. As with Montaigne, Pater admired Browne's uneven style: "it has its garrulity, its various levels of painstaking, its mannerism, pleasant of its kind or tolerable, together with much, to us intolerable" ("Sir Thomas Browne," *Appreciations,* V, 469). Besides Browne's spontaneous style (the stuttering syntax of Pater's critique emulates an irregular "garrulity"), Pater appreciated his egocentric temperament: "it is certain that Browne's works are of a kind to directly stimulate curiosity about himself — about himself as being manifestly so large a part of those works" ("Sir Thomas Browne," *Appreciations,* V, 471). Woolf's reading of Browne coincides in some ways with Pater's assessment of him as a writer of sincerity and modern subjectivity; she considered him "among a variety of other things, one of the first of our writers to be definitely himself."[25]

Browne himself called his best-known work a portrayal of the inner movements of his personality. This is the reason Emerson liked him — for his informal exploration of the self.[26] *Religio Medici* was putatively not composed for immediate publication. Browne refers to it as a collection of "retired imaginations" written as a "private exercise."[27] It is more a personal document about the intellectual journey of a questioning mind than a rigorous account of its ostensible subject matter. Portions of Browne's work are written under the guise of Montaignean sincerity. His preface "To the Reader" provides an example of the similarity in tone and intention to Montaigne's "Au Lecteur" in its claim to be a disarming and humble exercise in self-understanding:

> He that shall peruse that work, and shall take notice of sundry particularities and personall expressions therein, will easily discern the intention was not publik; and being a private exercise directed to my selfe, what is delivered therein was rather a memoriall unto me then an example or rule into any other. (*Religio Medici*, 59-60)

Much of *Religio Medici* is thus highly self-descriptive; Browne discusses the distinguishing features of his temperament and writes in the provisional introspective manner of Montaigne. Browne was also a connoisseur of doubt and skepticism, a writer "divers et ondoyant," whose claims can never be taken at face value and often remain paradoxically volatile. Browne's favorite image is Janus, who reminds him that there is an other side to every thing and event.[28] Like Montaigne he held in check the excessive claims of dogmatic reason in order to explore the inner configurations of his response to the world in the open and tentative context of the essay. Browne's skeptical and self-referential attitude, like Montaigne's, allowed him to make external concessions yet ultimately write for himself: "I have therefore one common and authentick Philosophy I learned in the Schooles, whereby I discourse and satisfie the reason of other men, another more reserved and drawne from experience, whereby I content with my own" (*The Garden of Cyrus,* 148). This type of paradoxical admission reproduces Montaigne's own ironic attitude on the interaction of the public and private dimensions of his work. Montaigne maintained the importance of social interaction and public service (in his case, in the form of pedagogy, law, politics, economics, tourism, and publishing), but wrote that "il se faut prester à autruy et ne se donner qu'à soy-mesme" (III, x, 1003). His life was a constant struggle to maintain a satisfying relationship between the two.

It was thus Browne's image of Janus, the custodian of the universe and god of beginnings ("January"), that ushered Montaigne's work into the mainstream of English letters. Browne's position is another modulation on the interactive relation between innovation and custom in the equivocal mode. Yet Browne was a doctor — after professors, the second of Montaigne's authoritative culprits. He was of a more scientific and empirical temperament, and also more explicitly preoccupied with spiritual matters than was Montaigne (he carried on an open religious debate with Milton for several years). He made more concessions to custom than did Montaigne; yet, as a more systematic thinker, he develops his arguments while discussing the weighty problems of scientific, religious, and philosophical importance in disarming, self-abnegating terms, maintaining an awareness of the difficulty of resolution and of the flexibility needed to accept the diversity of the world and still be able to express oneself in a serious way. In this, Browne's reception of the "*Montaignesque* element" into the mainstream of English letters in the seventeenth century is significant. The provisional, introspective qualities of the *Essais* served Browne in the development of his own medium, one structured yet supple enough to follow the inner movement of his thought.

As with Montaigne, Browne's introspection was often harshly received: "What should I say of his making so particular a Narration of personal things, and private thoughts of his owne; the knowledge whereof can not much conduce to any man's betterment?"[29] Browne produced a work that at first was considered useless or even dangerous by some, yet which eventually became canonized as monumental. Browne and Montaigne both developed flexible modes of thought and forms of expression to suit their self-conscious temperaments — an attitude that opened the way for the elusive search for psychic integration that has characterized "modernist" writing ever since. Montaigne was the more radical proponent of this new mode of writing. Browne thus serves as an important intermediary between Montaigne's baroque skepticism, Pater's aesthetic mannerism, and Woolf's cornucopian satirical rendition of the issues in *Orlando*. He offered Pater a more approachable model and practical inroad toward redeveloping the *Essais*. What Browne learned from Montaigne is how to try out an idea in conjunction with loosened textual structures flexible enough to pursue his roving skeptical consciousness.[30] The portrayal of the mind's movement in a spontaneous and immediate style was an important lesson learned by Browne from the *Essais*. Pater and Woolf adopted this sensibility into their own work through their readings of both authors as well as from Carlyle, Lamb, and Hazlitt, who redeveloped Montaigne, Browne, and Bacon in their highly influential works.[31] This strain of essay-writing in the skeptical mannerist mode of Montaigne's British readers demonstrates the *Essais* to be a source for writers whose concerns intersect, diverge, and replenish each other in an intertextual field in which self-portraiture and mobility have become the important guiding principles. Hazlitt perhaps most directly acknowledges Montaigne as the founder of the English essay:

> In treating of men and manners, he spoke of them as he found them, not according to preconceived notions and abstract dogmas; and he began by teaching us what he himself was … in a word, the first author who was not a book-maker, and who wrote not to make converts of others to established creeds and prejudices, but to satisfy his own mind of the truth of things.[32]

As we have seen, it is first in the work of the lesser known Browne that this tendency in English letters had its beginnings. It has since proved itself an inestimable catalyst for much Anglophone writing.

Several important studies have been written on the modernity of baroque and mannerist tendencies in the work of Montaigne and Browne.[33] It is a useful vantage point from which to develop stylistic criteria by which intertextual comparative analysis between writers of different histories, genders, and nationalities, yet similar aesthetic strategies, can be assessed in greater particularity. Morris Croll first established Montaigne as one of the founders of the "Anti-Ciceronian" or "explosive" style of the late sixteenth century. Literary style in this instance, according to Croll, transgressed Ciceronian strictures on choice of words, figures, and form in favor of looser structures that could better express ideas closer to their point of origin in the writer's mind, thereby achieving spontaneity and dynamism of expression. Anti-Ciceronian textuality "has the appearance of having been disrupted by an explosion within."[34] This is certainly a conspicuous quality of the *Essais*, of which we have seen an example in *Gaston*. The opening paragraph of "Du repentir" is a highly visible instance of Montaigne's attitude toward the instability of experience and an example of this "explosive" stylistic quality:

> Toutes choses y branlent sans cesse: la terre, les rochers du Caucase, les pyramides d'Aegypte, et du branle public et du leur. La constance mesme n'est autre chose qu'un branle plus languissant. Je ne puis asseurer mon object. Il va trouble et chancelant, d'une yvresse naturelle. Je le prens en ce point, comme il est, en l'instant que je m'amuse à luy. (III, ii, 805)

Disorderly and spontaneous syntax, the multiple substantive and adjectival qualifiers, and the variations of "branle" reflect the "yvresse naturelle" of the thought process. The broken symmetry of the semantic unit, the omission of conjunctions, and the sudden rhythmic shifts are manifestations of Montaigne's "anti-Ciceronian" style. The disorder and lack of logical connections in the passage are typical of Montaigne's attempts to catch the spontaneity and diversity of his thoughts in process. The *Essais* do not emulate the less inhibited Rabelaisean flow of language: beneath the spontaneous movement there is considerable structured consistency, which communicates Montaigne's attempts at ordering the instability of his experience. It is Montaigne's attempt to stabilize flux, yet to let the flux remain, that has demanded the rereading of his work by writers, philosophers, historians, and journalists for over four hundred years. He understood intimately the official rhetorical styles of his time, and often used them to his advantage, having learned Latin as his first language, having been educated in the humanist mode, trained as a lawyer, and employed as a magistrate; yet, he often derided the Ciceronian art of persuasion and sought refuge in a private discursive world of his own creation: "J'ay naturellement un stile comique et privé, mais c'est d'une forme mienne, inepte aux negotiations publiques" (I, xl, 252). The construction of a private space in language in one's own image has become an important common denominator of the modernist experience. Montaigne is clearly an essential forerunner of this phenomenon.

For Croll, Montaigne is one of the founders of "the modern prose style," and a writer who structured his text in a language uniform enough "to be called a style and also adaptable enough to adjust itself to the changing life of the modern world — a style which may grow and change in later generations without losing its recognizable features."[35] Instead of conforming to a prevailing model of stylistic acceptability, Montaigne developed a style more adaptable to his intellectual instability. Although Montaigne was a political and religious pragmatist, and although his enthusiasm most often yearned for the greatness of the past while remaining guarded against "nouvelletez" in all of its manifestations, he concomitantly created a countercurrent in his work by developing a novel mode of textual production, one outside of the accepted discursive modes of his time or of his own literary canon. The *Essais* thus became and created paradoxically a *new tradition*. Montaigne's duality and diversity spawned both a conservative in public matters ("Je vous conseille, en vos opinions et en vos discours, autant qu'en vos moeurs et en toute autre chose, la moderation et l'attrempance et la fuite de la nouvelleté et de l'estrangeté" — II, xii, 558) and a daring practitioner in private ones, since excess, dynamism, innovation, and uniqueness are the most dominant qualities of his writing.

Of Croll's "later generations" who pick up on Montaigne's stylistic innovations, Bacon, Burton, but especially Browne are the principal figures in the century following Montaigne's. A working definition of Montaigne's innovative style is the impulse to give more independence and autonomy to textual components in the attempt to capture the subject's thought patterns as they develop. The loose syntactical connections in both Montaigne and Browne help the development of their provisional thinking and demand of readers more attention to what the text is trying to say. Montaigne's transgression of rules, his playful attitude toward formal discursive systems resurfaces in Pater's undulancy in *Gaston* and, as we will see, in Woolf's phantasmagoric multiplication of discursive codes in *Orlando*.

Self-centered expression and a mobile writing style have been variously defined as baroque, mannerist, libertine, or decadent textuality. The self-referential, auto-critical, and textually parasitic world of the Montaignean experience provides an essential model for the production of all of these discursive modes. Montaigne sat alone in his tower, perused his books, and wrote in accord with his eccentricities, manifesting obsessions with death, melancholy, bodily functions, morals, and imaginative writing. Yet he only did so for a time, eventually returning to a socially active life, witnessing and participating in the extraordinary events of his time: witch burnings, religious wars, massacres, revolts, riots, plagues, famines, moral licentiousness as well as fanatical piety, thriving humanism juxtaposed with stultifying ignorance. For what kind of person was this to create a shrine to pagan culture in the midst of an illiterate population gorged on dogmatic Christianity and provincial superstition? We can imagine the noble luxury in which Montaigne lived compared to the culturally impoverished condition of the common people and even of many of his peers. His retreat into an ethereal atmosphere of cultural hedonism is not unlike that of the Duc Jean Floressas des Esseintes' attempt to reject the vulgarity and aesthetic barbarism of his times. Montaigne's simulacrum of Graeco-Roman antiquity in such a rustic setting has of course its charm, but also evokes the urgency and literalness with which he went about his project of living and writing. It is here that this *kritische* antiquarian struggled to live in as great a state of equanimity as possible. Montaigne could thus be considered as an earlier des Esseintes of the highly influential *A Rebours,* save for the glaring difference of Montaigne's valorization of the "natural" to Huysmans's glorification of "artifice." Yet Montaigne was not completely straightforward about naturalizing artifice; his quilt-like text is very mannered in bizarre ways and it must be considered that Huysmans was satirizing the artificiality that des Esseintes pursued. These correlations between the Montaignean and the *fin-de-siècle* experiences are not indisputable, but neither are they entirely dismissable.[36] Even Des Esseintes must return to the world of bourgeois materialism after his eccentric pursuit of self-fulfillment. Montaigne's work functions as an indirect model for *A Rebours,* a catalyst in the development of the literary generations that include Pater and Woolf. Living in a domestic retreat, however temporary this respite may be, with a sufficient income to do so, reading in an idiosyncratic manner while searching for self-understanding are circumstances shared by the authors of the *Essais* and *A Rebours* — an issue that could be explored elsewhere. Here, however, I would like to turn to Woolf's work, which has a particularly intriguing relationship to the *Essais.*

♦ ♦ ♦

Much of Woolf's critical writing is in the manner of the Montaignean essay and her aims and means are often produced in a skepticist mode. The weighing of probabilities, the suspension of dogmatic judgment, and the exploration of different sides of a question, qualities essential to her essayistic techniques, are attempts (*essais*), not closed systems of understanding.[37] The extent of Woolf's relation to Montaigne's work will emerge in an analysis of her reception of the *Essais*. Reflective lyricism abounds in her writing, chances are taken in the desire to explore flexible coalitions of thoughts that invite engaged redevelopment. These are elements of Pater's and Browne's writing, but Woolf takes a leap further than they do in confronting the *Essais*, assumes a more *kritische* position, and ultimately produces a more enigmatic reception of Montaigne's work. Her techniques have their models, yet are at the same time highly original in their outlook. Woolf's vision of narrative practice is outlined in "Modern Fiction" and "The Modern Essay," as well as in her essay on Montaigne. Her relationship to the *Essais* can thus be examined through her own "essays." Her contribution to the tradition of the English essay is substantial and numerous strategies found in the *Essais* can be seen operating in her work. In many of her over three hundred and fifty essays, Woolf proposed more radical modifications of the literary tradition of the previous two centuries than Montaigne could have imagined. She experimented radically with the forms she learned from the literary canon handed down by the Victorian guardians of culture and, although approaching the problematic of innovation and tradition more radically than Montaigne, Woolf's essaying attempted to recreate and revitalize the past through dynamically creative writing in a Montaignean mode. Her aesthetic of expressing the textures of self-consciousness was developed on a wide reception of cultural models, yet it is the tension between past and present that is highlighted in the attempt to develop her unique literary self through an engagement with past writers. In "How One Should Read a Book," Woolf's notion of participatory reading is very much in line with Montaigne's, namely, that the reader must be the writer's "fellow worker and accomplice."[38] This collaboration is more than ever necessary for Woolf's *suffisant lecteur*, since the artistic enterprise was for her an endless struggle, as it was for Montaigne and Pater, one that was never resolved.

Woolf awarded Montaigne the first single-author essay of *The Common Reader*. Yet why should she reach out across the boundaries of history, culture, and especially gender to this Catholic *seigneur* raised in the classical culture of renaissance humanism? Woolf's reasons were complex. Her fascination seemed to come from Montaigne's enterprise of attempting to communicate his sense of self, a project often at odds with his time and culture. To overcome the apparent incompatibility of discussing the interrelationship Woolf and Montaigne, let us remember that before Woolf, Montaigne's *suffisant lecteur* was, in fact, a *suffisante lectrice,* in the person of Marie de Gournay. Montaigne would have perhaps not been astonished at this since he seems to have appreciated the penchant that intellectual women had for recognizing the value of his special ability to communicate in a private way. Woolf, like Gournay and Montaigne, wrote within the tradition of male education and culture in which she was raised and with which she was saturated, but also against it. Like Gournay, she remade the language of her male predecessors (in her case Montaigne *and* Pater) in her own image. She did more than to simply recuperate Montaigne's writing; she reformulated it to suit her own needs. Reading was thus for Woolf, as it was for Montaigne, not just an attempt to decipher the past, but simultaneously a gesture of self-inscription into its various meanings. Woolf faced a cultural establishment as rigid toward women as it was toward Montaigne's writing. Their intellectual environments were different yet produced strikingly similar notions; this can clearly be seen in *A Room of One's Own.*

In *A Room,* Woolf proposes a more engaged relationship between innovation and tradition, between reader and text. She disclaims that great works are "single and solitary births" and proposes that artists produce original works only in the context of a shared cultural heritage: "masterpieces are the outcome of many years of thinking in common, of thinking by the body of the people, so that the experience of the mass is behind the single voice."[39] The writer's uniqueness is thus his or her *transformation* of a common tradition. The innovative self is not a pure subjectivity producing a solipsistic discourse, but rather an individual participating in "the common life which is the real life and not the little separate lives which we lead as individuals" (*A Room,* 117). The tension created by innovation and tradition is a space within which the activity of modulating new configurations arises from the confrontation of past examples. Woolf emphasized shared historical vision over individual uniqueness; the creative self develops in the context of the literary and cultural traditions that permeate it. At the same time, she radically diverged from tradition and produced unprecedented modes of writing.

In *A Room*, many of Woolf's pronouncements on education, style, innovation, and tradition resemble Montaigne's in thought and manner of presentation. Woolf found a paradoxical solution for the problem of the individual's ability to flourish in the shadow of custom; the writer must develop the paradoxical equation of the "habit of freedom" (*A Room*, 117). Woolf valued the "common life," the writer's relation to humanity and shared reality, yet ultimately posited conformity to personal motivation. In the context prepared by Montaigne and Nietzsche, she saw the role of education as a tool to be used to essay the "vastness and variety of the world" and to "bring out and fortify the differences rather than the similarities" (*A Room*, 91). She called for the rejection of dogmatic professors and antiquarian, rationalizing ideologies in favor of the freedom of the individual to develop his or her own provisional genre for the most authentic production of the self in writing:

> So long as you write what you wish to write, that is all that matters; and whether it matters for ages or only for hours, nobody can say. But to sacrifice a hair of the head of your vision, a shade of its colour, in deference to some Headmaster with a silver pot in his hand or to some professor with a measuring rod up his sleeve, is the most abject treachery, and the sacrifice of wealth and chastity which used to be said to be the greatest of human disasters, a mere flea-bite in comparison. (*A Room*, 110)

Like Montaigne, Woolf sought to escape the rigorous models of hegemonic discourse in order to peregrinate at her leisure through the literary tradition and develop inherited cultural tradition in her own particularized manner, with minimal regard to external stylistic strictures. She digresses freely in *A Room*, modulating idiosyncratically on materials drawn from both her reading and her lived experience. Like Montaigne, she seeks to share the common life of monumental creativity, yet remain committed to personal vision. She reaches, however, far beyond Montaigne's outwardly pragmatic attitude toward authority and tradition. She is less cautious than he or Pater in the personalizing of tradition and in the liberation from conformity, more on the side of Nietzsche in the openness and intense dynamism of her discursive practice.

In "De l'institution des enfans," Montaigne expressed dislike for the dogmatic attitude of traditional education toward books and learning and attempted to promote the student's natural understanding and practical implementation of inherited materials over bookish eloquence. In the next generation, Ben Jonson castigated such loose reading habits in his belief that they led to too much irregular and, thereby, unworthy writing: "Such are all Essayists, even their master Mountaigne."[40] Jonson's professionalist's attack is directed to the very quality that Woolf admired most in the *Essais*. In pursuing his own liberated method of reading, Montaigne released his text into the service of his readers. What disturbed Jonson as a refusal of authority over one's cultural tradition, is central to Woolf's notion of the writer's task: "To admit authorities, however heavily furred and gowned, into our libraries and let them tell us how to read, what to read, what value to place upon what we read, is to destroy the spirit of freedom which is the breath of those sanctuaries. Everywhere else we may be bound by laws and conventions — there we have none" ("How Should One Read a Book?" — 258). Freedom to pursue such reading is also an invitation to write in a similar manner — Montaigne's irregular textual development is alien to the patriarchal school of logic and rhetoric. Linear progress was a false construct for him; his circular manner of writing is a transgression of authoritarian (masculine) discourse. In *A Room*, Woolf proposes a similar aesthetic, but recast as a feminine one in place of the strictures of Johnsonian formalism (her own model for the stultifying univocalism of masculine discourse). In doing so, she calls forth Montaigne's notion of *essayer*, which is in Dr. Johnson's view, and even in David Hume's, a very inferior, even feminine sort of writing.[41]

In a diary entry written at the time she was working on the Montaigne essay, Woolf claimed: "But the truth is — no, I don't think I know the truth. Undoubtedly my chief prop is my writing, which can't foil me here or in London. But according to Montaigne, one is various. I can't lay down a law for my own feelings."[42] Within her Montaignean skepticism, Woolf developed a reciprocal means needed for the production of a modernist feminism, in which Montaigne was a central source:

> We hear of but two or three of the ancients who have beaten this road [said Montaigne]. No one since has followed the track; 'tis a rugged

> road, more so than it seems, to follow a pace so rambling and uncertain, as that of the soul; to penetrate the dark profundities of its intricate internal windings; to choose to lay hold of so many little nimble motions; 'tis a new and extraordinary undertaking, and that withdraws us from the common and most recommended employments of the world.[43]

Montaigne's success in partially withdrawing from society in order to pursue the "nimble motions" of his consciousness is important to Woolf's Montaigne. She too traveled down the "rugged road" of innovative literary production in the quest to experiment with a labyrinthine textuality in the expression of her personal vision: "to penetrate the dark profundities of its intricate internal windings," namely, her attempts to develop new and complex writing in the service of self-expression.

Woolf's essay "Montaigne" exposes the shared concerns and common ground between the *Essais* and her own writing; it is a work that can help us to examine Woolf's reception of Montaigne in the context of her own essayistic techniques. In "Montaigne," she is especially interested in his self-portraiture, the uncanny ability he has to be able "to write himself down" ("Montaigne," 59). She values his suspension of finalistic conclusions, his interest in particularities, as opposed to the abstract "rash assumptions of human judgement," and his "perpetual experiment" in communication ("Montaigne," 67). In Woolf's own project of deviating from what she saw as the constraint of convention, a point most clearly delineated in "Modern Fiction," she seeks, much like Montaigne, to convey the myriad impressions of life: "a shower of innumerable atoms, in order to henceforth allow form to be determined by content and not by conventions external to the work" (154). For Woolf, the writer must rely on "every feeling, every thought, every quality of brain and spirit ... no perception comes amiss ("Modern Fiction," 150). This modernist conviction of an intimate portrayal of the variegated self emulates Montaigne's "Je regarde dedans moi, je me considere sans cesse, je me contrerolle, je me gouste" (II, xvii, 657). Woolf and Montaigne thus share a diminished concern for narrative sequentiality and a desire to show the movements of consciousness — in Montaigne's terms, not the recounting of a static self, but the depiction of the immediacy of the mind's unfolding: "Je ne peints pas l'estre. Je peints le passage: non un passage d'aage en autre, ou comme dict le peuple, de sept en sept ans, mais de jour en jour, de minute en minute" (III, ii, 805). Neither Woolf nor Montaigne claim to resolve the problem of self-portrayal, preferring to explore it and attempt provisional judgments toward its resolution. In Cave's terms, the Montaignean text is one of abundant play which empties the cornucopia by the very gesture of extending itself indefinitely until the last word of the *Essais*: "it turns itself inside out and ironizes itself infinitely, blocking the reader's attempt to make it a moral handbook."[44] Plenitude is never attained in the *Essais* and final meaning is always absent, waiting to be reconsidered by further readings. The enigmatic quality of the Montaignean text is useful to Woolf in her attempts to play with elements of the *Essais* in her writing of *Orlando*, a text paradoxically fixed in perpetual and inexhaustible movement.

Woolf's essay, "Montaigne," stands as one of the few specific instances in which she acknowledged explicitly the importance of the *Essais* to her own notions of literary expression. She touches on many different aspects of Montaigne's life and writing in the essay: it is a vivid, whirlwind panorama of the importance of Montaigne's work to her own, showing how Montaigne maintained a vital place in Woolf's canon of the literature of personality and how well she understood his work and used it throughout her *oeuvre*:

> After all, in the whole of literature, how many people have succeeded in drawing themselves with a pen? Only Montaigne and Pepys and Rousseau perhaps. The *Religio Medici* is a coloured glass through which darkly one sees racing stars and a strange and turbulent soul. A bright polished mirror reflects the face of Boswell peeping between other people's shoulders in the famous biography. But this talking of oneself, following one's own vagaries, giving the whole map, weight, colour, and circumference of the soul in its confusion, its variety, its imperfection — this art belonged to one man only: to Montaigne. As the centuries go by, there is always a crowd before that picture, gazing into its depths, seeing their own faces reflected in it, seeing more the longer they look, never being able to say quite what it is they see. ("Montaigne," 58)

Woolf's painterly attitude is reflected in the palette of her paragraph as she splashes it with parts of herself and of literary history. She concludes by highlighting one of the central issues of this study: how readers keep looking into the *Essais* and simultaneously understand, misunderstand, or not fully understand what they read. Her perception of how generations of writers look into the depths of the

Essais and never fully succeed in coming to a clear understanding of what they examine is an apt characterization of many receptions of Montaigne's work — writer after writer has read the *Essais* and complained of the difficulty of not "being able to say quite what it is they see." This is in fact the dynamic that Montaigne tried to produce in his writing: he wished to generate further readings by never really concluding many of his arguments and by always leaving room for further critical articulation ("il y a tousjours place pour un suyvant"). In *Orlando*, Woolf, to a greater degree than in any of her other works, forges her attempt in "giving the whole map, weight, colour, and circumference of the soul in its confusion, variety, its imperfection." These final three qualities are what most readers experience when confronting *Orlando*. It is especially the "imperfect" (L. *imperfectus*, "incomplete") qualities of great writing that Woolf sees as the key to providing an inexhaustible textual apparatus for the engagement of future readers.

In stating further that "[n]ew editions testify to the perennial fascination," Woolf demonstrates her own interest in Montaigne's mode of seductive aesthetics. She says that it is through perpetual experiment that the writer can achieve the communication of his or her soul, an activity best accomplished in Montaigne's "parfaite et entière communication" ("Montaigne," 65). In Woolf's attempts to characterize Montaigne's role in literary history, she follows his paradoxes and tries to evaluate exactly what he said. She thereby embeds the paradoxes in her own conceptions as she reformulates them. She only gives up the argument by resorting to Montaigne's "'Que sçais-je'" ("Montaigne," 68), as she refuses her own conclusion. Woolf's diverse and undulating essay on Montaigne emulates the *Essais*, which for Woolf never reach their end but attain "suspension in full career" ("Montaigne," 66), demonstrating again her Montaignean penchant for mobility and inconclusiveness: "We should start without any fixed idea where we are going to spend the night, or when we propose to come back; the journey is everything" ("Montaigne," 65). This is in line with Montaigne's precept that the quest and not the destination is the goal of the philosophical life: "nous sommes nais à quester la verité; il appartient de la posseder à une plus grande puissance … [l]e monde n'est qu'une escole d'inquisition" (III, viii, 928).

Woolf presents Montaigne's work in a negligently diligent style (Montaigne's "nonchallante de l'art" — I, xxvi, 172), spontaneously, and multiply. She follows her own impulses and attempts to explore the circumference of the self in its "confusion, its variety, its imperfection" ("Montaigne," 62). She quotes Montaigne both in English (the Charles Cotton translation) and in French (the Armaignaud edition). She is whimsical in her pursuit of Montaigne's significance in literary history and her arguments revolve around the contradictions involved in the confrontation of convention and freedom. Her conception of the writer's desire to formulate the private life in a public context relies in great part on what she reactivates from the *Essais*:

> Let us simmer over our incalculable cauldron, our enthralling confusion, our hotch-potch of impulses, our perpetual miracle — for the soul throws up wonders every second. Movement and change are the essence of our being; rigidity is death; conformity is death: let us say what comes into our heads, repeat ourselves, contradict ourselves, fling out the wildest nonsense, and follow the most fantastic fancies without caring what the world does or thinks or says. For nothing matters of course except life; and of course, order. ("Montaigne," 63)

Woolf concludes this miniature modernist manifesto provisionally, and with an obvious contradiction: "nothing matters of course except life; and of course, order." She does so perhaps ironically ("of course ... of course"), since Montaigne was very much concerned with "what the world does or thinks or says." Woolf seems to adopt Montaigne's sense of humor, which so many commentators seem to miss or ignore ("J'ay naturellement un stile comique"). The private impulse toward freedom must be controlled, claim the text's signifieds. Yet the text's signifiers are pluralistic, linked by free use of punctuation and the mixing of concrete and abstract, thereby transgressing well-ordered syntactic progression and stylistic regularity. The tension between order and disorder generates an appropriate style and genre to express itself. This textual dynamism comes into greater prominence in Woolf's "Montaigne." The repetition of the plural imperative ("Let us ... let us") insists outwardly on the relevance of the issues to the collective intellectual community. Yet the multiple use of the hyphen and of the semi-colon helps to produce an outpouring of personal and spontaneous pronouncements. For Woolf, the witch-like alchemy ("incalculable cauldron," "hotch-potch," "fantastic fancies") of the Montaignean literary enterprise helps her to abnegate more rationalistic literary conventions, which she transcends in her writing in order to more fully examine the "enthralling confusion" of human experience. The private is valorized by the signifiers while the signifieds valorize the public. Woolf redevelops the "Satanic" element that Pater saw in Montaigne in a woman's manner, reformulating certain qualities of the *Essais* in her own work and drawing from them the justification for a personalized writing of fantastical dimensions. Her production of Montaigne's modernity helps her to develop the sense of freedom needed to write an innovative work such as *Orlando* in which *doubleness* (of gender, of the self) and the relationship between fact and fiction, literature and history, and biography and fiction become her central problematics.

Woolf thus saw Montaigne's work as an attempt to create a new space, a private world of consciousness that reaches, however indirectly, across gender lines. Woolf's perception of the potential of his writing for her own work was that Montaigne created a previously unexplored landscape within the division and fragmentation of his own psyche ("nous sommes doubles en nous-mesmes") rather than blindly adhere to the notion of the *whole man* commonly associated with renaissance humanism, so enthusiastically adopted by his father. Woolf understood how hard the task to communicate oneself is and that Montaigne's exposure of the conflict between the public world of action and the private world of language, the dislocation of words and things, along with his opposing of outward convention to inner idiosyncracy, provided the hidden possibilities for a modernist project: "For beyond the difficulty of communicating oneself, there is the difficulty of being oneself. This soul or life within us, by no means agrees with the life outside oneself" ("Montaigne," 59). Montaigne's indication of the instability of his own discourse, the lack of accord between his desire to communicate himself and his failure to ever completely do so, provided Woolf with a model for an alternative discourse which, although produced by a heterosexual male, an "uneasy chauvinist," indirectly subverted the patriarchal hegemony of his time.[45] Although Montaigne was outwardly inhospitable to women, his calling into question of his own discourse and writing at odds with the literary establishment, provided Woolf with a model of alternative literary production, which she adopted in a female mode (Gournay's "c'est une femme qui parle").

Montaigne often spoke of his lack of confidence as an intellectual and often defined himself as a man with qualities that have generally been attributed to women, positing for instance the particular over the universal, the private over the public, fickleness over constancy, haphazardness over design, and fortune over reason.[46] Within these oppositions, Montaigne constantly placed himself on the side of the binarism traditionally allotted to women. He thus indirectly provided the opportunity for a feminist discourse to be constructed by Woolf.

Since he attempted to construct his unique personality in an inflexible world of male intellect, Woolf and Gournay saw Montaigne as an ally in their experiences as women writers in quest of new (feminist) discourses. Montaigne, in fact, as Gournay perspicaciously understood, unsettled the stratification of gender when claiming, as almost no man of his time would, that gender is constructed, that it is an artificial limitation placed on females by the male hegemony ("les femmes n'ont pas tort du tout quand *elles refusent les reigles de vie* qui sont introduites au monde, d'autant que *ce sont les hommes qui les ont faictes sans elles*" — emphasis added), and can thus be reconstructed. Montaigne shook the ideological roots of the male humanist tradition just enough to allow women such as Gournay and Woolf to constitute their own feminist personalities within the discursive spaces opened up by the *Essais*. Woolf's Montaigne is one significant instance of her modernist revisionary activity — celebrating Montaigne's surreptitious dismantling of a chauvinistic culture devoted to dogmatic unity, order, and truth. Montaigne's idiosyncratic freedom helped Woolf to rewrite the male standards of culture in her own time, as Montaigne, in a subtler way, did in his.

There is no evidence that Woolf ever read the work of Gournay or knew of her relationship with Montaigne and his work. Yet the two women would seem to share a common attitude in their respective receptions of the *Essais*. While Woolf was undertaking to recuperate what is useful from the *Essais*, she was ever aware that she was treading on treacherous ground, since Montaigne's variableness and "Satanic" mutability could be used against her. For even he, like Browne "humane and tolerant in almost every respect, was nevertheless capable of a mood of dark superstition in which he would pronounce that two old women were witches and must be put to death" ("Sir Thomas Browne," 30). Woolf chose to make this claim in discussing Browne who, along with Montaigne, most likely did vote to execute witches during his political career. In doing so, along with Gide and before Leschemelle, she evoked indirectly the dark side of Montaigne, her French version of Browne. Woolf feared that the witch-like aesthetics of the "incalculable (feminist) cauldron" would ultimately threaten Montaigne and move him to outwardly reject both Gournay's and Woolf's writing projects, and worse, relegate them to a deadly silence ("pronounce that two old women were witches and must be put to death") by ignoring them, as Montaigne did Gournay's *Proumenoir,* thus impeding its acceptance into the male literary canon.

In considering *Orlando* in the context of the issues that connect Woolf's writing to the *Essais* through the essay "Montaigne," we can witness a Montaignean presence in many of her narrative strategies, thematic configurations, and ideological positionings. It is difficult to recognize Montaigne outwardly in Woolf's work beyond her essay "Montaigne" and in several instances in *A Room*. Yet there are suggestive intertextual points of contact between *Orlando* and the *Essais,* that are less evident, but highly active. Most critical commentary on *Orlando* has centered on two recurring issues: the androgynous nature of the text's protagonist and Woolf's sexual politics. Woolf's love affair with Vita Sackville-West, and her struggle toward a feminist discourse, are also important to consider in approaching *Orlando.*[47] The contributions of critical analyses carried out on these issues are central in understanding the implications of a text as complex as *Orlando*. Yet one should also consider other issues raised by *Orlando,* especially when taking into account the extremely complex nature of Woolfian textuality ("variety and confusion") and the problems Woolf encountered in her innovative modifications of cultural models — models needed, in the case of *Orlando,* to develop the history of the protagonist's life and literary career. Readings of *Orlando* should attempt to remain heuristic enough to better understand the complex network of its intertextual apparatus. A reception of *Orlando* in a Montaignean context may be able to ask such questions, explore the answers and better understand the text's resistance to univocal interpretation. Like the *Essais* or *Gaston, Orlando* is a prototype of the *scriptible* text of Barthes —

embodying that provisional mode of literature which always demands further analysis, a mode Pater considered to be the central quality of the modernist point of view: "What we have to do is to be forever curiously testing new opinions and courting new impressions, never acquiescing in a facile orthodoxy, of Comte, or of Hegel, or of our own" (*The Renaissance*, I, 219). As in *Orlando Furioso,* the search in *Orlando,* both for the protagonists and for the reader, is for something that perhaps does not exist, where the quests for understanding are only partially fulfilled. Both works are cornucopian and insist on innovative vision rather than unequivocal textual unity. Like the *Essais, Orlando* does have definite meanings, yet many of its aspects defy definitive explanation.

Montaigne himself commented on Ariosto's *Orlando Furioso* in a seemingly unfavorable characterization:

> Cette mienne conception se reconnoit mieux qu'en toute autre lieu, en la comparaison de l'*Aeneide* et du *Furieux*. Celuy-là, on le voit aller à tire d'aisle haut et ferme, suyvant toujours sa pointe; cettuy-cy, voleter et sauteler de conte en conte comme de branche en branche, ne se fiant à ses aisles que pour une bien courte traverse, et prendre pied à chaque bout de champ, de peur que l'haleine et la force luy faille. (II, x, 412)

Montaigne critiqued the lack of substantial coherence and regularity in *Orlando Furioso,* preferring the more balanced, sustained, and elevated style of the *Aeneid.* Yet Montaigne himself produced a type of writing closer to the style of *Orlando Furioso* than to that of the *Aeneid* and admits this in his description of the irregular discontinuity and overall imperfections of his writing: "Au demeurant, mon langage n'a rien de facile et poly: il est aspre et desdaigneux, ayant ses dispositions libres et desreglées" (II, xvii, 632). The clash between Montaigne's description of *Orlando Furioso* and his irregular manner of textual production could serve to characterize much of what Woolf does in *Orlando,* in which she takes her cue from this aspect of the *Essais* and produces narrative flights of discontinuous proliferation. Woolf herself is essayistic to an extreme in the writing of *Orlando.* In the early stages of the work, she described it as "an escapade; the spirit to be satiric, the structure wild ... half laughing, half serious: with great splashes of exaggeration."[48] Her satire is in fact of such a patriarchal convention as biography, a genre in which, she believed one can never fully capture the inexpressible particularities of the human experience, as Montaigne would claim, only pursue them. During a candid moment in *Orlando,* the biographer satirizes the biographical conventions of her literary fathers while setting up a new aesthetics for biography that decries any attempt to harmonize the personal self with history:

> The biographer is now faced with the difficulty which it is perhaps better to confess than to gloss over. Up to this point in telling the story of Orlando's life, documents, both private and historical, have made it the first duty of a biographer, which is to plod, without looking to right or left, in the indelible footprints of truth; enticed by flowers; regardless of shade; on and on methodically till we fall plump into the grave and write *finis* on the tombstone above our heads ... . Our simple duty is to state the facts as far as they are known, and so let the reader make of them what he may. (65)

Orlando is thus the Montaignean work "ayant ses dispositions libres et desreglées;" it is more *scriptible* portraiture than *lisible* biography and is very much concerned with questions of language and identity that are closely related: the protagonist works on a poem for centuries, is read like a book, reflects on her life in terms of her reading and writing, and concludes that she is only, like her work "in the process of fabrication" (175).

The intersection of Woolf and Montaigne in the context of *Orlando Furioso* thus raises the question again of intertextual genealogy. In *Orlando Furioso* itself, there are numerous moments that seem to point to Woolf's innovative adoption of its title and reworking of its stylistic, narrative, and thematic elements. Fantastic adventure, heroic exaggeration, a fascination of the strange and illustrious, historical and mythical dimensions in constant flux — *Orlando Furioso,* like its namesake *Orlando,* has multiple plots, heterogeneous variety in its arabesque vision of reality. There is much narrative rambling in both works, in which characters move about in a spectrum of uncertainty, as does the reader, struggling, like the protagonists, to distinguish between possibility and probability, certainty and uncertainty, discovery and loss of self-identity. Yet most importantly, of all of these oppositions, the most important is perhaps that of gender. The problematic of androgyny in *Orlando* has inevitably fascinated most readers and critics of the work, and its metaphoric dimensions are useful in understanding its relationship to Ariosto, Montaigne, and Woolf. There is a certain impulse toward sexual equality embodied in Ariosto's tendency to transpose attributes of the sexes in *Orlando Furioso*. This can be seen in Ariosto's introduction of the dual role to be played by Marfisa: "Costei (non piú costui detto vi sia)."[49] The antagonism between the "femine gentile" and "uomo vile" is also highlighted when Bradamante unhorses knights dressed like a man: "tu séi saper che ti levò di sella/l'alto valor d'una gentil donzella" (I, 69, 18). There is a startling resemblance between her and Ricciardetto, who later dresses like Bradamante and fabricates a story about his sexual transformation (XXV, 40-64) at the end of which he claims "Io 'l veggo, io'lsento, e a pena vero parmi:/sento in maschio, di femina mutarmi" (XXV, 64, 645). It is at this intersection that we can consider the gender instability in *Orlando,* in which there is not only a blurring of literary genres and historical periods, but also of sexual identity. The shifting between masculine and feminine in the development of an androgynous discourse recuperates all of the other ambiguities in the text, since it is not only a sexual problematic, but also a textual one. The androgyne, in Barthes's terms, is a threat to the unequivocal practice of univocal signification since it breaks down the constrictions of sexual as well as aesthetic boundaries, finding the way through the rock of antithesis,"le mur sans porte," that allows readers to make necessary distinctions during the interpretive process.[50]

Textual andrgogyny, as DiBattista has discussed, is not so much freedom from the tyranny of sex as much as freedom from the tyranny of a reified mode of referentiality. Orlando's androgyny is not just symptomatic of a questioning of conventional sexuality, but of language itself. Very concerned with the unstable relationship of *verba* and *res,* Woolf, like Montaigne, questions the reference theory of meaning. By focusing on transsexuality, she hyperbolizes the whole problem of self-identity since, like Montaigne, she manifests an admixture of the literal and figurative in her writing. The struggle between gender opposition is a very important part of Montaigne's work; although generally banishing women from intellectual pursuit, he provided catalytic openings toward a feminist project, as we have seen, by developing an aesthetic *anima*. Gournay and Woolf, like Shakespeare's imaginary sister, lived in worlds hostile to intelligent, talented women. Montaigne's "nous sommes double en nousmesmes" takes on a very new meaning in the context of Woolf's androgyny, which is, in a sense, Montaigne's "que sçay-je" — a refusal to choose, a non-dichotomy that provides an endless oscillation between contrary positions while unsettling platitudes, norms, and conventional forms. How androgyny, which is both literal and metaphoric for Woolf, functions in her aesthetic system and ideological positions can be seen in her discussion first of Coleridge, then of Shakespeare in *A Room*. Woolf sees the former's aesthetics of "man-womanly" and "woman-manly," as meaning "that the androgynous mind is resonant and porous; that it transmits emotion without impediment; that it is naturally creative, incandescent and undivided" (*A Room*, 102). The prototype of this mode of intellectual orientation would be Shakespeare, a "man-womanly mind" (*A Room*, 102). Montaigne did not of course claim to be as naturally prolific as an androgynous mind; yet he can be considered in this context especially after one experiences the vibrancy of expression he achieved in the *Essais*. Woolf, in fact, considers that Montaigne indirectly produced this mode of feminine expression. While reading the work of a well-known writer, the narrator in *A Room* is delighted "to read a man's writing again. It was so direct, so straightforward after the writing of women" (*A Room*, 103); yet is soon disappointed in his work since "it is the power of suggestion that one most misses" (*A Room*, 105). The very qualities that Woolf valorizes are those of the *Essais*. Montaigne's narcissism questioned the inherent masculinity of writing during his time; writers like Gournay and Woolf embraced his self-referential discourse and saw its potential for the development of a feminist mode of writing.

Montaigne's intellectual androgyny thus helped Woolf to break new ground toward the construction of a feminist aesthetics. Yet Woolf's androgynous spirit goes beyond what Montaigne could have imagined to radically question gender identity — a strategy that exposes, as Montaigne did somewhat differently, the duplicity of discourse. Woolf tells us much about her aesthetics in discussing the androgynous identity of great artistic creation: "Some marriage of opposites has to be consummated. The whole of the mind must lie wide open if we are to get the sense that the writer is communicating his experience with perfect fullness" (*A Room*, 108). The "perfect fullness" Woolf seeks is undermined by the undulancy of human nature; one can only watch life float past, grabbing what he or she can of it: "pluck rose petals from the rose or *watch the swans float calmly down the river*" (*A Room*, 108 — emphasis added). In the end, the narrator is caught in the current of words and cannot escape to control his thoughts, as Woolf had difficulty in controlling hers during bouts of mental instability: "And I saw again the current which took the boat and the undergraduate and the dead leaves; and the taxi took the man and the woman, I thought, seeing them come together across the street, *and the current swept them away*, I thought, hearing far off the roar of London's traffic, *into that tremendous stream*" (*A Room*, 108-09 — emphasis added). The uncertainty of the narrator's mental state while faced with the power of the androgynous vision can be seen stylistically in the comma splices and general subversion of clear syntactical structure. The equivocal "I thought" has no clear object and is repeated twice in the effort to capture thoughts in a moment of heightened awareness (brought on by a consideration of the sublimity of "the marriage of opposites"). Yet the "I thought" cannot order reality and is swept away into that "tremendous stream" of problematic being — it is impossible to produce perfect human fullness. The culminating vision of Woolf's tragic modernity, her *consumatum est*, is her despair as a writer whose swan song was literally to float down a river. In French "cygne" (swan) is pronounced the same as "signe" (sign) — Woolf's psychic catastrophe is brought on by her linguistic crisis — this intertextual puzzle is thus both literal and metaphoric.

Woolf and Montaigne thus share this penchant for textual mobility and free play, though with different goals. The intermediary text is *Gaston*, which provides Woolf with an essayistic example of modernizing narrative founded in part on the *Essais*.[51] The way in which the protagonist of *Orlando* cultivates his and her self through contact with historical models is an extreme example of Montaigne's and Nietzsche's ideal student who actively develops the past in the service of life in the present and a satiric development of the obsessive search for self-identity developed through historical understanding, as seen in Pater's *Marius* and *Gaston*. The stylistic and historical quest in *Orlando* further demonstrates the importance of Woolf's reception of the *Essais*. Skeptical expressionism plays a key role in *Orlando*, where narrative, self-portraiture, and history become hopelessly blurred in a phantasmagoric textual whirlpool, where the intensity with which "toutes choses vont coulant et roulant sans cesse" generates an intertextual cornucopia of *morceaux choisis* from the work of Montaigne, Browne, Pater, and an array of other writers and historical moments. In *Orlando,* androgyny is thus Woolf's metaphor for the shifting roles the self plays in its lifetime.

Orlando is the journey of a multiple, evolutionary protagonist who lives through different bodies, minds, and historical circumstances. In this case, the very body of the living and writing self is infused with historical existence. This brings to mind Pater's image of Mona Lisa whose summation of history makes her the quintessential model for modernist interiority and recollection. She represents for Pater the moment in present consciousness in which unfolds all of the disparate moments of the past:

> The fancy of a perpetual life, sweeping together ten thousand experiences, is an old one; and modern philosophy has conceived the idea of humanity as wrought upon by, in summing up in itself, all modes of thought and life. Certainly Lady Lisa might stand as the embodiment of the old fancy, the symbol of the modern idea." (*The Renaissance,* I, 99)

Mono Lisa embodies for Pater his notion of literary modernism: personal memory joined with a sense of history; she spans centuries and embodies history in a culminating vision of the present moment.[52] *Orlando* is the narrative embodiment of such a symbolic figure of multiple selfhood, a prime example of the text as living organism in diversity: the textual production of the self through the matrix of the past, which produces a unique eccentric vision nourished textually (and in Orlando's case, biologically and biographically) by literary history. What is Orlando looking for? What does she experience while attempting to write a poem for over four centuries?[53] Woolf's use of models is a cornucopian satire of all previous thought about the intellectual development of a writer in the context of the opposition of innovation and custom. Boundaries between past and present dissolve, syntactical ligatures are exploded, the narrative contract raises its stakes in a radically problematic text that demands the impossible task of fully unraveling its contradictory, often bewildering textuality. Orlando lives through this undulating and diverse experience as she attempts to understand the world and produce a literary work of merit.

The presentation of multiple personalities through literary contemplation, as developed in *Gaston*, was another useful point of departure for Woolf in composing *Orlando*, an essayistic narrative about a protagonist who lives through history from the sixteenth to the twentieth century. Yet Woolf undoes Gaston's quest for self-understanding and totally abnegates conventional boundaries. Orlando becomes her own tradition and lives many lives over a period of four hundred years, each stage of existence producing an intertextual labyrinth of narrative action infused with historical circumstance, literature, and other writers and their works. As Orlando evolves and carries the past with her, she attempts to finish a poem and to resolve the texts of her writing and of her life, but is constantly foiled. The diverse and undulating Montaignean element intensifies in *Gaston* and reaches cosmic as well as comic proportions of multiplicity in *Orlando*. Woolf's depiction of the interaction between history and innovation takes on expanded dimensions in the service of her revisionist project. She attempts to overcome the antiquarian and the monumental, yet her *kritische* modernism as produced in *Orlando* is vitally connected to an understanding of Pater's "*Montaignesque* element" recast in her own redevelopment of the *Essais*. *Orlando* was in part a useful context in which to develop Montaigne's and Pater's less explicit modernism and formulate the tradition-innovation paradigm in a radical way, assuming some antiquarian and monumental positions that are no more than catalysts in comparison to the web of cornucopian and mannerist abandon that she produces in rupturing the strictures of textual convention and formulating a radical complexity.

Whereas Pater seriously develops the problem of multiple selves, Orlando's multiplicity is hyperbolic. Woolf describes "these selves of which we are built up, one on top of another as plates are piled on a waiter's hand."[54] The concept of the multi-layered selves of an individual and the precariousness of their balance reminds one of Montaigne's concern to find his "assiete": a stable locus of certainty from which unequivocal decisions can be made. Orlando's selves are hyperbolic representations of Gaston's self as well as of the different layers of Montaigne's "evolutionary" self in the *Essais*, codified by Villey and others as the stoic, skeptical and epicurean stages of his career and expressed in terms of an A, B, and C layer. The evolutionary approach toward comprehending Montaigne's intellectual development has important implications. As discussed in Chapter One, the possibility of reading the A, B, and C layers of the *Essais* and arriving at an understanding of the evolutionary unity of Montaigne's work is useful in coming to terms with how Montaigne composed the *Essais*. Yet the evolutionary systematization of Montaigne's work also simplifies paradoxical aspects of the *Essais* that it cannot encompass. Villey's contribution is important but also has its shortcomings, setting up at the same time as it tries to schematize a precarious balance that increases the multiple ways in which the *Essais* can be read.[55]

Greater textual precision in understanding the undulant *Essais* in their more authentic entirety is clearly an important concern in Montaigne studies. But the evolutionary scheme is also in movement since it allows the exploration of Montaigne's paradoxes more fully, as earlier arguments unravel and often contradict themselves in the later additions. Paradox and openness, unintentionally exposed by the evolutionary concept, have subsequently become modernist qualities to be admired. Pater and Woolf freely pursued the *Essais* as they wanted and redeveloped their modernist implications as it suited them. The narrator in *A Room*, for instance, struggles to understand life and writing in clear categorical terms, but fails, and is only able to produce her own unraveled attempts:

> It was impossible to make head or tail of it all, I decided, glancing with envy at the reader next door who was making the neatest abstracts, headed often with an A or a B or a C, while my own notebook rioted with the wildest scribble of contradictory jottings. It was distressing, it was bewildering, it was humiliating. Truth had run through my fingers. Every drop had escaped. (*A Room*, 30)

To attempt to understand *Orlando* is to face "the wildest scribble of contradictory jottings" of modernist textuality, as well as a complication of the neat disciplinary categorizations of history, literature, and philosophy. This pseudo-echo of Villey's evolutionary scheme ("headed often with an A or a B or a C"), which was being formulated at about the same time as *Orlando* and *A Room*, shows two contemporaneous readings of the same author to be of very different purpose and design. The *Essais* produce, on the one hand their own evolutionary reception (Villey's), and on the other, their revolutionary one (Woolf's). At the same time, Woolf's scheme is more representative of the "evolution" of Montaigne's modernism. The *Essais* are more than ever at this time a "double" text by virtue of these diametrically opposed receptions. Montaigne of course did not propose an aesthetics of "the wildest scribble" — he wrote in the accepted mode of the *leçon* or *florilège* for the 1580 edition, in the spirit of Erasmus's *Adages*, and only amplified it later, even calling his own writing a sort of *scribbling* ("cette fricassée que je barbouille icy" — III, xiii, 1079).

In her preface, Woolf calls *Orlando* a "book," avoiding greater generic specificity, a fact that readers struggle with as they interact with the text's demands for reconstitution. *Orlando* is a work embodying a radical phenomenology of reading in which the reader must surrender to the imaginative world of the author and then attempt to reconstitute his or her own experience of that world. Yet Woolf realizes at the same time that her imaginative world is only a reconstitution of past cultures, periods, and individuals. She admits in fact the importance of antiquarian background, "the profound historical knowledge" contained in the work, yet at the same time undermines her own authority by disclaiming precision of historical detail: "whatever degree of accuracy they may attain" (*Orlando*, ix). Woolf's self-professed innovative attitude is explicit in the "Preface" and goes well beyond Montaigne's contradictory evasiveness in the "Avis au lecteur," in which he attempts to concomitantly valorize and discredit his own project: "*Ainsi, lecteur, je suis moy-mesmes la matiere de mon livre: ce n'est pas raison que tu employes ton loisir en un subject si frivole et si vain*" ("Au Lecteur," 3). In concluding her preface, Woolf thanks her "American correspondent" who "generously and gratuitously corrected the punctuation, the botany, the entomology, the geography, and the chronology" (*Orlando*, ix). She thus admits to having *Orlando* normalized on points important to scholarly discourse. As Montaigne submitted to the French and Italian censors, Woolf was jokingly very concerned with the public propriety of her work. Yet Woolf's innovation broke through codified structures of literary expression and produced an experimental narrative journey far beyond the more conservative modernizing of Pater and Montaigne. She admits to both the consistent and the inaccurate textual status of *Orlando*. The paradoxical movement in the conclusion of the preface hardly prepares readers for the enigmatic narrative that is to follow. Woolf thus turns what Montaigne did guardedly into an open mockery of the conventions of the preface.

Woolf's concern for the elusive nature of truth ("every drop had escaped") underscores her skeptical attitude toward logocentric understanding and is magnified in the decentered text of *Orlando*. In order to demonstrate the difficulty of using creative language to express the fluidity of the human self, and the impossibility of using rigorous categories of mind to understand the variegated quality of the modernist literary experience, Woolf produces a dialectic of intuition and doubt, historical renovation compensated for by imaginative fantasy. In *Orlando*, Woolf's deployment of the "*Montaignesque* element" helps her to portray the flux of the writing subject as she conceptualized it. The liquid metaphors of Montaigne and Nietzsche are reproduced and unleashed in Woolf's narrative development of the truly problematic nature of literary understanding — all is "movement and confusion" for Orlando, her mind is "a fluid, an incessant stream" of impressions (*Orlando*, 123). The text's polyvocal qualities push the critical enterprise to either participate in this textual multiplicity or relegate the text's multifarious elements to reduced dimensions.

Orlando lives both chronologically and simultaneously through specific periods of time. She is permeated with the past, with writers, and with literary history. She carries around periods of historical time in her mind as she develops intellectually and physically through four centuries, each literary and social period briefly characterized in a satirical manner. She is an aristocrat, a courtier, an ambassador, and a writer, and in the 1920s completes the poem she has been working on since the sixteenth century. Orlando's life revolves around the public tasks imposed by a prominent rank in society, yet it does not prevent her from indulging in the private pleasures of home, reading, and writing. Through this profusion of shifting identities Orlando always returns to her estate and seeks stability and comfort as she attempts to write herself down as a coherent unity. These literary attempts, however, always fall short. As a young man, Orlando attempts to write, but both conventional and poetic discourse fail to capture reality:

> "The sky is blue," he said, "the grass is green." Looking up, he saw that, on the contrary, the sky is like the veils which a thousand Madonnas have let fall from their hair; and the grass fleets and darkens like a flight of girls fleeing the embrace of hairy satyrs from enchanted woods. "Upon my word," he said (for he had fallen into the bad habit of speaking aloud), "I don't see that one's more true than another. Both are utterly false." And he despaired of being able to solve the problem of what poetry is and what truth is and fell into a deep dejection. (*Orlando*, 102)

After affirming his skepticism, Orlando continues to ponder the problem and finally decides to abandon the quest for certainty and conventional writing, thereby claiming: "bad, good, or indifferent, I'll write from this day forward, to please myself" (*Orlando*, 103). The impossibility of certainty motivates Orlando to continue writing. He attempts to embellish the empty center of his philosophical impasse with literary production. His quest, like Montaigne's, is less concerned with definite understanding than with exploring understanding.

The *Essais* prepare the ground for Woolf to cultivate her most extreme piece of writing, whose innovative dimensions represent a radical example of newness: the overflowing of the skeptical personality. Woolf's irreverence for canons, explosive symmetrical structures, free-rhythm, hybrid textuality, and especially the abnegation of a rational hermeneutics places *Orlando* clearly in the network of a paradoxical modernist writing where the decentered nature of textual experience cannot achieve a satisfying resolution. This is how Woolf uses Montaigne's work, as a justification for "perpetual experiment and observation." Orlando searches constantly for stability and a firm identity and is constantly undermined in her quest. Her existence is alternately filled and emptied and the cornucopia of information about her never achieves a plenitude of understanding. She is the comic embodiment of the literary artist drawing from all sources in attempts at self-expression. She reproduces much of Montaigne's essayistic nonchalance and is in some ways emblematic of his attempt at mediating between the public and the private.

Orlando's literary quest comes to an end when she finishes composing "The Oak Tree," a text whose main concerns are the shifting, open qualities of history and identity that embody the qualities of Orlando's personality. In the nineteenth century, Orlando resumes interest in her manuscript in progress and gives it new consideration:

> Then Orlando felt in the bosom of her shirt as if for some locket or relic of lost affection, and drew out no such things, but a roll of paper, sea-stained, blood-stained, travel-stained — the manuscript of her poem, "The Oak Tree." She had carried this about with her for so many years now, and in such hazardous circumstances, that many of the pages were stained, some were torn, while the straits she had been in for writing paper when with the gipsies, had forced her to overscore the margins and cross the lines till the manuscript looked like a piece of darning most conscientiously carried out. She turned back to the first page and read the date, 1586, written in her own boyish hand. She had been working at it for close on three hundred years now. It was time to make an end. (*Orlando*, 236)

Orlando's poem has lived with her and evolved as she evolves, the various stages of its composition being inscribed in its intricate interwoven texture. Her text resembles the manuscript of the 1580 edition of the *Essais*, which were carried by Montaigne on his journeys through France, Germany, Switzerland, and Italy, as well as their battered quality, if one considers the extant manuscript of the *Essais* (the 1588 edition a copy to which Montaigne added until his death), with its marginal additions, some of which were glued on small strips of paper, and many of which are missing. The history of the *Essais* has seen their erroneous pagination, new bindings, and fragmentation of its contents. The actual text has taken on a life of its own, producing a certain textual ontology. We should not forget that it was during the Enlightenment that one third of his "scribbling" in the margins was cut of by the bookbinder in order to conform to the publication formats of the day. The final manuscript, the "Exemplaire de Bordeaux," is today the source for the "definitive" edition of the *Essais*. We see Montaigne composing them, yet never the ultimate version he wrote — the textual authenticity of parts of the *Essais*, and the difficulty of reading them in their problematized, multi-layered dimensions, will always impede finalized consensus.[56] The definitive edition of the *Essais* is actually missing, for the "Exemplaire de Bordeaux" is suspect: many editors after Gournay have written in its margins and the Gournay edition of 1595 may in fact have been prepared from another copy of the *Essais*, one never found, and which Montaigne was perhaps preparing for publication.

"The Oak Tree," Orlando's life-long masterpiece, is likewise finished in "definitive" form, although the life of its undulating author seems to be starting on a new, perpetual adventure at the end of

Orlando. Yet the reader never really gets to see the text of "The Oak Tree," only the life of the writer writing the work; it is the missing centerpiece of *Orlando.* After submitting the manuscript to a publisher, Orlando senses that it is now out of her control. *Orlando* itself moves in and out of control, often weaving into its narration an intertextual reception of the *Essais* that may or may not be intentional, and is perhaps more than coincidental. The year 1586 is when Montaigne was preparing the last version of the *Essais* to be published in his lifetime, two years later. The three-hundred-year correlation of 1586 to 1886 is also interesting as 1886 is the year Pater began to work on *Gaston de Latour.* In this period of Orlando's literary development, she struggles to assimilate contact with literary models and historical understanding into her own writing. The relationship of historical dates coyly points to *Orlando* as the meeting ground for the work of Montaigne and Pater in a new setting, which helps Woolf to produce her own notion of the intertextuality of literary production. Orlando's poem is like a "piece of darning most conscientiously carried out" (Montaigne's "fagotage de tant de diverses pieces"). Woolf's admiration of Montaigne's polyvocal impetus ("hotch-potch of impulses") is seen in particularized prominence as it is put into narrative practice.[57]

Orlando next resumes writing "The Oak Tree" in the early twentieth century. She attempts to maintain "a deep obeisance to the spirit of the age," even as she tries to be original (*Orlando,* 265). She finally strikes the right balance between her writing-self and the spirit of the age: "she was of it, yet remained herself" (*Orlando,* 266). This final arranging of her compositional energies allows Orlando to write with a flourish, complete her manuscript, and place it in the hands of Nick Greene, "the most influential critic of the Victorian age" (*Orlando,* 277), a passing joke on her father, on Pater, and on other antiquarian men of letters, self-serving critics, and self-glorifying literary artists. The evolving Nick Greene (the Edmund Gosse of an earlier time of literary dogmatism) passes very favorable judgement on a work with "no trace in it, he was thankful to say of the modern spirit" (*Orlando,* 280). This is directly contrary to what Pater and Woolf admire in the *Essais.* Nick Greene, in the sixteenth century, mourns the inferiority of the age to that of Greek antiquity, and in the nineteenth century complains about the loss of the cultural splendor of the sixteenth century. The *kritische* writing of Woolf produces a protagonist who embodies a more conservative mode of antiquarian writing: Orlando is a writer who refuses "nouvelletez" in her own textual production and is accepted by the conventional arbiters of literary taste. "The Oak Tree" undergoes assimilation into the literary canon at the same time that *Orlando* is upsetting its conventions. After having her manuscript praised, Orlando, grateful and perplexed about literature and her identity, finally reaches the year 1928, "the present moment" (*Orlando,* 298). Woolf thus embeds a fantastical dynamic of both custom and innovation in this multiple intersection of texts: Woolf's, the biographer's, and Orlando's.

Woolf's text within a text is thus a conservative, classically composed one, surrounded however by an innovative exfoliation of "crotesques." As Montaigne originally wrote around the poems of Etienne de la Boétie, adding his experiences and observations around them, the original centerpiece eventually became subsumed by the embellishments that surrounded it, as he points out, in the style of mannerist painters: "Il choisit le plus bel endroit et milieu de chaque paroy, pour y loger un tableau élabouré de toute sa suffisance; et, le vuide tout au tour, il le remplit de *crotesques,* qui sont peintures *fantasques,* n'ayant grace qu'en la varieté et *estrangeté*" (I, xxviii, 183 — emphasis added). Like Montaigne's persona, Orlando becomes the fantastical and strange matter of her book. Woolf was also looking to develop the importance of Vita-Sackville West in her life as Montaigne tried to develop La Boétie's in "De l'amitié." Both writers ultimately digress to produce the "crotesques" after resigning themselves to the fact that capturing in writing the monochrome, veritable quintessence of these one-of-a-kind friends was impossible.

"The Oak Tree," which parallels Orlando's growth as a literary artist, survives the three hundred years of Orlando's personal and cultural history — it represents for her the continuity and endurance of the past even as she has undergone radical changes in her life. The poem's absence of any "trace ... of the modern spirit," its success in avoiding any "unscrupulous eccentricity" (*Orlando,* 280), is the deciding factor in its acceptance by Nick Greene. On one level, then, *Orlando* is an aesthetic history of a writer writing a text. "The Oak Tree" is the personal and aesthetic evolution of a protagonist who must write to order her existence while fulfilling the demands of the historical moment. She conforms "by loving nature and being no satirist, cynic, or psychologist," and is rewarded in the production of a worthy text: "Orlando had so ordered it that she was in an extremely happy position; she need neither fight her age, nor submit to it; she was of it, yet remained herself. Now, therefore, she could write, and write she did. "She wrote. She wrote. She wrote" (*Orlando*, 266). But even after all of her study, thoughts, and composition, even after the successful publication of her manuscript and ensuing fame, Orlando maintains that all she has said is only provisional and in the process of becoming: "Yet still, for all her travels and adventures and profound thinkings and turnings this way and that, she was only in process of fabrication" (*Orlando,* 275). Orlando, in contrast to Montaigne, conforms to tradition as a writer while transgressing social norms as an eccentric individual. Woolf turns the innovation/tradition opposition on its head, yet even in doing so, arrives at a similar impasse in the dialectics of becoming.

"The Oak Tree" is to *Orlando* what the sonnets of La Boétie were to the *Essais* — a classically oriented centerpiece around which the writer produces an eccentric exercise in literary production that eventually relegates the original center to a minor role. The "crotesques qui sont peintures fantasques" become the principal text that renders the writer's vision of human nature, which is, in Woolf's terms, "variable, complex, and infinitely mysterious" ("Montaigne," 64). The "crotesques" are thus the result of an attempt to communicate that which is ultimately incomprehensible in definitive terms — an attitude that Woolf adapts in part from Montaigne and deploys in her experimental text *Orlando*: "To communicate is our chief business; society and friendship our chief delights; and reading, not to acquire knowledge, not to earn a living, but to extend our intercourse beyond our own time and province" ("Montaigne," 64). The active use of cultural material in order to perpetuate one's self-understanding is one of Woolf's principal aesthetic goals. The extension of the *Essais* beyond their own "time and province" is one of the accomplishments of Woolf's writing of *Orlando,* a work whose intertextual parallels, affinities, and connections with the *Essais* helps to perpetuate Montaigne's modernity. *Orlando* embodies the qualities that Woolf admires in her reading of the *Essais*: the "incalculable cauldron," "enthralling confusion," and "hotch-potch of impulses" ("Montaigne," 63). Woolf's protagonist Orlando becomes the Montaignean adventurer in life, thought, and writing and, like Montaigne, Woolf invites the reader to approach her experience in a constructive manner: "it is plain enough to those who have done a reader's part in making up from bare hints dropped here and there, the whole boundary and circumference of a person" (*Orlando*, 73). The relationship of *Orlando* to the *Essais* is then an essayistic one and justifies itself by virtue of the "bare hints" left by the narrator. Woolf's choice of the renaissance gentleman unsure of absolute understanding draws on Montaigne as a model — one who satisfies the role better than any other.

As Orlando experiences the modern world, she continues to fail to definitively establish her own identity, and finally solves the crisis by accepting her multiple selves and the impossibility of attaining final understanding of them. The narrator poses the problem of the necessary incompleteness of her project since the subject matter of the biographer is inexhaustible: "For she had a great variety of selves to call upon, far more than we have been able to find room for, since a biography is considered complete if it merely accounts for six or seven selves, whereas a person may well have as many thousand" (*Orlando*, 309). Montaigne's "mille visages," and Gaston's "thousand repeated modifications" of the self, have now become Orlando's "thousand" multiple selves. At thirty-six years old, she finally basks in her impending fame as a writer; she then retires to the haven of her home after a life of literary quest, historical change, philosophical upheaval, and biological metamorphosis. Orlando retreats into a private world and is relieved: "Yes she thought, heaving a deep sigh of relief, as she turned from the carpenter's shop to climb the hill, I can begin to live again" (*Orlando*, 322). Orlando finds the way back to understanding her inner self by climbing the hill (a "montagne") toward inner harmony. She finally arrives at the source of her literary life, the oak tree itself: "The ferny path led, with many turns and windings, higher and higher to the oak tree, which stood on the top. The tree had grown bigger, sturdier, and more knotted since she had known it, somewhere about the year 1588, but it was still in the prime of life" (*Orlando*, 324). 1588 is the year in which Montaigne published the final version of the *Essais* (in his lifetime) and therefore an important year in Montaignean textual criticism whose quadrennial symposiums were held in 1988. Perhaps Woolf is wryly pointing to the *Essais* as a source for the outgrowth of important aspects of *Orlando*.

At the locus of Orlando's literary origins, she decides to bury her book "The Oak Tree." Yet she finally rejects the vanity of the gesture and of the secret, personal quality of literary creation and lets her book "lie unburied and dishevelled on the ground" (*Orlando*, 325). Her literary enterprise abandoned, Orlando achieves ecstasy as she is reunited with her husband on "the twelfth stroke of midnight, Thursday, the eleventh of October, Nineteen Hundred and Twenty-eight" (*Orlando*, 329). Her concomitant affirmation and abnegation of the importance of her text points to the type of Montaignean skeptic who produces a continual emptying and replenishing of belief in his or her writing project. Orlando's failure to consciously destroy her work leads to the "forgetting" of it completely so as to be able to begin a new life. Yet what are we to make of this ending with its Geese and ellipsis and peroration — is it a wild goose chase? We never really get a good look at her husband; like Montaigne's silence on Françoise de la Chassaigne, the missing spouse is a loud absence, the silencing of the other sex to promote one's own.

At this point in her life, Orlando is thirty-six years old and, having finally published her first work, is at the new beginning ("stroke of midnight") of a potential literary life. In Montaigne's thirty-sixth year, he inaugurated his literary career with his first publication, a translation for his father of the *Théologie naturelle* of Raymond Sebond. From this point onward, he began to take himself seriously as a literary writer and retired to his château, as does Orlando, in order to write. This concurrence is perhaps incidental or coincidental, yet its recurrence is striking in its relationship to important dates in the lives and works of Montaigne and Orlando. Woolf, of course, is playing with such an abundance of historical and textual codes that Montaigne's presence among them plays a necessarily fragmentary role; yet it also helps to highlight her attitude toward Montaigne and how she may have modulated her own writing on some of the dimensions of his work: "No fact is too little to let it slip through our fingers, and besides the interest of facts themselves there is the strange power we have of changing facts by the force of the imagination" ("Montaigne," 66). Woolf again and again puts into practice what she admires in Montaigne's work by changing in innovative ways textual lessons learned from the *Essais* that were important to her in the writing of *Orlando*. Yet like Montaigne's evocation of children playing with mercury, much does slip through any reader's fingers (III, xiii, 1067).

Orlando, as a youth and throughout his and her life, although an aristocrat, spends much time with servants, workers, and the common people living near the family estate and in London, learning from their candid and often profound thoughts, words, and actions. He appropriates their insights on life and learns what he never could from books. In this, he learns from life during the first thirty years of his life by living fully in the historical moment — an experience which will serve him later as he writes "The Oak Tree." Orlando explicitly abandons book-learning for a time (although he loves books and reading) in favor of the school of life, echoing Montaigne's "un cabinet, un jardin, la table et le lit, la solitude, la compaignie, le matin et le vespre, toutes heures luy seront unes, toutes places luy seront estude." In the meantime he engages in literary writing. His first attempts at literary production are in the fixed genres of expression: tragedies, epics, romances, histories — all written with great ease but with little satisfaction since the production of texts in preestablished genres never allows him to capture the essence of his experience. Like Montaigne, who began his literary career with a translation, Orlando gets a conventional start. Later in her literary career, Orlando attempts to embellish nature with works of literature, but soon realizes that literary artifice can never capture what is natural and essential in human experience: "Nature and letters seem to have a natural antipathy; bring them together and they tear each other to pieces" (*Orlando*, 17). Orlando strives to understand literature but fails to arrive at any satisfying conclusions: "And in truth, his mind was such a welter of opposites" (*Orlando*, 20). Orlando, unable to adequately mediate between literature and the lived moment, thus abandons literary pretensions for a time and enters into a successful diplomatic career. His impasse is in response to the vanity of literary writing, which conflicts with an authentic understanding of life. Although not in identical chronological order, Orlando's experience, like

Montaigne's, is a struggle to mediate between the private life of a writer and the public life of social responsibility.

During his tenure as Treasurer and Steward to Queen Elizabeth, Orlando falls in love with a Russian princess named Sasha and the description of his emotions is a prolific outpouring of rapturous sentiments: "Orlando stared; trembled; turned hot; turned cold; longed to hurl himself through the summer air; to crush acorns beneath his feet; to toss his arms with the beech trees and the oaks. As it was, he drew his lips up over his small white teeth; opened them perhaps an inch as if to bite and shut them as if he had bitten" (*Orlando*, 38). This passage is a good example of how Woolf uses the "explosive" style to communicate Orlando's groping toward the expression of his thoughts. The passage itself is a "welter of opposites" — heat vs. cold, flying vs. gravity, the human vs. the material world — all linked together by the semicolon which, gives the individual semantic groupings a tentative meaning: they are not mutually exclusive entities, yet neither are they sequentially related through commas. The reader is provoked to relate the "hotch-potch of impulses" and to visualize the ambiguous presentation of Orlando's facial expressions ("as if ... as if"). There are numerous other passages throughout the pages dealing with Orlando's love for Sasha in which Orlando's language fails to capture reality in satisfying expressions. This is another manifestation in *Orlando* of a severe crisis in the relationship of *verba* and *res,* which shakes Orlando's faith in his ability to adequately communicate his lived experience: "Ransack the language as he might, words failed him" (*Orlando*, 47).

Woolf, in her descriptions of Orlando's and Sasha's activities together, relies on figurative abundance. She supplies her descriptions with copious catalogs of material objects that serve as a backdrop for the most stable and tangible moments of Orlando's life. It is when focusing on the nominal world that the text is certain of itself; when this occurs there is an outpouring of quotidian experience. As Orlando and Sasha, for example, stroll through London, they are

> shouldered by apprentices; tailors; fishwives; horse dealers; cony catchers; starving scholars; maid-servants in their whimples; orange girls; ostlers; sober citizens; bawdy tapsters; and a crowd of little ragamuffins such as always haunt the outskirts of a crowd, screaming and scrambling among people's feet — all the riff-raff of London streets

> indeed was there, jesting and jostling, here casting dice, telling fortunes, shoving, tickling, pinching; here uproarious, there glum ... . (*Orlando*, 56)

The copious description, the flow of people and their actions, is striking in the tangibility of its composition. Unwilling to attempt to describe the inner-workings of the relationship of Orlando and Sasha, Woolf chooses to describe their physical surroundings as they walk through London. The spontaneous force of the passage is one of "irrepressible vivacity" ("Montaigne," 59), something that Woolf so much admired in the *Essais*. Woolf pursues her "fantastic fancies" ("Montaigne," 63) and at this point in the narrative produces a moment of stability in Orlando's existence. The passage, with its colorful agglomeration of the commoner's revelry, is one of Woolf's attempts to startle readers with liberated, pluralistic innovation ("fling out the wildest nonsense" — "Montaigne," 63), something she does again and again in *Orlando*. The passage provides a plenitude of experience for Orlando — it helps him to shake off the historical burden from which he was suffering (the abandonment of the past and his aristocratic responsibilities) and to recapture the memory of who he is and his purpose in life: "He remembered everything. The time had come" (*Orlando*, 57). The descent into the "yvresse naturelle" of the common experience of London helps Orlando to remember the higher purpose in his life and inspires him to make the decision to marry Sasha. The cornucopian description of the London populace, the fertility of the discursive moment, provides the experience Orlando needs in order to understand and assume greater control of his life. He thus makes the decision to meet at midnight and elope with Sasha. Certainty is now established in Orlando's life as he waits for his beloved; yet as the clock strikes midnight, Sasha fails to arrive, and an ensuing flood washes away not only Orlando's plans, but also the very people who had helped him in arriving at his decision: "The river had gained its freedom in the night... . All was riot and confusion... . Now, eddying and swirling like a tortured serpent, the river would seem to be hurtling itself between the fragments and tossing them from bank to bank... . But what was the most awful and inspiring of terror was the sight of the human creatures who had been trapped in the night and now paced their twisting and precarious islands in the utmost agony of spirit" (*Orlando*, 62).

There is a metatextual moment in "Des cannibales" in which Montaigne demonstrates the Heraclitean dimensions of his discourse; it is a metaphoric key that complicates yet clarifies a problematic as reformulated by Woolf:

> Il semble qu'il y aye des *mouvmens,* naturels les uns, les autres *fievreux,* en ces grands *corps* comme aux nostres. Quand je considere l'impression que ma *riviere* de Dordogne faict de mon temps vers la rive droicte de sa descente, et qu'en vingt ans elle a tant gaigné, et *desrobé le fondement à plusieurs bastimens,* je vois bien que c'est *une agitation extraordinaire*: car, si elle fut tousjours allée ce train, ou deut aller à advenir, *la figure du monde seroit renversé.* (I, xxxi, 204 — emphasis added)

The energetic dynamism of the *Essais* often defies univocal interpretation: its irreducible textuality is constantly in movement. Its deferment of coherence is both "natural" (in the sense that Montaigne attempts to present his *coeur mis à nu*) and "feverish" (in the sense that the essay form as invented by him embodies a discursive condition of heightened activity). Montaigne compares the movement of the essay's textual body ("corps comme aux nostres") to the Dordogne river, whose endless movement eventually erodes the firm foundations of many buildings and, if allowed to continue, would eventually reverse the order of the world. The terms Montaigne uses are feverish with Heraclitean dynamism; the fluid quality of his thoughts are suggestive and never produce an immediate presence. Montaigne's Dordogne river slowly washes away previous physical characteristics of the earth; yet the Thames sweeps away the temporary certainty of Orlando's life, as the river Ouse eventually carries away Woolf. Orlando's experience thus undergoes an "agitation extraordinaire" (I, xxxi, 204), and as the river washes away the people and places in which he had found certainty, his life is in complete tumult ("la figure du monde [est] renversée"). Montaigne's river, however effective, is gradual compared to the torrent of Woolf's accelerated dynamism. She appropriates what she needs from Montaigne and then accelerates into high gear. Her river washes away the cornucopia of textual multiplicity that provided Orlando with a period of stability, however brief. Now, it is literally that "toutes choses vont roulant et coulant sans cesse" and Orlando's plans, as well as his linguistic and literary capacities, are swept away in the torrent: "The swirling waters took his words, and tossed at his feet a broken pot and a little straw" (*Orlando*, 64). Not only the recent reality that had stimulated him to action, but also Orlando's ability of self-expression along with his literary capacities ("words" … "broken [ink] pot" … "little [pen] straw") are carried away as he hopelessly watches the world float out of control.

Textual abundance produces a saturated discursive experience in Chapter I of *Orlando* and now creates the flood that pushes Orlando's life quickly from the psychic and physical integration ("perfect fullness") of a whole being, to its absence. The paradigm of wholeness washes away in this flood of language and Orlando is left alone to begin another stage of life. This ending is thus another beginning — a clean slate provided by the flood. As with the *Essais*, *Orlando* is filled with cornucopian plenitude that then empties itself out, thereby valorizing the emptiness of discourse that attempts to celebrate its plenitude but ultimately exposes the reality of its vapidity. The writing-self continues to accept the challenge of replenishing this emptiness of discourse. Gaston's desire to float down the river to the sea is now realized by Orlando. Woolf extends Pater's quest to a point where he would never have dared to venture. By putting into narrative practice the moment of intellectua! mobility as developed in *A Room* ("and the current swept away … into that tremendous stream"), Woolf ironically foreshadows her own death, literally swept away by a river.

After the flood, Orlando retires to his château in order to recover from the downfall of his previous plans. He begins to read Sir Thomas Browne and spends a great deal of time meditating on his "most marvellously contorted cogitations" (*Orlando*, 73). Orlando feels affinities with Browne and with the type of writing he produces; reading his work causes him to believe that he himself is also "strangely composed of many humours — of melancholy, of indolence, of passion, of love, of solitude, to say nothing of those contortions and subtleties of temper" (*Orlando*, 75). As Montaigne would claim of all human beings, Orlando's most universal quality is that of diversity and instability. He can never remain satisfied with anything for too long and lives a life based on movement and flux. After reading Browne, Orlando thus becomes "afflicted with a love of literature" and also writing, "that other scourge which dwells in the inkpot and festers in the quill" (*Orlando*, 75). It is a pastime that causes the nobleman Orlando to manage his household barely adequately enough (like Montaigne), as he gives his life over to the production of elegant but useless writing since it takes us away from self-presence and is devoid of any true attempt to help people live a better life; in Montaigne's terms: "L'eloquence faict injure aux choses, qui nous destourne à soy" (I, xxvi, 172). As the literary impulse grows, Orlando "begged paper as he begged ink" (*Orlando,* 76) and appears to be taking Montaigne's joke about writing until there is no more ink and paper in the world all too seriously: "thus had been written before he was twenty-five, some forty-seven plays, histories, romances, poems; some in prose, some in verse; some in French, some in Italian; all romantic, and all long" (*Orlando,* 77). The hyperbolic description of Orlando's literary output recalls Montaigne's belief in the nonsense of writing which inevitably produces more writing *ad infinitum.*

The narrator then asks how it is possible to order this outpouring of textual "confusion," the "rag-bag of odds and ends within us" (*Orlando,* 78). The answer is memory; yet memory, the textual "seamstress," is "capricious" and "inexplicable" (*Orlando,* 79). Orlando has the same problem of ordering historical learning and private experience into a coherent whole as do Montaigne, Nietszche, and Gaston. The narrator berates memory as "idiotic and out of keeping" (*Orlando,* 80) and after several months of feverish attempts at producing a more personalized work, abandons the project in despair; the failure of his memory to synthesize "a thousand odd, disconnected fragments" (*Orlando,* 78) provokes him to renounce the type of historicizing texts that he had written and to burn the "fifty-seven" manuscripts on which he had been working. He retains only the autobiographical work that he had been struggling to write since a young boy, "The Oak Tree." Fifty-seven is the same number of essays in Book I of the *Essais.* Montaigne (as far as we know) never burned his works, yet he too sought to surpass the more antiquarian mode of production of his first fifty-seven writing attempts (where the emphasis was on the glossing of ancient texts) in favor of the more personally revealing essays of Books II and III. Orlando's ultimate *kritische* act of "forgetting" his work by burning it, in order to allow himself the space in which to create something new and vital, is related to Montaigne's attempt to assert the development of his self-portraiture over the tyranny of the *Historische*. Woolf again makes suggestive references to the *Essais*, which, as she interprets them, provide her a literary antecedent of a text founded on "movement and change" ("Montaigne," 63). The text of *Orlando* itself suffers from poor memory: Orlando changes identities so often, moving back and forth between political and literary lives and aristocratic leisure, between admiration and scorn for literature, and even between different sexual identities. The text constantly "forgets" its protagonist's previous status in order to forge some new event. It does so likewise with its various genres — mingling biography, essay, lyric, narrative, and history — each layer seemingly ignoring the others and the inconsistencies that this practice generates. The abrupt shifts in Orlando's life, and the demands put on the reader to accept such discontinuities and constant surprises, are in part the result of how Woolf develops what she considers to be the most innovative and provocative aspects of the *Essais*. Montaigne's A, B, and C layers have a similar effect: one layer may often supplement another yet just as often may negate or subvert what was previously stated; this is one factor that produces textual tension and incongruity in the *Essais*.

While at a social gathering, Orlando meets several entertaining noblemen, one of whom is a "Mr. M." She converses at length with him and finds "Mr. M. amusing" (*Orlando*, 193). Yet the next morning, when she tries to recollect the specific substance of their conversation the previous evening, she has completely forgotten what it consisted of. She now depends so completely on the present moment that she lives an overly developed *kritische* life — unable to retain past experiences that would have encumbered the flourishing of her personality in the present. Immediately after praising "Mr. M.," Orlando tries to remember which of his qualities were so praiseworthy: "But when she tried to recollect in what their gallantry, politeness, charm, or wit had consisted, she was bound to suppose her memory at fault, for she could not name a thing. It was always the same. Nothing remained over the next day, yet the excitement over the moment was so intense" (*Orlando*, 193). Woolf again wittily points to Montaigne's work as an operative element in the textual fabric of *Orlando*, yet never makes explicit references to the *Essais* or to Montaigne ("Mr. M"), only veiled ones — she must necessarily "forget" them in order to achieve the necessary freedom to produce her own innovative essayistic text. As she states in the "Preface," some of her debts to other authors are so important that she hesitates to tell us who they are, perhaps to escape the specter of their presence, which explicit reference would make more difficult: "Some are dead and so illustrious that I scarcely dare to name them" (*Orlando*, vii).

As with Montaigne's life, we have very little knowledge of Orlando's public existence: "when he played a most important part in the political life of his country, we have least information to go on" (*Orlando*, 119). The narrator thus must depend on the "imagination" to reconstruct Orlando's life: "It is with fragments such as these that we must do our best to make up a picture of Orlando's life and character at this time" (*Orlando*, 174). The narrator, who claims to be ignorant of the historical facts, creates nevertheless an elaborate description of Orlando's life as Ambassador to Turkey; we are not told what actually happened, but what could have happened. What Montaigne says he prefers to do in "De la force de l'imagination," is what Woolf chooses to accomplish by following his suggestions in the writing of *Orlando*: "Il y a des autheurs, desquels la fin c'est dire les evenemens. La mienne, si j'y sçavoye advenir, seroit dire sur ce qui peut advenir" (I, xxi, 105-06). Woolf pieces together fragments of Orlando's life into a "marqueterie mal jointe" and could claim, like Montaigne, in the writing of *Orlando*: "qu'il n'est rien si contraire à mon stile qu'une narration estendue" (I, xxi, 106). Memory, not capable of producing the plenitude of Orlando's existence, the narrator, in relying on her essayistic imagination, can only produce a fragmentary protagonist, one buffeted along by a kaleidoscope of circumstances: "What a phantasmagoria the mind is and meeting-place of dissemblables" (*Orlando*, 176). Woolf produces the Montaignean penchant for multiple contrarieties while developing a narrative text infused with movement and paradox.

As in Pater's *Gaston*, Woolf literalizes Orlando's contact with past writers and has her spend several months in the company of Addison, Pope, and Dryden, the canonical triumvirate of eighteenth-century English literature. At first, Orlando absorbs all that they have to teach by virtue of the many conversations and dinner parties. She feels especially honored in the company of Pope and thinks about emulating him as a writer. Yet she soon becomes disillusioned with the "high opinion poets have of themselves" (*Orlando,* 213) and ends up by despising their vanity and marveling at the contradictory nature of literary intellectuals who possess great minds yet are less than admirable human beings. She begins to feel stifled in their company and realizes that she must cease to see them if she is to allow her own personality to flourish. Orlando had for a time denied herself by being overly burdened with too much "history," in the form of the anxiety of influence provided by Addison, Pope, and Dryden, the monumental, neoclassical models of the time. She must "forget" them so as not to suppress her own personality and to be able to produce a unique literary work. Following Montaigne and Nietzsche, she must go beyond her precursors by negating their existence. Unlike Gaston, she is not susceptible to overly naive identification with, nor total self-absorption in the greatness of previous writers. She breaks away from the historical chain as Gaston could not do and moves onward to the next sequentially disconnected episode of her life where she again becomes a writer (this time in the nineteenth century) and finally finishes her only work of original quality, "The Oak Tree."

Orlando experiences life in the late nineteenth century, roughly at the same time Pater was writing, and has many fragmentary recollections of the Elizabethan age while she is adjusting to her new Victorian surroundings. The house and its lands have changed, as well as her servants and the fashions of the time. Yet as Orlando ponders what to do with her life, she comes across the three-hundred year old manuscript of "The Oak Tree," which she decides to finally complete. She thus contemplates that the Victorian and Elizabethan ages were not so different after all; like Pater, she conflates the two into one impulse: the type of writing that Orlando was developing in 1586, she can as easily develop in 1886: "'After all,' she thought, getting up and going to the window 'nothing has changed... . True, Queen Victoria is on the throne and not Queen Elizabeth, but what difference ... '" (*Orlando,* 237). History may have progressed, but a link to an earlier mode of innovative writing has been reformulated. Montaignean textuality continues in the late nineteenth century and Woolf, like Pater, considers the modernist attitude as more of a recurring impulse than an historically delineated period. As soon as Orlando comes to this realization, she is able to pick up a pen and begin working on her manuscript. She would now finish in the modernist period what was started in the renaissance, thereby connecting the two historical periods. This event in Orlando's literary career recalls Pater's desire to produce a rearticulation of the renaissance by redeveloping the *Essais* in *Gaston*. On one level then, Orlando is carrying out a renaissance of her own writing; on another, Woolf is pointing to the plausibility that she is rewriting the "*Montaignesque* element" in *Orlando,* albeit in a radical deployment of their textual suggestiveness. The correspondence of dates previously indicated points to the confluence of the *Essais* and *Orlando,* as well as to the way in which Woolf appears to fulfill the criteria for writing about the self that she sets up in "Montaigne," and which she develops, more than in any of her other works, in *Orlando.*

As Orlando thus picks up the pen to begin finishing "The Oak Tree," she is interrupted by her housekeeper and spills a huge inkblot and "was much annoyed to be impeded by that" (*Orlando,* 237). The blot spreads over her manuscript and becomes larger and larger. She decorates the blot as it spreads until it becomes a "monster." She realizes that it is impossible to write with her housekeeper in the room. Her presence disturbs Orlando's writing and causes the ink with which the poem should have been written to metamorphose into horrific proportions. The housekeeper's name is Mrs. Bartholomew. She is not the locus of any massacre, yet her presence impedes Orlando's literary accomplishments from flourishing. In the next moment, Orlando begins to compose her poem and continues to write, realizing after some time that she is alone in the room. She forgets about Mrs. Bartholemew while absorbed in composition. Her "forgetting" of "Bartholemew" permits her to create successfully and not become the victim of Montaigne's "monstres fantasques." This is certainly not the same manner of "forgetting" as in Montaigne's choice to ignore the Saint Bartholemew's Day massacre in his writing, nor as in Gaston's failed attempts to respond effectively to the circumstances surrounding his experience of the event. Yet Woolf again embeds another surreptitious reference to what we now see as an important intertextual link in the work of Montaigne, Pater, and Woolf. Forgetting "Bartholemew," in whatever form it appears (literal or metaphoric), allows Montaigne, Gaston, and Orlando to live their own lives and to write literary texts. Had Montaigne divulged more of the possible role he may have played in the event, it would have been a "blot" on his reputation and he may well have been considered to be in complicity with the "monsters" who carried out the massacres. The Bartholemew intertext is at once gratuitous and significant since it shows how the *Essais, Gaston,* and *Orlando* are linked by a similar problematic: how to achieve self-expression while in the shadow of threatening external influence.[58]

As Orlando continues writing, she feels that she has become too absorbed in literature and that she has been "poisoned through and through" (*Orlando,* 243) and must seek greater stability in her life than writing can provide. She claims that she needs some support, someone to provide her a greater sense of security than does writing: "But whom could she lean upon" (*Orlando,* 245)? As she searches for a husband, she considers "Mr. M," but he is unsuitable for religious reasons since "he was become a Catholic" (*Orlando,* 245). Woolf is perhaps figuratively rejecting the more conservative aspects of Montaigne's life and work as she valorizes their more innovative ones. His putative orthodoxy is his great paradox, and Woolf would outwardly reject it while quietly appropriating that which is unorthodox in his writing, thereby foregrounding the radical potential embodied in the *Essais.* Orlando thus retreats again from the world and spends a great deal of time out of doors on her estate and ruminates that, although she has had great experiences, met many people, traveled, read, written, and discoursed with great minds, she is nevertheless prompted to arrive at a skeptical conclusion of life: "'I have sought happiness through many ages and have not found it... . I have known many men and many women,' she continued; 'none have I understood'" (*Orlando,* 248-9). She then meets her husband whose eccentric name, Marmaduke Bonthrop Shelmerdine, Esquire, does not quite rival Woolf's explosive description of the "wild, dark-plumed name — a name which had in her mind, the steel blue gleam of rook's wings, the hoarse laughter of their caws, the snake-like twisting descent of their feathers in a silver pool, and a thousand other things besides ..." (*Orlando,* 250-1). The polyvocal suggestiveness of his name is what Orlando finds so attractive in her fiancé. As with Montaigne's titles, a name most often fails to encompass its object. At this point, Woolf is again valorizing the Montaignean penchant for the "school of life" over that of writing in Orlando's experience. Yet this does not prevent Orlando from writing. The description of the fiancé's name is a sentence swollen with multiple imagery. Orlando has finally found an "assiete" yet it is one of suggestive multiplicity that language cannot capture ("a thousand other things besides"). The narrator thus ends Orlando's first encounter with Shelmerdine by stating the problematic nature of modernism. She shifts from the biographical mode to the critical and states that language is unable to capture what needs to be said. She claims that there is always a disjuncture between *verba* and *res*, that language can and cannot communicate, that one must write and refuse to write, that the text is empty and that the text is full, that there is meaning and that there is its lack: "For it has come about, by the wise economy of nature, that our modern spirit can almost dispense with language, the commonest expressions do, since no expressions do … for which reasons we have a great blank here, which must be taken to indicate that the space is filled to repletion" (*Orlando*, 253).

Orlando is thus a work filled even while empty, empty in the sense that it is so abundant in possibilities that the interpretive apprehension of any number of them will always be lacking a full and coherent understanding of the text as a whole. Even the opening word of *Orlando* points to the paradoxical quality of its full emptiness: "He —" (*Orlando*, 13). The text undoes itself from the very start, positing a full-blooded presence through the capitalized masculine subject pronoun, then juxtaposing it with a large dash. The reader attempts to fill in this typographical lacuna (L. *lacuna*, "pool") for the next three hundred pages and four centuries of Orlando's life. The "modern spirit" then, characterized by Pater in his reception of the *Essais* as Montaigne's superior ability to express his inner-self (Woolf says much the same thing in the opening of "Montaigne"), is turned into aporia by Woolf's "He —" and by the claim that the "great blank" is already full, full of emptiness. Montaigne's ability to "draw himself with a pen" is what Woolf admires in his work, yet she also claims that "when we attempt the task, the pen falls from our fingers; it is a matter of profound, mysterious, and overwhelming difficulty" ("Montaigne," 58). Orlando picks up and drops her pen again and again in her attempts to write. She would finally complete "The Oak Tree," though the reader never gets to see the poem. This locus of Orlando's full understanding of her life is left blank and one must be satisfied with the narrator's claim that it is "filled to repletion." In the same way, Montaigne constantly claims that his text is unworthy and devoid of any firm understanding; yet he seduces readers to continue to fill in the blanks with more and more interpretations. He can't paint an authentic portrait of himself, try as he may, as the painter captured the Duke of Sicily on canvas. Woolf redevelops a similar *scriptible* paradigm in *Orlando*; the full picture is never present and one must therefore connect the dots in order to complete what will always be differing concretizations of the text.

Orlando marries at the age of thirty-two, the same age when Montaigne married. She does so, not out of great love, but more in order to establish stability in her life and especially the security that conformity to "the spirit of the age" provides. In this, she follows Montaigne who maintained that friendship, and not passion, is the most stable basis for a marriage whose highest purpose was propagation of the species. This is very much the relationship of Orlando and Shelmerdine. They are more friends than lovers; after the wedding ceremony Shelmerdine departs on a sea-voyage and Orlando will give birth to their child in his absence, only seeing Shelmerdine again on the final page of *Orlando*. After the marriage, the abrupt departure of her husband, and the birth of her child, Orlando feels that quotidian life is complete and she is finally capable of sitting down to write once again. After finding the stability that she sought, she now "forgets" it in order to resume work on her manuscript. It is another *kritische* act that allows her to change from wife and mother back into writer. This is another of the many times that the focus of Orlando's life shifts from career or status in life (diplomat, wife, nobleman, ambassador) to that of a struggling literary writer. Yet this final time she is successful and begins the completion of "The Oak Tree."

The motif of paper, pen, and ink, repeated over a dozen times in *Orlando*, occurs once again as she composes the poem. Woolf commented on Montaigne's desire to write "so long as ink and paper exist" ("Montaigne," 67) and, throughout the narrative, Orlando remains obsessed with the writing activity that she will now complete. After the satisfaction she experiences on the successful publication and popularity of "The Oak Tree," she can begin her life anew, once again. After four hundred years of undulating literary experience, Orlando wishes to start over. She cannot understand what praise and fame have to do with poetry and realizes that she has written "The Oak Tree" solely as an exercise in self-understanding, thereby redeveloping Montaigne's "je suis la matière de mon livre" into another textual embodiment of self-portraiture: "was not writing poetry a secret transaction, a voice answering a voice" (*Orlando*, 325)? The narrative thus abruptly ends with an enigmatic "conclusion" in the year 1928. Orlando is reunited with Shelmerdine and what will follow are readers' attempts to engage the text's various meanings. The reunification of Orlando and Shelmerdine occurs exactly four hundred years after the marriage of Montaigne's parents, Pierre Eyquem and Antoinette de Louppes in 1528 — the union from which emanated the author of the *Essais* and their four-hundred-year journey to the publication of *Orlando* in 1928. This is certainly not *the* hermeneutic key that explains the work, but the numerous references to Montaigne are too obvious to ignore. Woolf would berate any search for the definitive closure of this narrative — the adventure of the literary experience was foremost in her mind as she wrote *Orlando*. The belief that "the journey is everything" ("Montaigne," 65) is nowhere more apparent in her work than in *Orlando*. Woolf's radical innovation and "perpetual experiment" in writing, by virtue of the many intertextual confluences with the *Essais*, is founded on concepts that she delineated in "Montaigne." All of these factors point to Woolf's significant involvement with a Montaignean mode of thought and writing — she uses it as an architectural garland into which she weaves other intertextual constructs.

Woolf's characterization of Montaigne's life could almost as easily apply to Orlando's:

> Here is someone who succeeded in the hazardous enterprise of living; who served his country and lived retired; was landlord, husband, father, entertained kings, loved women, and mused for hours over old books. By means of perpetual experiment and observation of the subtlest he achieved at last a miraculous adjustment of all these wayward parts that constitute the human soul. ("Montaigne," 67)

Orlando as a protagonist shares many characteristics with Montaigne — both are aristocratic landowners, lovers of nature, sporadically involved in politics, but mostly engaged in the problematics of literary production. Woolf clearly understands that Montaigne wrote at a time when there was very little notion of specified practice or of fixed discursive categories: "literature" for him was inseparable from politics, history, philosophy, and science. Woolf regenerates this notion found in the *Essais* in *Orlando*, indicating Montaigne as a significant component, hitherto little regarded, in the development of Woolf's most challenging text. Montaigne provides Woolf with the model of experimentation in literature, with an example that helps to justify her own pluralistic, multifaceted attempts to show the variety and confusion of the human experience in all of its diverse unity. In "Montaigne," she claims that the literary enterprise should be to "vary our state as much as possible; turn now this; now that" ("Montaigne," 65). Woolf thus produces a paradoxical evaluation of the *Essais* by first stating that Montaigne achieved a unity of being ("miraculous adjustment of all these wayward parts"), then claiming that his work is founded on variability ("vary our state as much as possible"). It is this unity of diversity that best characterizes Woolf's reception of Montaigne, which is, in part, a justification for the writing of a text like *Orlando* whose multiple enigmas and incongruities continue to pose problems for critical interpretation. Woolf seeks to unify Montaigne's importance to her in "Montaigne," then disperse it in her own innovative deployment of the *Essais* in *Orlando*. Pater may have provided Woolf with a prototype of the undulating and essayistic protagonist who nourished self-cultivation through historical literary contact with the *Essais*. Yet it is Montaigne who supplied the textual challenge that Woolf answers by magnifying the skeptical pluralism of the *Essais* into one of the most problematic modernist texts ever written. She uses Montaigne's work and ideas as skeletal *florilège* around which she produces an abundance of mulifaceted intertextual relationships. Yet following Montaigne, Woolf's use of the past in *Orlando* is subordinated to the protagonist's search for self-understanding. *Orlando* is the most visible fulfillment in Woolf's *oeuvre* of the criteria set up in "Montaigne." If one thus considers Woolf's profound influence on twentieth-century literature, then it can be said that Montaigne's work is implicated in the receptions of her work and should be given its due. Woolf's modernizing reception of Montaigne's life and writing thus allows the

Essais to merit a more pronounced consideration in twentieth-century literature.

Woolf makes explicit references in *Orlando* to many other writers and their work, yet nowhere does she do so with Montaigne (only mentioning Pater in the preface).[59] To propose that Pater and Montaigne are the key intertexts for *Orlando* would be excessive; yet taking into consideration Woolf's reception of the work of both writers, added to the intertextual exfoliation that their work undergoes in hers and the manner in which Woolf calls attention to certain aspects of their work, causes the reader to reconsider the *Essais* and *Gaston* in the context of Woolf's reception of them. The points of contact of Woolf's reception of the *Essais* and her textual innovations modulated upon them are Woolf's unique case: she modernizes the *Essais* for her own project, yet at the same time it is the openings in the *Essais* that help her to assert her own positions. As with other readers of Montaigne, Woolf develops the *Essais* to suit her needs, yet as a woman in England in the early twentieth century — contrary to the academic Montaigne being developed at the same time in France, or the spiritual kinship felt by Pascal, Sainte-Beuve, and Gide, or even a more officially consecrated "modern" Montaigne as developed by Pater — she reproduces the roving skeptical consciousness of the *Essais* in a unique way as she searches for direction in her literary life and the textual structures needed to represent it. She articulates Montaigne's writing by the power of her literary imagination, produces an innovative work founded in part on suggestions in the *Essais*, which Montaigne encouraged future writers to continue in their own manner: "Les discours sont à moy, et se tiennent par la preuve de la raison, non de l'expérience: *chacun y peut joindre ses exemples*: et qui n'en a point, qu'il ne laisse pas de croire qu'il en est, veu le nombre et varieté des accidens. Si je ne comme bien, qu'un autre comme pour moy" (I, xxi, 105 — emphasis added). Woolf adds the examples of her own literary experience to Montaigne's discourse and reformulates his work in a new context; the *Essais* are consequently both modernist and modernized.

Yet what of "The Oak Tree?" It is Orlando's most cherished possession, yet always absent from view in *Orlando*: "she felt *in the bosom of her shirt* as if for some locket or *relic of lost affection*, and drew out no such things, *but a roll of paper … the manuscript* of her poem." Woolf's reception of Montaigne is this poem. After his father's death in 1568, Montaigne dropped the family name "Eyquem" and replaced it with the name of his land and seigniory. This gave him the advantage of the newly arrived bourgeois to be able to confuse his name with feudal territory and nobility. He dropped the name of his father, and thus of the family lineage. The name "Montaigne" was subsequently propagated, through no male heir, the quintessence of patriarchal culture, but biologically through his daughter Léonor, and spiritually and intellectually by Gournay, and in this century by Woolf. The name "Eyquem" or "Ayquem" or "Aiquem" was very common in Montaigne's *Gironde*, long inhabited by the English. The name is a transmuted variation of "Ockham," "hamlet of oaks."[60] The equivocal Michel *Eyquem* de Montaigne, the "Hamlet of Oaks," is the missing acorn of Woolf's female *Hamlet*; the enigmatic intertextual dynamic of "Eyquem," the kernel of Montaigne's name, is buried in the narration of *Orlando* from which exfoliates Woolf's Montaignean identity. Orlando as a woman keeps the cherished piece of the Montaigne intertext next to her breast — the manuscript of "The Oak Tree" ("Eyquem") — and a phallic one at that ("a roll of paper"). The narrative literalization of this androgynous dynamic between male and female (read Montaigne and Woolf) underscores Woolf's aesthetics as developed in the context of the *Essais*. Woolf escapes her "fathers" (Shakespeare, Coleridge, Browne, Hazlitt, Dryden, Sir Leslie Stephen, Pater, among others, *and* Montaigne) to produce a feminine discourse in response to them; she does not idolize the "roll of paper" too long, but goes on to produce what her male ancestors would never even have thought of, much less understood. Montaigne dropped his father's name and the Eyquem and Montaigne families were soon to disappear, not only literally, but also metaphorically. Montaigne realized that he was not the "renaissance man" that his father so wanted him to be and that he was somehow little qualified to be a *seigneur*. By overcoming his own paternal oppression, Montaigne was free to essay his life, yet this also led to his disregard of the family lineage and of its well-being after his death. Yet the *Essais* have lived on, both Montaigne and Eyquem have been redeveloped. Gournay perhaps more vitally than anyone first promoted the "*Montaignesque* element," but it is Woolf who most innovatively reformulated it in her work by rearticulating Montaigne's oblique meanings, thereby producing a feminized reception of the *Essais*.

Woolf's work, so intimately related as it is to Montaigne's, regenerates the *Essais* in a far-reaching spectrum of twentieth-century intellectual history, particularly in the essay, the modern novel, and most importantly, in the birth of modernist feminism. Montaigne's role in these phenomena as seen through Woolf's reception of him is problematic, and not definitive; yet neither is it unsubstantial.

♦ ♦ ♦

Orlando ends in mid-air, as does its predecessor *Gaston*. Like Montaigne and Pater, the narrator of *Orlando* downplays or even abolishes conclusions. The ironic tone and vacillating narration of Orlando's life prevents the reader from taking things too seriously. *Orlando* ends elliptically, and in modulating on Montaigne's attitudes, themes, and style achieves a suspension of closure that challenges the conventions of linear narration. Specific borrowings from Montaigne's subjects and themes may be elusive and difficult to pinpoint, since the *Essais* and Montaigne's sensibility operate freely in *Orlando* and provide Woolf a useful textual model that enriches her already prismatic sensibility for the writing of *Orlando*. Her use of Montaigne and Pater is carried out in indirect and unusual ways, playing with intertextual codes and leaving them undecideable, infusing her text with the *Essais* while multiplying their points of contact and extending their dimensions. In the attempt to develop her own personalized renaissance, while seeking innovative positionings between past and present, Woolf continues to interpret interpretation and produces more literary endeavor whose parameters, like all writing true to itself, are, in the words of Montaigne, "poursuites qui sont sans terme, et sans forme; son aliment c'est *admiration, chasse, ambiguité*" (III, xiii, 1068 — emphasis added). This is the facet of Woolf's modernism that demonstrably arises from her contact with the *Essais*. Montaigne's work in the context of Pater's and Woolf's becomes a source for their innovative literary productions and also expands certain of its own qualities that have had less development by other readers of the *Essais*.

Pater was a more conservative adherent to Montaigne than was Woolf, being original, yet cautiously so. In this sense, his approach is more related to Emerson's reception of Montaigne. Woolf is more Nietzschean in her reception of the *Essais* and exceeds Pater's approach by virtue of her *kritische* and more radical modulations of the notions of style, tradition, and innovation as developed by Montaigne. She uses Pater and Montaigne, even as she surpasses their more conservative solutions, to promote her unique vision of literary production: a concept that revolves around the dynamic opposition of self and history learned in part from the teachers that she exceeds and even abnegates. In *Orlando,* Woolf breaks many of the rules yet still operates in the context of the lessons she adapted from Pater and Montaigne; she concretizes the more philosophical receptions of Emerson and Nietzsche by producing a narrative of the problems of history and writing as first developed in the *Essais.* Both Pater and Woolf reproduced the "*Montaignesque* element" and wrote mobile, personalized texts that rely heavily on their receptions of Montaigne's writing. The parasitic originality of the work of Montaigne, Pater, and Woolf links them as important practitioners of literary modernism and makes the collective value of their writing relevant to the discussion of how modernist writers struggle with the opposition of mimesis and expression, history and self, repetition and originality. The modulation of the past through *kritische* response, through an attempt to use history and presentness in a reciprocally productive way in order not to be tyrannized by the "shadow of events," and also to avoid solipsistic self-referentiality, are important elements in the attempt to understand that which is "modernist," both as a literary period and, more importantly, as a writing phenomenon less dependent on chronological specificity than on an impulse to produce something that is lacking, namely, a new and vitalized response to one's historical moment. Pater and Woolf became modernist classicizers of the *Essais,* appropriating them as monumental, yet pursued their *kritische* implications in order to produce original narratives. It is widely accepted that Pater and Woolf played a central role in literary modernism, yet it is their modification of the "*Montaignesque* element" that makes their contributions as receivers of Montaigne's work unique and that propels the "under-texture" of the *Essais* into the foreground of modernist writing.

Montaigne, Woolf, and Pater were wary of logocentric utterances to varying degrees, and in their essayistic techniques meanings are often decentered, deferred, setting up a dynamic interplay of forces necessitating further elucidation. Pater's "mannerism," Montaigne's "baroque," Huysmans's "decadence," Woolf's "modernism" are related phenomena that should generate further critical examination. An important source of this modernist problematic is Montaigne's essayistic practice, in which self-conscious textuality filtered through a reciprocal relationship with past writers produces a network of problematic questions and shows the mind attempting to grapple with them. The *Essais* intoxicate readers with the force of their expressiveness, yet this textual energy is often overwhelming and leaves readers dissatisfied and restless with their own critical responses. Montaigne goes beyond the practice of *florilège* and develops a style that allows him to address the problems of his historical milieu in his own unique way, something that preexisting genres did not permit him to do. Woolf, through her readings of the *Essais*, and through the intermediaries Browne and Pater, transforms the implications of their work into her own expressive fabric as embodied in the innovative vision of *Orlando*. This is of course only one way to approach a text as complex as *Orlando*, yet it has shown how certain of its aspects operate in a light not considered by other of Woolf's critics.

Pater's and Woolf's receptions of the *Essais* and their use of several of their elements in their own writing once again extend Montaigne's work beyond its "time and province." This is one side of their "receptions." Yet the way in which they read Montaigne — as an innovative model for their own work — is another side of their receptions. The ability of later writers to influence earlier ones, in the sense that they expose aspects of works that may have not been previously understood in a formulated manner, makes Pater and Woolf creators of Montaigne's modernism; the *Essais* are thus read differently after Pater's and Woolf's receptions of them. In this sense, their receptions of the *Essais* are active and constructive, producing an open dialog with the significance of Montaigne's writing. In Jauss's terms: "the perspective of the present constitutes the coherence of literature as the prehistory of its present manifestation."[61] In examining Pater's and Woolf's transformation of the *Essais* in their own work, one can better understand such problematic texts as *Gaston* and *Orlando* in the enhanced light that their receptions of the *Essais* produce. Montaigne could thus be subsequently discussed in a wider context than previously considered, and for some time to come. It is especially significant that Montaigne's genre, the essay, has had more marked instances of redevelopment by Anglo-American writers than by French. Montaigne's informality and playful use of language seem to be more congenial to the Anglo-American tradition than to the French, whose more formal, serious essay writing is in contrast to a greater degree of whimsical indulgence that characterizes many Anglo-American essayists.[62] Beyond their "time and province," Montaigne's *Essais* have often been significantly appropriated outside of France's borders; this is one reason why their discussion in a comparative context can be so rewarding.

None of the three writers ever really reached the goal of their quests: Montaigne added to his work until his death, Pater was thinking about Montaigne during the last days of his life as he worked on the unfinished "Pascal," and Woolf could no longer bear the burden of the creative life and committed suicide by walking into the river with a large stone ("une pierre") in her pocket. Montaigne's death was ultimately caused by symptoms related to his kidney stones ("des pierres"). As we have seen, such strange intertextual correlations between the lives and works of Montaigne and Woolf illuminate striking interrelationships between their respective notions of living and of writing. Since the 1970s Woolf of course has become one of the most prestigious writers in scholarly and literary activity of the twentieth century — there have even been recent cinematic and theatrical versions of *Orlando*.[63] In recent years she has become the object of numerous studies of great insight and gained widespread attention, both in and outside of the academy.[64] Woolf's *oeuvre* has become the "literary feminist bible" for a new generation of writers and scholars, both men and women.[65] She has become a sainted mother, a revolutionary feminist, a leading intellectual figure who first provided the means to remake repressive male ideology into a feminist strategy of empowerment, thereby allowing herself (and other women) to discard the identity of the "'daughter of an educated man.'"[66] Woolf so canonized, however, as Bette London has argued, could lead to a newly repressive hegemony, that of an official feminist Woolf, whereby allowable readings of her work become institutionalized.[67] It is therefore the unpredictable juncture of Montaigne and Woolf that could perhaps help us to consider how feminine and masculine discourses can interact and enrich each other. Like the *Essais,* Woolf's work is beginning to be more fully understood; yet, like Montaigne's, it is so complex that we should be wary of reducing its polyvocal dynamism. Echoing Baudier's pronouncement at the end of the sixteenth century that no writer produced commentary "aussi divers or plutôt aussi contraires" than Montaigne, C. Ruth Miller, at the end of the twentieth, has claimed much the same for Woolf: "Virginia Woolf never systematically outlined her aesthetic priorities: the terms of her argument changed continually and the attitudes she held towards the relationship between life and art are so various that *it is quite easy to find support for contradictory conclusions*" (emphasis added).[68] Woolf's ideal that the "whole of the mind must lie wide open if we are to communicate our experience with perfect fullness" is the impossible goal for which many strive. There will be as many responses to this challenge as there are attempts. Woolf's work, like Montaigne's, is as personally expressive as it is historically and ideologically revealing: personality as consciousness has indeed been one of the dominant modes of modernist and subsequently of postmodernist writing. We can perhaps now see more clearly how reading Montaigne through Pater, and especially through Woolf, is vitally connected to our understanding of interrelated intellectual and literary phenomena of the twentieth century.

Notes to Chapter 3

1. See Thomas Wright, *The Life of Walter Pater* (New York, Haskell House, 1907).
2. Perry Meisel's provocative study, *The Absent Father: Virginia Woolf and Walter Pater* (New Haven: Yale UP, 1980), discusses Woolf's eventual access to her father's library, previously forbidden by him, as a catalytic event in her development as a writer.
3. See Jane Spirit's "Nineteenth-Century Responses to Montaigne and Bruno: A Context for Pater," *Pater in the Nineties*, eds. Laurel Brake and Ian Small (Greensboro, NC: ELT Press, 1991), 43-61.
4. There are great differences as well as similarities between Pater, Nietzsche, and Emerson. Evidence of Pater's reading of them is available in Billie Andrew Inman's *Walter Pater's Reading: A Bibliography of His Library Borrowings and Literary References* (New York: Garland Publishing, 1981). Pater's notion of modernity is very much involved in Nietzsche's notion of *kritische* history as well as with Emerson's impulse toward an active renewal of tradition.
5. Walter Pater, *Appreciations, Complete Works*, 10 vols. (London: MacMillan and Company, 1910-1912), V, 116-117. All further references to Pater's work appear in text with references to title, volume, and page number.
6. Meisel, xvii.
7. See Quentin Bell, *Virginia Woolf: A Biography* (New York: Harcourt Brace Jovanovich, Inc., 1972).
8. See Juliet Dusinberre's suggestive reading of Montaigne's role in Woolf's *The Common Reader*: "Virginia Woolf and Montaigne," *Textual Practice* 5, 2 (1991): 219-241.
9. John M. Robertson, *Shakespeare and Montaigne* (London: The University Press, 1891), 113-14.
10. Walter Landor, *Imaginary Conversations*, ed. T. Earle Welby (London: Chapman and Hall, 1928), VII, 148.
11. Thomas Carlyle, *Montaigne and Other Essays, Chiefly Biographical* (London: James Gowan, 1897), 3.
12. Matthew Arnold, "On Translating Homer," *The Complete Prose Works of Matthew Arnold*, ed. R.H. Super (Ann Arbor: University of Michigan Press, 1960), I, 174.
13. F. C. McGrath's work on Pater and modernism lists the twelve essential points of Pater's work that influenced writers of the next generation. See *The Sensible Spirit: Walter Pater and the Modernist Paradigm* (Tampa: University of South Florida Press, 1986). Among those most pertinent to Pater's reception of Montaigne would be the subjectivity and relativity of knowledge, epistemological relativism, the primacy of sensory experience, and a functionalist attitude toward all productions of imagination and intellect (6).
14. Dédéyan, Chapter VI.

15. It has in fact now been established that Pater was refused a university proctorship as a result of his philosophical stance in *The Renaissance* as well as his homosexuality. See Billie Andrew Inman, "Estrangement and Connection: Walter Pater, Benjamin Jowett, and William M. Hardinge," *Pater in the Nineties*, 1-20.

16. In *The Cornucopian Text,* Cave has demonstrated the notion of *copia* as a mode of literary expression. In Montaigne's case, the "text represents the emptying of the cornucopia by the very gesture of extending itself indefinitely until the moment of *egressio* or elimination" (321). Montaigne fills his horn of plenty, yet empties it as he goes, whereby "the possibility of fruition is continually held in suspense, as the writing extends and points toward some ultimate unfolding" (274). Montaigne's fondness for *amplificatio* functions in a generative way, continually extending its topic.

17. See Pierre Bonnet, "Montaigne et le maniérisme et le baroque," *Bulletin de la Société des Amis de Montaigne* 5 (1973): 45-58.

18. Sir Leslie Stephen, "Art and Morality," *Cornhill* 32 (1875): 91-101.

19. "Pensées of Pascal," *Selected Essays*, 362.

20. See Wolfgang Iser, *Walter Pater: The Aesthetic Moment* (Cambridge: Cambridge UP, 1987), 168.

21. McGrath demonstrates, more thoroughly than any other critic, Pater's relationship to many of his philosophical and literary precursors. Although he does mention Montaigne's importance to Pater's work, it is only in passing. An extraordinary minimal reference to Montaigne's role in the work of Pater occurs in John J. Conlon's *Walter Pater and the French Tradition* (East Brunswick, NJ: Associated University Presses, 1982).

22. Gerald Monsmon has recently shed light on this issue in "Editing Pater's *Gaston de Latour*: A Fragment of Perfect Expression," *Pater in the Nineties*, 21-31. In his current project of establishing a definitive edition of Pater's complete works, Monsmon has chosen to publish the unfinished drafts of *Gaston* in order to counteract the edited version of Charles Shadwell, Pater's colleague at Oxford (who chose to polish the completed parts and leave the rest unpublished), that has been the standard edition for nearly a hundred years. In doing so, Monsmon felt that a more authentic version of Pater's work would be restored to us, one that would privilege Pater's compositional process over the artificially perfected text as carried out by Shadwell. *Gaston* will thus be read, more than ever, as a work *en mouvement*, in the process of becoming, always seeking further supplementation by the reader engaging its incompleteness, in the manner of the *Essais' scriptibilité*.

23. Fokemma, 683.

24. In Harold Bloom's terms: "He gives us a vision of art through his own unique sensibility, and so his writings obscure the supposed distinction between criticism and creation." "Introduction," *Selected Writings of Walter Pater*, ed. Harold Bloom (New York: Columbia UP, 1974), vii. In this sense, one can draw a similarity between Pater and Montaigne, who are both "creative" "critics" of their respective cultural traditions.

25. Virginia Woolf, *Collected Essays* (London: Hogarth Press, 1960), II, 28.

26. See Matthiessen's discussion of Browne's importance to Emerson in *American Renaissance.*

27. Sir Thomas Browne, *Religio Medici, The Works of Sir Thomas Browne* (Chicago: The University of Chicago Press, 1964), 81. All further references to Browne refer to this edition and appear in text.

28. For relevant discussions of Browne's philosophical skepticism and penchant for paradox, see *Approaches to Sir Thomas Browne,* ed. C.A. Patrides (Columbia: University of Missouri Press, 1982).

29. Sir Kenelm Digby, *Observations upon "Religio Medici,"* quoted in Patrides, 33.

30. See Jonathan F. S. Post, *Sir Thomas Browne* (Boston: G.K. Hall & Co., 1987), especially Chapter IV, "Elements of Style": "If Browne was a connoisseur of doubt, he achieved this destination by using a frequently rarefied diction, which lent an elevated tone to his prose, in conjunction with a loose or libertine syntax especially as exemplified in the recently discovered essay form" (63).

31. See Good, *The Observing Self.*

32. William Hazlitt, "Lecture on the English Comic Writers," *The Complete Works of William Hazlitt,* Centenary Edition, ed. P. Howe (London and Toronto: Dent Publishers, 1931), VI, 92-93. Hazlitt's discussion of Montaigne in an essay on comedy is a curious foreshadowing of Woolf's comic *Montaignerie* in *Orlando.* Is Montaigne perhaps joking more than is generally thought?

33. See Croll, Cave, and especially Richard Sayce, "Mannerism and Baroque," *The Essays of Montaigne: A Critical Exploration,* 313-334.

34. Croll, 209.

35. Croll, 184.

36. See Michele Federico Sciacca, "Montaigne e i libertini come antecedente dell'ertismo moderno," *Libro de homenaje à Luis Alberto Sanchez* (Lima: Universidad Mayor Nacional de San Marcos, 1967), 223-33 and Maria Luisa Belleli, *Modernità di Montaigne* (Rome: A.F. Formiggini, 1933).

37. One of the most helpful studies on Woolf of recent date is Pamela L. Caughie's *Virginia Woolf and Postmodernism: Literature in Quest and Question of Itself* (Chicago: University of Illinois Press, 1991). See also *New Feminist Essays on Virginia Woolf,* ed. Jane Marcus (Lincoln: University of Nebraska Press, 1981).

38. Virginia Woolf, "How One Should Read a Book," *The Common Reader,* Second Series (London: The Hogarth Press, 1932), 259. All further references to the essays in this work appear in text.

39. Virginia Woolf, *A Room of One's Own* (New York: Harcourt, Brace & World, 1929), 98. All further references appear in text.

40. Ben Jonson, *Discourses* (Edinburgh: Edinburgh UP, 1966), 31.

41. See Good, "Johnson: The Correction of Error," 55-70.

42. Virginia Woolf, *The Diary of Virginia Woolf: 1920-1924,* ed. Anne Olivier Bell (New York: Harcourt Brace Jovanovich, 1980), II, 285.

43. Virginia Woolf, "Montaigne," *The Common Reader* (New York: Harcourt, Brace, Jovanovich, 1925), 59. All further references to the essays in this work appear in text.

44. Cave, 319.

45. The term is Robert M. Adams's, from "Montaigne and the Ladies," *Hudson Review* 43, 2 (1990): 193-211.

46. Such systematic binarism constructed on gender lines has been amply delineated in MacLean's *The Renaissance Notion of Woman.* I am aware of the limitations of binary thinking in discussing writers as complex as Woolf and Montaigne.

47. See for example Maria DiBattista, "Androgyny," *Virginia Woolf's Major Novels: The Fables of Anon* (New Haven: Yale UP, 1980); Jean O. Love, "Orlando and Its Genesis: Venturing and Experimenting in Art, Love, and Sex," *Virginia Woolf: Revaluation and Continuity*, ed. Ralph Freedman (Berkeley: University of California Press, 1980), 189-218; and Sandra M. Gilbert and Susan Gubar, *No Man's Land: The Place of the Women Writer in the Twentieth Century* (New Haven: Yale UP, 1989).

48. Virginia Woolf, *Diary: 1925-1930*, III, 167-68.

49. Ludovico Ariosto, *Opere*, ed. Cesare Segre (Rome: Arnoldo Mondadori Editore, 1964), XXVI, 8, 656. All further references appear in text.

50. Barthes, *S/Z*, 71.

51. Paul Barolsky discusses *Gaston* as *the* precursor of *Orlando*: "From Mannerism to Modernism," *University of Hartford Studies in Literature* 16 (1984): 47-57.

52. See Carolyn Williams, *Transfigured World: Walter Pater's Aesthetic Historicism* (Cornell Ithaca UP, 1989).

53. Both gender pronouns are used at different times to refer to the androgynous Orlando according to the context in the work under consideration.

54. Virginia Woolf, *Orlando* (New York: Harcourt, Brace, Jovanovich, 1929), 308. All further references appear in text.

55. Villey's evolutionary scheme, for example, posits Montaigne's development from a position of stoicism, to one of skepticism, to one of epicurianism. He coincides the A, B, and C layers (the two editions published in Montaigne's lifetime and the "Exemplaire de Bordeaux") with this putative evolution of Montaigne's philosophical attitudes. Yet an examination of almost any essay exposes aspects of all three of these attitudes operating simultaneously throughout the *Essais* in autonomous layers. It is in fact the tension of these categories that paradoxically produces a disseminate instability. Villey's very model allows one to read the *Essais* not only horizontally, but vertically, progressing in time as well as space; he thus unintentionally provides for multivocal readings of the *Essais*; the three layers interacting in harmonious dissonance.

56. See Frame, *Montaigne: A Biography* for his discussion of the impossibility of ever determining the actual edition of the *Essais* that Montaigne would have authorized.

57. The numerological model here is neither gratuitous nor unfounded — witness the plausibility of Butor's *Essais sur les "Essais"* (Paris: Gallimard, 1968) and more recently Daniel Martin's *Architecture des "Essais" de Montaigne* (Paris: Librairie A.-G. Nizet, 1992).

58. Another strange symbolic permutation of the Bartholemew motif, also caught up in transgressive river imagery, is the fact that in the fall of 1572, soon after the

massacres, some of which took place near Montaigne's city residence on rue de la Rousselle in Bordeaux, the Garonne river swelled over into his neighborhood up to the fourth step of the Eglise St.-Michel. The overflowing river, such a key event in *Orlando,* has its bizarre historical counterpart which Montaigne himself experienced. In line with the genesis of Montaigne's writing of the *Essais,* 1572 is also the year in which Simon Millanges ("a thousand angels") began to publish in Bordeaux — he printed the first edition of the *Essais* eight years later. For a recounting of these events see Jean de Gaufreteau, *Chronique Bordelaise*: *1240-1636* (Bordeaux: Archives municipales de la Gironde, 1878).

59. See Beverly Ann Schlack, *Continuing Presences: Virginia Woolf's Use of Literary Allusion* (University Park: The Pennsylvania State UP, 1979). In the chapter concerning *Orlando,* the focus is on Sackville-West, Shakespeare, and Shelley.

60. See Théophile de Malzevin, *Michel de Montaigne: son origine, sa famille* (Bordeaux: G. Counouilhon, 1874) for the etymology of "Eyquem" as well as for other little known details of Montaigne's life. Malzevin asserts, inconclusively, that Montaigne's ancestors may have been of English origin. He was perhaps speculating on Montaigne's declaration that "les miens se sont autre-fois surnommez Eyquem, surnom qui touche encore une maison cogneuë en Angleterre" (II, xvi, 627).

61. Jauss, 39.

62. See a comparison of the traditions in Theodore P. Fraser's *The French Essay* (Boston: Twayne Publishers, 1986).

63. Sally Potter, *Orlando* (Great Britain: Adventure Pictures, 1992) and Robert Wilson, *Orlando* (L'Odéon-Théâtre de l'Europe, 1993).

64. Witness a recent 1991 edition of *Diacritics* (2, 3) in which Woolf is the subject of several comprehensive articles that discuss dozens of newly minted books dedicated to her life and work.

65. See Jane Marcus, *Virginia Woolf and the Language of Patriarchy* (Bloomington: Indiana UP, 1987), 5.

66. Marcus, *Language of Patriarchy*, 133.

67. Bette London, "Guerilla in Petticoats or Sans-Culotte? Virginia Woolf and the Future of Feminist Criticism," *Diacritics* 2, 3 (1991): 16.

68. C. Ruth Miller, *Virginia Woolf: The Frames of Art and Life* (New York: St. Martin's Press, 1989), 3.

Chapter Four

Conclusions: Montaigne among the Postmoderns

Outside his library window he could see
A gentle landscape terrified of grammar,
Cities where lisping was compulsory
And provinces where it was death to stammer.

— W.H. Auden, *The Double Man*, 1941.

Some of the more salient issues that have been dealt with in this study are the problems of consistency in the *Essais* and the qualities of several of their more problematic receptions: ambivalent resolution, eccentric rearticulation, cornucopian textuality, and free appropriation of cultural models. The *Essais* were written in a time of great political and cultural insecurity, a period marked by conflicts in religion and politics — civil war, famine, plague, and economic instability were the historical circumstances surrounding Montaigne's life that inspired him in part to question orthodox values and dogmatic ways of thinking.[1] Thus skepticism, relativism, and textual multiplicity reflect the sense that reality, even of the self, is a shifting, subjective, and impermanent phenomenon — haphazard since Montaigne chooses inconsistency to depict his world view, which is perhaps the dominant epistemological mode of our own time. It is thus possible to begin to understand Montaigne's project and its relevance to our "postmodern condition," an age in which

> It is no longer possible to maintain the economy of truth and representation in a world where reality is entirely constructed through forms of mass-media feedback, where values are determined by consumer demand (itself brought about by the endless circulation of meanings, images and advertising codes) and where nothing could serve as a means of distinguishing true from merely true-seeming (or ideological) habits of belief.[2]

Sixteenth-century France began with vigor and optimism, inspired by the advent of the printed book, the discovery of the "new world," and the humanist project; yet it ended in pessimism and despair, rife as it was with political chaos, bloody civil war, the evident treachery of colonialism, and the budding neoclassical suppression of renaissance exuberance.[3] Although Montaigne assumed a conservative pose on religion, politics, and culture, he implicitly critiqued societal and political affiliations. The *Essais* are in fact, by virtue of their unprecedented title, a radical critique of the officially accepted discourses of their time. Yet Montaigne's outward faith in the dominant religious and political orders permitted him an existential security whereby he could revolt discursively against the normalizing proscriptions of erroneous dogmatisms by demanding from himself and his readers an attempt toward authentic self-awareness, which could hopefully reform reified cultural practices and the illusions of common opinion.

It is at the end of the twentieth century, which began with great potential — the extraordinary technological advancements in transportation, communication, medicine, science, industry, by the move toward national consolidation, and by the general improvement of human life in many parts of the world — that we can begin to understand the relevance Montaigne's time to our own. This nascent century's optimism also dissipated during the most atrocious wars the world has ever experienced and, in the 1990s, is apparently an optimism lost in a widespread sense of the dissolution of social, ethical, and political stability. There is currently a general loss of faith that we will ever be able to remedy the situation, faced as we are with a technocracy that appears to be increasingly dehumanizing its citizenry and with ever-growing world populations perpetually at odds with each other. From one *fin de siècle* to another, at the "end of history," we live in a time whose historical dynamics are not so dissimilar to Montaigne's. It is suggestive to consider how he may have also experienced a postmodern "crisis of information," brought on by the advent of printing and the new availability of books, saturated with more knowledge than he could ever hope to understand as a coherent whole. His collection of over a thousand printed volumes, in a time before public libraries, would have been impossible for his grandfather's generation. This opportunity to gather such a prolific, private collection of writings helped bring him to the realization that he would never harmonize the superabundant contradictoriness of history and of life itself, and could only use the copious printed information of the past idiosyncratically, in order to preserve his mental integrity. Montaigne would have perhaps understood Eliot's desperate claim in the "The Waste Land" that our inability to live an organic relationship with our cultural traditions can only lead to an imperfect ordering of its contents, one that nevertheless helps to avoid psychic disintegration: "These fragments I have shored against my ruin."[4] This is an aesthetics not so unlike Montaigne's activity of piecing together his personality through a collage-like appropriation of texts and events ("une marqueterie mal jointe") as the only way, in Nietzsche's terms, to attempt to organize the chaos. The *Essais* stand perhaps as a late-sixteenth-century signpost to the postmodern age, unintentionally indicating what was to occur at a later time. Erich Auerbach's characterization of Montaigne's circumstances seem somehow applicable to our own:

> His [Montaigne's] newly acquired freedom was much more exciting, much more of the historical moment, directly connected with the feeling of insecurity. The disconcerting abundance of phenomena which now claimed the attention of men seemed overwhelming. The world — both outer world and inner world — seemed immense, boundless, incomprehensible. The need to orient oneself in it seemed hard to satisfy and yet urgent.[5]

Numerous Montaigne commentators have identified so closely with the *Essais* that they often continued their textual dimensions as if they were their own. Others, while resisting total identification with the *Essais,* attempt to establish clear reductive frameworks within which to interpret them. Others admit to the impossibility of ever clearly analyzing Montaigne's work and thereby dismiss the *Essais* as an aberrant text, unworthy of sustained critical attention. And still others, Nietzsche and Woolf being the two most prominent members of this fourth group, radically appropriate the "*Montaignesque* element" and reactivate it in ways that bring to light the more innovative dimensions of the *Essais*. Their redevelopment of Montaigne's work in their own has subsequently had a significant impact, direct and indirect, on other modernist and postmodernist writers. The latest receptive field of the *Essais* in some ways continues the Woolfian or Nietzschean appropriation of Montaigne's work, while adding further problematic inquiries to the continually growing body of critical and creative receptions of Montaigne's life and writing.

♦ ♦ ♦

As during the modernist period of the late nineteenth and early twentieth centuries, contemporary receptions of the *Essais* are characterized by both official academic criticism and by literary writers who produce creative commentary on, as well as narrative redevelopment of the *Essais*. Several current attitudes in receptions of the *Essais* can be found in Michel Butor's *Essais sur les "Essais,"* Jean-Yves Pouilloux's *Lire les "Essais" de Montaigne*, Michel Chaillou's *Domestique chez Montaigne*, and Philippe Sollers's *Portrait du joueur* and *Théorie des Exceptions*. Butor is one of the first contemporary writers to consider the *Essais* in what has now become widely considered a poststructuralist light: the valorization of Montaigne's work as a heterogeneous configuration of dynamic proportions. As a result of interacting with the *Essais*, these are some of the dominant qualities highlighted and operative in "Vom Nutzen und Nachteil," *Gaston*, and *Orlando*. Butor continues the tradition of creative-critical response to Montaigne's writing and in his reception of it pays closer empirical attention to the *Essais* themselves than did either Nietzsche, Pater, or Woolf.[6] He is one of the first contemporary writers to accept Montaigne's irregularity as a quality to be admired and strives to allow the diversity of the *Essais* to speak for itself, without filtering it through a critical system of reductive unity. Yet at the same time, he does paradoxically attempt to order the disorder through numerical systematization, thereby producing a conflictual reading of the *Essais* as a model for essaying their textuality. In this sense, Butor reaches back to Woolf's reception, which provided, along with Pater's and Nietzsche's, the possibility of considering Montaigne as a writer who embodies that which is new and daring.

At the same time, Butor anticipates critical attitudes toward the *Essais* outside of a mimetic frame of reference, in a poststructuralist attitude where the text is no longer privileged as an integrated presentation of human consciousness, nor as a unified textual vision, but rather as a multifaceted agglomeration of dynamic intertextual relationships whose gaps in coherence should be enjoyed as such and vicariously filled in by the attentive reader. Yet Butor's attempt to produce a rational scheme of numerical coherence also reproduces previous efforts to establish the unity of the *Essais*. This conflictual attitude is not lacking in the approaches to the *Essais* of Emerson, Nietzsche, Pater and Woolf; it is now only more pronounced. It is also not absent in the receptions of earlier readers of the *Essais*, who often became victims of the Montaigne's enigmas in attempting to valorize only one half of the dual status of the *Essais*: either their concomitant heterogeneity ("divers et ondoyant") or homogeneity ("mon livre est tousjours un" — III, ix, 964). In a more systematic formulation than developed by either Nietzsche or Woolf, Butor insists on the creative response of readers needed in order to grapple with the slipperiness of the *Essais*: "Invinciblement le lecteur est amené à revenir en arrière, à se promener dans le texte, dans cet ensemble qui forme un cercle ou mieux une guirlande circulaire."[7] Butor does not characterize the status of the *Essais* as a *classicisme manqué,* but prizes their incompleteness as a truer representation of human experience. The diverse and undulating qualities of various receptions of the *Essais* now play a more prominent role in a revised notion of their dimensions as proposed by Butor.

What existed in the receptions of Pascal, Rousseau, and Sainte-Beuve, or more explicitly in the radical reformulations of Nietzsche, Pater, and Woolf, now becomes the new "horizon-of-experience" within which the *Essais* are revaluated. Butor's concern for the mannerist textuality of the *Essais,* and his description of their compositional organization according to a scheme of incessant modification arranged around catalytic centerpieces (particularly the work of La Boétie and Sebond), proposes a "unity" of the *Essais,* yet one of movement and dynamic structure. *Essais sur les "Essais"* thus reaches back to Thibaudet's *Montaigne* yet also anticipates Starobinski's *Montaigne en mouvement.* It is an affirmation of the *Essais*' multiplicity, eccentricity, and dispersion, yet at the same time is an attempt to stabilize these very qualities. This dialectical mode of critical apprehension thereby seeks to engage the *Essais* on the level of rules that they themselves establish. Butor strives to formulate that which resists formulation and thus to order the disorder. He posits, however, unlike many of his predecessors such as Villey, Strowski, and Friedrich, a formulated disorder as a "unifying" principle.

Butor's *Essais sur les "Essais"* is a series of prefaces to the central themes of the *Essais* in which Butor emulates Montaigne's extended style and penchant for categorical enumeration while drawing attention to Montaigne's writing as a textual puzzle. Butor reads the relationship of Montaigne's life and work as central to a valid understanding of the *Essais*. In this sense, Butor does impose a certain structural unity onto the *Essais*, yet it is a dynamic unity: the structure oscillates between the painterly (openness of form) and the architectural (a systematic totality); it is variegated and symmetrical at the same time. Butor maintains that Montaigne solves the structural problem of his textual composition by arranging his fragments around a central portrait; the "crotesques" are thus related by "un entrelacement de lignes qui vont conduire perpétuellement l'oeil du spectateur de l'un à l'autre" (69). Butor's reception thus succeeds in producing an interactive understanding of the *Essais*, yet his valorization of the movement and incompleteness of Montaigne's writing project, over its impulse to produce stability and unity out of the chaos of experience, is very much an effort to relativize absolute positions. Butor's examination of the *Essais* is thus determined in part by what he finds in Montaigne's writing, but also by what he projects onto it. He is, like all Montaigne commentators, and Montaigne himself, distanciated yet derivative, repetitive yet unique. As he attempts to redevelop Montaigne's ability to play one position off another, he brings Montaigne's innovative identity into greater focus, yet at the same time becomes implicated in the *Essais'* dynamics of textual seduction. He seeks to find the unifying principal of the *Essais* while suggesting that readers develop this unity for themselves. Although he presents a schema toward the understanding of Montaigne's writing, he claims simultaneously that within this positivist armature, one can develop personalized meaning. Following Montaigne's interactive mediation between self and history,

Butor modulates between tradition (adherence to the text's parameters) and innovation (the liberty accorded to individual readings).

What is now more pronounced in the contemporary period of Montaigne's receptions, beginning with the work of Butor, is that the *Essais'* polyvalent features, as well as the important role accorded to the reader in formulating their significance, have now come into the foreground of critical response. The innovative elements of Montaigne's writing now appear in an enhanced context by virtue of a wider acceptance of the open, intertextual quality of literary production. Pascal's "Ce n'est pas dans Montaigne mais dans moi que je trouve tout ce que j'y vois" appears to hold truer than ever and Butor's essayistic mode of critical apprehension is perhaps symptomatic of contemporary critical attitudes toward them. In his conclusion, Butor insists on the *scriptible* attitude needed to approach Montaigne's writing. The self-abnegating proposal of his attempt at reading the *Essais* in his own idiosyncratic way is based upon the permission of Montaigne himself: "il nous convie à entrer dans cette galerie d'où le monde apparaît à travers un air nettoyé, et, comme il a si bien su faire siennes les citations qu'il empruntait aux auteurs de l'antiquité, il nous invite à faire nôtres ses sentences" (216). Butor identifies very closely with Montaigne, as can be seen in his appropriation of the *Essais* to a highly personal degree: "Pour retrouver cette origine rêvons et fantastiquons" (23). Butor's preference to insist upon the dynamic structure of the *Essais* leads him to draw the parallel between them and the renaissance gardens admired by Montaigne on his Italian journey: "labyrinthes remplis de délices et de dangers" (111), a characterization that demonstrates Butor's wariness of the complexity of the *Essais* and of the problematic nature of critically apprehending them. Butor's "danger and delight" in reading the *Essais* shows how their daring textuality motivates him to generate his own attempt at reading them, while at the same time to develop an accompanying skeptical awareness that this attempt can only be provisional. He invites a new generation of readers to make the *Essais* their own, but warns of the perils of not finding one's way out of Montaigne's hermeneutic labyrinth.

Butor's approach to the *Essais,* although an important event in highlighting the acceptance of the "modernist" dimensions of Montaigne's work in the contemporary period, is still one involved in ordering Montaigne's disorder. For even as Butor's reception can, on the one hand, be construed as emblematic of a current climate of acceptance of the modern openness of the *Essais*, it also demonstrates an impulse toward a systematic unification of their textuality. Butor thus concomitantly points to the *Essais'* movement and dynamism as well as to their structured coherence. He proposes that the *Essais* are not simply a collection of discontinuous observations on the human condition written according to the whims of their author, but rather a concretely conceived writing project: Book I was originally a supporting text for La Boétie's *Discours de la servitude volontaire*, Book II a response to Sebond's *Théologie naturelle*, and Book III written around the seventh of its thirteen essays "De l'incommodité de la grandeur" — Montaigne's defense of his private, political, and literary activities. It is especially in Butor's chapters "Diptyque" and "Figure générale du troisième livre" that he attempts to develop his numerological theory for the composition of the *Essais* — proposing that, although his writing was one of painterly composition, it is still a "guirlande *circulaire*" and an "*encadrement* maniériste," ordered symmetrically in relation to various central subjects and numerological patterns. He observes, for example, that the first book of fifty-seven chapters has in its center number twenty-nine, in which Montaigne placed the twenty-nine sonnets of La Boétie. Book II, composed of thirty-seven chapters, is organized around the nineteenth essay, on Julien the Apostate, whom Montaigne considers to be an earlier La Boétie. The central piece of Book III, number seven, "De l'Incommodité de la grandeur," is a strikingly much shorter chapter than the others in which Montaigne links together the theme of the "liberté de conscience" (173) found in Book I and in the last essay of Book III. Butor continues in this vein with other suggestive numerological correlations that open onto endless possibilities.

Butor's numerical scheme and geometrical approach, in contrast to his admiration of the dynamic mobility of Montaigne's writing, thus proposes a structured regularity for the *Essais*; the sense of irregularity *and* consistency that one experiences in reading the *Essais* is calculated in terms of an ordered text whose seeming disseminate qualities are actually diversifications of structured paradigms. In this way, Butor valorizes a dialectical reading of the *Essais* whereby one should consider that the dictum "nous sommes doubles en nous-mesmes" is to be extended to readings of the text itself — a dualistic apprehension of its elements, which are arranged in an ordered disorder. The *Essais* are thus multifarious only to an extent and Butor proposes that his relational interpretation will help readers to interact with the multidimensional, yet coherent nature of Montaigne's writing project, thereby producing readings closer to the essayist's intentions of helping his readers achieve self-understanding. Butor's Montaigne is thus a problematized approach, in which readers must engage the *Essais* in a continuously reciprocal mode of apprehension in order to avoid producing a reductive reading of the text and also not to succumb to a facile acceptance that the *Essais* are simply too "divers et ondoyant" to be adequately comprehended. Yet Butor's very title (an "essai" on "essais") nevertheless points to the provisional nature of even his own approach to the problem of reading Montaigne's work.

Butor's *Essais sur les "Essais"* preceded the next important contemporary reception of the *Essais*, Pouilloux's *Lire les "Essais" de Montaigne*, by several years. Pouilloux is one of the first contemporary academic critics to approach the *Essais* as a self-reflective text, one always needing to be supplemented by further critical engagement: "la vérité n'est pas donnée, elle est à construire."[8] Pouilloux, going beyond Butor's qualified readerly approach, more readily accepts the status of the *Essais* as open and antisystematic, and proposes a "double" reading of the *Essais* whereby Montaigne's skeptical approach (his impetus to often undermine his own pronouncements) generates a manner of reading in which the contradictory, self-reflexive nature of the text must first and foremost be taken into account: "rien ne peut être affirmé sans avoir reçu une seconde lecture qui détermine les conditions de validité de la première affirmation" (36). This circular method of reading the *Essais* is a significant valorization of the mobile text that problematizes all affirmations toward its understanding. Pouilloux propels these problematic qualities of Montaigne's writing into the foreground of his reception of the *Essais*. What was often suppressed, repressed, ignored, and even brought to life in isolated incidents in the numerous commentaries on the *Essais* for over four centuries now becomes the central focus of Montaigne studies at the present time. The more radically innovative characteristics of the *Essais*, as seen in the irregular degrees of success of many writers' attempts at critically articulating them, or in the receptions by such unlikely heirs to Montaigne as Nietzsche and Woolf, now appear with greater visibility beginning with the receptions of Butor and Pouilloux. Montaigne is now read more often as a heterodox writer who problematizes all categorizations of his work. This attitude has been prepared by Montaigne's presence in the work of writers engaged in the modernist problematics of the *Essais* as discussed in the preceding chapters.

Yet what could be considered a shift (Montaigne's modernism has its own "evolution" and becomes more fully developed in the last hundred years), a triumph (modernist receptions of Montaigne's work have finally produced the *Essais* in their truest light), or a repetition of the same (Baudier's pronouncement of 1601: "Il n'y a aucun écrivain sur lequel on porte des jugements aussi divers ou plutôt aussi contraires que Michel de Montaigne") is what ultimately produces the impasse of attempting to univocally interpret the *Essais*, for each possible model has its own degree of truth. The last twenty-five years have seen the flourishing of the second of the above three choices. Yet contemporary receptions, even as they enhance understandings of the *Essais*, also reproduce the schemas of evolution or repetition, thereby perpetuating the chain of problematization. A telling example of the current state of the Montaignean impasse can be seen in Pouilloux's reading of the *Essais*, in which he admits to the value of unifying critical evaluations such as Villey's and Friedrich's while proposing a new approach that would avoid repeating the synthesizing attitude to Montaigne's writing and its desire to establish an inclusive understanding of the *Essais'* multiple dimensions. Pouilloux thus proposes a more heuristic mode of critically rearticulating the *Essais* and is satisfied with a partial understanding of what they have to offer, one that can better generate what is both a critical inventory and a creative modulation of some of their thornier aspects:

> Cette lecture a pour objectif de faire apparaître, de constituer par son propre développement, ce que les *Essais* se sont donné à poser comme question, comme problème. Il ne sera pas ici demandé à Montaigne compte seulement de ses réponses, mais surtout de ses questions et des questions de ses questions. (15)

Pouilloux attempts to work against what he sees as the falsifying image of many critical readings of the *Essais* which strive to order the disorder of Montaigne's writing and thus establish its organizational principle.[9]

Opposing Villey, Pouilloux maintains that the examination of the temporal evolution of the *Essais* exposes not their definitive meaning, but rather the evolution of their contradictions, which renders interpretive certainty evasive. In order to demonstrate his point, Pouilloux proposes a triadic process of affirmation, distinction, and dissolution that ultimately forbids both univocal and unequivocal interpretations of the *Essais.* Thus the only responsible reading of the *Essais* would be one that "constitue le désordre du texte comme son objet" (41). Pouilloux proposes that readers submit to the scandalous nature of Montaigne's writing and consider it a work of humor and insignificance: the aberrant product of an experiment in liberated writing. He proposes the acceptance of Montaigne's avowal of the illegitimacy of his own discourse and maintains that centuries of univocal readings of the *Essais* have produced one radical misunderstanding of the text after another and that the remedy for such critical distortion is to accept the "modernity" of Montaigne's work, in the sense that the *Essais* are a nontotality — a text whose iconoclastic nature must be experienced on its own terms in a mode of critical apprehension that is both supple and tenacious — all of its serious readings will be, at best, good misreadings.

Montaigne is thus, for Pouilloux, the incarnation of the modernist impulse of discontinuity, discursive freedom, and above all, of the dissolution of reductive critical understanding:

> La coexistence de ces trois schémas (affirmation, distinction, dissolution) interdit toute tentative univoque d'interprétation. Ces différents ordres se distinguent selon leur référence à la connaissance; de la dissolution d'un savoir naïf, pour la dissolution d'un savoir averti, naît le plaisir d'écrire l'inanité humoristique des pensées humaines. (118)

Pouilloux, some forty years after Woolf's "Montaigne," is one of the first university critics in France to develop such a notion of Montaigne's writing and thus sets the tone for subsequent receptions of Montaigne's work of the last twenty years, which are carried out in the context of the more radically innovative dimensions of the *Essais.* Pouilloux is thus the first of the new wave of poststructuralist

Montaigne commentators to systematically acclaim the postmodern heterogeneity of the *Essais*. Yet even Pouilloux's putative heterodox approach depends on a stratified tripartite structure ("affirmation, distinction, dissolution") and inevitably repeats the impulse to establish the *Essais* as a systematically comprehensible entity. His reception is a further problematization of an already problematic text. His formalistic armature, although more flexible and essayistic than others, nevertheless maintains a schematizing attitude toward the *Essais*, thereby conflicting with his belief in the heterogeneous nature of the *Essais* and reiterating Montaigne's conviction that interpretation is inescapably contradictory, and therefore endless.

There have been several other works over the last twenty years that have continued this problematized vein of Montaigne commentary. Although varying in great degree in concern, approach, and result, these works are related in their attempts to regard the *Essais* in new interpretive formulations provided by critical strategies that focus on the question of textuality, moving away from the monumental shadow of Villey's insistence on the thinker Montaigne and on the coherence of the evolutionary status of his text, as well as from Friedrich's thematically ordered *Essais*, and toward a greater consideration of the open-endedness, plurality of meaning, and textual aporia characteristic of the *Essais*. Richard Regosin's assessment of the important works of Jules Brody (*Lectures de Montaigne*), Lawrence Kritzman (*Déstruction/Découverte: le fonctionnement de la rhétorique dans les "Essais" de Montaigne*), Terence Cave (*The Cornucopian Text*), Michel Beaujour (*Miroirs d'encre: Rhétorique de l'auto-portrait*), Antoine Compagnon (*Nous, Michel de Montaigne*), and Mary McKinley (*Words in a Corner: Studies in Montaigne's Latin Quotations*) aptly summarizes the trends in Montaigne studies in a poststructuralist context: "Recent studies have moved away from biography, or ideas as intellectual biography, in a concern for the strategies of writing, for rhetorical composition and the disposition of figures, for lexical and stylistic dimensions of discourse, for etymology and the semantic potential of grammar and syntax."[10] This cursory characterization of these works, which vary in approach, interests, and results, shows how the vitality of the *Essais* is currently generating new critical readings today and how receptions of Montaigne's work are now more attentive than ever to textual problematics inscribed in the *Essais* by Montaigne. They are companion works to the more contextualized studies of critics such as Bellenger, Schaefer, Bauschatz, Nakam, and Leschemelle, which have analyzed the complex relationships of the *Essais* to their historical and cultural milieu.[11]

The latest receptive field of the *Essais* is thus predominantly concerned with what was considered unworthy of serious attention for so many generations of commentators: Montaigne's "modernism." The affirmation of the forces of multiplicity, eccentricity, and dispersion of the *Essais* is the latest version of the status of Montaigne's receptions. From protest against Montaigne's novelty, through the systematic establishment of the *Essais* as a unified canonical text of consistent meaning, and finally to a wider critical acceptance of Montaigne's writing as a case study in textual problematics, critics are essaying the *Essais* in academic discourse on the level of their ability to problematize the questions of the writing-subject, reading, and the relations of self and text, as well as of history and its use. This latest "horizon-of-experience" was foreshadowed in the equivocal receptions of Pascal, Rousseau, and Sainte-Beuve, and more significantly in the modulations of the *Essais* as carried out by Emerson, Pater, Nietzsche, and Woolf: a group of Montaigne commentators whose interpretive dimensions drew attention to the *Essais* as an uncanny and unresolvable text. Montaigne's ability to generate new and problematic approaches in writers of subsequent generations is now produced by many of the authoritative arbiters of the *Essais*. Reading four-hundred years of the *Essais* receptions has prepared the background for what has become valorized by a proliferation of readers as Montaigne's modernism: the richly suggestive fabric of a text that perpetually produces renewed interpretive activity. The work of such critics as Cave, Brody, Kritzman, Beaujour, McKinley, and Compagnon, and more recently those of François Rigolot (*Les Métamorphoses de Montaigne*) and Gisèle Matthieu-Castellani (*Montaigne et l'écriture des "Essais"*) have thus moved beyond the convention of reading the *Essais* as a text that reflects the personality of its author and left behind the obsession with the referent in order to examine the level of the signifier, the operation of rhetorical and linguistic devices, intertextual systems, and the nature and role of Montaigne's thoroughly unresolvable discourse.[12] These recent Montaigne receptions fulfill yet surpass the moderns' contributions by continuing to articulate the *Essais'* problematic status while doing so with more particularized and refined attention, thereby enhancing our contemporary self-awareness as readers in the process of critical activity.

Roland Barthes is an example of a writer who does not explicitly approach the work of Montaigne in his own, yet develops several interesting relationships to the *Essais* in his writing. His notion of the polyvalent text generates a system, or standard of procedure, that ultimately renders indeterminate the final authoritative understanding of a text:

> Interpréter un texte, ce n'est pas lui donner un sens (plus ou moins fondé ou plus ou moins libre), c'est au contraire apprécier de quel pluriel il est fait. Posons d'abord l'image d'un pluriel triomphant, que ne vient appauvrir contrainte de représentation (d'imitation). Dans ce texte idéal, les réseaux sont multiples et jouent entre eux, sans qu'aucun puisse coiffer les autres; ce texte est une galaxie de signifiants, non une structure de signifiés; il n'y a pas de commencement; il est réversible; on y accède par plusieurs entrés dont aucune ne peut être à coup sûr déclarée principale; les codes qu'il mobilise se profilent *à perte de vue*, ils sont indécidables (le sens n'y est jamais soumis à un principe de décision, sinon par un coup de dés); de ce texte absolument pluriel, les systèmes de sens peuvent s'emparer, mais leur nombre n'est jamais clos, ayant pour mesure l'infini du langage.[13]

Is this another surreptitious development of the "*Montaignesque* element" in the contemporary period? Is Barthes's "texte idéal" not an apt description for many of the *Essais'* textual characteristics? In considering the oppositions of philosophy and literature, innovation and custom, the search into the self as both a positivist and an idealist quest, as well as the plurality of the text, Barthes establishes a renewed trend in his work of many qualities essential to the *Essais*. *Roland Barthes par Roland Barthes* is his most Montaignean book in its open analysis of the self and of literature. The relation between the work of Barthes and Montaigne is very indirect in comparison to the other contemporary writers discussed here, and for this very reason, more heuristic, suggestive, and perhaps indicative of Montaigne's ubiquitous presence, though not always empirically visible, in other contemporary literary, critical, and theoretical thought and writing at the present time. *Roland Barthes par Roland Barthes* is a work that decries rigid systems, develops the movements of the consciousness of its author, and abandons linear argument in the quest to invent a renewed genre of essayistic autobiography. It is a work that "registers new forms of dramatic stress of a self-referring kind and becomes the record of compulsions and resistances to write."[14] To consider Barthes as an important heir to the *Essais* in the contemporary period would require lengthy justification; it has been admirably discussed by Réda Bensmaïa in *The Barthes Effect.*

There are similarities and affinities in the textual strategies of Barthes and Montaigne that relate their work in essential ways. The very duality of the writing project itself, as proposed by Barthes, points to Montaigne's claim that humans and their writing accomplishments, even when they have dogmatic aims, are unstable and undulating. Writing in the Montaignean mode is a process of tension and resonance of competing dispositions, characteristics that generate the powerful productivity of both Barthes's and Montaigne's formulation of an aesthetic of *complicatio.* In the short first essay for example, "Actif/réactif" of *Roland Barthes par Roland Barthes,* Barthes establishes a trend for the type of irreducible writing that is characteristic of many of the dimensions of both his work and Montaigne's. For both writers, textuality is the production of a polyphonic galaxy of signifiers that brings into play the possibility of plural networks of movement:

> Dans ce texte qu'il écrit, il y a deux textes. Le texte I est réactif, mû par des indignations, des peurs, des ripostes intérieures, de petites paranoïas, des défenses, des scènes. Le texte II est actif, mû par le plaisir. Mais en s'écrivant, en se corrigeant, en se pliant à la fiction du Style, le texte I devient lui-même actif; dès lors il perd sa peau réactive, qui ne subsiste plus que par plaques (dans de menues parenthèses).[15]

The generative power of the double text, the *Essais,* has been witnessed in many of their receptions throughout this study — the constancy of this theme is its diversity. Operating in the work of many receivers of the *Essais* is the struggle with a style of thought and writing that has been commonly recognized as one crucial aspect of a modernist mode of literary production: maximal fluidity, generated through the production of discourse characterized by the pluralization of codes, and the dispersion of ideas among many fragments. As Bensmaïa has demonstrated, Barthes's textual practice is closely related to Montaigne's essayistic heterogeneity, which continues to persist in twentieth-century thought and writing.[16]

Flux and variability are central notions in contemporary receptions of Montaigne's work. Yet there is a paradoxical constancy in the mobility of these receptions. It is Jean Starobinski who has presented most decisively this dimension of Montaigne's work in his reception of the *Essais*. For Starobinski, the *Essais* are a text that contain the same words on the page for all readers, yet their elusiveness, the loose interconnections of the many texts woven into them, and the ways in which readers constitute their receptions, reasserts the dynamic, productive capacity of Montaigne's writing. Starobinski reminds us of Montaigne's warning to all commentators about the pitfalls of interpretation and of the continual self-referentiality involved in the attempt at textual exegesis, as well as the lamentable fact that more books written about books only exacerbate the problem of critical understanding ("plus de livres sur les livres que sur autre subject"). Starobinski concludes his preface to *Montaigne en mouvement* by cautiously authorizing readers to produce meaning while interacting with the text. The participatory reader who plays a subjective yet informed role in the generation of the text's meaning is clearly promoted by Starobinski in his redevelopment of the *Essais*; yet he too attempts to remain skeptical of any totalizing interpretive function. This tentative participatory attitude both fulfills Montaigne's wishes and respects his demonstration that total understanding is elusive:

> D'autre part, Montaigne souhaite un suffisant lecteur, qui saura imaginer, à partir des *Essais*, les *infinis essais* dont ce livre offre le prétexte. Ce lecteur tirerait parti de la *fortune* qui a collaboré avec l'écrivain, et qui s'est manifesteé par des traits *surpassant sa conception et sa science*. J'ai composé ce livre dans le souci de respecter à la fois l'avertissement et la permission qui me venaient de Montaigne.[17]

For Starobinski, the unity of Montaigne's writing is to be found in its diversity — more essaying takes place in the various receptions of the *Essais* where reactivation of the scheme of mobility continues to play itself out in new interpretive configurations. Starobinski's discussion of the movement of the *Essais*, however, is one of coherent structure — it is neither linear nor evolutionary. The open structure proposed by Starobinski extends in some ways the receptions of Pater and Woolf. In the context of a general paradigm of the *Essais*' textuality, Pater and Woolf loosely generated their own configurations within its dimensions and produced new texts that were reworkings of old ones. Starobinski thus develops his own version of Montaigne, yet as he does so, dispels the belief that it will ever be free of paradox.

There are two recent important receptions that have catapulted Montaigne's presence more visibly into the contemporary literary scene. Michel Chaillou and Philippe Sollers have drawn significantly on the *Essais* in several of their own works. Chaillou's 1982 publication of *Domestique chez Montaigne* marks the latest narrative redevelopment of the *Essais* as well as of Montaigne's life and historical moment.[18] Chaillou's narration of the real and imagined life and work of Montaigne combines in some ways the tendencies of both Pater's and Woolf's receptions. His interest is in reproducing the *Essais* by using dates, places, and people important in Montaigne's life as the material around which to construct a fictional account of the crisscrossing experiences of several protagonists. They become the barometer of the geographical, historical, and literary landscapes in and around Montaigne's château during his life as well as through four succeeding centuries. Their experiences are abundant in imagined recuperations of the life of Montaigne, and of his family, peasants, servants, and most importantly of their descendants between 1530 and 1980. They are witnesses to what may have occurred during Montaigne's lifetime and draw on the *Essais* as a textual source from which to create their own essayistic understanding of the world and of their selves. Chaillou's narration is both fragmentary and cornucopian, presenting the multiple details of a loosely associated group of characters as well as an abundance of intertexts important to the history of Montaigne's time and place. The novel both begins and ends *in medias res* and what occurs in between is a kaleidoscopic journey through four centuries of discontinuous narrative experience, which takes place on a single day. *Domestique* seeks to recapture historical significance and at the same time strives to understand its overwhelming multiplicity. Chaillou's protagonists emulate Gaston in his effort to understand himself in relation to his spiritual guide, Michel de Montaigne, and Orlando in his effort to understand herself in the ludic narrative journey of Woolfian Montaigneanism. As in *Gaston,* there are numerous references to the *Essais,* which culminate or introduce various episodes, and likewise, at the end of *Domestique,* the successes of the protagonists' quests are left unresolved, in the process of development. Chaillou's reception of the *Essais* is perhaps the most unique and active yet, as seen in his claim: "j'ai glissé mon propre tempérament dans les *Essais*, ma propre culture, Montaigne était mon inconscient."[19] His effort "refaire la vie de Montaigne" has provided one of the most committed and explicit literary renovations to date. The *Essais* permeate every fiber of *Domestique* — witness Chaillou's avowal that they are "la bible de ce roman" ("Chaillou").

For Chaillou, Montaigne is above all "le maître de la digression" whose writing manifests "l'élaboration d'une digression constante par rapport au sujet proposé" and whose innovative use of language has a modern suppleness to it that was "pas encore figé dans le moule classique ("Chaillou"). His writing project in *Domestique* is much like that of Montaigne's in the *Essais* of giving new life to dead writers: "communiquer avec les morts, retrouver une oralité de ceux qui ont précédé" ("Chaillou"). Chaillou spent five summers in and around St. Michel de Montaigne and Bordeaux, collecting information, interviewing the guardian of the Château de Montaigne, studying departmental archives, and generally immersing himself in the history, psychogeography, and quotidian ambiance of the region. After starting to write an account of his subject matter, which was to have been the basis for a film on Montaigne (never made), he came to see himself implicated in the results of his research and began to infuse the material with the heredity of his own family, pursuing the quest for his personal as well as authorial identity in response to Montaigne's work. It is thus that Chaillou, the narrator, as well as the three protagonists (Alex and Jeanne Lambert, the married caretakers of the château, and Gabriel Lorgerie, a scholarly tourist in search of a more intimate understanding of Montaigne's life and work), interrogate themselves on human experience and reality in general. The first sentence of *Domestique* ends in fact with a question and opens up a series of questions as the uncultivated Alex wakes up one morning to deal with the "pénombre," not only of awakening in his dark room, but also of his perplexed life and its relationship to the haunting memories of his ancestors, servants at Montaigne's estate (*Domestique,* 9). This is something Alex will attempt to understand (unsuccessfully) throughout the work. His ignorance complements the reader's, the other protagonists', as well as the narrator's on their way to an incomplete self-knowledge. The experience for Chaillou writing of *Domestique* was similar to Alex's life: "un tâtonnement dans l'obscurité" ("Chaillou"). In Chaillou's terms, Alex is Caliban to the narrator's Prospero. Montaigne is of course Ariel, from whom Chaillou explicitly borrows the ethereal liberty that he finds in the *Essais* (a reformulation of Montaigne's "je jette la plume le plus souvent au vent ... et m'abandonne à la mercy de la fortune") and regenerates it in the textual "vagabondage" of *Domestique*: "J'ai essayé de rémémorer la phrase de Montaigne comme une espèce de chewing-gum" ("Chaillou"). They are the glue for Chaillou's narrative collage of the many intertextual levels operating in *Domestique*. He thus regenerates the immediacy of the quotidian tangibility of the *Essais* as well as their digressive form, freely mingling past and present, philosophy and self-analysis, history and contemporary events.

Chaillou thus traces that which is mostly absent, yet ever present in the *Essais*: Montaigne's laconic references to his family and servants. Alex Lambert descends in fact from a man named Donval — Montaigne's secretary, whom he brought back from Italy and who started a family of his own during a ten-year residence at Montaigne's estate. Chaillou mixes historical fact with imaginative fiction and this allows him to infuse the work with the history of his own ancestors who were of an "origine très populaire" ("Chaillou"). Thus, instead of the "discours des maîtres," Chaillou produces "le bruit de la vaisselle" ("Chaillou") — the common people's experience in relation to Montaigne, who is now the background of their lives. He takes literally Montaigne's claim that his life was mediocre and common ("Je propose une vie basse et sans lustre" — III, ii, 805) and pushes it in an oblique direction by producing a proletarian reformulation (L. *proles*, "offspring") of the *Montaignesque* element. Chaillou adeptly brings to life an imaginative reconstruction of what might have been, as inspired by Montaigne's register of suggestivity. He makes an engaged attempt to come to serious terms with Montaigne and with his own writing; his textual pyrotechnics can be disconcerting for any but a *suffisant lecteur* since one day and four centuries are woven together in a "digression multiple mais avec une direction précise" ("Chaillou"). The manipulative polyvocalism of *Domestique* is not always easy to decipher (in accord with

Chaillou's commitment that the novel should be a defiant "acte de résistance" in the face of commonplace cultural conventions — "Chaillou"). He develops a narrative complexity similar to Montaigne's by explicitly adopting the *Essais*' digressive movement (even calling Montaigne's *Essais* "un *roman* de sa vie profonde" — "Chaillou"). Chaillou's free translation of the past into the present, infused with his own personal family history, is consequently embodied in the experiences of Alex, Jeanne, and Gabriel, all of whom mix their own lives with their individual experiences of the *Essais*: "ils essaient à mener leurs propres vies aux *Essais* ("Chaillou"). As we know, Montaigne's family after his death was perpetuated through his daughter Léonor. This female generation could not perpetuate the patronymic Montaigne (the novel of the descendants of Montaigne's daughter is waiting to be written). It is thus a woman in *Domestique*, Jeanne Lambert, who actually gives the visitor tours of Montaigne's tower and who knows the *Essais* and Montaigne's life thoroughly. She is the true guardian of Montaigne's legacy (in contrast to Alex's cultural illiteracy), and is another important instance of the role of women role in perpetuating the life of the *Essais*. The feminization of Montaigne's modernism continues in this instance of Chaillou's reception, which is, as we will see, in marked contrast to Sollers's involvement in sexual politics.

Gabriel, the tourist, comes to the château in order to decipher the hieroglyphics of Montaigne's life (metaphorically embodied in the layers of centuries of visitors' signatures which still cover the wall of Montaigne's sitting room next to his tower library — hundreds of names layered upon each other, a palimpsest of Montaigne's legacy as well as a collective monument to his project of writing over that which was previously written, much the same as one reception after the next has added its own "crotesques" to the garland of Montaigne's heritage). It is Gabriel, living through Chaillou's attempt to produce a mysterious evocation of Montaigne, who asks: "Si l'on pouvait tirer les morts de leur mort?" (*Domestique*, 115). The *Essais* are the textual source that motivates Chaillou's essayistic experience of triangulating between Montaigne's life, his own, and that of his characters, who all have something of Chaillou in them. Yet it is Gabriel who seems to best emulate Chaillou's own quest — his departure from St. Michel de Montaigne occupies the last chapter, in which he is moving on and "roulant et coulant sans cesse" toward a future that is unknown to all: "Que devient Gabriel? … Il roulait, sa tête à la portière, la vôtre, la nôtre, quatre roues, un changement de vitesse, la vie derrière, tuyau d'échappement, la vie consumée" (*Domestique*, 277). The *Essais* are thus given new life, regenerated in another textual construction that strives to stimulate a collective response both to the *Essais* and to Chaillou's creative rearticulation of them. Chaillou's notion of "une nouvelle méthode romanesque qui se rapporte sur un grand écrivain" ("Chaillou") involves him in the endless flow of Montaigne's receptions. He ultimately characterizes the writing of the fantastical *Domestique*, like that of the *Essais*, as a "ruisseau dans la prairie" ("Chaillou") — a fluid text that winds through the historical fields of Montaigne's legacy while reproducing the *Essais*' innovative modernity and emulating Montaigne's claim of the oscillation and inconsistency of the human experience: "Nous n'allons pas, on nous emporte, comme les choses qui flottent" (II, ii, 333).

The case of Sollers has perhaps broader implications than that of Chaillou due to the former's literary as well as theoretical interest in Montaigne, along with his central position in French intellectual life of the last thirty years.[20] As does Chaillou, Sollers speaks from outside of the academy. He has accomplished perhaps the most unique and prolific understanding of Montaigne at the present time. He is by no means the new Montaigne (Chaillou prefers to call him "Philippe Voltaire"), yet he has relied on the *Essais* time and again in his own literary and intellectual development. Sollers, a Bordelais, first undertook an absorbed study of the *Essais* while a student at the *Lycée Montaigne* in Bordeaux, making the obligatory pilgrimage to the tower library at the age of twelve: "L'étude de Montaigne? on n'étudiait que ça."[21] Sollers has at once a symbiotic yet exfoliating relationship to the *Essais*; his essay, "Montaigne, le mutant," admirably delineates in a few pages Montaigne's "modernité" and his importance to contemporary intellectual debates as well as to Sollers's own thought and writing.[22] Sollers begins "Montaigne le mutant" by playing with the titles of various *Essais* and writing a series of "haïkus" with them. In this ludic approach to Montaigne's work, Sollers, in a parodic manner, emulates Montaigne's own use of the past: "comme une horloge à remonter le temps et à le dissoudre" ("Mutant," 18). In Sollers's understanding of the *Essais*, Montaigne's monumental contribution to literature is to have gathered history into the present in order to make it his own: "Montaigne: le premier qui signe vraiment en son nom. Et qui le sait. Et qui l'affirme" ("Mutant," 19). Montaigne's liberated essaying of the past in the present, his ability to wryly preserve the past in himself is, for Sollers, an event of extreme importance, since in doing so, Montaigne "commence le temps de l'ouvert" ("Mutant," 20). Openness is Montaigne's essential modernist quality — he did not seek to interpret the world, but rather to recite it in himself and thereby produce a dynamic, revolutionary work: "une forêt de réflexion en marche" ("Mutant," 21). For Sollers, the *Essais* are the "fricassée" in which Montaigne produces an enchanted textual field: a modernist paradise of playful narrativity. The question of Montaigne's unique textual development is thus central to Sollers's conception of his modernity: "Pour enchainer? C'est très simple: 'mais revenons à nos bouteilles.' Ou, vraiment sans complexes: 'mais suivons'" ("Sollers"). Montaigne's aesthetic of discontinuity is his ultimate challenge, in which the enigmatic textual idiosyncrasy is so unrestrained. He asks us to undertake the exercise of self-discovery with him in the protean development of the *Essais*; it is this challenge that informs Sollers's concept of "le sujet mutant." Yet Montaigne's work has also been *mutilated* by four hundred years of receptions, from which Sollers seeks to free him by making him an avatar of postmodern *jouissance*.[23] What struck Sollers as audacious and unforgettable in the *Essais*, even while a student at the *Lycée Montaigne*, was Montaigne's total commitment to himself: "'C'est une absolue perfection et comme divine, de savoir jouir loyalement de son être' ... Je me rappelle que je ne croyais pas à mes yeux" ("Mutant," 23). This is Montaigne's singular accomplishment and, for Sollers, his contribution of combining history and self-referentiality is more important than ever: "Pour les siècles des siècles. Ici même. Dans ce paysage du temps filtré. 'Savoir jouir.' Je vous laisse là" ("Mutant," 23).

Sollers's frequent defiance in maintaining controversial positions is significantly posited on his appropriation of Montaigne's thought and writing. Sollers was editor of (as well as a contributor to) the influential *Tel Quel* during the 1960s and 1970s, a journal that sought to question traditional norms and ideological assumptions about literature, reality and human identity in all of its psychological and linguistic precariousness. There are shared traits of Sollers's work and much of that published in *Tel Quel*— writing is no longer the recounting of some adventure or other, it *is* the adventure. Sollers thus welcomes the unsubmissive, ludic nature of the *Essais* as qualities to be affirmed rather than condemned since they help to free literature from mimetic constraints. Montaigne is thus surprisingly in the company of Sade, Mallarmé, Lautréamont, Artaud, and Bataille, the authors who surface repeatedly in the work of Sollers and many of the other contributors to *Tel Quel* by virtue of their radical interrogation of Western intellectual and aesthetic traditions. Sollers maintains that we can now begin to understand Montaigne's hidden radical potential from the vantage point of our much enhanced historical awareness and critical acumen. It is Montaigne's discursive experience (F. *expérience*, "experiment"), which challenges inherited modes of thinking by going to extreme efforts in attempting to understand the human condition, that makes him such an integral part of Sollers's writing project.

Montaigne plays an explicit role in the *Portrait du joueur* and is implied in other of Sollers's works that have been instrumental in shaping the landscape of recent French literary history. Sollers wrote "Montaigne, le mutant" as he was writing *Portrait* ("en marges" according to Sollers). It serves as a sort of manifesto for *Portrait,* a work not only copious in stylistic effects and philosophical perspectives of Montaigne's, but one that also makes explicit references to him, even quoting the *Essais* at various points in the narration. *Portrait,* polemical, charged with eroticism, engaging ambiguously contemporary events and personalities, rewrites the *Essais' jouissance* and propels them into the bestseller market in France. The narrator-protagonist, a writer and native of Bordeaux who resides in Paris, returns to visit the places that inform his childhood memories. Yet the cityscape has changed drastically: an enormous supermarket has replaced the homes and gardens of his former neighborhood. In reaction to the transformation, his "souvenirs brûlants d'autrefois" provoke him to lament the disparity between past and present and to examine the "drôlerie grinçante du temps" ("Preface" to *Portrait*).[24] The grandfather who dominates his most intense memories sounds like a distant spiritual heir of both Pierre and Michel Eyquem: "mobile et fantasque, escrimeur, amateur de chevaux et joueur de cartes" ("Preface," 7). Yet the Proustian attempt at recapturing time is thwarted and the narrator is propelled into the present and into a relationship with a Genevan doctor, Sophie, who writes him letters charged with a verbal eroticism in which love becomes a game, as do life and death.

The *joueur,* like Montaigne, plays with many levels of cultural reference and especially with the self-*portrait* (Montaigne's "je *peints* le passage"). There is of course a *jeu* played with the *je* in *Portrait* — a novel of essayistic memory as well as a metaphysical meditation on life, culture, and civilization that produces a "bon vivant" exuberance that Sollers takes from his own and from Montaigne's Gasconism:

> "Qu'est-ce que ça veut dire: *gascon*? Fanfaron, hâbleur, craqueur, vantard? Oui, mais aussi: plaisant, railleur, moqueur... . Le mot gascon par excellence? *Cadet.* Qui porte avec lui la bravoure, l'éclat, l'étourderie... . Synonyme de: gaillard, délibéré, hardi... . La marque la plus durable du gascon dans le français qui l'a recouvert? L'emploi transitif des verbes: *entrer, sortir, tomber, fixer...* . (*Portrait,* 275)

Bold, flamboyant, and dynamic, Montaigne's hardy, irregular Gasconism helps Sollers to formulate his own textual configurations of skepticist self-portraiture based on rupture, verbal crisis, and fluid narration. Multiple and dynamic, there is no total vision of the self or of the world. Montaigne's manner of expression, elliptical and anecdotal, is *jouissant,* the *res* spilling over the brim of the *verba.* He goes to extreme lengths to capture the essence of things, to produce a dynamic orality of textual vehemence that overwhelms almost any reader with its Longinian flashes of brilliance. Sollers quotes the following passage at length to support his own attempts at a similar manner of literary expression:

> "C'est aux paroles à servir et à suivre, et que le Gascon y arrive, si le Français n'y peut aller! Je veux que les choses surmontent et qu'elles remplissent l'imagination de celui qui écoute de façon qu'il n'ait aucune souvenance des mots. Le parler que j'aime, c'est un parler simple et naïf, tel sur le papier qu'à la bouche: un parler succulent et nerveux, court et serré, non tant délicat et peigné comme véhément et brusque ... déréglé, décousu, hardi ... ." (*Portrait,* 43)

Montaigne transgresses fixed discursive systems ("le Français") and puts to use a marginal discourse ("le Gascon" — metaphorically his own unprecedented style) in order to produce his work, which is so catalytic for Sollers's own aesthetics.

Following Montaigne, the narrator eventually makes an aesthetic plea for a more direct mode of writing that can better respond to his own problematic times:

> Il faut bien que la littérature avance. On branche directement sur la vie quotidienne. Un personnage réel peut être maintenant dix fois plus intéressant et subversif qu'un personnage de fiction. Le roman traîne en longueur à cause de la timidité des romanciers ... . Il faut qu'on voie tout ensemble, les contradictions les plus prononcées. La vie est impossible. L'impossible devient possible. (*Portrait,* 283)

The epicurean embrace of quotidian life, some instances of which scandalized many readers and caused outcries against Montaigne as an irreligious *libertin,* as well as his impulse to treat equally all subjects in their enhanced contradictoriness ("les contradictions les plus prononcées," an echo of Woolf's "our enthralling confusion, our hotch-potch of impulses"), is Sollers's version of the Montaignean *chasse de cognoissance.* Yet Sollers's development of a *jouissant* or *libertin* Montaigne has another problematic dimension, as can be seen in the former's mischievous narrative eroticism, attacked as misogynist and pornographic, especially in the case of the ever-controversial *Femmes,* a work that has scandalized his own times as Montaigne's did his by virtue of an explicit frankness in sexual matters, as seen in "Sur des vers de Virgile," which conflicted radically with the official codes of moral virtue established in the seventeenth century (Sollers claims that its importance is to have "ruiné le paysage de la vertu morale" — "Sollers"). The current feminist antipathy for Sollers (especially in the wake of *Femmes*) shows the flip side of Gournay's feminization of the *Essais* —Sollers own personal attitudes toward women are, like Montaigne's, ambivalent, ironic, and provoke strong reactions. The drama of his reception of the *Essais* in this controversial ideological field is still being played out in contemporary debates on sexual politics.

Sollers's position concerning the *Essais* thus goes against the trend of academic dogmatism that often surrounds its most cherished authors. For Sollers, Montaigne should not be categorized as a representative of "la libre pensée" or as a "Protestant masqué" in the manner of Gide ("Sollers"). Montaigne's modernity is not an evolutionary flourishing of the subject liberated from hegemonic constraints bringing us ever closer to refined self-understanding. Montaigne, on the contrary, fully embraces tradition, and especially Catholicism (formally asserting his faith by placing an *ex-voto* in Notre Dame de Lorette and by kissing Pope Gregory XIII's slipper) — outward signs of devotion, yes, but for Sollers a misunderstood point since what Montaigne is most afraid of, faced with Calvinist innovation, is that "Rome" will disappear — not the Holy Apostolic Church, but the whole of Graeco-Roman Christian civilization, and with it all of his cherished cultural past. This is one reason Montaigne submitted his work to the Church's censors: to ensure their place in the Vatican library, next to the manuscripts of Seneca, Plutarch, and Virgil, which he had the opportunity to peruse during his stay in Rome. This is the same pope who continued to hold elaborate celebrations commemorating the Saint Bartholomew's Day massacre years after the event; Montaigne was apparently undisturbed by this as he paid hommage to one of the most repressive authorities of his time.

Yet Montaigne's engagement of "coûtume" is impertinent in Sollers's eyes: it is a paradoxical response of total commitment that then left the essayist totally free for himself: "C'est un geste très étrange et singulier qui consiste à l'idée que d'abord il faut s'occuper du soi, conforté par une reprise de tout le passé qui risque de disparaître" ("Sollers"). This is Montaigne's crucial gesture for Sollers: the past is threatened with defiguration and total misinterpretation; he thus seizes history and attempts to save it by inscribing it in the *Essais*. Even with his modest intellectual and literary means, Montaigne believed that he is the only one capable of doing so — an audacious claim. After his demonstrations of total conservatism, he believed that his spiritual sovereignty was answered for and was thus mentally at ease. His preservation of the past thus allowed him the freedom to rely on himself as the measure of all things and to consequently affirm, in what Sollers considers to be Montaigne's quintessential undertaking, the quotidian aspects of his life: "Montaigne nous dit: 'il faut qu'on se branche sur la vie quotidienne'" ("Sollers"). Montaigne's act of retreat into the immediately tangible, safeguarded by his embrace of tradition through idiosyncratic quotation, is not a diminishing of the subject, nor a limitation of the quest for self-understanding, but rather an opening onto its infinitude. Montaigne is thenceforth able to develop whatever means he chooses to express his newly found freedom. This is for Sollers the *Montaignesque* element postmodernized: "... collage en collage, récupération en récupération, recyclage en recyclage, citation en citation" ("Sollers"). Montaigne's château tower, divided as it is into chapel, bedroom, and library, is the literal manifestation of his efforts to write the past within himself — the walls of his tower once covered with frescoes depicting literary and mythological events of antiquity, his shelves of books, the fifty-seven Greek and Latin inscriptions engraved on the library's ceiling beams (a literal correlation with the fifty-seven chapters of Book I), like his writing, are protective devices against the outside world. Yet this retreat is also an engagement, since he constructs literally and figuratively a sanctuary in which he can "promener son esprit" ("Sollers") and thereby come to a more authentic realization of what life should be. Montaigne's desire to make the necessary tributes to religion yet remain independent can be seen symbolically in the tower's air shaft, through which Montaigne could hear the daily chapel services without leaving the comfort of his bedroom.

Montaigne's paradoxical achievement is to completely appropriate the past by relying on "la grande batterie de la linguistique classique" ("Sollers") — which is however a "retour *innovateur*" ("Sollers") since it is a radical and complete appropriation. Montaigne becomes the past and the past becomes him; his gesture to write the past through himself in a private manner ("je ne m'y suis proposé aucune fin, que domestique et privée" — "Au Lecteur," 3) is like Proust's claim, as paraphrased by Sollers, "c'est moi Racine, Baudelaire, Madame de Sévigné," or Céline's "c'est moi Rabelais, c'est moi Villon" ("Sollers"). Montaigne's modernity for Sollers is that he totalized the objective world in a subjective mode of writing, thereby dissolving the distinctions between mind and body, body and soul, subjective and objective, innovation and tradition. Montaigne's uniqueness is this paradoxical recapturing of the past, yet for himself: "La modernité de Montaigne c'est ni la sensualité, ni la force de la métaphore, ni la reconstruction du passé permanente ... c'est le temps retrouvé" ("Sollers"). Montaigne's personalized enterprise is very much in line with Proust's arguments in *Contre Sainte-Beuve* that literature has no public destination — it is not a sociological phenomenon, but a private one. Montaigne's engaged commitment, but to himself, is the refusal of collective action that made him so unsuitable for the Jansenists; his individualism ran completely counter to the collective project of the adherents of Port-Royal: "reprocher à Montaigne son isolement, il n'a pas de projet collectif et c'est le projet de Port Royal, la petite communauté des justes" ("Sollers"). Montaigne's relativism and textual "fricassé" were much closer to the casuistry of the Holy Roman Church than to the more severely rigorous discourse of the Jansenists. Montaigne's privatism was equally threatening to the centralization process underway in France during the seventeenth century, which was eager to put an end to the last vestiges of the independent, mutinous nobility (as seen in the wars of *La Fronde,* whose last gasps took place in the provinces, particularly around Bordeaux).

Montaigne *libertin*? Yes, in so many eyes, but his *libertinage* is not a progressive liberation of libidinal textuality and political anarchy; in Sollers's reception, Montaigne's modernity is to be found in the constant unfolding of his paradoxical position between tradition and innovation. His acceptance of history ("tous les pesanteurs du passé," "Sollers") is done to preserve himself, to preserve the past in himself. He is not Rousseau, who wrote to revindicate or to justify himself, but has a much different project: "moi, Michel de Montaigne, je vais sauver le passé si j'existe" ("Sollers"), thus emulating Nietzsche's *überhistorische* gathering of the past into the present. Montaigne's work has none of the eternal melancholic neuroses of romanticism; he is rather *jouissant,* in Sollers' nuancing of the term: "l'écriture comme agitation, éveillée, vive, et gaie" ("Sollers"). Montaigne's agitated textuality, his ability "jouir de soi-même" ("Sollers") is not to produce his *être* in writing like Rousseau, but rather to depict its movement. In this, the romantic left misinterpreted Montaigne's "conservatism" since, in Sollers's eyes, the very attempt to retreat into language is in itself a revolutionary act. Montaigne's fragmentary, open form is the natural expression of his quest for absolute subjectivity — a mode of non-teleological expression that would conflict with the neoclassical doctrine of a common, purified administrative language (cultural, economic, and religious). Montaigne also shocked the romantics' sense of literary propriety by the "quotidienneté" of his writing — French literary history would have to await Sade and Baudelaire to see explicit physiological experiences presented in a literary text — an activity that has since flourished in the modernist and postmodernist obsession with the particularities of everyday life.

Barthes sees Sollers's principal challenge as a refusal to inherit the dominant philosophical and aesthetic models of the Western tradition.[25] Sollers's dismissal of preexisting modes of literary configuration (the tradition of the *lisible*), his radical *scriptibilité*, is what makes him in Barthes's eyes a crucial revolutionary writer, since he has produced, like Montaigne, the possibility that life and writing should not be separate, that the relationship between public action and self-commitment should not be analogous, but one and the same thing: "Un écrivain ne peut se définir que par son travail. Au regard de ce travail, la révolution est essentiellement une forme, celle de la dernière différence, *la différence qui ne ressemble pas.*"[26] Montaigne's act of discursive defiance has thus fully surfaced in the work of Sollers to clear a new ground from which to reformulate many of the fossilized, and ineffective, Western systems of thought and cultural practice.

The question of Montaigne's "revolutionary" writing project ("le geste de se réfugier dans le langage" — "Sollers") is central to understanding Sollers' reception as well as the landscape of French intellectual history of the last thirty years, in which the latter has played a key role. The notion that a revolution can take place within language and consequently catalyze a rebirth of the human subject in its political existence, that significant ideological gestures can occur in discursive acts, has colored much of the theoretical and creative work of the contemporary French intelligentsia. Kristeva's concept, as developed in *La Révolution du langage poétique* and elsewhere in her work, characterizes many of this generation's preoccupations and also resonates, in Sollers terms, with a certain "Montaignerie."[27] For Kristeva, the "language of the semiotic" is a pleasurable, creative excess of fluid textual plurality, opposed to the discovery of transcendental significations, which harasses the secure domain of language ("the symbolic"), thereby disrupting the hegemonic sign systems that enforce the fixed power systems of patriarchal civilization: God, father, state, property, law, etc. Decentering thus becomes an alternative to revolution by virtue of its slow dismantling of reified consciousness. Montaigne's conservative radicalism as envisioned by Sollers is an earlier manifestation of this very notion. Yet this raises the question of how a depoliticized intelligentsia can participate in political power. Alex Callinicos, in *Against Postmodernism*, concludes that it is the "disillusionment of the generation of 1968" and its failed attempts at cultural revolt that are the very beginnings of a "postmodern culture."[28] The hopes of a socialist revolution gone, the intellectual community of the left (Sollers, Kristeva, Derrida, Foucault, Lyotard, and Baudrillard among others) has retreated into a critique of logocentrism and historical teleology, seeking to aestheticize theory, criticism, and ethics, thereby articulating its political disillusionment in a postmodern rhetoric of ironic detachment in the belief that we live in a period of unreconciled realities that cannot be changed for the better. The struggle to resolve the contradictions of modernity while awaiting the realization of a social revolution is in a sense a refusal to understand or to transform existing social reality. These contradictions inherent in the postmodern experience still await resolution. Montaigne and the *Essais* are thus both a precursor and a catalyst, playing a significant role in these current, and to date unresolved problematics.

♦ ♦ ♦

Thus the *Essais*: marginal and useless or central and useful, how and to whom? Montaigne's reception by the postmoderns now makes the *Essais* more than ever a text with "mille visages," yet with one — a constant intertextual source whose historical journey has not diminished its capacity to renew again and again attempts to redevelop its continually pertinent discourse and refreshing perspectives. The destabilized realities of contemporary receptions (using Montaigne's work to produce innovative writing, conflating genres into essayistic textuality) are gestures that embrace his penchant toward fragmentation and relativistic skepticism. They maintain that the *Essais* cannot be understood from a totalizing viewpoint, but that they must be dispersed in order to reproduce Montaigne's strategy of assembling the fragments of antiquity through the synthesizing power of his self-portrait. Pater, Woolf, Chaillou, and Sollers use this strategy in works of essayistic fiction as they reformulate *morceaux choisis* of the *Essais* into narrative entities. They refuse to submit the *Essais* to a reductive interpretive scheme in their receptions, preferring to pursue the *Essais*' plurality, essay their multiplicity, and produce new writing through intertextual exfoliation. Their receptions are interrelated in the refusal of totalizing gestures (although they too inevitably produce their own more or less coherent approaches to Montaigne's writing) and establish several approaches to a problematic text, which have now become viable characterizations, in the wake of modernism, of the postmodern phenomenon: historical pastiche (Jameson), collage/montage (Derrida), end of meta-narrative (Foucault and Lyotard), process and participation (Hassan), and individual autonomy (Newman).[29] In receptions of Montaigne by Nietzsche, Pater, Woolf, Butor, and Chaillou these are several of the factors that have been produced from contact with the *Essais*. Receptions of Montaigne's writing thus continue to play an actively problematic role in the development of literary and intellectual history in the late twentieth century.

To ask whether the *Essais* are therefore modernist or postmodernist touches upon one of the most complex issues of recent literary and cultural history. It can perhaps be put forth that Montaigne is more postmodern than modern. One useful way to approach the questions of whether there is a current shifting in the structure of being and of what distinguishes modern from postmodern is to consider that most current characterizations of the techniques of postmodernism are very similar to that of modernism — they simply can no longer fill the ontological void. It is thus the epistemology that has changed: modernist convictions maintained that truth is elusive, yet through an aesthetics of expanded consciousness believed that some satisfying degree of reality could be attained. The postmodern impasse, on the contrary, is that truth is impossible to determine, leading the writer to either despair or playfulness: "If reality is no longer linked to logic or words, one might as well die — or dance."[30] And Montaigne, although an innovator, certainly did not believe in cultural progress or in a modernist nostalgia for truth. He had no sense of faith that he would ever achieve a total aesthetics of presence and could only celebrate its absence, claiming that his work would always need supplementing, another "allongeail" (III, 9,

963), by either himself or, after his death, by his *suffisants lecteurs.* The modernist epistemology is thus at odds with the postmodern attitude (Montaigne's?) that truth can never be attained and that self-exploration will only lead to a perpetual deferral of meaning in which the activity of juxtaposing various cultural codes (psychological, historical, philosophical, and literary) in a written text will go on indefinitely, demanding constant resituation of one's previous pronouncements.

If the concepts on non-linearity, instability, and fluctuation, so diffuse today in literary but also in scientific and social thinking, have any plausibility at all, then Chaillou, Sollers, and others, with Montaigne as one of their guides, have certainly developed these qualities in key places in their work. Montaigne's "parler succulent et nerveux ... non tant délicat et peigné comme véhément et brusque" perhaps permeates contemporary French writing more than we have previously considered. The opening passage of Sollers's novel *H* playfully underscores Montaigne's role in postmodern literature in France, in which the gestural rhythms of writing and non-linear movement across themes, allusions, and scenes from past and present explore the possibilities opened up by Montaigne's essaying four hundred years ago:

> qui dit salut la machine avec ses pattes rentrées son côté tortue cata socle ses touches figées accents toniques hors de strophe elle a rêvé cette nuit que je lançais la balle très haut et très loin elle ne s'arrête plus elle allume en passant les cerceaux disposés méridiens plus ronds quand elle les traverse et voilà la bombe qui retombe toute chaude enfumée grillée tiens *on est en pleine montagne.*[31]

Montaigne's presence in the contemporary period thus continues in many ways the modernist receptions of Nietzsche, Pater, and Woolf. Recent responses to Montaigne's work often valorize the modernity of the *Essais,* and what were once claimed as aberrations are now thought of as meritorious. The path leading to the new official status of Montaigne in France was prepared in many ways by non-French writers — hence the value of a comparative approach, which has helped to demarcate these cross-cultural interrelationships. The international impact of Montaigne is evident in his receptions in Germany, England, and the U.S., and in the fact some of his most prolific interpreters are not French: for instance, the American

Frame, German Friedrich, and Swiss Starobinski. The interest in paradoxical and problematic writing as worthy of serious consideration on its own terms is a critical attitude prepared by the writers most closely examined in this study. Many of the analytical models that have been developed by postmodern critics, especially in France, are in response to the radical nature of works such as Joyce's, Nietzsche's, Woolf's, and as is now more evident, Montaigne's. Their writing has necessitated new critical approaches in order to better understand these writers and their ability to be so bothersome that "any reader cannot but feel that the text constantly overreaches the landmarks established by the best critical constructions."[32] The ways in which Montaigne helped at least two major writers of the modernist period to develop their widely influential aesthetic notions is a key toward understanding how literary modernism continues to operate at the present time, as seen in the field of contemporary receptions of the *Essais*.

Critical studies of a comparative nature concerning Montaigne's work and its receptions should continue, as readers recognize the significant intertextual contacts between the *Essais* and other writers of the nineteenth and twentieth centuries. Further work could be carried out on many of the writers discussed in this study. Stefan Zweig's *Die Welt von Gestern*, Max Frisch's *Homo Faber*, Heinrich Mann's *Henri IV*, Proust's *A la Recherche du temps perdu*, and Michel Leiris' *L'Age d'homme*, (Sollers even considers Joyce's *Finnegans Wake* to be a very Montaignean text) have appropriated certain aspects of Montaigne's work and could thus be added to the list of works that have played a role in the continuing fortunes of the *Essais*. All of these authors' receptions of the *Essais* deserve further critical attention. For Montaigne's modernity is the very conflict of the new and the old; more than a monument of self-conscious recognition, more than an ahistorical exercise in self-referentiality, his achievement is to break down barriers in order make way for the possibility of a new relationship of the cultural codes tradition and innovation. Although he explicitly takes a conservative stand on culture and society, he implicitly problematizes the authority of officially acceptable discourse. This negative category of Montaigne's is at once an acceptance and a critique of the world as it is. Montaigne, like Galileo, plays it safe — conforming to ruling powers yet fully aware that his transgressive discourse will flourish at a later time: "Ma raison n'est pas duite à se courber et flechir, ce sont mes genoux" (III, viii, 935). Montaigne's modernity is to define himself in relation to the past in order to view himself as the result of a transition from old to new. His demand for authentic self-experience conflicted with his professional life: he rejected his family name, gave up his privileged professional career, and became a reluctant and aloof participant in political activities in order to pursue his writing project. His is a paradoxical revolt against the normalizing proscriptions of cultural tradition. His conservatism provides him an identity and an existential security in which he can pursue his imperfect, yet fulfilling humanism.

This study has thus attempted to prepare the ground for further inquiry into Montaigne's role in modernist and postmodernist thought and writing and has by no means exhausted its subject. It serves as a preparatory task for future work since its very subject is its downfall as well as its most valuable contribution. Each case-study as undertaken here perhaps needs its own book-length inquiry to more fully apprehend Montaigne's presence in the complete works of the writers considered. Pursuing Montaigne's concept of *des pertes triomphantes,* succeeding while failing, flirting with critical relativism, paradox, and hermeneutic uncertainty has produced nevertheless new perspectives on the *Essais* and their receptions. Yet after considering his interrelationships with Nietzsche, Woolf, and the contemporaries, even in the enhanced perspective that this activity provides, the *Essais* seem more difficult to read than ever. Inevitably one is the victim of one's "horizon-of-experience," and it is difficult to claim absolute validity for an assumed point of view that is not exempt from distorting the texts under consideration. Yet these shortcomings arise from the necessary activity of analyzing a grouping of issues in a new light. Attempts at critically evaluating Montaigne's writing and its receptions are thus essays in seeing the final results not so much of a "successful" interpretation of the *Essais,* but of the rearticulated positioning of critical concerns in various historical contexts. Decentered, yet stable, mobile, yet structured, receptive critical reception of the *Essais* succeeds neither through monumental, antiquarian, nor *kritische* engagement of the text, but through a combination of these strategies in a constantly open examination of issues in the belief that it is equally the quest as well as the destination that is the essence of the Montaignean challenge. This study has demonstrated, in any case, that Montaigne has played a significant intertextual role in several important writers and that the *Essais,* while a monumental text, will continue to produce problematic engagements of its *kritische* dimensions.

The *Essais* are certainly only one possible perspective from which to witness the development of several issues active in the notion of literary modernism and postmodernism as developed here. Current readers of Montaigne's work can consider his implicit innovatory moves, his explicit pronouncements of conformity, and modulate on the interactive movement between these phenomena as they continue the struggle to articulate such fruitful tensions toward self-understanding in what is more than ever a complex and paradoxical world. The virtue of considering Montaigne in modernist and postmodernist contexts is embodied in the various ways that the *Essais* have affected writers, how they continue to do so and, most significantly, how receptions of the *Essais* have modified the landscape of literary history. As with the many writers who feel that they own Montaigne and attempt to make him theirs, a conclusive grasp of the *Essais* is quite often elusive. No sooner does one understand some aspect of the *Essais* that this understanding begins to erode — Montaigne's "meaning" shifts and the critic inevitably arrives at another "new" formulation. Montaigne anticipated this problematic of meaning and understanding dissolving in attempts to dominate them in his realization that the multiplicity of the text ("l'infinité des figures et si menuës partitions" — III, xiii, 1067) defies its ultimate comprehension ("aucune certaine intelligence" — III, xiii, 1067): "Qui a veu des enfans essayans de renger à certain nombre une masse d'argent vif? Plus ils le pressent et petrissent et s'estudient à le contraindre à leur loy, plus ils irritent la liberté de ce genereux metal: il fuit à leur art et se va menuisant et esparpillant au delà de tout compte" (III, xiii, 1067). The encounter of this problematic (the refusal of absolute authority) necessitates *scriptible* reception which is invited by Montaigne and at the same time rejected in his desire to end the multiplicity of opinion: "Il falloit effacer la trace de cette diversité innumerable d'opinions, non poinct s'en parer et en entester la posterité" (III, xiii, 1067). The *Essais* will remain both complete and to be completed. Montaigne's use of the conditional tense maintains that we *should* cease to write about writing. Yet as he continued to comment on others' writings, so do others in the quest for particularized understandings of his.

At the present time, the dimensions of Montaigne's work are particularly relevant to current discussions of language and writing. In the current plethora of critical approaches, many writers today search for the order of the disorder and often discover the disorder of the order. The *Essais* teach that both sides of the equation are needed in order to maintain an attentive understanding of their uncanny qualities as its dimensions are reproduced through new "horizons-of-experience." The case of Montaigne among the moderns has demonstrated how the present need to write about the *Essais* is a perpetuation of the modernists' opening up of the text as well as a manifestation of our ongoing attempts to comprehend imperfectly the *Essais*' implications. Even as valuable lessons have been learned, new attempts will struggle, in Woolf's terms, to describe what it is that they see. In contemporary receptions of the *Essais*, Barthes's "texte idéal" appears to be a *modus operandi* for those who interact with Montaigne's writing "par plusieurs entrés dont aucune ne peut être à coup sûr déclarée principale." Each new reading of the *Essais* produces its own methods while dealing with them theoretically and especially *analytically* (Gk. *analuein*, "to break up, to dissolve"). In this sense the *Essais* are "ideal" since their textual dynamism and problematization of artistic writing are in many ways "absolument pluriel ... jamais clos," providing opportunities for new readings to examine the nature of the modernist and postmodernist experiences. The *Essais* will never let critics rest since, as Montaigne claims, glossing Cicero, all great works of art extend beyond themselves infinitely: "Toute art jette sa fin hors d'elle" (III, 6, 903) and defy the oblivion of time. This is another reason why Montaigne, knowing he would have no male heir, was so concerned to have the *Essais* accepted into the sanctuary of the Vatican library for posterity.

Officially consecrated studies on Montaigne are now often essays in the Montaignean sense; these new receptions of the *Essais* are often works of an innovative approach, attempting to face the challenge of Montaigne's discourse and, at the same time, continuing to regenerate the *Essais* "beyond their time and province" in newer and newer formulations, challenging readers to reread the *Essais* as well as to question their own responses while engaging them. At the same time, the new-historicist approach to the *Essais* (Desan's "contextualist"), while transcending a more vulgar historicism, is currently formulating the complex interrelations of Montaigne's life and work and the specific historical events and cultural practices of his time — a pursuit that enriches our particularized understanding of the *Essais* as well as of their author. The *Essais* thus concomitantly remain a fixed masterpiece in the Western literary canon as well as a disturbing, unresolvable text.

Receptions of Montaigne at the present time, in their claims and demonstrations of a polyvalent "modernist" Montaigne, revolve around the fairly stable set of issues operative in Baudier's prediction of the four-hundred year history of the *Essais'* receptions. Montaigne's "modernism" has been a recurring factor in the *Essais'* receptions from their beginning, to varying degrees, and in positive and negative lights. At present, its seems that in the widening scope of the *Essais'* presence in literary and intellectual history, their receptions have encompassed the modernizing aspects of the text more than ever before. Having expanded the lessons learned from Montaigne's receptions of the modernist period, the contemporary scene is witnessing readers discussing the *Essais* in more and more innovative and articulate ways. At the same time that this event could be conceived as a triumphant shift in the life of the *Essais,* it is also a repetition of concerns and continuity of issues. Attitudes have changed and refined methods of reading have helped to clarifiy a text that is now understood in greater detail. Yet one must still confront Baudier's pronouncement, Gournay's, Pascal's, Sainte-Beuve's, and Rousseau's predicaments, Gide's, Thibaudet's, Merleau-Ponty's identifications, and Emerson's, Nietzsche's, Pater's, Woolf's, Chaillou's and Sollers's experiments in the attempt to reproduce the *Essais* in the shadow of the problems that they have raised for their most committed readers. The *Essais* thus remain on a course of monumental constancy in progress. In the postmodern clash of historical continuities and contemporary innovations, the formulation of the *Essais'* relationship to past and present are more important than ever. Montaigne's modernity is a significant force in current intellectual history and literary production and, if the world is "une perpetuele vicissitude de formes" (III, vi, 908) and on a path of constant change, then critical engagement of the *Essais* helps to see how Montaigne speaks to the present moment and provides opportunities to participate with him by engaging the *Essais*, while moving toward an enhanced understanding of their importance to the modern age.

♦ ♦ ♦

Their "importance to the modern age?" For what relevance can the *Essais* have, belonging as they do, in many eyes, to "the compost-heap of cultural archaelogy."[33] On the contrary, Montaigne's general popularity appears to be very healthy at the present time. Witness the longevity of the *Bulletin de la Société des Amis de Montaigne*, the newly established *Montaigne Studies*, the constant proliferation of quality books on Montaigne, the many conferences commemorating special quadrennial dates: 1980, 1988, 1992, the popularity of the *Château de Montaigne* (10, 000 visitors a year), the *Bibliothèque de Bordeaux*'s enshrinement of the most prized editions of the *Essais* as well books from Montaigne's own library, sealed from public access in the *Coffre Montaigne*, and the *Archives Municipales de la Gironde*'s supervision of its priceless catalog of documents concerning Montaigne's life and times. In 1988 there were Montaigne conferences held in France, England, the U.S., and Greece; his reception in Italy, which is significant, has yet to be written. Outside of the West there have been six different translations of the *Essais* in Japan alone during the twentieth century, and there is most likely a wealth of material, as of yet untapped, on Montaigne's reception by writers of many other countries throughout the world. The *Essais* are being read by an ever widening audience: from the numerous scholarly works of the last twenty-five years, to the popular *La Fête de l'esprit* of Bellenger, *Montaigne: le mal à l'âme* of Leschemelle, and *Autour de Montaigne* of Stéphane, works written for more general readers, and finally to the bestseller *Portrait du joueur* of Sollers. His *Journal de voyage* is being read with renewed interest toward the understanding of Montaigne the person and of Europe's cultural landscape of the late sixteenth century — witness François Rigolot's new critical edition.[34] Almost any teacher in the humanities, whether "traditionalist" or "innovative," would want to make at least a nod toward Montaigne's problematic formulations of literary production and political engagement. Any study of French literary history must still accord at least a dozen or so of the *Essais* their central place. Among the general reading public, Montaigne is more than ever the embodiment of what is most lofty in French culture. At the same time he has been a model for many "anticlassical" writers of the last four hundred years. The *Essais* will most likely continue to flourish in the coming century. If one of the only hopes for world concord seems to rest in tolerance and compromise, then Montaigne (without overstating his importance as a thinker), can perhaps make a difference in pedagogical terms. Montaigne tells us himself that the *Essais* are not a work to be passively read, in the sense that they are a quantifiably consumable, but one to be interacted with as a springboard toward self-understanding and consequently perhaps toward a better regulation of daily affairs. We should thus read him as he did Tacitus: "Ce n'est pas un livre à lire, c'est *un livre à estudier et à apprendre*; il est si plain de sentences qu'il y en a à tort et à droict: c'est *une pepiniere de discours ethiques et politiques,* pour la provision et ornement de ceux qui tiennent rang au *maniement du monde*" (III, viii, 941 — emphasis added).

Perhaps the *Essais* need to be recast in more accessible formats and translated into many languages in order to perpetuate the proliferation of Montaigne's thought and thereby touch people from all walks of life in diverse cultures, and move them toward some *harmony of contradictions*: "Nostre vie est composée, comme l'harmonie du monde, de choses contraires … ." Yet in a world with more problems than answers, where Western technological consumerism has eroded literature's educational and social role, can reading any literary text make a difference? If Alvin Kernan's claim is true that "[t]elevision and other forms of electronic communication have increasingly replaced the printed book, especially in its idealized form, literature, as a more attractive and authoritative source of knowledge,"[35] then perhaps it is time for someone to make that film of Montaigne's life or to develop computer software with which readers can explore the *Essais* in their social and historical context. Montaigne's project is more than a literary experience; engaging the *Essais* in almost any format is a crucial awakening to intellectual growth. They perpetuate the consideration of the many aspects of any topic judiciously, and then the attempt to make as informed decisions as possible, which may not always be distinctly black and white, but often many shades of gray.

Montaigne has, in fact, even made recent appearances in the United States in popular contexts, outside of the academy where he is still a staple of scholarly inquiry as well as a fixture in many university world-literature curriculums. Monroe Spears, in the *Hudson Review* for instance, has recently claimed: "Reading Montaigne, then, can absolve us from some of our dreadful freedom and diminish the isolation, the weight of responsibility for defining and making ourselves … ."[36] Even more recently, Robert Fulghum in his bestseller, *Uh-Oh* reveals: "I'm still wrestling with dilemmas that are not easily resolved … . I am not finished with them. And may never be. This attitude is inspired by … Michel Eyquem de Montaigne."[37] These two writers have thus helped to propel Montaigne into the awareness of the American reading public at large. Yet the consideration of Montaigne's role in American intellectual life raises the question of the efficacy of the *Essais'* message in a mass-media society in which the study of moral philosophy has all but disappeared. Many graduates from American universities are technically sophisticated yet culturally illiterate and, more importantly, devoid of any authentic concern for ethical values, for individual and collective responsibility, for tolerance and mutual respect of difference, and for self-fulfillment within a framework of common values. Is Montaigne's message thus a dangerous one, preaching selfish egoism, hedonistic fulfillment, and withdrawal from social action, a poor example for the intellectual formation of a nation? Or is it a vital one toward the reformulation of a multicultural humanism in which we may better understand our limits as well as our potential and consequently be able to work toward a more moderate and rational basis for a shared sense of values, a will for ethical action, and a more tolerant mode of human communication and interaction?[38]

Thus, the *Essais* — irresponsible relativism or urgent realism? Whether aesthetic, political, or philosophical, Montaigne's lessons are for us perhaps not such bad ones to consider. For he can soothe *and* shock and propel us into a mode of presocratic dynamism that may be more than ever needed again, not to find the first principles of things, but to find some principles that work in the ever growing complexity of the world, and perplexity of the human experience.

Notes to Chapter 4

1. A particularly informative account of these events can be found in *Montaigne and his Age*, ed. Keith Cameron (Exeter: The University of Exeter Press, 1981).
2. Christopher Norris paraphrasing Jean Baudrillard in "Baudrillard and the Politics of Postmodernism," *What's Wrong with Postmodernism*, 168.
3. See *Humanism in Crisis: The Decline of the French Renaissance*, ed. Philippe Desan (Ann Arbor: The University of Michigan Press, 1991).
4. T.S. Eliot, *"The Waste Land" and Other Poems* (New York: Harcourt, Brace, & World, 1934), 46.
5. Erich Auerbach, "L'Humaine Condition," *Mimesis: The Representation of Reality in Western Literature* (Princeton: Princeton UP, 1946), 310.
6. See Georges Dupéyron, "Montaigne vu par un écrivain d'aujourd'hui: Michel Butor," *Bulletin de la société des amis de Montaigne* 3 (1965): 20-25: "Ainsi Montaigne collabore avec Michel Butor et *vice versa:* tous deux travaillent ensemble à organiser les *Essais*: l'intellectuel rejoint le sensible" (24).
7. Michel Butor, *Essais sur les "Essais"* (Paris: Editions Gallimard, 1968), 71. All further references appear in text.
8. Jean-Yves Pouilloux, *Lire les "Essais" de Montaigne* (Paris: F. Maspero, 1969), 36. All further references appear in text.
9. Two more recent works pursue the aesthetics of disorder by innovatively reformulating the *Essais*. Joseph-Guy Poletti, in *Montaigne à batons rompus: le désordre d'un texte* (Paris: Librairie Josi Corti, 1984), sees Montaigne's project as one that promotes the reader to create "une forme supplémentaire" (11) in his or her critical apprehension of the *Essais*. He thus pursues an aesthetics of dispersion in his critical supplementation of them. Roger Stéphane's *Autour de Montaigne* (Paris: Editions Stock, 1986) is a meditation on Montaigne's life and work in the spirit of self-contemplation in which Montaigne's and Stéphane's experiences converge in the latter's exploration, while copiously quoting the *Essais*, of the significance of Montaigne's work for his own life, and while maintaining that the *Essais* lend themselves with ease to such creative *re-essaying* of their contents.
10. Richard Regosin, "Recent Trends in Montaigne Scholarship: A Post-Structuralist Perspective," *Renaissance Quarterly* 37 (1984): 54.
11. See Philippe Desan, "Montaigne en lopins ou les *Essais* à pièces décousues" *Modern Philology* 88, 4 (1991): 278-291 for his delineation of the two dominant trends in contemporary Montaigne studies: the "poetic" approach that privileges the textual tensions and structural dynamism of Montaigne's paradoxes, and the "contextual" in which Montaigne's work is read in relation to the history of ideas, sixteenth-century social practices, and religious and political events of his time.
12. In *Les Métamorphoses de Montaigne* (Paris: Presses Universitaires de France, 1988), François Rigolot argues that the metamorphic poetics of the *Essais* functions as an act of resistance against the formulation of a completed discursive product. Gisèle Matthieu-Castellani, *Montaigne et l'écriture des "Essais"* (Paris:

Presses Universitaires de France, 1988), develops a phenomenological Montaigne whose achievement is to carry out "la première exploration psychosomatique de l'homme," (22) thus becoming "le premier philosophe existentialiste des temps modernes" (60).

13. Barthes, *S/Z,* 11-12.

14. Susan Sontag, "Introduction," *A Barthes Reader* (New York: Hill and Wang, 1982), xvii.

15. Roland Barthes, *Roland Barthes par Roland Barthes* (Paris: Editions du Seuil, 1975), 47.

16. Bensmaïa: "They preserve throughout the mark of their original fragmentation: an arrangement of heterogeneous elements, a mélange of discussion with oneself, of free conversation, of letter or address, and also of sententiae and maxims" (4).

17. Starobinski, *Montaigne en mouvement,* 9.

18. Michel Chaillou, *Domestique chez Montaigne* (Paris: Editions Gallimard, 1982). All references appear in text.

19. From a personal interview with Chaillou on 25 May 1992. All further references appear in text indicated by "Chaillou."

20. For an account of Sollers's current reputation, see Leslie Hill, "Philippe Sollers and *Tel Quel,*" *Beyond the Nouveau Roman,* ed. Michael Tilby (Oxford/Providence, RI: Berg Publishers, 1990), 100-120.

21. From a personal interview with Sollers on 22 May 1992. All further references appear in text indicated by "Sollers."

22. Philippe Sollers, "Montaigne, le mutant," *Théorie des Exceptions* (Paris: Editions Gallimard, 1986), 18-23. All further references appear in text.

23. I will begin with Barthes's notion of a "text of bliss" from *Le Plaisir du texte* (Paris: Editions du Seuil, 1973): "Texte de jouissance: celui qui met en état de perte, celui qui déconforte (peut-être jusqu'à un certain ennui), fait vaciller les assises historiques, culturelles, psychologiques, du lecteur, la consistance de ses goûts, de ses valeurs et de ses souvenirs, met en crise son rapport au langage" (25-6). It is one so close to what we have seen in the history of Montaigne's receptions as to be unavoidably quotable.

24. Philippe Sollers, *Portrait du joueur* (Paris: Editions Gallimard, 1984). All further references appear in text.

25. See Roland Barthes, *Sollers, écrivain* (Paris: Editions du Seuil, 1979).

26. "Le refus d'héritier," *Sollers, écrivain,* 53.

27. See Julia Kristeva, *Desire in Language: A Semiotic Approach to Literature and Art,* ed. Léon S. Roudiez (New York: Columbia UP, 1980).

28. Alex Callinicos, *Against Postmodernism: A Marxist Critique* (New York: St. Martin's Press, 1990), 166.

29. See David Harvey, "Postmodernism," *The Condition of Postmodernity* (Oxford: Basil Blackwell, 1989), 39-65 for a comprehensive evaluation of the most pervasive theories, theorists, and practitioners of postmodernism.

30. David Galef, "Shifts and Divides: The Modernist-Postmodernist Scale in Literature," *Studies in the Literary Imagination* XXV, 2 (1992): 83-93.
31. Philippe Sollers, *H* (Paris: Editions du Seuil, 1973), 9 — emphasis added.
32. Derek Attridge and Daniel Ferrer, "Introduction," *Poststructuralist Joyce*, eds. Derek Attridge and Daniel Ferrer (Cambridge: Cambridge UP, 1984), 10. The collected essays in this work demonstrate the French reception of Joyce as symptomatic of how the more problematic modernist authors have helped to generate poststructuralist theory and postmodernist practice in France.
33. Dusinberre, 2.
34. François Rigolot, *Journal de voyage de Michel de Montaigne* (Paris: Presses Universitaires de France, 1992). Rigolot has produced an exemplary edition that is indispensable for anyone interested in Montaigne and in the cultural consciousness of late sixteenth-century Europe.
35. Alvin Kernan, *The Death of Literature* (New Haven: Yale UP, 1990), 3.
36. Monroe K. Spears, "Montaigne Our Contemporary," *The Hudson Review* XLI, 2 (1988): 318.
37. Robert Fulghum, *Uh-Oh: Some Observations from Both Sides of the Refrigerator Door* (New York: Random House, 1991), 30.
38. This opposition is humorously set forth in a relatively obscure article by Theodore Spencer, "Montaigne in America," *The Atlantic Monthly* 177, 3 (1946): 91-97, in which Montaigne comes alive in a committee room of a prestigious American university as the topic for a session of the "University Committee on Humanism and Society." The evening's debate is on whether Montaigne is a worthy example for students' intellectual formation or whether his ideas are subversive. Whether or not Montaigne belongs on the university's list of selected books is passionately argued by all sides, with Montaigne defending himself. As the meeting adjourns, no consensus has been reached, and the issue is to be reconsidered the following week. More recently, Nannerl O. Keohane, in her inaugural address as President of Duke University, has encouraged students to read Montaigne, and more importantly, to cultivate a Montaignean mode of intellectual sovereignty in order "to embark on a lifelong odyssey in which you will keep learning, keep experimenting, remain mentally adventurous and continually update and redecorate the backroom of your mind." See Nannerl O. Keohane, "Exploring the Backroom of Your Mind," *Viewpoints* (27 August 1993): 7.

Bibliography

Adam, Antoine. *Histoire de la littérature française au XVIIe siècle*. Paris: Editions Mondiales, 1962.

Adams, Robert Martin. "What Was Modernism?" *The Hudson Review* 35 (1978): 97-118.

______, "Montaigne and the Ladies." *Hudson Review* 43, 2 (1990): 19-33.

Andler, Charles. *Nietzsche: Sa vie et sa pensée*. Paris: Nouvelle Revue Française, 1920.

Arac, Jonathan. "F.O. Matthiessen: Authorizing an American Renaissance." *The American Renaissance Reconsidered*. Eds. Walter Benn Michaels and Donald E. Pease. Baltimore: The Johns Hopkins UP, 1985, 90-112.

Ariosto, Ludovico. *Opere*. Ed. Cesare Segre. Rome: Arnoldo Mondadorie Editore, 1964.

Arnauld, Antoine and Lancelot, Claude. *Grammaire générale et raisonnée de Port Royal*. Paris: Chez Perlet, 1803.

Arnauld, Antoine and Nicole, Pierre. *La Logique ou l'art de penser*. Paris: Garnier Flammarion, 1970.

Arnold, Matthew. "On Translating Homer." *The Complete Prose Works of Matthew Arnold*. Ed. R.H. Super. Ann Arbor: University of Michigan Press, 1960.

Attridge, Derek and Ferrer, Daniel. eds. *Poststructuralist Joyce*. Cambridge: Cambridge UP, 1984.

Auerbach, Erich. *Mimesis: The Representation of Reality in Western Literature*. Princeton: Princeton UP, 1946.

Baillon, Emmanuelle. "Montaigne et Pascal: deux esprits si proches par les prémisses et si distant par les conclusions." *Montaigne et la révolution philosophique au XVIe siècle*. Brussels: Editions de l'Université de Bruxelles, 1992. 93-104

______, "The Gender of Genre." *Montaigne Studies* II, 1 (1990): 26-47.

Baraz, Michael. *L'être et la connaissance selon Montaigne*. Paris: Librairie Josi Corti, 1965.

Barolsky, Paul. "From Mannerism to Modernism." *University of Hartford Studies in Literature* 16 (1984): 47-57.

Barthes, Roland. *S/Z*. Paris: Editions du Seuil, 1970.

______, *Roland Barthes par Roland Barthes*. Paris: Editions du Seuil, 1975.

______, *Le Degré zéro de l'écriture*. Paris: Editions du Seuil, 1953.

______, *Le Plaisir du texte*. Paris: Editions du Seuil, 1973.

______, *Sollers, écrivain*. Paris: Editions du Seuil, 1979.

Bauschatz, Cathleen M. "'Leur plus universelle qualité, c'est la diversité': Women as Ideal Readers in Montaigne's *Essais*." *Journal of Medieval and Renaissance Studies* 19 (1989): 83-101.

Beaujour, Michel. *Miroirs d'encre: Rhétorique de l'auto-portrait*. Paris: Editions du Seuil, 1980.

Beckman, Diane. "The Wild Man: Images of Liminality. Prolegomena to a Study of *Gilgamesh* and Montaigne's 'Des cannibales.'" Ph. D. Dissertation. The University of North Carolina at Chapel Hill, 1993.

Bell, Quentin. *Virginia Woolf: A Biography*. New York: Harcourt, Brace, Jovanovich, 1972.

Belleli, Maria Luisa. *Modernità di Montaigne*. Rome: A.F. Formiggini, 1933.

Bellenger, Yvonne. *Montaigne: Une fête pour l'esprit*. Paris: Editions Balland, 1987.

Bensmaïa, Réda. *The Barthes Effect: The Essay as Reflective Text*. Minneapolis: The University of Minnesota Press, 1987.

Bergson, Henri. *Matière et mémoire: essai sur la relation du corps à l'esprit*. Paris: Presses Universitaires de France, 1982.

Bimbenet, Jean-Eugène. "Montaigne-Montesquieu." *Société d'agriculture, sciences, belles-lettres et arts d'Orléans* 54 (1882): 1-23.

Bloom, Harold, ed. "Introduction." *Selected Writings of Walter Pater*. New York: Columbia UP, 1974.

______, ed. *Modern Critical Views: Ralph Waldo Emerson*. New York: Chelsea House Publishers, 1985.

______, ed. *Modern Critical Views: Montaigne*. New York: Chelsea House, 1987.

Boase, Alan M. *The Fortunes of Montaigne: A History of the "Essais" in France: 1580-1669*. New York: Octagon Books, 1970.

Bomer, John M. *The Presence of Montaigne in the "Lettres Persanes."* Birmingham, AL: Summa Publications, Inc., 1988.

Bonnet, Pierre. "Montaigne et le maniérisme et le baroque." *Bulletin de la Société des Amis de Montaigne* 5 (1973): 45-58.

______, *Bibliographie méthodique et analytique des ouvrages et documents relatifs à Montaigne*. Geneva: Editions Slatkine, 1983.

Bossuet, Jacques-Bénigne. *Oeuvres Complètes*. Paris: J. A. Lebel, 1815.

Bouillier, Victor. *La Renommée de Montaigne en Allemagne*. Paris: Librairie Ancienne Edouard Champion, 1921.

Braak, Sybrandi. *André Gide et l'âme moderne*. Amsterdam: Firma A.H. Kruyt, 1923.

Bradbury, Malcolm and McFarlane, James, eds. *Modernism: 1890-1930*. Great Britain: Penguin Books, 1976.

Brake, Laurel and Small, Ian, eds. *Pater in the Nineties*. Greensboro, NC: ELT Press, 1991.

Brody, Jules. *Lectures de Montaigne*. Lexington, Kentucky: French Forum, 1982.

Brown, Frieda S. "Peace and Conflict: A New Look at Montaigne and Gide." *French Studies* 1 (1971): 1-7.

Browne, Sir Thomas. *Religio Medici. The Works of Sir Thomas Browne*. Chicago: The University of Chicago Press, 1964.

Brunetière, Ferdinand. *Essais sur la littérature contemporaine*. Paris: Calmann-Lévy, 1892.

Brunschvicg, Léon. *Pascal et Descartes: Lecteurs de Montaigne*. Neuchâtel: Baconnière, 1945.

______, "Introduction aux *Pensées* de Pascal." *Grands écrivains de la France*. Paris: Librairie de la Hachette, 1904.

Busson, Henri. *La Pensée religieuse française de Charron à Pascal*. Paris: Librairie Philosophique, 1933.

Butor, Michel. *Essais sur les "Essais."* Paris: Editions Gallimard, 1968.

Callinicos, Alex. *Against Postmodernism: A Marxist Critique*. New York: St. Martin's Press, 1990.

Cameron, Keith, ed. *Montaigne and His Age*. Exeter: The University of Exeter Press, 1981.

Camus, Jean-Pierre. *Diversitez*. Paris: Claude Chapellet, 1609.

Carlyle, Thomas. *Montaigne and Other Essays, Chiefly Biographical*. London: James Gowan, 1897.

Carpenter, Frederick Ives. *Emerson Handbook*. New York: Hendrick House, 1953.

Caughie, Pamela. *Virginia Woolf and Postmodernism: Literature in Quest and Question of Itself*. Chicago: University of Illinois Press, 1991.

Cave, Terence. *The Cornucopian Text*. Oxford: Oxford UP, 1979.

______, "Problems of Reading in the *Essais*." *Montaigne: Essays in Memory of Richard Sayce*. Eds. I.D. McFarlane and Ian Maclean. Oxford: Clarendon Press, 1982.

Chadbourne, Richard M. *Sainte-Beuve*. Boston: G.K. Hall & Co., 1977.

Chaillou, Michel. *Domestique chez Montaigne*. Paris: Editions Gallimard, 1982.

______, Personal interview with author. Paris: 25 May 1992.

Chambers, Frank M. "Pascal's Montaigne." *PMLA* 65 (1950): 790-804.

Charron, Pierre. *De la Sagesse*. Ed. Barbara de Negroni. Paris: Librairie Arthème Fayard, 1986.

Christodoulou, Kyriaki. "Pascal Critique de Montaigne." *Montaigne et les "Essais": 1580-1980*. Paris: Librairie Honoré Champion, 1983.

Clements, Robert J. *Comparative Literature as Academic Discipline*. New York: The Modern Language Association of America, 1978.

Clive, H. Peter. *Bibliographie annottée des ouvrages relatifs à Montaigne: 1976-1985*. Paris: Librairie Honoré Champion, 1986.

Colie, Rosalie. *Paradoxica Epidemica*. Princeton: Princeton UP, 1966.

Coleman, Dorothy Gabe. "Montaigne: The Living Text." *French Studies* 40, 4, (1986): 393-400.

Compagnon, Antoine. *Nous, Michel de Montaigne*. Paris: Editions du Seuil, 1980.

______, "A Long Short Story: Montaigne's Brevity." *Yale French Studies* 64 (1983): 24-50.

______, *La seconde main ou le travail de la citation*. Paris: Editions du Seuil, 1979.

Conlon, John J. *Walter Pater and the French Tradition*. East Brunswick, NJ: Associated University Presses, 1982.

Cottrell, Robert. "Gender Imprinting in Montaigne's *Essais*." *L'Esprit Créateur* XXX, 4 (1990): 85-95.

Couchman, Jane. "Twentieth-Century Responses to Montaigne." Ph. D. Dissertation. University of Toronto, 1971.

Courcelle, Pierre. *L'Entretien de Pascal et Sacy*. Paris: Librairie Philosophique J. Virin, 1960.

Croll, Morris. *"Attic" and Baroque Prose Style*. Princeton: Princeton UP, 1966.

Croquette, Bernard. *Pascal et Montaigne: Etude des réminiscences des "Essais" dans l'oeuvre de Pascal*. Genève: Librarie Droz, 1974.

Van Croumphout, Gustaaf. *Emerson's Modernity and the Example of Goethe*. Columbia: University of Missouri Press, 1990.

Curtius, E. R. *European Literature and the Latin Middle Ages*. Princeton: Princeton UP, 1973.

Cuvillier-Fleury, Alfred-Auguste. *Dernières études historiques et littéraires*. Paris: M. Lévy, 1859.

Dédéyan, Charles. *Montaigne chez ses amis Anglo-Saxons*. Paris: Editeurs Boivin, 1943.

Defaux, Gerard. "Readings of Montaigne." *Yale French Studies* 64 (1983): 73-92.

Deleuze, Gilles. *Nietzsche et la philosophie*. Paris: Presses Universitaires de France, 1962.

De Man, Paul. "Literary History and Literary Modernity." *Blindness and Insight*. Minneapolis: University of Minnesota Press, 1983. 142-65.

______, "Montaigne et la transcendence."*Critique* IX, 79 (1953): 1012-22.

______, "Pascal's Allegory of Persuasion." *Allegory and Representation: Selected Papers from the English Institute*. Ed. Stephen Greenblatt. Baltimore: The Johns Hopkins UP, 1981.

Derrida, Jacques. *Disseminations*. Chicago: The University of Chicago Press, 1981.

______, "Like the Sound of the Sea Deep Within a Shell: Paul de Man's War." *Responses*. Eds. Werner Hamacher, Neil Hertz, and Thomas Keenan. Lincoln: University of Nebraska Press, 1989. 127-64.

______, *Spurs: Nietzsche's Styles/Eperons: Les styles de Nietzsche*. Chicago: The University of Chicago Press, 1978.

Desan, Philippe. "Montaigne en lopins ou les *Essais* à pièces décousues." *Modern Philology* 88, 4 (1991): 278-91.

______, ed. *Humanism in Crisis: The Decline of the French Renaissance*. Ann Arbor: The University of Michigan Press, 1991.

Descombes, Vincent. *Le même et l'autre*. Paris: Les Editions de Minuit, 1979.

Dezon-Jones, Elyane. *Fragments d'un discours féminin*. Paris: Librairie Josi Corti, 1988.

DiBattista, Maria. *Virginia Woolf's Major Novels: The Fables of Anon*. New Haven: Yale UP, 1980.

Diderot, Denis. *Oeuvres Complètes*. Eds. J. Assézat and M. Tourneux. Nendeln, Liechtenstein: Kraus Reprint Ltd., 1966.

Dionne, James Robert. *Pascal et Nietzsche: Etude historique et comparée*. New York: Burt Franklin and Co., 1965.

Donaldson-Evans, Lance K. "Montaigne and Poetry." *Neophilologus* 58 (1974): 360-67.

Donellan, Brendan. "Nietzsche and Montaigne." *Colloquia Germanica* 19 (1986): 1-20.

Dowden, Edward. *Montaigne*. London: J. B. Lipincott, 1905.

Dréano, Mathurin. *La Renommée de Montaigne en France au XVIIIe Siècle: 1677-1802*. Angers: Editions de l'Ouest, 1952.

______, *La Religion de Montaigne*. Paris: A.-G. Nizet, 1969.

Du Bellay, Joachim. *La Deffence et illustration de la langue françoyse*. Ed. Henri Chamard. Paris: Classiques Larousse, 1966.

Dupéyron, Georges. "Montaigne vu par un écrivain d'aujourd'hui: Michel de Butor." *Bulletin de la Société des amis de Montaigne* 3 (1965): 20-25.

Dusaulx, J. *De mes rapports avec J. J. Rousseau*. Paris: Didot, 1978.

Dusinberre, Juliet. "Virginia Woolf and Montaigne." *Textual Practice* 5, 2 (1991): 219-41.

Duval, Edwin. "Rhetorical Composition and Open Form in Montaigne's Early Essays." *Bibliothèque d'Humanisme et Renaissance* 43 (1981): 269-87.

______, "Lessons of the New World: Design and Meaning in Montaigne's 'Des Cannibales' (I:31) and 'Des Coches' (III:6)." *Yale French Studies* 64 (1983): 95-122.

Eco, Umberto. *The Role of the Reader*. Bloomington: Indiana UP, 1979.

Eliot, T. S. *Selected Prose of T. S. Eliot*. Ed. Frank Kermode. New York: Harcourt, Brace, Jovanovich, 1975.

______, *"The Waste Land" and Other Poems*. New York: Harcourt, Brace & World, 1934.

Ellman, Richard and Feidelson, Charles, eds. *The Modern Tradition*. New York: Oxford UP, 1965.

Emerson, Ralph Waldo. *Complete Works*. 11 vols. Boston: Houghton Mifflin Company, 1903.

______, *Journals of Ralph Waldo Emerson*. 10 vols. Boston: Houghton Mifflin Company, 1911.

Faguet, Emile. *Rousseau penseur*. Paris: Boivin et Compagnie, 1910.

Fernandez-Morera, D. "The Term 'Modernism' in Literary History." *Actes du Dixième Congrès de l'Association Internationale de Littérature Comparée*. New York: Garland Publishing, 1985.

Fleury, Colette. *Rousseau et Montaigne*. Paris: A.-G. Nizet, 1980.

Fokkema, D. W. "The Code of Modernism." *Actes du Huitième Congrès de l'Association Internationale de Littérature Comparée*. Stuttgart: E. Bieber, 1980.

Foster, John Burt. *Heirs to Dionysus: A Nietzschean Current in Literary Modernism*. Princeton: Princeton UP, 1981.

Foucault, Michel. *Les Mots et les choses*. Paris: Gallimard, 1966.

Frame, Donald. *Montaigne in France: 1812-1852*. New York: Columbia University Press, 1940.

______, *Montaigne: A Biography*. New York: Harcourt, Brace & World, 1965.

Fraser, Theodore P. *The French Essay*. Boston: Twayne Publishers, 1986.

Freedman, Ralph, ed. *Virginia Woolf: Revaluation and Continuity*. Berkeley: University of California Press, 1980.

Friedrich, Hugo. *Montaigne*. Paris: Editions Gallimard, 1968.

Fromillage, R. *La Vie de Malherbe*. Paris: Armand Colin, 1954.

Fulghum, Robert. *Uh-Oh: Some Observations from Both Sides of the Refrigerator Door*. New York: Random House, 1991.

Galef, David. "Shifts and Divides: The Modernist-Postmodernist Scale in Literature." *Studies in the Literary Imagination* XXV, 2 (1992): 83-93.

Gaufreteau, Jean de. *Chronique Bordelaise: 1240-1636* (Bordeaux: Archives municipales de la Gironde, 1878).

Genette, Gérard. *Figures of Literary Discourse*. New York: Columbia UP, 1982.

Gide, André. "Essai sur Montaigne." *Oeuvres Complètes.* Vol. 15. Paris: Nouvelle Revue Française, 1939. 3-31.

______, *Les pages immortelles de Montaigne choisies et expliqués par André Gide.* Paris: Editions Gallimard, 1948.

______, "Suivant Montaigne." *Oeuvres Complètes.* Vol. 15. Paris: Nouvelle Revue Française, 1939. 35-63.

______, *Les Journaux d'André Gide.* Paris: Editions Gallimard, 1948.

Gilbert Sandra M. and Gubar, Susan, eds. *No Man's Land: The Place of the Woman Writer in the Twentieth Century.* New Haven: Yale UP, 1989.

Glidden, Hope. "The Theory and Practice of Reading." *L'Esprit Créateur* 21 (1981): 25-36.

Good, Graham. *The Observing Self: Rediscovering the Essay.* New York: Routledge, 1988.

Gougenheim, Georges. *Grammaire de la langue française du seizième siècle.* Paris: A. & J. Picard, 1973.

Gournay, Marie de. "Préfaces sur les *Essais* de Michel, Seigneur de Montaigne." *"Essais" de Michel de Montaigne.* Paris: A l'Angelier, 1595.

—. "Préfaces sur les *Essais* de Michel, Seigneur de Montaigne." *Montaigne Studies* II, 2 (1990): 68-98.

______, *Le Proumenoir de Monsieur de Montaigne.* Paris: Librairie de la Hachette, 1906.

______, *Les Advis ou les presens de la Demoiselle de Gournay.* Paris: Toussainct Du-Bray, 1624.

Grace, Ruth. "Montaigne's Twentieth-Century Critics." Ph. D. Dissertation. University of Michigan, 1964.

Gracey, Phyllis. *Montaigne et la poésie.* Paris: Presses Universitaires de France, 1935.

Gray, Floyd. *Le Style de Montaigne.* Paris: Librairie Nizet, 1958.

Guggenheim, Michel. "Gide and Montaigne." *Yale French Studies* 7 (1951): 107-14.

Harvey, David. *The Condition of Postmodernity.* Oxford: Basil Blackwell, 1989.

Hayden, Hiram. *The Counter-Renaissance.* New York: Scribner, 1950.

Hayman, David. *Mallarmé et Joyce.* Paris: Librairie de la Hachette, 1947.

______, *Nietzsche: A Critical Life.* New York: Oxford UP, 1980.

Hazlitt, William. "Lecture on the English Comic Writers." *The Complete Works of William Hazlitt.* Ed. P. Howe. London and Toronto: Dent Publishers, 1931.

Heller, Erich. *The Importance of Nietzsche.* Chicago: The University of Chicago Press, 1988.

Heraclitus. *The Art and Thought of Heraclitus.* Ed. and Trans. Charles H. Kahn. Cambridge: Cambridge UP, 1979.

Howe, Irving. *The American Newness: Culture and Politics in the Age of Emerson.* Cambridge: Harvard UP, 1986.

Hummel, Hermann. "Emerson and Nietzsche." *New England Quarterly* XIX, 84 (1946): 60-82.

Huysmans, Joris-Karl. *A Rebours.* Paris: Union Générale D'Editions, 1975.

Inman, Billie Andrew. *Walter Pater's Reading: A Bibliography of His Library Borrowings and Literary References.* New York: Garland Publishing, 1981.

Insdorf, Cecile. *Montaigne and Feminism.* Chapel Hill: North Carolina Studies in the Romance Languages and Literatures, 1977.

Iser, Wolfgang. *The Act of Reading.* Baltimore: The Johns Hopkins UP, 1978.

______, *Walter Pater: The Aesthetic Moment.* Cambridge: Cambridge University Press, 1987.

Isley, Marjorie. *A Daughter of the Renaissance: Marie le Jars de Gournay.* La Haye: Mouton, 1963.

Jauss, Hans Robert. *Toward an Aesthetic of Reception.* Minneapolis: University of Minnesota Press, 1982.

Jonson, Ben. *Discourses.* Edinburgh: Edinburgh UP, 1966.

Keohane, Nannerl O. "The Backroom of Your Mind." *Viewpoints* (27 August 1993): 7.

Kernan, Alvin. *The Death of Literature.* New Haven: Yale UP, 1990.

Koelb, Clayton, ed. *Nietzsche as Postmodernist: Essays Pro and Contra.* Albany: State University Press of New York, 1990.

Kristeva, Julia. *La révolution du langage poétique.* Paris: Editions du Seuil, 1974.

______, *Desire in Language: A Semiotic Approach to Literature and Art.* Ed. Léon S. Roudiez. New York: Columbia UP, 1980.

______, *Semiotikè: Recherches pour une sémanalyse.* Paris: Editions du Seuil, 1969.

Kritzman, Lawrence D. *Déstruction/Découverte: Le fonctionnement de la rhétorique dans les "Essais" de Montaigne.* Lexington, Kentucky: French Forum, 1980.

Kwant, Rémy C. *The Phenomenological Philosophy of Maurice Merleau-Ponty.* Pittsburgh: Duquesne UP, 1963.

Kyriaki, Christodolou. "Pascal critique de Montaigne." *Montaigne et les "Essais": 1580-1980.* Paris: Champion, 1983.

Landor, Walter. *Imaginary Conversations.* Ed. T. Earle Welby. London: Chapman and Hall, 1928.

Lanson, Gustave. *Les "Essais" de Michel de Montaigne.* Paris: Mélotté Editeur, 1930.

Leschemelle, Pierre. "Montaigne et les femmes." *Montaigne et la révolution philosophique du XVIe siècle.* Ed. Jacques Lemaire. Brussels: Editions de l'Université de Bruxelles, 1992. 75-92.

______, "La Passion des femmes." *Montaigne, ou le mal à l'âme.* Paris: Editions d'Images, 1991. 83-134.

L'Homme, Charles Edmund. "The Influence of Walter Pater: A Study in the Making of a Modern Literary Mind." Ph. D. Dissertation. Columbia University, 1965.

London, Bette. "Guerilla in Petticoats or Sans-Culotte? Virginia Woolf and the Future of Feminist Criticism." *Diacritics* 2,3 (1991): 11-42.

Luthy, Hubert. "Montaigne on the Art of Being Truthful." *Encounter* 1, 2 (1953): 11-28.

MacLean, Ian. *The Renaissance Notion of Women*. Cambridge: Cambridge UP, 1980.

Maine, La Croix du. *Bibliothèque française*. Paris: Rigolet de Juvigny, 1772.

Malebranche, Nicolas. *La Recherche de la vérité*. Paris: Boivin et Compagnie Editeurs, 1938.

Mallarmé, Stéphane. *Oeuvres Complètes*. Paris: Editions Gallimard, 1945.

Malraux, André. "The Cultural Heritage." *Yale French Studies* 18 (1957): 31-38.

Malzevin, Théophile de. *Michel de Montaigne: son origine, sa famille*. Bordeaux: G. Counouilhon, 1874.

Marcu, Eva. *Repertoire des idées de Montaigne*. Genève: Librairie Droz, 1965.

Marcus, Jane, ed. *New Feminist Essays on Virginia Woolf*. Lincoln: University of Nebraska Press, 1981.

Marcuse, Herbert. *Negations: Essays in Critical Theory*. Boston: Beacon Press, 1968.

______, *Virginia Woolf and the Language of Patriarchy*. Bloomington: Indiana UP, 1987.

Marr, David. *American Worlds Since Emerson*. Amherst: The University of Massachusetts Press, 1988.

Martin, Daniel. *Architecture des "Essais" de Montaigne*. Paris: Librairie: A.-G. Nizet, 1992.

______, *Essais: Réproduction photographique de l'édition originale de 1580 avec une introduction et des notes sur les modifications apportées ultérieurement au texte en 1582, 1587, 1588 et sur l'exemplaire de Bordeaux*. Paris: Librairie Honoré Champion, 1976.

Matthiessen, F.O. *American Renaissance*. New York: Oxford UP, 1941.

Matthieu-Castellani, Gisèle. *Montaigne et l'écriture des "Essais."* Paris: Presses Universitaires de France, 1988.

McGrath, F.C. *The Sensible Spirit: Walter Pater and the Modernist Paradigm*. Tampa: University of South Florida Press, 1986.

McKinley, Mary. *Words in a Corner*. Lexington, Kentucky: French Forum, 1981.

Meisel, Perry. *The Absent Father: Virginia Woolf and Walter Pater*. New Haven: Yale UP, 1980.

Melchiori, Giorgio. *The Tightrope Walkers: Mannerism in Modern English Literature*. London: Routledge and Kegan Paul, 1956.

Ménager, Daniel. "Jugements sur Montaigne et sur les *Essais*." *Montaigne: "Essais."* Paris: Librairie Larousse, 1973.

Merleau-Ponty, Maurice. "Lecture de Montaigne." *Les Temps Modernes* 3 (1947): 1044-60.

Mermier, Guy. "Inconstance et relativité pièces maîtresses de la modernité de Montaigne." *Bulletin de la Société des Amis de Montaigne* 25 (1978): 51-56.

Michel, Pierre. *Montaigne.* Bordeaux: Ducros, 1969.

Miller, C. Ruth. *Virginia Woolf: The Frames of Art and Life.* New York: St. Martin's Press, 1989.

Miller, Perry. "Emersonian Genius and American Democracy." *The New England Quarterly* XXVI, 1 (1953): 27-44.

Monsmon, Gerald. "Pater and His Younger Comtemporaries." *Victorian Newsletter* 48 (1975): 1-12.

Montaigne, Michel de. *Essais.* Eds. V. L. Saulnier and P. Villey. Paris: Presses Universitaires de France, 1978.

Montesquieu, Charles de Secondat. *Oeuvres Complètes.* Ed. André Masson. Paris: Les Editions Nagel, 1950.

Mowitt, John William. "From Montaigne to Nietszche: Towards a Theory of the Essay." Ph.D. Dissertation. University of Wisconsin, 1982.

Nakam, Géralde. *Montaigne et son temps: les événements et les "Essais."* Paris: Librairie A.-G. Nizet, 1982.

Nicolaï, Alexandre. *Les Belles amies de Montaigne.* Paris: Editions Dumas, 1950.

Nicolas, Marius Paul. *From Nietzsche Down to Hitler.* New York: Kennikat Press, 1938.

Nietzsche, Friedrich. *Werke in drei Bänden.* Ed. Karl Schlechta. Munich: Carl Hanser, 1956.

Noguères, Henri. *La Saint Barthélemy.* Paris: Editions Robert Laffont, 1959.

Norris, Christopher. *What's Wrong with Postmodernism: Critical Theory and the Ends of Philosophy.* Baltimore: The Johns Hopkins UP, 1990.

Norris, Margot. *The Decentered Universe of "Finnegans Wake."* Baltimore: The Johns Hopkins UP, 1976.

Pascal, Blaise. *Oeuvres Complètes.* Eds. Léon Brunschvicg and Pierre Boutroux. Paris: Librairie de la Hachette, 1904.

Pasquier, Etienne. *Oeuvres choisies.* Ed. Léon Feugère. Geneva: Slatkine Reprints, 1968.

Pater, Walter. *Complete Works.* 10 vols. London: MacMillan and Company, 1910-12.

Patrides, C. A., ed. *Approaches to Sir Thomas Browne.* Columbia: University of Missouri Press, 1982.

Payen, Jean-François. *Recherches et documents inédits ou peu connus sur Montaigne.* Genève: Slatkine Reprints, 1970.

Pierrot, Jean. *The Decadent Imagination: 1880-1900.* Chicago: The University of Chicago Press, 1981.

Plato. *The Collected Dialogues of Plato*. Eds. E. Hamilton and E. Cairns. Princeton: Princeton UP, 1961.

Poletti, Joseph-Guy. *Montaigne à batons rompus: le désordre d'un texte*. Paris: Librairie Josi Corti, 1984.

Porteau, Paul. *Montaigne et la vie pédagogique de son temps*. Paris: Librairie Droz, 1935.

Porter, Laurence. "Literary Structure: The Concept of Decadence." *The Centennial Review* 2 (1978): 189-200.

Post, Jonathan F. S. *Sir Thomas Browne*. Boston: G. K. Hall & Company, 1987.

Potter, Sally. *Orlando*. Great Britain: Adventure Pictures, 1992.

Pouilloux, Jean-Yves. *Lire les "Essais" de Montaigne*. Paris: F. Maspero, 1969.

Rabelais, François. *Pages choisies*. Eds. Chappon et Pons. Paris: Classiques Larousse, 1955.

Regosin, Richard L. "Recent Trends in Montaigne Scholarship: A Post-Structuralist Perspective." *Renaissance Quarterly* 37 (1984): 34-54.

______, "Conceptions of the Text and the Generation(s) of Meaning: Montaigne's *Essais* and the Place(s) of the Reader." *Journal of Medieval and Renaissance Studies* 15 (1985): 101-14.

Rigolot, François. *Les Métamorphoses de Montaigne*. Paris: Presses Universitaires de France, 1988.

______, *Journal de voyage de Michel de Montaigne*. Paris: Presses Universitaires de France, 1992.

Robertson, John M. *Shakespeare and Montaigne*. London: The University Press, 1891.

Rousseau, Jean-Jacques. *Oeuvres Complètes*. Eds. B. Gagnebin and M. Raymond. Paris: Editions Gallimard, 1959-1969.

Rousset, Jean. *La littérature de l'âge baroque en France*. Paris: Josi Corti, 1953.

Sainte-Beuve, Charles Augustin. *Nouveaux Lundis*. Paris: M. Lévy, 1883.

______, *Port Royal*. Ed. Maxime Leroy. Paris: Librairie Gallimard, 1952.

Sayce, Richard. *The Essays of Montaigne: A Critical Exploration*. London: Weidenfeld and Nicholson, 1972.

Schacht, Richard. "Nietzsche's Coming of Age." *The German Book Review*. Munich: Goethe Institute, 1991. 45-46.

Schaefer, David. *The Political Philosophy of Montaigne*. Ithaca: Cornell University Press, 1990.

______, "Montaigne and Leo Strauss." *Montaigne Studies* II, 2 (1990): 34-57.

Schiffman, Zachary. "Montaigne and the Rise of Skepticism in Early Modern Europe: A Reappraisal." *Journal of the History of Ideas* 3 (1984): 499-516.

Schlack, Beverly Ann. *Continuing Presences: Virginia Woolf's Use of Literary Allusion*. University Park: The Pennsylvania State UP, 1979.

Schwartz, Jerome. *Diderot and Montaigne: The Shaping of Diderot's Humanism.* Genève: Librairie Droz, 1966.

Sciacca, Michele Federico. "Montaigne e i libertini come antecedente dell'ertismo moderno." *Libro de homenaje à Luis Alberto Sanchez en los ãnos de su docencia universitaria.* Lima: Univ. Mayor Nacional de San Marcos, 1967. 223-233.

Silber, Ellen. "Rousseau and Montaigne: The Evolution of a Literary Relationship." Ph. D. Dissertation. Columbia University, 1968.

Smith, Malcolm. *Montaigne and Religious Freedom: The Dawn of Pluralism.* Geneva: Librairie Droz, 1991.

Sollers, Philippe. *Portrait du joueur.* Paris: Editions Gallimard, 1984.

———, *Théorie des exceptions.* Paris: Editions Gallimard, 1986.

———, *H.* Paris: Editions du Seuil, 1973.

———, Personal interview with author. Paris, France, 22 May 1992.

Sontag, Susan, ed. "Introduction." *A Barthes Reader.* New York: Hill and Wang, 1982.

Sorel, Albert. *Montesquieu.* Paris: Hachette et Compagnie, 1887.

Spears, Monroe K. "Montaigne Our Contemporary." *The Hudson Review* XLI, 2 (1988): 301-318.

Spencer, Theodore. "Montaigne in America." *The Atlantic Monthly* 177, 3 (1946): 91-97.

Starobinski, Jean. *Montaigne en mouvement.* Paris: Editions Gallimard, 1982.

Stéphane, Roger. *Autour de Montaigne.* Paris: Editions Stock, 1986.

Stephen, Sir Leslie. "Art and Morality." *Cornhill* 32 (1875): 91-101.

Stern, J.P. "Introduction." *Friedrich Nietzsche, Untimely Meditations.* Trans. R.J. Hollingdale. Cambridge: Cambridge UP, 1983.

Strowski, Fortunat. *Montaigne: sa vie publique et privée.* Paris: Editions de la Nouvelle Revue Critique, 1938.

———, *Montaigne.* Paris: Librairie Honoré Champion, 1906.

———, ed. *Les Grands philosophes: Montaigne.* Paris: Librairie Honoré Champion, 1906.

Suleiman, Susan R. and Crosman, Inge, eds. *The Reader in the Text.* Princeton: Princeton UP, 1980.

Tetel, Marcel. *Montaigne: Updated Edition.* Boston: Twayne Publishers, 1990.

Thibaudet, Albert. *Montaigne.* Paris: Editions Gallimard, 1963.

———, *Physiologie de la critique.* Paris: Editions de la Nouvelle Revue Critique, 1930.

Thomas, Jean. *L'Humanisme de Diderot.* Paris: Société d'Edition "Les Belles Lettres," 1938.

Tilby, Michael, ed. *Beyond the Nouveau Roman.* Oxford/Providence, RI: Berg Publishers, 1990.

Tilley, Arthur. "Montaigne's Interpreters." *Studies in the French Renaissance.* New York: Barnes and Noble, 1968. 259-93.

Tocqueville, Alexis de. *Democracy in America.* 2 vols. Ed. Phillips Bradley. New York: Alfred A. Knopf, 1985.

Tompkins, Jane P, ed. *Reader-Response Criticism.* Baltimore: The Johns Hopkins UP, 1980.

Tournon, André. *La glose et l'essai.* Lyon: Presses Universitaires de Lyon, 1983.

______, "Montaigne et 'l'alleure poétique.'" *Bibliothèque d'Humanisme et Renaissance* 33 (1971): 155-62.

Guy Turbet-Delof, ed. *Entre Montaigne et Montesquieu: les écrivains bordelais et la vie intellectuelle au XVIIe siècle.* Bordeaux: L'Imprimerie Biscaye, 1985.

Ulstick, W. L. "Emerson's Debt to Montaigne." *Washington University Studies* 9 (1922): 245-62.

Villey, Pierre. *L'Influence de Montaigne sur les ideés pédagogiques de Locke et de Rousseau.* Paris: Librairie de la Hachette, 1911.

______, *Montaigne devant la postérité.* Paris: Boivin Editeurs, 1935.

______, "La place de Montaigne dans le mouvement philosophique." *Revue Philosophique* (1926): 338-59.

______, *Les Sources et l'Evolution des "Essais" de Montaigne.* Paris: Librarie de la Hachette, 1933.

Voizard, Eugène. *Etude sur la langue de Montaigne.* Geneva: Slatkine Reprints, 1969.

Voltaire, François-Marie Arouet. *Oeuvres Complètes.* Paris: Chez Lefèvre, 1834.

Weinraub, Ruth. "Structural Techniques in *A Rebours.*" *The French Review* 49 (1974): 222-33.

Weisstein, Ulrich. *Comparative Literature and Literary Theory.* Bloomington: Indiana UP, 1968.

White, Hayden. *Metahistory: The Historical Imagination in Nineteenth-Century Europe.* Baltimore: The Johns Hopkins UP, 1973.

Whitman, Walt. *Leaves of Grass.* Eds. Harold W. Blodgett and Sculley Bradley. New York: New York University Press, 1965.

Williams, Carolyn. *Transfigured World: Walter Pater's Aesthetic Historicism.* Cornell: Ithaca UP, 1989.

Williams, W. D. *Nietzsche and the French: A Study of the Influence of Nietzsche's French Reading on His Thought and Writing.* Oxford: Basil Blackwell and Mott Limited, 1952.

Wilson, Robert. *Orlando.* L'Odéon-Théâtre de l'Europe, 1993.

Woolf, Virginia. *Collected Essays.* London: Hogarth Press, 1960.

______, *The Common Reader.* New York: Harcourt, Brace, Jovanovich, 1925.

______, *The Common Reader,* Second Series. London: The Hogarth Press, 1932.

———, *The Diary of Virginia Woolf.* Ed. Anne Olivier Bell. New York: Harcourt, Brace, Jovanovich, 1980.

———, *Orlando.* New York: Harcourt, Brace, Jovanovich, 1929.

———, *A Room of One's Own.* New York: Harcourt, Brace, & World, 1929.

Wright, Thomas. *The Life of Walter Pater.* New York: Haskell House, 1907.

Young, Charles Lowell. *Emerson's Montaigne.* New York: The MacMillan Company, 1941.

Zenn, Fritz, "Remodeling Homer." *Light Rays: James Joyce and Modernism.* Ed. Heyward Ehrlich. New York: New Horizon Press, 1984, 70-92.

Index

Addison, Joseph, 258–259
Amyot, Jacques, 170
Andler, Charles, 126
Androgyny: and textuality, 235–37
Ariosto, Ludovico, *Orlando Furioso*, 234: and androgyny, 235–36
Arnauld, Antoine, 45–47, 202
Arnold, Matthew, 188, 194
Auerbach, Erich, 280

Barthes, Roland, 233: and *jouissance*, 319n.23; and modernism, 12; *Roland Barthes par Roland Barthes*, 291–92; and *scriptible*, 102n.133; and Sollers, 302; and "texte idéal," 291, 313
Bauschatz, Cathleen, 27
Baudier, Dominique, 20–21, 24, 272, 287
Beaujour, Michel, 289
Bellenger, Yvonne, 315
Bensmaïa, Réda, 291–92, 319n.16
Bergerac, Cyrano de, 40
Bergson, Henri, 80
Bibliothèque Nationale, 76
Bloom, Harold, 274n.24
Boétie, Etienne de la, 70, 248: as centerpiece, 247; *Discours de la servitude volontaire*, 170, 285
Bonaparte, Napoléon, 70
Bonnefon, Paul, 76
Bossuet, Jacques-Bénigne, 47, 202
Bouillier, Victor, 132
Brach, Pierre de, 30
Browne, Sir Thomas, 197, 221, 232–33, 255: *The Garden of Cyrus*, 217; as heir to Montaigne, 216–17; influence on Pater and Woolf, 216–21; and "*Montaignesque* element," 218; *Religio Medici*, 217; and skepticism, 217; and style, 219
Brunetière, Ferdinand, 78
Bruno, Giordano, 195, 215
Butor, Michel, 10, 281: *Essais sur les "Essais,"* purpose of, 282–83; reception of Montaigne, 281–87; theory of *Essais*, 283

Callinicos, Alex: and post-modern condition, 307

Camus, Jean-Pierre, *Diversitez,* 38
Carlyle, Thomas, 188, 193, 219
Cave, Terence, 6, 115–16, 196, 228, 274n.16, 289
Chaillou, Michel, 281: *Domestique chez Montaigne*, 293–98; and "*Montaignesque* element," 296; reception of *Essais,* 293–98
Charron, Pierre, *De la Sagesse,* 36–37
Charles IX, 168–69, 172
Chassaigne, Françoise de la, 250
Château de Montaigne, 209, 304, 315
Cicero, 128, 201, 219–20, 313
Coleridge, Samuel Taylor, 237
Coste, Pierre, 52
Cottrell, Robert, 28, 96n.24
Croll, Morris: and style, 219–21

Dédéyan, Charles, 111, 195
De Man, Paul, 105, 142, 177, 210: *Blindness and Insight,* 174; "blindness and insight," 175; and forgetting, 172–73; and modernist predicament, 173; and modernity 141, 153; "Montaigne et la transcendance," 167–73; on Montaigne's modernism, 151; war-time articles, 171
Derrida, Jacques, 91, 171, 307
Desan, Philippe, 313–14, 318n.11
Descartes, René, 40, 51
Dezon-Jones, Elyane, 34
DiBattista, Maria, 236
Diderot, Denis: "Sur la diversité de nos jugements," 57; "De l'Interprétation de la nature," 57; "Pensée XXX," 56; *Pensées philosophiques,* 56; "Pyrrhonisme," 55; reception of Montaigne, 55–59; "Réflexions sur le livre de l'esprit," 57; and skepticism, 56–57; "Supplément du voyage de Bougainville," 58
Discourse: definition of, 92
Dréano, Mathurin, 21, 51, 62, 99n.66
Dryden, John, 258–59
Du Bellay, Joachim, 116, 197
Dupéyron, Georges, 318n.6

Eliot, T.S., 112, 150, 180n.15, 190, 196: as critic of Montaigne, 202–03; and Pascal, 202–03; "Tradition and the Individual Talent," 117; "The Wasteland," 280
Emerson, Ralph Waldo, 103, 175–77, 189, 195, 208: and American culture, 106, 119; "The American Scholar," 122–23; and books, 105; and Browne, 217; and cultural reformation, 120; and democracy, 120, 123; "Education," 111; and the essay tradition, 110; and individualism, 123; "Montaigne; Or, the Skeptic," 106–09; "Nature," 121; and Nietzsche, 124–25; "Plutarch," 111; and privatism, 121; "Quotation and Originality," 112, 115, 117, 120; reception of Montaigne,

105–25; "Self Reliance," 113–14, and skepticism, 106–09; stylistic qualities, 110; tradition and innovation, 114
Empiricus, Sextus, 46
Encyclopédie, 55, 56
Enlightenment, 52
Erasmus, Desiderius, 242
Essais (Montaigne): and critical uncertainty, 72; and diverse opinion, 83; and dynamism, 72; editions in eighteenth century, 50, 52; edition of 1580, 31; editions in seventeenth century, 37-38; and evolution, 79–80, 241–42; history of manuscript, 245; interpretations of, 20; modernist qualities, 231, 286–88; and numerical scheme, 285; problem of reading, 90–92; problem of reception, 73–74; receptions of, 23; receptions in nineteenth century, 77, 83; stylistic qualities, 77, 110, 282; and unity, 82, 283
Essay: definition of, 3, 83–84, 92, 136
Eyquem, as family name, 267
Eyquem, Pierre, 264, 300
Exemplaire de Bordeaux, 245

Fideism, 43–44
Fleury, Colette, 59, 64, 67
Fokkema, D.W., definition of modernism, 207
Foucault, Michel, 182n.39, 307
Frame, Donald, 69, 74, 77, 95n.12, 309
Friedrich, Hugo, 138, 282, 287, 309
Frisch, Max, 310
Fronde, La, 38
Fulghum, Robert, 317

Galileo, 310
Garonne river, 277n.58
Gide, André, 82, 189, 195, 233, 302: and Catholicism, 86–87; "Essai sur Montaigne," 85; reception of Montaigne," 84–88; and skepticism, 85; "Suivant Montaigne," 84
Gosse, Edmund, 246
Gournay, Marie le Jars de, 175, 186, 192, 231–32, 233: *Les Advis ou les presens de la Demoiselle de Gournay*, 35; defense of *Essais*, 24–25; "Défense des pères Jésuites," 35; as editor of *Essais*, 29, 245; *De l'Education des enfants en France*, 33; "Egalité des hommes et des femmes," 28–29, 33–34; as heir to Montaigne, 28–36; "L'Ombre de la Damoiselle de Gournay," 34; Preface to 1595 *Essais*, 32; Preface to 1635 *Essais*, 36; *Le Proumenoir de Monsieur de Montaigne*, 29, 33, 233; "Quatrains pour la maison de Montaigne, 97n.28; and social emancipation, 68; *Traité sur la poésie*, 35; and Woolf, 224
Gray, Floyd, 80

Harvey, David, 319n.29
Hayden, Hiram, 189n.27
Hazlitt, William, 219

Helvétius, Claude-Adrien, 55
Henri III, 170
Heraclitus, 129, 204, 208
Historicism, 71, 78
Hitler, Adolf, 174
Huët, Bishop of Avranches, 40
Hume, David, 226
Huysmans, Joris-Karl, 222

Influence, 5–6, 15: and fluidity, 76
Intertextuality: definitions of, 5–6

Jansenism, 46
Janus, 217, 218
Jauss, Hans Robert, 75, 147, 270: and reception theory, 4, 14–15, 21
Johnson, Samuel, 226
Jonson, Ben, 226
Joyce, James, 93, 196: and *Finnegans Wake*, 4, 310

Keohane, Nannerl O., 320n.38
Kernan, Alvin, 316
Kristeva, Julia, 306–07: and intertextuality, 5
Kritzman, Lawrence, 289

Lamb, Charles, 218
Lanson, Gustave, 78, 86, 189: and reception, 21
Leiris, Michel, 310
Leschemelle, Pierre, 315
Lestonnac, Jeanne de, 97n.35
Ligue, La, 168, 171
London, Bette, 271–72
Louppes, Antoinette de, 264

Maine, La Croix du, 22
Malebranche, Nicolas, 55, 202: *La Recherche de la vérité*, 47–49
Mallarmé, Stéphane, 93
Malraux, André, 112
Malzevin, Théophile, 277n.60
Mann, Heinrich, 310
Marcuse, Herbert: and affirmative culture, 121
Matthiessen, F.O., 118
Matthieu-Castellani, Gisèle, 290, 318–19n.12
McGrath, F.C., 273n.13, 274n.21
McKinley, Mary, 180n.13, 289
Medeci, Catherine de, 168, 172
Meisel, Perry, 191
Merleau-Ponty, Maurice, 88–89: and subjectivity, 89
Mermier, Guy, 182n.37
Miller, C. Ruth, 272
Modernism: characteristics of, 207; definitions of, 2–3, 8–9, 11–12; as predicament, 142–43; and reader-response criticism, 143
Mona Lisa, 239
Monsman, Gerald, 7, 274n.22
Montaigne, Léonor de, 30, 267, 297
Montesquieu, Charles de Secondat: reception of Montaigne, 54–55
Montaigne, Michel de: and the *Aeneid*, 234; and androgyny, 236–37; and anti-Ciceronian style, 220; "Apologie de Raymond Sebond," 42, 43, 107–08, 158, 160; "Au lecteur," 217, 242, 304; and books, 105; "Des cannibales,"

54, 58, 116, 142–43, 208, 254; "Des coches," 50, 54, 58; concept of natural, 149–50; conflict of innovation and tradition, 144–45; "De la coustume," 137–38, 144, 145–46; and cultural reformation, 120; and current reputation, 315–16; and custom, 303–04; and decadence, 222; and Delphic oracle, 163; and diversity, 75; and dogmatism, 48; and education, 134–36, 148–49; and education in France, 118–119; and eloquence, 256; and essayistic structure, 226; "De l'experience," 65, 156; and "explosive style," 219; family religion, 169; and forgetting, 210; as founder of essay, 219; and Gasconism, 301; and Gournay, 28–36; and historical circumstances, 278; on historical education, 152; and Humanism, 119, 122; and ideal reader, 145; and impressionism, 193; incompatibility with Nietzsche, 155; and individualism, 157; and influence, 94; influence on essay genre, 271; "De l'institution des enfans," 25, 62, 112, 115, 116, 132–33, 159, 276; and interpretation, 153; and irregular style, 234; and Jansenists, 305; and *jouissance*, 300, 301, 305; *Journal de voyage*, 315; and language, 128; and learning, 136; as libertine, 302, 305; and linguistic skepticism, 128–130, 132; and marriage, 263; on memory and forgetting, 158–61; and modernism, 13, 16, 76, 89, 92–93, 138, 150–51, 168, 200, 203–04, 207, 269, 272, 290, 293, 298–306, 310–312, 314–15; and modernist impulse, 177; and modernist problematic, 147; and "*Montaignesque* element," 280; and movement, 81; "Nos affections s'emportent au delà de nous," 64; and "nouvelletez," 87, 137, 178; "De l'oisiveté, 170; and originality, 52, 221; originality as writer, 190–91; and *Orlando Furioso*, 234; and paradox, 156–67, 241; "Du pedantisme," 60, 62; and political order, 123; and postmodernism, 166–67, 278–79, 303–09; and poststructuralism, 281; as protomodernist, 186; and public discourse, 217; and pyrrhonism, 40, 51; and quotation, 194; and reader-response criticism, 89, 93; reception in England, 193–94; relation to feminism, 231–32; relationship with Gournay, 96n.27; and religion, 97n.35; and religious wars, 168–71; "Du repentir," 220; and self-portraiture, 62–63; and skepticism, 80, 83, 107–09, 200; and social events, 221–22; and Socrates, 43; as split subject,

175; and stream of consciousness, 207; and style, 90; and subjectivity, 167–68, 193; "Sur des vers de Virgile," 50, 302; and suspension of judgement, 159; and uncertainty, 153–154, 201; in United States today, 317; "De la vanité," 137–38; and women, 26–28, 33; and teachers, 140; on tradition and innovation, 114; travels to Italy, 21, 305; use of history, 137–140

National Socialism, 174
Navarre, Henri de, 170
Nazi Party, 174
Nicole, Pierre, 45–47
Nietzsche, Elizabeth Foerster, 174
Nietzsche, Friedrich, 103, 187, 189, 190, 208, 214, 225, 280, 305, 310: "Aus dem Nachlass der Achtzigerjahre," 153; concept of natural, 149–50; conflict of history and modernity, 154–55; and critical history, 75, 141–42; and cultural decadence, 147; and cultural health, 149; and Delphic oracle, 162; and Delphic teaching, 150; "Die Philosophie im tragischen Zeitalter der Griechen," 130; *Ecce Homo*, 125–26, 156; and education, 134–36, 148–49; and Emerson, 124–25, 127; and forgetting, 157–61, 166; and French writers, 126; *Die Geburt der Tragödie*, 126, 165–66; and German culture, 154, 165; *Götzen-Dämmerung*, 127; and Greek culture, 163–64; and hermeneutic instability, 159; and historical antidote, 160–62; and history, 213; and ideal reader, 160; "Jenseits von Gut und Böse," 154; and linguistic skepticism, 127–30; "Menschliches, Allzumenschliches," 129; and modernism, 131, 165; and monumental history, 138–39; and newness, 155; and paradox, 160; and Pascal, 142; and postmodernism, 165, 166–67; on quotation and originality, 177; reception of Montaigne, 125–67; and Schopenhauer, Arthur, 127; and skepticism, 126; and teachers, 140; and truth, 158; and uncertainty, 153–54; use of *Essais*, 156, 164–65, 176; use of history, 147, 153; "Über Wahrheit und Lüge im aussermoralischen Sinne," 126, 127–28; "Vom Nutzen und Nachteil der Historie für das Leben," 11, 131, 132–64; and Woolf, 225, 256; *Zur Genealogie der Moral*, 166
Norris, Margot, 4

Orlando (Woolf), 191, 192, 199, 206, 216, 218, 221, 228, 229, 231, 233–68: and *aporia*, 261–63; characteristics of, 239; and dates, 246, 249–50, 264; and forgetting,

259, 261; and *Gaston*, 240; and linguistic instability, 262; and memory, 256–58; and mobility, 239–240; and modernism, 243; and "*Montaignesque* element," 240, 260; notion of renaissance, 260; "The Oak Tree," 244–49, 266–67; Orlando as protagonist, 243; and stylistic qualities, 241

Papal Index, 49
Pascal, Blaise, 189, 195, 201–03, 201, 284: and ambivalence, 42–43; "L'Entretien de Pascal et Sacy," 43; and fideism, 43–44; *Pensées*: (62), 41; (63), 42; (64), 42; (66), 43; (93), 142; (233), 44; (282), 44; (347 & 348), 44; (684), 142; reception of Montaigne, 41–45
Pasquier, Etienne, response to *Essais*, 22–23
Pater, Clara, 192
Pater, Walter, 178, 185: "Charles Lamb," 197; "Coleridge," 200; "Conclusion," 195; and the essay, 198, 199; and expressionism, 197; *Gaston de Latour*, 186, 194, 195, 199, 204, 205–16, 220, 221, 238, 240, 246, 249, 258, 260–61, 268; *Gaston* and style, 211–14; *Marius the Epicurean*, 195, 196, 204, 207; *Miscellaneous Studies*, 204; and modernism, 234; and modernist predicament, 200; and "*Montaignesque* element," 189, 198, 206; on Montaigne's modernism, 196–97; notion of modernism, 204, 239; notion of renaissance, 196, 204, 260; and reception, 195; reception of Montaigne, 187–216; reception of Pascal, 201–03; "The Renaissance," 197, 210, 234, 239; "Pascal," 189, 199, 201–03, 207, 271; *Plato and Platonism*, 195, 198, 199; and pyrrhonism, 204; "Sir Thomas Browne," 197–98; and subjectivity, 197; and "undertexture," 189; use of *Essais*, 216–16; and Victorian age, 200; and Woolf, 224, 225
Payen, Dr. Jean-François, 76
Périgord, 205
Philosophes, 51
Plato, 128: and *furor poeticus*, 208
Plutarch, 170, 201, 303
Poletti, Joseph-Guy, 318n.9
Pope, Alexander, 258–59
Pope Gregory XIII, 303
Post, Jonathan F.S., 275n.30
Postmodern Condition, 279–280
Pouilloux, Jean-Yves: reception of *Essais*, 286–89
Pound, Ezra, 196
Protomodernism, 7
Proust, Marcel, 93, 196, 310
Pyrrhonism, 46

Rabelais, François, 116, 220
Reader-response criticism, 146, 187–88

Reception theory, 84, 186
Regosin, Richard: *Essais* and poststructuralism, 289
Rigolot, François, 290, 315, 318n.12, 320n.34
Robertson, John, 193
Ronsard, Pierre, 214
Rousseau, Jean-Jacques, 51, 305: *Confessions*, 63; "Discours sur l'inégalité, 60–61; "Discours sur les sciences et les arts," 60; *Emile*, 61, 62; *Lettres morales*, 61; reception of Montaigne, 59–68; *Rêveries du promeneur solitaire*, 64–66

Sackville-West, Vita, 233, 247
Saint Bartholomew's Day Massacre, 168–70, 172, 210–11, 260, 303
Sainte-Beuve, Charles Augustin, 45, 77, 195, 201, 203: and modernism, 73; *Port Royal*, 71; reception of Montaigne, 70–74; and skepticism, 73
Scriptible: notion of, 93, 123, 147, 174–75, 182n.45, 233, 284, 306, 312
Sebond, Raymond, *Théologie naturelle*, 250
Seneca, 201, 303
Sévigné, Marie de: comments on Montaigne, 39
Shakespeare, William, 237
Socrates, 111,
Sollers, Philippe, 281, 315: *Femmes*, 302; *H*, 309; "Montaigne, le mutant," 298–300; *Portrait du joueur*, 300–02; reception of *Essais*, 298–307; and *Tel Quel*, 299–30
Spears, Monroe, 317
Starobinski, Jean, 181–82n.34, 282, 309; *Montaigne en mouvement*, 292–93
Stéphane, Roger, 315, 318n.9
Stephen, Sir Leslie, 196: critique of Pater, 200
Strowski, Fortunat, 79–80, 282
Suffisant lecteur: notion of, 121, 176, 203, 224

Tacitus, 316
Taine, Hippolyte, 71, 78–79
Thibaudet, Albert, 80–82, 189, 282
Tocqueville, Alexis de, 122

Viau, Théophile de, 40
Villey, 80, 189, 282, 287: and evolution of *Essais*, 240–41, 276n.55; receptions of *Essais*, 23
Virgil, 303
Voltaire, reception of Montaigne, 53–54

Wagner, Cosima, 126
White, Hayden, 166, 183n.51
Whitman, Walt, 124
Wilde, Oscar, 190
Woolf, Virginia, 178, 185, 190, 202, 302, 310: as academic subject, 271–72; adaptation of *Essais*, 248–49, 264–66, 271; and androgyny, 235–237; *The Common Reader*, 191, 224; and the essay, 223; and "explosive style," 252; "How One Should Read a Book," 223,

226; on innovation and tradition, 224–225; "The Modern Essay," 223; "Modern Fiction," 223, 227; and modernism, 269; modernist qualities, 261–62; and modernist style, 230–31, 238; "Montaigne," 192, 227–231, 250–51, 253, 257, 263, 264–65; and "*Montaignesque* element," 268; and Montaigne's style, 229; notion of biography, 235; and reading, 223; reception of Montaigne, 222–268; relation to Pater, 191; *A Room of One's Own*, 191, 224–25, 226, 233, 237–38, 241; "Sir Thomas Browne," 232–33; and skepticism, 223; use of *Essais*, 224, 244, 255;

Young, Charles Lowell, 109, 112–13, 179, 179–80n.8, 195

Zweig, Stefan, 310